Internet Routing Architectures

Bassam Halabi

CISCO SYSTEMS

CISCO PRESS

New Riders

New Riders Publishing
201 West 103rd Street
Indianapolis, IN 46290 USA

Printed in the United States of America   2 3 4 5 6 7 8 9 0

Library of Congress Cataloging-in-Publication Data

CIP data available upon request

Warning and Disclaimer

This book is designed to provide information about **Internet routing architectures**. Every effort has been made to make this book as complete and as accurate as possible, but no warranty or fitness is implied.

The information is provided on an "as is" basis. The author, New Riders Publishing, and Cisco Systems Inc. shall have neither liability nor responsibility to any person or entity with respect to any loss or damages arising from the information contained in this book or from the use of the disks or programs that may accompany it.

Publisher:	Don Fowley
Publishing Manager:	Julie Fairweather
Executive Editor-in-Chief:	Ann Trump Daniel, Macmillan
Cisco Systems Representative:	H. Kim Lew, Cisco Systems
Marketing Manager:	Mary Foote
Managing Editor:	Carla Hall
Project Managers:	Tracy Turgeson
	Gina Brown
Senior Editors:	Sarah Kearns
	Suzanne Snyder
Development Editor:	Laurie McGuire
Copy Editor:	Geneil Breeze
Technical Editor:	Ravi Chandra
	Robert Craig
Cover Designer:	Sandra Schroeder
Cover Production:	Aren Howell
Cover Art:	Provided by Cisco Systems
Interior Layout and Design:	Argosy
Indexer:	Bront Davis

Contents
at a Glance

Foreword

To say that the Internet has changed in the past 10 years is a vast understatement. The Internet today is the single most influential phenomenon in computing. The way in which it continues to evolve is likely to affect every form of data communication on a global scale. Internet information-handling strategies, such as Web-based customer support and secure networked commerce, will permanently alter business and consumer behavior.

As the Internet and networking have evolved, so too has Cisco Systems' role. Cisco has become the premier worldwide provider of networking for the Internet. In this role, Cisco helps network managers build reliable, scalable, and cost-effective solutions for networks that span the requirements of small offices to globally-dispersed enterprises. Over the years, Cisco has assembled the largest and most experienced staff of networking experts who serve customers in planning, implementing, and troubleshooting large networks. Bassam Halabi is one of those experts.

Although Cisco's expertise is primarily delivered directly to customers, it also can be shared through other means. A new and important medium for sharing Cisco's networking expertise is the Cisco Press. In creating this new forum, New Riders Publishing and Cisco Systems jointly plan to build a library of publications that provide practical information about the design and implementation of routers, switches, servers, and connectivity software.

Bassam Halabi's *Internet Routing Architectures* is the first of these books. Bassam provides his keen insight into interdomain routing, Internet service provider requirements, and the changing Internet infrastructure. He touches on issues that affect everyone connecting networks to or through the Internet. Bassam's many years of consulting experience with Cisco's largest IP-based networks contribute to this book's useful design recommendations. He brings a pragmatic perspective to the process of building links between domains and selecting network designs for specific situations.

Internet Routing Architectures is a readable distillation of essential design and implementation guidelines. We trust you will find it a valuable addition to your networking library.

Edward R. Kozel

Chief Technology Officer
Cisco Systems, Inc.

Trademark
Acknowledgments

Acknowledgments

I wish to acknowledge Ravi Chandra from the BGP4 development team for being a key reference for the protocol. I would also like to thank Robert Craig from the consulting team for his help in reviewing parts of the material; Kim Lew for motivating and leading this book project and for his guidance in organizing the material; and Laurie McGuire for her excellent input in the book development editing. Finally, this book couldn't have been written without the support and patience of my family who put up with the extra work hours during the last year.

A portion of the proceeds from this book will be donated to Cisco Networking Academies, a non-profit educational fund.

Introduction

The Internet, an upstart academic experiment in the late 1960s, struggles with identity and success in the late 1990s. From the ARPANET to the NSF-NET to ANYBODYSNET, the Internet is no longer owned by a single entity; it is owned by anybody who can afford to buy space on it. Millions of users are seeking connectivity and thousands of companies are feeling left out if they do not tap into the Internet. This has put network designers and administrators under a lot of pressure to keep up with networking and connectivity needs. Learning about networking, and especially routing, has become a necessity.

People get surprised when networks fail and melt down; I get surprised when they don't. I say that because there is so little useful information out there. Much of the information on routing that has been available to designers and administrators up until now is doubly frustrating: The information makes you *think* that you know how to build your network until you try, and find out that you don't. I wrote *Internet Routing Architectures* to be the first book that addresses real routing issues, using real scenarios, in a comprehensive and accessible treatment.

OBJECTIVES

The purpose of this book is to make you an expert on integrating your network into the global Internet. By presenting practical addressing, routing, and connectivity issues both conceptually and in the context of practical scenarios, the book aims to foster your understanding of routing so that you can plan and implement major network designs in an objective and informed way. Whether you are a customer or provider (or both) of Internet connectivity, this book anticipates and addresses the routing challenges facing your network.

AUDIENCE

This book is intended for any organization that might have the need to tap into the Internet. Whether you are becoming a service provider or you are connecting to one you will find all you need to integrate your network. The perspectives of network administrators, integrators, and architects are considered throughout this book. Even though this book addresses different levels of expertise, it progresses logically from simplest to most challenging concepts and problems, and its common denominator is straightforward, practical scenarios to which anyone can relate. No major background in routing or TCP/IP is required. Any basic or background knowledge needed to understand routing is developed as needed in text discussions, rather than assumed as part of the reader's repertoire.

ORGANIZATION

The book is organized into four parts:

- **Part 1—The Contemporary Internet.** Chapters 1–3 cover essential introductory aspects of the contemporary Internet with respect to its structure, service providers, and addressing. Even if you are already familiar with the general structure of the Internet, you are encouraged to read the portions of Chapter 1 concerning Network Access Points, the Route

Arbiter Project, and Network Information Services. The pressures that precipitated these components of the Internet have continuing practical implications for routing design problems faced by administrators. Chapter 2 provides valuable criteria by which to evaluate Internet service providers. If you represent such a provider, or are already a customer of one, some of the information may be familiar to you already.

- **Part 2—Routing Protocol Basics.** Chapters 4 and 5 cover the basics: Why interdomain routing protocols are needed and how they work. These topics are covered both generally, and in the specific context of BGP—Border Gateway Protocol—the de facto standard interdomain routing protocol of today. BGP's particular capabilities and attributes are thoroughly introduced.

- **Part 3—Effective Internet Routing Designs.** Chapters 6–9 delve into the practical, design-oriented applications of BGP. The attributes introduced in Part 2 are shown in action, in a variety of representative network scenarios. BGP's attributes are put to work in implementing design goals such as redundancy, symmetry, and load balancing. The challenges of making intradomain and interdomain routing work in harmony, managing growing or already large systems, and maintaining stability are addressed.

- **Part 4—Internet Routing Device Configuration.** Chapters 10 and 11 contain numerous code examples of BGP's attributes and of various routing policies. The code examples will make the most sense to you after you have read the earlier chapters, because many of them address multiple concepts and design goals. However, so that you can juxtapose textual discussions from earlier chapters with code examples in Chapters 10 and 11, pointers entitled "Configuration Example," have been placed in the earlier chapters. When you see one, you may wish to fast forward to the referenced page to see a configuration example of the attribute or policy being discussed.

APPROACH

It is very hard to write about technical information in an accessible manner. Information that is stripped of too much technical detail loses its meaning, while complete and precise technical detail can overwhelm readers and obscure concepts. This book introduces technical detail gradually and in the context of practical scenarios whenever possible. The most heavily technical information—configuration examples in the Cisco IOS language—is withheld until the final two chapters of the book, so that it is thoroughly grounded in the concepts and sample topologies that precede it.

Although your ultimate goal is to design and implement routing strategies, it is critical to grasp concepts and principles before applying them to your particular network. This book balances conceptual and practical perspectives by following a logical, gradual progression from general to specific, and from concepts to implementation. Even in chapters and sections that necessarily take a largely descriptive approach, hands-on interests are addressed through pointers to configuration examples, frequently asked questions, and scenario-based explanation.

The scenario-based approach is an especially important component of this book: It utilizes representative network topologies as a basis for illustrating almost every protocol attribute and routing policy discussed. Even though you may not see your exact network situation illustrated, the scenario is specific enough to facilitate learning-by-example, and general enough that you can extrapolate how the concepts illustrated apply to your situation.

FEATURES AND TEXT CONVENTIONS

This book works hard not to withhold protocol details and design-oriented information, while at the same time recognizing that building general and conceptual

understanding necessarily comes first. Two features are included to help empha-
size what is practical and design-oriented as underlying concepts are developed:

- Pointers to configuration examples—located in the margins next to
  pertinent text discussions, these references point forward to places in
  Chapters 10 and 11 where related configuration examples can be found.

- Frequently Asked Questions—located at the end of every chapter, these
  questions anticipate practical and design-oriented questions you may
  have, for your particular network, after having read the chapter.

In addition, this book utilizes several other conventions:

- Troubleshooting margin notes—these brief references are placed adjacent
  to text discussions that are especially relevant to preventing or correcting
  common routing problems and programming mistakes.

- Notes—these set-off passages include elaborations that will further illu-
  minate text passages, but which can be skipped without loss of understanding of core topics.

PART 1

The Contemporary Internet

The complexity of routing problems and solutions is tied closely to the growth and evolution of the contemporary Internet. Thus, before delving into specifics about routing protocols, you will find it extremely useful to have some general perspective and background information. Such historical developments as the Route Arbiter project, Network Access Points, and Network Information Services, covered in Chapter 1, continue to have extremely practical implications for organizations that want to be connected to global networks. General and network topology issues associated with Internet service providers are introduced in Chapter 2. Concepts of addressing and Classless Interdomain Routing, which are needed to control the depletion of the IP address space, are covered in Chapter 3.

Chapter 1—Evolution of the Internet

Chapter 2—ISP Services and Characteristics

Chapter 3—Handling IP Address Depletion

**THIS CHAPTER COVERS
THE FOLLOWING KEY TOPICS:**

- **Origins of the Internet; the Internet Today**

  Very brief history of the early Internet, with emphasis on its implementors and users, and on how it has evolved in the last decade.

- **Network Access Points**

  Internet service providers must connect, directly or indirectly, with Network Access Points (NAPs); customers will need to know enough to evaluate how their providers connect to the NAPs.

- **Route Arbiter Project**

  Overview of concepts central to the rest of this book: Route servers and the Routing Arbiter Database. Route servers are architectural components of NAPs, Internet service providers, and other networks.

- **Regional Providers**

  Background on the current Internet layout with respect to regional connection service and goals.

- **Network Information Services**

  Description of information collected and offered by central and distributed Internet information services. Includes description of templates that customers and providers must fill out to get connected.

CHAPTER 1

Evolution of the Internet

The structure and makeup of the Internet has adapted as the needs of its community have changed. Today's Internet serves the largest and most diverse community of network users in the computing world. A brief chronology and summary of significant components are provided in this chapter to set the stage for understanding the challenges of interfacing the Internet and the steps to build scalable internetworks.

ORIGINS OF THE INTERNET

The Internet started as an experiment in the late 1960s by the Advanced Research Projects Agency (ARPA, now called DARPA) of the U.S. Department of Defense. DARPA experimented with the connection of computer networks by giving grants to multiple universities and private companies to get them involved in the research.

In December 1969, the experimental network went online with the connection of a four-node network connected via 56 Kbps circuits. This new technology proved to be highly reliable and led to the creation of two similar military networks, MILNET in the U.S. and MINET in Europe. Thousands of hosts and users subsequently connected their private networks (universities and government) to the ARPANET, thus creating the initial "ARPA Internet." ARPANET had an Acceptable Use Policy (AUP), which prohibited the use of the Internet for commercial use. ARPANET was decommissioned in 1989.

By 1985, the ARPANET was heavily used and congested. In response, the National Science Foundation (NSF) initiated phase one development of the NSFNET. The NSFNET was composed of multiple regional networks and peer networks (such as the NASA Science Network) connected to a major backbone that constituted the core of the overall NSFNET.

In its earliest form, in 1986, the NSFNET created a three-tiered network architecture. The architecture connected campuses and research organizations to regional networks, which in turn connected to a main backbone linking six nationally funded super-computer centers. The original links were 56 Kbps.

The links were upgraded in 1988 to faster T1 (1.544 Mbps) links as a result of the NSFNET 1987 competitive solicitation for a faster network service, awarded to Merit Network, Inc. and its partners MCI, IBM, and the state of Michigan. The NSFNET T1 backbone connected a total of 13 sites that included Merit, BARRNET, MIDnet, Westnet, NorthWestNet, SESQUINET, SURANet, NCAR (National Center of Atmospheric Research), and five NSF supercomputer centers.

In 1990, Merit, IBM, and MCI started a new organization known as Advanced Network and Services (ANS). Merit Network's Internet engineering group provided a policy routing database and routing consultation and management services for the NSFNET, whereas ANS operated the backbone routers and a Network Operation Center (NOC).

By 1991, data traffic had increased tremendously, which necessitated upgrading the NSFNET's backbone network service to T3 (45 Mbps) links. Figure 1–1 illustrates the original NSFNET with respect to the location of its core and regional backbones.

As late as the early 1990s, the NSFNET was still reserved for research and educational applications, and government agency backbones were reserved for

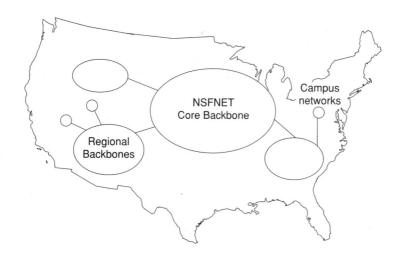

Figure 1–1
*NSFNET-based
Internet
environment.*

mission-oriented purposes. But new pressures were being felt by these and other emerging networks. Different agencies needed to interconnect with one another. Commerical and general-purpose interests were clamoring for network access, and Internet service providers (ISPs) were emerging to accommodate those interests, defining an entirely new industry in the process. Networks in places other than the U.S. had developed, along with interest in international connections. As the various new and existing entities pursued their goals, the complexity of connections and infrastructure grew.

Government agency networks interconnected at Federal Internet eXchange (FIX) points on both the east and west coasts. Commercial network organizations had formed the Commercial Internet eXchange (CIX) association, which built an interconnect point on the west coast. At the same time, ISPs around the world, particularly in Europe and Asia, had developed substantial infrastructures and connectivity. To begin sorting out the growing complexity, Sprint was appointed by NSFNET to be the International Connections Manager (ICM)—to provide connectivity between the backbone services in the U.S. and European and Asian networks. NSFNET was decommissioned in April 1995.

THE INTERNET TODAY

The decommissioning of NSFNET had to be done in specific stages to ensure continuous connectivity to institutions and government agencies that used to be connected to the regional networks. Today's Internet structure is a move from a core network (NSFNET) to a more distributed architecture operated by commercial providers such as Sprint, MCI, BBN, and others connected via major network exchange points. Figure 1–2 illustrates the general form of the Internet today.

The contemporary Internet is a collection of providers that have connection points called POP (point of presence) over multiple regions. Its collection of POPs and the way its POPs are interconnected form a provider's network. Customers are connected to providers via the POPs. Customers of providers can be providers themselves. Providers that have POPs throughout the U.S. are called national providers.

Providers that cover specific regions (regional providers) connect themselves to other providers at one or multiple points. To enable customers of one provider to reach customers of another provider, Network Access Points (NAPs) are defined as interconnection points. The term ISP is usually used when referring to anyone who provides service, whether directly to end users or to other pro-

Figure 1–2
*The general
structure of today's
Internet.*

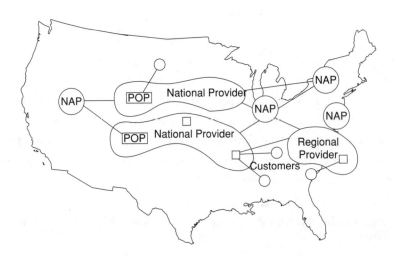

viders. The term NSP (network service provider) is usually restricted to providers who have NSF funding to manage the Network Access Points, such as Sprint, Ameritech, and MFS. The term NSP, however, is also used more loosely to refer to any provider that connects to all the NAPs.

NSFNET SOLICITATIONS

NSFNET has supported data and research on networking needs since 1986. NSFNET also supported the goals of the High Performance Computing and Communications (HPCC) Program, which promoted leading-edge research and science programs. The National Research and Education Network (NREN) Program, which is a subdivision of the HPCC Program, called for Gigabit-per-second networking for research and education to be in place by the mid 1990s. All these needs, in addition to the April 1995 expiration deadline of the Cooperative Agreement for NSFNET Backbone Network Services, lead NSF-NET to solicit for NSFNET services. This process is generally referred to as *solicitation*.

The first NSF solicitation, in 1987, lead to the NSFNET backbone upgrade to T3 links by the end of 1993. In 1992, NSF wanted to develop a follow-up solicitation that would accommodate and promote the role of commercial service providers and that would lay down the structure of a new and robust Internet model. At the same time, NSF would step back from the actual operation of the network and focus on research aspects and initiatives. The final NSF solicitation (NSF 93-52) was issued in May 1993.

The final solicitation included four separate projects for which proposals were invited:

- Creating a set of Network Access Points (NAPs) where major providers connect their networks and exchange traffic.

- Implementing a Route Arbiter (RA) project to facilitate the exchange of policies and addressing of multiple providers connected to the NAPs.

- Finding a provider of a very high-speed Backbone Network Service (vBNS) for educational and governmental purposes.

- Transitioning existing and/or realigned regional networks to support interregional connectivity (IRC) by connecting to NSPs that are connected to NAPs or by connecting directly to NAPs. Any NSP selected for this purpose must connect to at least three of the NAPs.

NETWORK ACCESS POINTS

The solicitation for this project was to invite proposals from companies to implement and manage a specific number of NAPs where the vBNS and other appropriate networks may interconnect. These NAPs should enable regional networks, network service providers, and the U.S. research and education community to connect and exchange traffic with one another. They also should provide for the interconnection of networks in an environment that is not subject to the NSF Acceptable Use Policy. (This policy was put in place to restrict the use of the Internet for research and education.) Thus, general usage, including commercial usage, can go through the NAPs also.

What Is a NAP?

The *NAP* is defined as a high-speed network or switch to which a number of routers can be connected for the purpose of traffic exchange. NAPs must operate at speeds of at least 100 Mbps and must be able to be upgraded as required by demand and usage. The NAP could be as simple as an FDDI switch (100 Mbps) or an ATM switch (155 Mbps) passing traffic from one provider to the other.

The concept of the NAP is built on the FIX (Federal Internet eXchange) and the CIX (Commercial Internet eXchange), which are built around FDDI rings with attached Internet networks operating at speeds of up to 45 Mbps.

The traffic on the NAP should not be restricted to that which is in support of research and education. Networks connected to the NAP are permitted to exchange traffic without violating the use policies of any other networks interconnected to the NAP.

There are four NSF-awarded NAPs:

- *Sprint NAP*—Pennsauken, NJ

- *PacBell NAP*—San Francisco, CA

- *Ameritech Advanced Data Services (AADS) NAP*—Chicago, IL

- *MFS Datanet (MAE-East) NAP*—Washington, D.C.

The NSFNET backbone service was physically connected to the Sprint NAP on September 13, 1994. It was physically connected to the PacBell NAP and Ameritech NAP in mid-October 1994 and early January 1995, respectively. The NSFNET backbone service was upgraded to the collocated FDDI offered by MFS on March 22, 1995.

Additional NAPs are being created around the world as providers keep finding the need to interconnect.

Networks attaching to NAPs must operate at speeds commensurate with the speeds of attached networks (1.5 Mbps or greater) and must be upgradable as required by demand, usage, and program goals. NAPs must be able to switch both IP and CLNP (ConnectionLess Networking Protocol). The requirements to switch CLNP packets and to implement IDRP-based (InterDomain Routing Protocol, ISO OSI Exterior Gateway Protocol) procedures may be waived depending on the overall level of service and the U.S. government's desire to foster the use of ISO OSI protocols.

NAP Manager Solicitation

A NAP manager should be appointed to each NAP with duties that include the following:

- Establish and maintain the specified NAP for connecting to vBNS and other appropriate networks.

- Establish policies and fees for providers that want to connect to the NAP.

- Propose NAP locations subject to the given general geographic locations.

- Propose and establish procedures to work with personnel from other NAP managers (if any), the Route Arbiter, the vBNS provider, and regional and other attached networks, to resolve problems and to support end-to-end connectivity and quality of service for network users.

- Develop reliability and security standards for the NAPs and procedures to ensure that these standards are met.

- Specify and provide appropriate NAP accounting and statistics gathering and reporting capabilities.

- Specify appropriate access procedures to the NAP for authorized personnel of connecting networks and ensure that these procedures are carried out.

At the NAP

The current physical configuration of today's NAPs is a mixture of FDDI/ATM switches with different access methods, ranging from DS3 for dedicated and FR/ATM/SMDS for switched. Figure 1–3 shows a possible configuration, based on some contemporary NAPs. The routers could be managed either by the NSP or the NAP manager. Different configurations, fees, and policies are set by the NAP manager. Connections from different LATA (Local Access and Transport Area) are provided by Inter eXchange Carriers (IXC).

Federal Internet eXchange (FIX)

Due to the decommissioning of the NSFNET backbone, federal regional networks faced the problem of transitioning to the new infrastructure where they have to be connected to new NSPs. The Federal Networking Council (FNC) Engineering and Planning Group (FEPG) was responsible for making a recommendation on how to transition to the new NAP-NSP operational environment

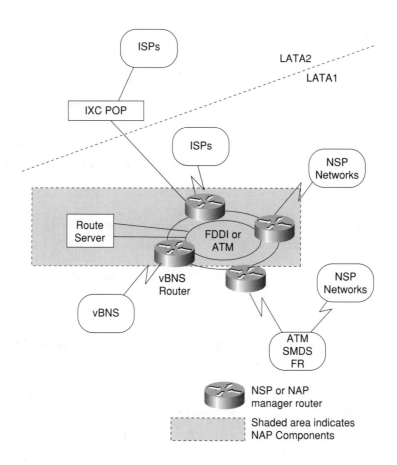

Figure 1–3
Typical NAP physical infrastructure.

with minimal disruption to users, specifically in federal agency communications with the U.S. academic and research communities.

Existing Federal Internet eXchanges (FIX West and FIX East) were to be connected to the major NSPs (MCInet, Sprintlink, ANS). The FIX West backbone formerly was maintained at NASA Ames. Now it is connected to the major NSPs, and route servers were installed to peer with the federal agencies. The FIX East backbone formerly was maintained at SURA (College Park, MD). Now it is connected to the major NSPs and is also bridged to the MAE-East facility (Tyson's Corner, VA) of MFS.

Commercial Internet eXchange (CIX)

The CIX (pronounced Kix) is a nonprofit trade association of Public Data Internetwork Service Providers. The association promotes and encourages the development of the public data communications internetworking services industry in both national and international markets. The CIX provides a neutral forum to exchange ideas, information, and experimental projects among suppliers of internetworking services. Some benefits CIX provides its members include:

- A neutral forum to develop consensus positions on legislative and policy issues.

- A fundamental agreement for all CIX members to interconnect with one another. No restriction exists on the type of traffic that can be routed between member networks.

- No "settlements" nor any traffic-based charges between CIX member networks.

- Access to all CIX member networks, greatly increasing the correspondents, files, databases, and information services available to them. Users gain a global reach in networking, increasing the value of their network connection.

With increasing ISP connectivity to NAPs, the CIX becomes essential in the coordination of legislative issues between members. In fact, the role of the CIX for physical connectivity is not as important as its role in coordination between parties. With the existence of a number of other high bandwidth connection points such as the NAPs, the CIX plays a minor role in the connectivity game. ISPs who still rely on the CIX as their only physical connection to the Internet are still way behind.

On July 13, 1994, the CIX board voted to block traffic from ISPs who are not CIX members. CIX membership costs approximately $7,500 annually.

Significance of the NAPs for Routing

Although NAP connectivity is primarily something ISPs have to worry about, the level of redundancy and diversity of NAP connections affects traffic patterns and trajectories in the whole Internet. As such, the delays or speed of access caused by ISPs' interconnectivity affect the performance of everyone's Internet access. As you will see in the rest of this book, speed of access to the NAPs and the distance an ISP or a customer is from the NAP affects routing behaviors and traffic trajectories.

ROUTE ARBITER PROJECT

Another project for which NSF solicited services is the Route Arbiter (RA) project, which is charged with providing equitable treatment of the various network service providers with regard to routing administration. The RA will provide for a common database of route information to promote stability and manageability of networks.

Multiple providers connecting to the NAP have created a scalability issue because each provider will have to peer with all other providers to exchange routing and policy information. The RA project was developed to reduce the full peering mesh between all providers. Instead of peering among each other, providers will peer with a central system called a *route server*. The route server will maintain a database of all information needed for providers to set their routing policies. Figure 1–4 shows the physical connectivity and logical peering between a route server and various service providers.

The following are the major tasks of the RA per the NSFNET proposal:

- Promote Internet routing stability and manageability.

- Establish and maintain network topology and policy databases by such means as exchanging routing information with and dynamically updating routing information from the attached Autonomous Systems

(AS)[1] using standard interdomain routing protocols such as BGP (Border Gateway Protocol) and IDRP (support for IP and CLNP).

- Propose and establish procedures to work with personnel from the NAP manager(s), the vBNS provider, and regional and other attached networks to resolve problems and to support end-to-end connectivity and quality of service for network users.

- Develop advanced routing technologies such as type of service and precedence routing, multicasting, bandwidth on demand, and bandwidth allocation services, in cooperation with the global Internet community.

- Provide for simplified routing strategies, such as default routing, for attached networks.

- Promote distributed operation and management of the Internet.

Figure 1–4
Route server handling of routing updates in relation to traffic routing.

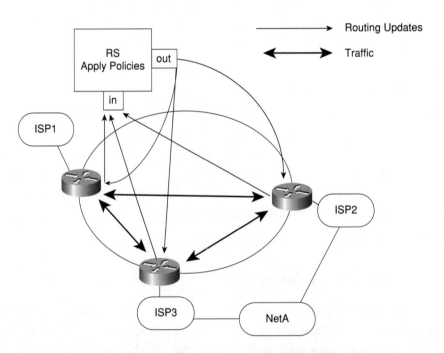

[1] An Autonomous System is a collection of routers under the same administration and sharing a consistent policy.

Today, the RA project is a joint effort of Merit Network, Inc.[1], the University of Southern California Information Sciences Institute (ISI)[2], Cisco Systems, as a subcontractor to ISI, and the University of Michigan ROC, as a subcontractor to Merit.

The RA service is comprised of four projects:

- *Route server*—The route server can be as simple as a Sun workstation deployed at each NAP. The route server exchanges routing information with the service provider routers attached to the NAP. Individual routing policies requirements (RIPE 181)[2] [3] for each provider are maintained. The route server itself does not forward packets or perform any switching function. Those functions are taken care of by the NAP's physical network.

  The server(s) facilitate interconnections between ISPs by gathering routing information from each ISP, applying the ISP's predefined set of rules and policies, and then redistributing the processed routing information to each ISP. This process saves the routers from having to peer with all other routers, thus cutting down the number of peers from $(n-1)$ to (1), where n is the number of routers.

  In this configuration, the routers of the different providers concentrate on switching the traffic between one another and do relatively little filtering and applying of policies.

- *Network management system*—This software monitors the performance of the RS. *Distributed rovers* run at each RS and collect information such as performance statistics. The central network management station (CNMS) at the Merit Routing Operation Center queries the rovers and processes the information.

---

[2] The RIPE language is covered in Appendix A.

- *Routing Arbiter Database (RADB)*[3] [1]—This is one of several routing databases collectively known as the Internet Routing Registry (IRR). Policy routing in the Routing Arbiter Database is expressed by using RIPE-181 syntax developed by the RIPE Network Coordination Center (RCC). The Routing Arbiter Database was deployed in dual mode with the Policy Routing Database (PRDB). The PRDB had been used to configure the NSFNET's backbone routers since 1986. With the introduction of the RIPE-181 language, which provided better functionality in recording global routing policies, the PRDB was to be retired in 1995 for full RADB functionality.

- *Routing engineering team*—This team works with the network providers to set up peering and to resolve network problems at the NAP. The team provides consultation on routing strategies, addressing plans, and other routing related issues.

As you have already seen, the main parts of the Route Arbiter concept are the route server and the RADB. The practical and administrative goals of the RADB apply mainly to service providers connecting to the NAP. Configuring the correct information in the RADB is essential in setting the required routing policies, as explained in Appendix A, "RIPE-181." As a customer of a provider, you may never have to configure such language. What is important, though, is not the language itself but rather understanding the reasoning behind the policies being set. As you will see in this book, policies are the basis of routing behaviors and architectures.

On the other hand, the concept of a route server and peering with centralized routers is not restricted to providers and NAPs, and could be implemented in any architecture that needs it. As part of the implementation section of this book, the route server concept will come up as a means of creating a one-to-many relationship between peers.

---

[3]   The RADB is covered in Appendix A.

THE VERY HIGH-SPEED BACKBONE NETWORK SERVICE (vBNS)

The very high-speed Backbone Network Service (vBNS) project was created to provide a specialized backbone service for the high-performance computing users of the major government-supported SuperComputer Centers (SCCs) and for the research community. The vBNS will continue the tradition that NSF-NET has provided in this field. The vBNS will be connected to the NSFNET-specified NAPs. On April 24, 1995, MCI and NSF announced the launch of the vBNS.

MCI duties include the following:

- Establish and maintain a 155 Mbps or higher transit network that switches IP and CLNP, and connects to all NAPs.

- Establish a set of metrics to monitor and characterize network performance.

- Subscribe to the policies of the NAP/RA manager.

- Provide for multimedia services.

- Participate in the enhancement of advanced routing technologies and propose enhancements in both speed and quality of service that is consistent with NSF customer requirements.

The five-year, $50-million agreement between MCI and NSFNET will tie together NSF's five major high performance communication centers:

- Cornell Theory Center (CTC), in Ithaca, New York

- National Center for Atmospheric Research (NCAR) in Boulder, Colorado

- National Center for SuperComputing Applications (NCSA) at the University of Illinois at Champaign

- Pittsburgh SuperComputing Center (PSC)

- San Diego SuperComputer Center (SDSC)

The vBNS has been called the R & D lab for the 21st century. The use of advanced switching and fiber optic transmission technologies, Asynchronous Transfer Mode (ATM), and Synchronous Optical Netwok (SONET) will enable very high-speed, high-capacity voice and video signals to be integrated.

The NSF is already in the process of authorizing use of the vBNS for "meritorious" high-bandwidth applications, such as using super-computer modeling at NCAR to understand how and where icing occurs on aircraft. Other applications at NCSA consist of building computational models to simulate the workings of biological membranes and how cholesterol inserts into membranes.

The vBNS will be accessible to select application sites through four NAPs in New York, San Francisco, Chicago, and Washington, D.C. Figure 1–5 shows the geographical relationships between the centers and NAPs. The vBNS is

Figure 1–5
Overall map illustrating vBNS geographical components.

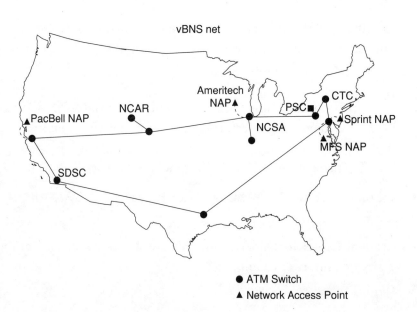

mainly composed of OC3 /T3 (OC12 is in the process of being deployed) links connected via high-end systems, such as Cisco routers and Cisco ATM switches.

The vBNS is a specialized network that emerged due to continuing needs for high-speed connections between members of the research and development community, one of the main charters of the NSFNET. Although the vBNS does not have any bearing on global routing behavior, the preceding brief overview is meant to give the reader background on how NSFNET covered all its bases before being decommissioned in 1995.

MOVING THE REGIONAL PROVIDERS

As part of the NSFNET solicitation for transitioning to the new Internet architecture, NSF requested that regional networks (also called *mid-level networks*) start transitioning their connections from the NSFNET backbones to other providers.

Regional networks have been a part of NSFNET since its creation and have played a major role in the network connectivity of the research and education community. Regional network providers (RNPs) connect a broad base of client/member organizations (such as universities), providing them with multiple networking services and with Inter Regional Connectivity (IRC).

The anticipated duties of the Regional network providers per the NSF 93–52 program solicitation follow:

- Provide for interregional connectivity by such means as connecting to NSPs that are connected to NAPs and/or by connecting to NAPs directly and making inter-NAP connectivity arrangements with one or more NSPs.

- Provide for innovative network information services for client/member organizations in cooperation with the InterNIC and the NSFNET Information Services Manager.

- Propose and establish procedures to work with personnel from the NAP manager(s), the RA, the vBNS provider, and other regional and attached networks to resolve problems and to support end-to-end connectivity and quality of service for network users.

- Provide services that promote broadening the base of network users within the research and communication community.

- Provide for, possibly in cooperation with an NSP, high-bandwidth connections for client/member institutions that have meritorious high-bandwidth applications.

- Provide for network connections to client/member organizations.

In the process of moving the regionals from the NSFNET to new ISP connections, NSF suggested that the regional networks be connected either directly to the NAPs or to providers connected to the NAPs. During the transition, NSF supported, for one year, connection fees that would decrease and eventually cease (after the first term of the NAP Manager/RA Cooperative Agreement, which shall be no more than four years.)

Table 1–1 lists some of the old NSFNET regional providers and their new respective providers under the current Internet environment. As you can see, most of the regional providers have shifted to either MCInet or Sprintlink. Moving the regional providers to the new Internet architecture in time for the April 1995 deadline was one of the major milestones that NSFNET had to achieve.

NSF SOLICITS NIS MANAGERS

In addition to the four main projects relating to architectural aspects of the new Internet, NSF recognized that information services would be a critical component in the even more widespread, freewheeling network. As a result, a solicitation for

Old Regional Network	New Internet Provider
Argone	CICnet
BARRnet	MCInet
CA*net	MCInet
CERFnet	CERFnet
CICnet	MCInet
Cornell Theory Ctr.	MCInet
CSUnet	MCInet
DARPA	ANSnet
JvNCnet	MCInet
MOREnet	Sprintlink
NEARnet	MCInet
NevadaNet	Sprintlink
NYSERnet	Sprintlink
SESQUINET	MCInet
SURAnet	MCInet
THEnet	MCInet
Westnet	Sprintlink

Table 1–1
Example regional transitions to new providers.

one or more Network Information Services (NIS) managers for the NSFNET was proposed. This solicitation invites proposals for the following:

- To extend and coordinate Directory and Database and Information Services.

- To provide registration services for non-military Internet networks. The Defense Information Systems Agency Network Information Center (DISA NIC) will continue to provide for the registration of military networks.

At the time of the solicitation, the domestic, non-military portion of the Internet included the NSFNET and other federally sponsored networks such as the NASA Science Internet (NSI) and Energy Sciences Network (ESnet). All these networks, as well as some other networks of the Internet, were related to the National Research and Education Network (NREN), which was defined in the

President's fiscal 1992 budget. The NSF solicitation for Database Services, Information Services, and Registration services were needed to help the evolution of the NSFNET and the development of the NREN.

Network Information Services

At the time of the proposal, certain network information services were being offered by a variety of providers; some of these services included the following:

- End-user information services were provided by NSF Network Service Center (NNSC) operated by Bolt, Beranek, and Newman (BBN). Other NSFNET end-user services were provided by campus-level computing and networking organizations.

- Information services for various federal agency backbone networks were provided by the sponsoring agencies. NSI information services, for example, were provided by NASA.

- Internet registration services were provided by DISA NIC operated by Government Services, Inc. (GSI).

- Information services for campus-level providers have been provided by NSFNET mid-level network organizations.

- Information services for NSFNET mid-level network providers have been provided by Merit, Inc.

Under the new solicitation, NIS managers should provide services to end users and to campus and mid-level network service providers, and should coordinate with mid-level and other network organizations, such as with Merit, Inc.

Creation of the InterNIC

In response to NSF's solicitation for NIS managers, in January 1993 the Inter-NIC [4] was established as a collaborative project among AT&T, General

Atomics, and Network Solutions, Inc. It was to be supported by three five-year cooperative agreements with the NSF. During the second year performance review, funding by the NSF to General Atomics stopped. AT&T was awarded the Database and Directory Services, and Network Solutions was awarded the Registration Services and the NIC Support Services.

Registration Services (RS)

The NIS manager will act in accordance to RFC 1174, which states the following:

> The Internet System has employed a central Internet Assigned Numbers Authority (IANA) for the allocation and assignment of various numeric identifiers needed for the operation of the Internet. The IANA function is performed by the University of Southern California's Information Sciences Institute. The IANA has the discretionary authority to delegate portions of this responsibility and, with respect to numeric network and autonomous system identifiers, has lodged this responsibility with an Internet Registry (IR).

The NIS manager will either become the IR or a delegate registry authorized by the IR. The Internet registration services to be provided will include:

- Network number assignment

- Autonomous system number assignment

- Domain name registration

- Domain name server registration

Today, NSI is providing assistance in registering networks, domains, AS numbers, and other entities to the Internet community via telephone, electronic mail, and U.S. postal mail. RS will work closely with domain administrators, network coordinators, ISPs, and other various users to register Internet domains, Autonomous System numbers, and networks.

The RS will provide databases and information servers such as WHOIS registry for domains, networks, AS numbers, and their associated Point Of Contacts (POCs). The RS also offers Gopher and Wide Area Information Server (WAIS) interfaces for retrieving information.

The documents distributed by the InterNIC registration services include templates, network information, and policies to request network numbers and register domain name servers.

Some of the templates include:

- Template for contact registration:

    This template is used to add, change, or delete a person who is to be registered in the InterNIC database as the main contact for a certain domain.

- Template for requesting an ISP CIDR[4] block:

    This is a template targeted for ISPs as part of the process in obtaining CIDR blocks of Internet Protocol (IP) network numbers. The template requests information on how the ISP is connected to the Internet and what, if any, IP blocks were previously allocated to it. This information is reviewed for efficient utilization prior to allocating additional addresses. The ISP has to allocate a technical Point Of Contact (POC) and indicate its network name, organization and geographic location, size of the block requested, and portable/nonportable address space.

    The information about portable and nonportable address space is requested to monitor the usage of IP address space. The portable option indicates that the ISP enables its customer to keep the IP address space in case the customer changes providers; the nonportable option indicates that the ISP requires its customers to return the IP address (and hence renumber) when the customer changes providers.

---

[4] CIDR will be discussed further in Chapter 3, "Handling IP Address Depletion."

The ISP is also required to provide at least two independent servers for translating address-to-name mapping for hosts in the domain (DNS). The servers should be in physically separate locations and on different networks if possible. A new form for IN-ADDR domain modification should be supplied.

- Template for requesting Internet Protocol (IP) numbers:

This template must be completed as part of the application process for obtaining Internet Protocol (IP) network numbers. Due to policy constraints on IP address number assignments, users are urged to take their IP addresses from their direct ISPs. IP addresses taken directly from the InterNIC might be subject to policies and might not be routable on the Internet.

Customers should provide an explanation of their Internet connection. In case of a connection to a provider, the customer should contact the provider for IP addresses. A technical POC should be provided, along with a network name, an organization name, type of network (research, educational, and so on), location and postal address, and a justification for the size of IP space requested.

In case 16 class C or more addresses are required, a network topology plan should be provided. In case a class B is requested (256 Cs), the whole network diagram should be included.

- Template for host registration:

This template is used to register a new name server in the ISP's domain. The template could be used to add, change, or delete the host records from the InterNIC database.

- Template for requesting Autonomous System (AS) numbers:

An Autonomous System is a group of IP networks/routers sharing the same policies. An AS number is an integer between 1 and 65535 with the range 64512 through 65535 reserved for private use. Due to the finite number of available AS numbers, justification should be presented before an organization is given an AS number. Today, the IANA is enforcing a policy whereby organizations connecting to a single provider and sharing the same policies as their providers use an AS number from the private pool. These private ASs can then be stripped at the provider level. Organizations connecting to multiple providers can request an AS number from the public pool.

Organizations that qualify for getting an AS number should provide an AS name, an organization name, and a technical point of contact.

- Template to register, delete, or modify an IN-ADDR domain:

The Internet uses a special domain to support address-to-name mapping, referred to as *inverse-addressing* (IN-ADDR). IN-ADDR domains are represented using the network number in reverse. The IN-ADDR domain for network 192.213.11.0, for example, is 11.213.192.IN-ADDR.ARPA.

The template indicates whether this is a new IN-ADDR registration, a modification, or a deletion of an existing IN-ADDR.

- Template for requesting or modifying Domain Name records:

This template is used for registering new domain names, making changes to existing domain name records, and removing domain names from the InterNIC database and root servers. The template asks for the purpose of the registration, with a justification for the domain name (com, edu, and so on) and a complete domain name according to RFC 1591 (ex: ABC.COM). RFC 1591 describes the distinction between different domains, for example:

- GOV is for United States federal government agencies.
- EDU is for four-year, degree-granting institutions.
- NET is for network infrastructure machines and organizations.
- COM is for commercial, for-profit organizations.
- ORG is for nonprofit organizations.

U.S. state and local government agencies, schools, libraries, museums, and individuals should register under the U.S. domain as described in RFC 1480.

GOV registrations are limited to top-level U.S. Federal Government agencies per RFC 1816.

The template also includes the name of the organization (or individual) using the domain name and the administrative, technical, and billing contacts.

Each domain must provide at least two independent DNSs, which need to be active before the application is submitted.

Directory and Database Services

The implementation of this service should utilize distributed database and other advanced technologies. The NIS manager could coordinate this role with respect to other organizations that have created and maintained relevant directories and databases. AT&T is providing the following services under the NSF agreement.

- Directory services (white pages):

  This provides access to Internet White Pages information using X.500, WHOIS, and netfind systems.

  The X.500 directory standard enables the creation of a single worldwide directory of information about various objects of interest—information about people, for example.

  The WHOIS lookup service provides unified access to three Internet WHOIS servers for person and organization queries. It searches the InterNIC Directory and Database Services server for non-military domain and non-Point-Of-Contact data. The search for MIL (military) domain data is done via the DISA NIC server, and the POC data is done via the InterNIC Registration Services server.

Netfind is a simple Internet white pages directory search facility. Given the name of a user and a description of where the user works, the tool attempts to locate information about the Internet user.

- Database services:

    This should include databases of communication documents such as Request For Comments (RFCs), For Your Information RFCs (FYI), Internet Drafts (IDs), Meeting Minutes, IETF Steering Committee (IESG) documents, and so on. This service could also contain databases maintained for other groups with a possible fee.

    AT&T also offers a database service listing of *public databases,* which contains information of interest to the Internet community.

    Access to database and directory services can be done via the Web at http://ds.internic.net/ds/dspgwp.html.

- Directory of directories:

    This service points to other directories and databases such as those listed previously.

    This is an index of pointers to resources, products, and services accessible through the Internet. It includes pointers to resources such as computing centers, network providers, information servers, white and yellow pages directories, library catalogs, and so on.

    As part of this service, AT&T stores a listing of information resources, including type, description, how to access the resource, and other attributes. Information providers are given access to update and add to the database. The information can be accessed via different methods such as telnet, ftp, gopher, e-mail, and www.

NIC Support Services

The original solicitation for "Information Services" was granted to General Atomics in 1993 and taken away in February 1995. At that time, Network

Solutions, Inc. took over the proposal, and it was renamed NIC Support Services.

The goal of this service is to provide a forum for the research and education community, Network Information Centers (NICs) staff, and the academic Internet community, within which the responsibilities, duties, and functions of the InterNIC may be defined. As of now, this service is divided into two components:

- Info Scout Service:

  NSI subcontracts to the University of Wisconsin, Madison for this service. The scout staff at the university and the NSI NIC support staff work together to serve both end-users and NICs in the higher-education community.

- NIC Support Service at NSI:

  The definition of NICs refers to individuals or organizations within the research and education community who provide a wide range of support for people within their client base who use the Internet.

  The focus of NSI is to provide an outreach program to the NIC community, soliciting input from the community on a regular basis and acting on the input by implementing new InterNIC services in support of NICs.

OTHER INTERNET REGISTRIES

Other Internet Registries (IR) were created outside the U.S.; these registries perform functions similar to those performed by the InterNIC in the U.S.

RIPE NCC (Reséaux IP Européens Network Coordination Center)

Created in 1989, RIPE[5] is a collaborative organization that consists of European Internet service providers. It aims to provide the necessary administration and coordination to enable the operation of the European Internet.

APNIC (Asia Pacific Network Information Center)

APNIC [6] is the IR for the Asia Pacific rim. It provides the IP registration and domain name services for that region. Created in 1993, APNIC started as a 10-month pilot project with the goal of providing Internet Registry functions and Routing Register functions (the RR function has not materialized to date). The pilot proved to be successful, and the APNIC is now in full operation serving as an IR.

Other Internet Registers are listed on the InternetNIC[4] home page.

INTERNETWORKING ROUTING REGISTRIES (IRR)

With the creation of a new breed of ISPs that want to interconnect with one another, offering the required connectivity while maintaining flexibility and control has become more challenging. Each provider has a set of rules, or policies, that describe what to accept and what to advertise to all other neighboring providers. Example policies include determining route filtering from a particular ISP and choosing the preferred path to a specific destination. The potential for the various policies from interconnected providers to conflict with and contradict one another is enormous.

To address these challenges, a neutral Routing Registry (RR) for each global domain had to be created. Each RR will maintain a database of routing policies created and updated by each service provider. The collection of these different databases is known as the Internetworking Routing Registries (IRR).

The role of the RR is not to determine policies, but rather to act as a repository for routing information and to perform consistency checking on the registered information with the other RRs. This should provide a globally consistent view of all policies used by providers all over the world.

Autonomous Systems (ASs) use exterior gateway protocols such as BGP to work with one another. In complex environments, there should be a formal way of describing and communicating policies between different ASs. Maintaining a huge database containing all registered policies for the whole world is cumbersome and difficult to maintain. This is why a more distributed approach was created. Each RR will maintain its own database and will have to coordinate extensively to achieve consistency between the different databases. Some of the different IRR databases in existence today are:

- RIPE Routing Registry (European Internet service providers)

- MCI Routing Registry (MCI customers)

- CA*net Routing Registry (CA*net customers)

- ANS Routing Registry (ANS customers)

- Routing Arbiter Database (all others)

- JPRR Routing Registry (Japanese Internet service providers)

Each of the preceding registries serves a limited number of customers except for the Routing Arbiter Database (RADB), which handles all requests not serviced by other registries. As mentioned earlier, the RADB is part of the Routing Arbiter (RA) project, which is a collaboration between Merit and ISI with subcontracts to Cisco Systems and the University of Michigan ROC.

LOOKING AHEAD

The decommissioning of the NSFNET in April 1995 marked the beginning of a new era. The Internet today is a playground for hundreds and thousands of providers competing for market share. For many businesses and organizations, connecting their networks to the global Internet is no longer a luxury but a requirement for staying competitive.

The structure of the contemporary Internet has implications for service providers and their customers in terms of speed of access, reliability, and cost of use. Some of the questions organizations that want to connect to the Internet should ask are: Are providers—whether established or relatively new to the business—well-versed with routing behaviors and architectures? For that matter, how much do customers of providers need to know and do with respect to routing architecture? Do we really know what constitutes a stable network? Is the bandwidth of our access line all we need to worry about to have the "fastest" Internet connection? The next chapter is intended to help ISPs and their customers evaluate these questions in a basic way. Later chapters get into details of routing architecture.

Interdomain routing is fairly new to everybody and is evolving every day. The rest of this book builds upon this chapter's overview of the structure of the Internet in explaining and demonstrating current routing practices.

FREQUENTLY ASKED QUESTIONS

Q— *Are there other NAPs besides the four NSF-awarded NAPs?*

A— Yes. As connectivity needs keep growing, more NAPs are being created. Many exchange points are spread over North America, Europe, Asia/Pacific, South America, Africa, and the Middle East.

Q— *If I am a customer of a provider, do I have to connect to a NAP?*

A— No. NAPs are mainly for interconnection between providers. If you are a customer of a provider, your connection will be to the provider only. But how your provider is connected to one or more NAP can affect the quality of your connection.

Q— *Is the function of the route server at the NAP to switch traffic between providers?*

A— No. The route server keeps a database of routing policies used by providers. Providers use the NAP physical media to exchange traffic directly between one another.

Q— *Do all providers that connect to a NAP have to peer with the route server?*

A— Although this is the recommended procedure, in some situations, major providers end up peering directly with each other, while smaller providers are required to peer with the route server.

Q— *What is the difference between IRs and IRRs?*

A— Internet Registries (IRs) such as the InterNIC are responsible for registration services such as IP address assignment. Internet Routing Registries are responsible for maintaining databases of routing policies for service providers.

Q—*How are database services different from the Route Arbiter Database?*

A—Database services are part of the Network Information Services. These databases include communication documents such as RFCs. The RADB is a database of routing policies.

REFERENCES

[1] www.merit.edu

[2] www.isi.edu

[3] RFC 1786; Representation of IP Routing Policies in a Routing Registry (Ripe-81++)

[4] ds.internic.net

[5] www.ripe.net

[6] www.apnic.net

THIS CHAPTER COVERS
THE FOLLOWING KEY TOPICS:

- **ISP Services**

  A basic categorization of Internet service providers in terms of physical access methods, basic services, and security options.

- **ISP Service Pricing**

  Survey of price ranges for different physical access methods.

- **ISP Backbone Selection Criteria**

  Criteria for evaluating ISPs in terms of their network topology and traffic exchange agreements.

- **Demarcation Point**

  Distinguishing the provider's network, equipment, and responsibilities from those of the customer.

CHAPTER 2

ISP Services and Characteristics

Before going deeper into the technical subject of interdomain routing, it is important to be familiar with some of the basic provider services and characteristics that affect the quality of Internet connections. Anybody who can offer Internet connectivity could claim to be a service provider; this description covers everything from a provider with a multimillion dollar backbone and infrastructure to a provider with a couple of routers and access servers in his garage.

Price should not be the main factor on which you base your decision. What really matters are factors such as the provider's services, backbone design, fault tolerance, redundancy, stability, bottlenecks, provider/customer equipment arrangement, and so on.

Routing behaviors on the Internet are affected by how routing protocols and data traffic behave over an already established physical connectivity. A good physical infrastructure design and maintenance is one of the main factors in achieving healthy routing on the Internet.

ISP SERVICES

Different ISPs offer different services depending on how big they are and the infrastructure of their networks. Mainly, providers can be categorized by their method of physical Internet access, the applications they provide, and the security services they provide.

The following physical access methods are the most commonly deployed throughout the Internet:

- *Leased lines*—Leased lines could be provided at 19.2 Kbps or 56 Kbps, with increments of 56 Kbps or 64 Kbps up to T1/E1 lines on the lower-end, and T3 and fractional T3 (in multiple T1s) on the higher-end of the bandwidth scale. Leased lines are usually used when traffic bandwidth is predictable and the frequency of network access is high enough to justify a line being up 24 hours a day. Of course, the trade-off is the cost, which is higher than any other connection type.

- *Frame relay*—Frame relay connections are one of the most economical ways for corporations to hook up to the Internet. Purchasing sufficient point-to-point leased line connections can be prohibitively expensive for some companies, in which case they may want to consider connecting to existing frame relay backbones on a per-need basis. With frame relay, corporations can buy enough bandwidth to meet their existing needs and to easily expand as traffic requirements increase. The trade-off is that you are limited by the bandwidth offered by your provider. Other wide area network services such as ATM are starting to be used and recognized, but do not have the success that frame relay has experienced.

- *Dialup services*—This includes Asynchronous dialup at 9.6, 14.4, and 28.8 Kbps, ISDN Basic Rate Interface (BRI), or Primary Rate Interface (PRI). Dialup services range from serving individual users to serving corporations that are subcontracting with providers to obtain all their remote login needs. ISDN BRI and PRI services have experienced great growth lately due to their on-demand nature and their capability to carry digital signaling essential for multimedia services.

Prices for ISP services are often predicated on physical access methods, as discussed further in the next section. Customers need to weigh costs and benefits of the different options against their needs.

Almost every single provider offers the following basic services: electronic mail, Usenet newsgroups, ftp, Gopher retrieval, and Wide Area Information Servers (WAIS) resource discovery tool. In addition, due to the phenomenal popularity of the World Wide Web, most ISPs provide this service in one form or another. Customers who do not want to maintain an in-house WWW server can buy space from a shared server on the ISP's premises. Some ISPs are even offering total Web solutions for companies that need a total package, such as advertising, enabling customers to order online, updating inventory, billing, and shipping.

ISPs can offer consulting for different security services. The easiest service would be providing packet filtering on the router level. More security measures involve firewalls and, usually, additional fees. ISPs can integrate their own firewalls or help you configure firewalls that you buy from outside vendors.

ISP PRICING AND TECHNICAL CHARACTERISTICS

Besides evaluating services, customers should consider pricing and technical characteristics of an ISP before choosing one. Although technical characteristics in particular may seem intimidating, they have enormous implications for the reliability and ease-of-use of the provider you eventually select. Technical issues that this section addresses include backbone issues and demarcation.

ISP Service Pricing

Prices for services can differ dramatically between ISPs, even for the same services and within the same service areas. The price is usually determined by the provider's relative strength and level of investment in a particular area. A provider, for example, that has an established frame relay service will probably give you a much better price for that service than a provider just setting up frame relay. The following price ranges, based on 1996 data, should give you a rough idea of what to expect:

- *56 Kbps*— First time setup fee is $1,000 on the average. Monthly fees range between $300 to $1,300, with an average of $1,000/month.

- *T1*— First time setup fee is $1,000 on the average. Monthly fees average $3,000/ month.

- *T3*—Prices for T3s vary widely; companies usually strike deals with providers and negotiate the price. The average monthly fee for a T3 link could go as high as $50,000 per month. Customers usually deploy fractional T3 because it is considerably less expensive.

- *Dialup Asynchronous Service*—Prices for dialup connections are becoming very inexpensive; prices could range from $10 to $29 per month per user. There is usually a small startup fee and a preset hour limit such as 30 or 60 hours. A small charge is added for additional hours. In some cases, major telephone carriers who are getting into the Internet business are offering free access to their customers, which is driving competitors' prices even lower.

- *ISDN*—Pricing is usually provided either as a flat rate between $300 and $500 per month, or based on an hourly rate of about $30 for 30 to 35 hours plus $1.50 to $2 for each additional hour.

The prices just described do not include the cost of access lines because access lines are provided by carriers such as phone companies. Thus, most ISPs do not include the price of the physical link in their quotes. Customers must negotiate prices of the access lines directly with the carriers, although ISPs usually help to get the ball rolling.

Getting the same price from different providers does not mean that you are getting the same service. Some providers include the Customer Premises Equipment (CPE), such as the router and CSU/DSU (Channel Service Unit/Data Service Unit), as part of the deal. Others charge you extra for the CPE, which could make the bottom line substantially different. You might save a lot of money if you provide your own CPEs and maintain them yourself or pay the provider to do the maintenance.

Large companies usually like to buy their national and international Internet services from the same provider. This means better control and better coordination of services between the different regions of the same network. Some providers offer consolidated billing for all their services, national and international. This means one bill and one check, which is considered a plus by many companies. If the convenience of consolidated billing or common services is not an important issue, companies might find better deals for national and international service, respectively, from different ISPs.

ISP Backbone Selection Criteria

An ISP's backbone encompasses many important technical characteristics. These include physical network topology—connections, network bottlenecks, level of redundancy, distance from destination networks—and traffic exchange agreements. This section is aimed at both customers and designers of ISPs. Customers should certainly evaluate these characteristics in choosing a provider; they are far more important than prices in predicting service quality. Designers should consider the potential benefits and pitfalls associated with these characteristics when setting up or expanding their networks.

Physical Connections

Customers should investigate the provider's physical connections, and the provider should be able to show a decent map of the network, with every connection indicated. With respect to connections, a healthy physical topology is one that can provide consistent, adequate bandwidth for the whole traffic trajectory. The existence of high-speed links such as T3 and OC3/12 does not by itself guarantee overall high-speed access for the customer. Your traffic might flow on the provider's network over some backdoor T1 or frame relay clouds that might slow down the overall access.

Potential ISP Bottlenecks

The provider's network is only as strong as its weakest link. A provider should not oversubscribe its connections. ISPs that save money by overloading their routers or their connections will end up losing customers and credibility in the long run.

Oversubscribing happens when the cumulative traffic of multiple links exceeds the bandwidth of the pipe used to carry the traffic to the rest of the Internet. A provider selling 20 T1s at the POP (Point Of Presence) and connecting to the NAP via a T1 link will experience a bottleneck at the NAP connection. As illustrated in figure 2–1, a rule of thumb is a 5 to 1 ratio: there should be no more than five T1 links for each T1 pipe. Even this ratio might not be accurate if most of the T1s get heavily loaded all at the same time. For ISP network designers, a better approach is to monitor the pipe and to start adding bandwidth whenever line utilization starts exceeding 50 percent of the pipe's capacity.

Another example of a bottleneck is high-speed sites trying to access information from low-speed sites. A Web server located at a site connected to the Internet via a 56 Kbps link can only be accessed at a maximum speed of 56 Kbps, even if you have a faster connection to the Internet. Figure 2–2 illustrates a client with T3 access to the Internet that will be limited to 56 Kbps access to its WWW server.

Figure 2–1
An ISP's weakest link limits performance.

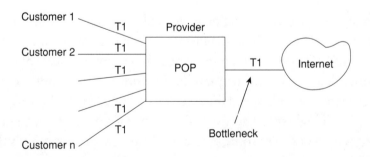

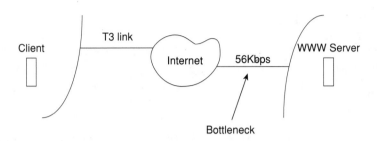

Figure 2–2
Access speed is limited by the smallest bandwidth.

If you are a provider, you had better watch the weak links for overutilization, and if you are a customer, understand what you are buying before you commit.

Level of ISP Internet Access Redundancy

Murphy is out there, ready to make your life miserable. Whether because of bad weather, carrier problems, or bad luck, an ISP's connection to a NAP or another POP might go down from time to time, with the potential for leaving customers without service. A redundant network will enable traffic to take another route until the problem is fixed. A well-designed ISP network is a network that has its POPs connected to multiple NAPs or to multiple other POPs, as illustrated in figure 2–3.

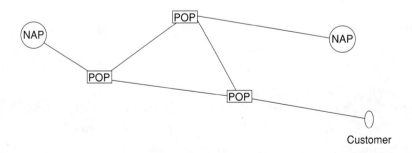

Figure 2–3
A redundant network provides more reliable connectivity.

Distance to Destinations

Customers should be concerned with the number of *hops*—that is, the number of interim networks—needed to reach a destination network through their ISP. In general, the more hops, the more potential for traffic to get delayed, misdirected, or garbled.

The distance to destinations depends on how the provider is connected to the NAPs. As you know by now, the Internet is a set of overlapping backbones from different providers, with the NAPs being the crossover between one provider and another. Small providers might connect to only one NAP or might not connect to any NAPs at all. In the latter case, a provider could offer service by being the customer of another provider who is connected to the NAP.

In general, providers that claim less than five hops to a destination are those who are connected to most of the NAPs and have a widespread backbone. Smaller resellers tap into major providers, and the traffic might end up hopping a couple of different backbones before reaching the final destination.

Traffic Exchange Agreements

It is important that an ISP be part of all traffic exchange agreements, such as the CIX. Every ISP has to pay its due; there is no free lunch out there. If an ISP is not part of an interexchange agreement with other ISPs, its traffic might be denied when it reaches other providers' networks.

Demarcation Point

Finally, in addition to pricing and backbone issues, customers will want to consider demarcation point (DP) issues in selecting an ISP and forming an agreement. A *demarcation point* is the point that differentiates the provider's network from the customer's network, as illustrated in figure 2–4. It is important to differentiate between the areas of responsibility of both parties, provider and customer. Demarcation points are defined down to the cables and connectors to make sure that no arguments occur in case of equipment or network problems.

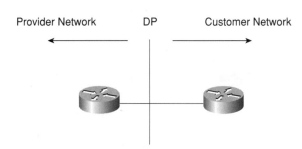

Provider Network   DP   Customer Network

Figure 2–4
Demarcation point.

Different providers define the DP differently depending on who is paying for the equipment and the access line.

Customer Premises Equipment (CPE)

Customer Premises Equipment (CPE) usually includes the router, the CSU/DSU, the cabling, and probably an analog modem for monitoring. ISPs typically offer customers the choice of buying the CPE and the access line, buying just the access line, or just paying a monthly fee with all equipment and access needs taken care of by the ISP. Any arrangement is available at a price. ISPs usually are responsible for maintaining equipment or packages that they provide. An ISP might have a predefined package that includes CPE and/or access. If the customer does not want to take the package, then the customer would be required to choose equipment that is pre-approved by the ISP. The customer would then be responsible for troubleshooting and maintaining its own equipment. The provider is always available to solve problems at an extra charge. Figures 2–5 through 2–7 illustrate some examples of ISP packages.

In the scenario illustrated in figure 2–5, the ISP is responsible for the access line and the CSU/DSU all the way up to the CSU's serial connector at the customer site. Restrictions might be imposed on the customer premises routers to meet some memory or software revision guidelines.

In the scenario illustrated in figure 2–6, the ISP has provided everything and its responsibility ends at the LAN port of the router at the customer's premises.

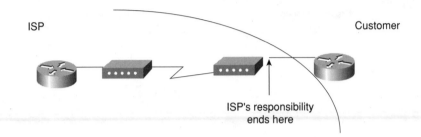

Figure 2–5
Example: ISP provides access and CSU/DSU; customer provides router.

ISP

Customer

ISP's responsibility
ends here

In the scenario illustrated in figure 2–7, the customer provides the CPE and the access line; the provider's responsibility will end at the POP's wiring closet where the ISP interconnects with the carrier's central office (CO).

Router Collocation

Collocation is the act of placing one party's equipment on another party's premises. An example of collocation is putting the customer's router on the provider's site, as illustrated in figure 2–8. The customer motivation for such a collocation scheme would be to have the ISP provide local monitoring of the equipment. Usually ISPs do not like to put customer routers on their premises unless they really have to in order to satisfy the customer. Real estate is becoming a real issue, and the ISPs are having problems finding places for their own equipment at the POP.

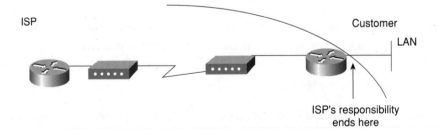

Figure 2–6
Example: ISP provides access, router, and CSU/DSU.

ISP

Customer

LAN

ISP's responsibility
ends here

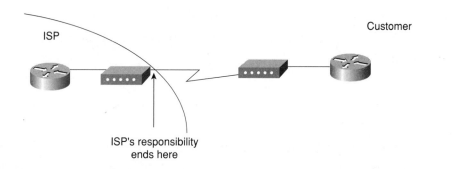

Figure 2–7
Example: customer provides everything.

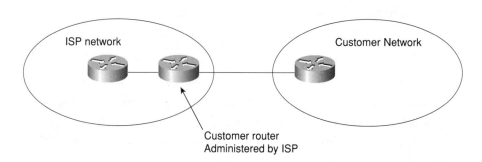

Figure 2–8
Example: customer router located at ISP site.

The opposite of the situation described in figure 2–8 is for the ISP to collocate its own POP router at the customer's site. This is shown in figure 2–9. Usually in this case, the ISP would pay for the access line and the router and would

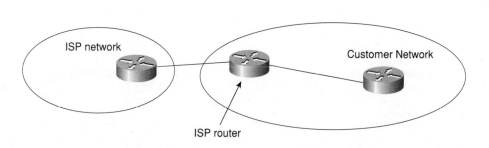

Figure 2–9
Example: ISP router located at customer site.

charge the customer a monthly fee for the whole service. The ISP in this case would benefit from more real estate at his premises while providing a total package to the customer.

Looking Ahead

Technical characteristics of an ISP's network have significant repercussions for the customer's service, including the quality of routing architecture. Because the customer might not have direct control over some of these technical characteristics, it is critical that the customer at least evaluate them and make sure that they will deliver the required connectivity and quality.

If you are an ISP customer whose demarcation point and collocation agreements stipulate that you are running and maintaining equipment on your premises—even if you do not own it outright—you are likely to be taking a significant hands-on role in developing the routing policies and architecture for your network. Even if you are not running and maintaining the equipment, there are decisions you will need to make and understand with respect to routing architecture.

The next chapter completes the foundational part of this book by discussing addressing and address depletion. After that, all the groundwork will have been established for an in-depth discussion of routing protocols in subsequent chapters.

FREQUENTLY ASKED QUESTIONS

Q— *Is higher price an indication that I will receive faster, better connection service from an ISP?*

A— Not neccessarily. Higher prices sometimes reflect the provider's having invested in fast connections, such as T3 or higher bandwidth links. The mere presence of such links, however, does not necessarily mean that your connections will be faster. A poorly designed combination of high-speed links and low-speed clouds, for example, might affect the overall performance of the provider negatively. The bottom line is that price is just one factor to consider; even more important is a sound network topology that offers enough redundancy and adequate bandwith to fit your needs.

Q— *What causes bottlenecks in the ISP's backbone?*

A— Bottlenecks are caused by oversubscription or overutilization of bandwidth on a physical link.

Q— *When I connect to an ISP, should I buy my own equipment?*

A— There are pros and cons to buying your own equipment; only you can decide whether this is the optimal approach for your organization's needs. First, find out whether your ISP insists on your using its equipment (some do). Even if the ISP will let you purchase your own, it probably will stipulate certain hardware and software that conform to its system. Cost issues are likely to factor significantly in your decision: Can your organization afford the capital investment, including upgrades and expansion as needed? By buying the equipment, you might also be committing yourself to maintaining it, although some ISPs will agree to maintain (for a fee) equipment owned by the customer.

Q— *If my connection to an ISP goes down because of equipment failure, who is responsible for what?*

A— It all depends on the service you are getting from the ISP. The preset demarcation point defines the line of responsibility between you and the provider.

CHAPTER 3

Handling IP Address Depletion

The overall model of address assignment continues to evolve. One of the major problems facing the Internet community is the depletion of IP addresses; this mandates the implementation of new IP addressing strategies. This chapter summarizes these strategies, their relative merits, and the issues surrounding address assignment on the Internet.

Addressing strategies are of direct and fundamental relevance to routing architecture. One of the basic functions of routing architecture and routers is to accommodate addresses for all the traffic that they direct. With the explosive growth of the Internet, the sheer number of addresses and the evolution of new addressing strategies have presented new challenges for routing architecture. Throughout this chapter, we will note particular routing rules and issues as they pertain to IP addressing.

This chapter begins with an overview of the basic IP addressing and subnetting models.

OVERVIEW OF IPV4 ADDRESSING

The IP addressing scheme that is widely used today is relevant to the IP version 4 (IPv4) implementation. This section discusses the following:

- Basic Addressing [1]

- Basic Subnetting [2]

- Variable Length Subnet Mask (VLSM) [3]

BASIC ADDRESSING

The IP address, a 32-bit address, is represented by a dotted decimal notation of the form X.Y.Z.T (for example, 10.0.0.1). The 32-bit address field consists of two parts: a network number and a host number whose boundaries are defined based on the class of the IP address. The different IP classes are: A, B, and C[1]. This addressing scheme is sometimes referred to as the *classfull* model. The different classes lend themselves to different network configurations, depending on the desired ratio of networks to hosts. The full implications of the different classes will become more apparent as this chapter proceeds. For now, the chapter focuses on basic definitions of each class.

Class A Addressing

A class A network is represented by a 0 in the first bit. The first 8 bits (0–7) represent the network number, and the remaining bits (8–31) represent a host number on that network. The outcome of this representation, indicated in Figure 3–1, is 128 (2^7) class A network numbers having 16777216 (2^{24}) hosts per network (ignoring the boundaries such as all 0s and all 1s hosts that have special meaning). An example of a class A network is 10.0.0.1, representing network 10.0.0.0 and host 1.

---

[1]   Classes D and E for multicast and reserved addresses are beyond the scope of this book.

Class B Addressing

A class B network is represented by a 1 and a 0 in the first two bits. The first 16 bits (0–15) represent the network number, and the last 16 bits (16–31) represent the host number on that network. The outcome of this representation, indicated in Figure 3–2, is 16384 (2^{14}) network numbers with 655366 (2^{16}) hosts per network (also ignoring boundaries). An example of a class B network is 172.16.0.1 where 172.16.0.0 is the class B network, and 1 is the host.

Class C Addressing

A class C network is represented by a 1 and a 1 and a 0 in the first three bits. The first 24 bits (0–23) represent the network number, and the last 8 bits (24–31) represent the host number on that network. The outcome of this representation, indicated in Figure 3–3, is 2097152 (2^{21}) network numbers with 256 (2^{8}) hosts per network (ignoring boundaries). An example of a class C network is 192.11.1.1, where 192.11.1.0 is the class C network and 1 is the host.

Basic Subnetting

Basic subnetting and variable length subnets are still quite misunderstood. This section first gives a brief introduction on how subnetting works and then tackles Variable Length Subnet Masks (VSLM), trying to make it as clear as possible.

Figure 3–1
General class A address format.

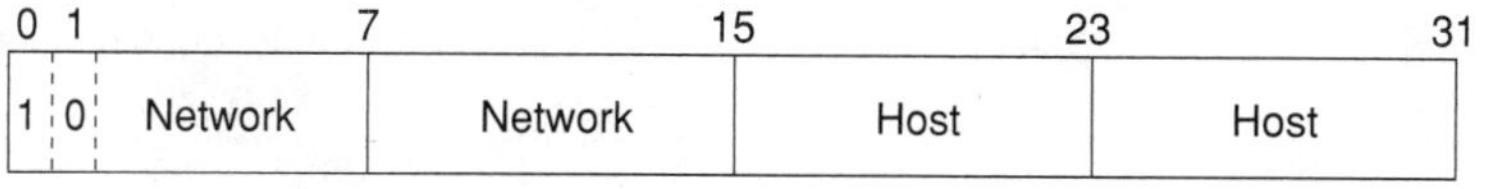

Figure 3–2
General class B address format.

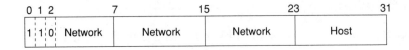

A *subnet* or *subnetwork* is a subset of class A, B, or C networks. To elaborate more, take a closer look at IP addresses. IP addresses are formed of a network portion and a host portion. A network *mask* is used to separate the network information from the host information.

In figure 3–4, the network mask 255.0.0.0 is applied to network 10.0.0.0. The mask in a binary notation is a series of contiguous ones followed by a series of contiguous zeros. The ones portion represents the network number, whereas the zeros portion represents the host number. This would split the IP address 10.0.0.1 into a network portion of 10 and a host portion of 0.0.1. As such, classes A, B, and C each have what is called a *natural mask,* which is the mask created by the very definition of the network and host portions of each class.

- Class A natural mask 255.0.0.0

- Class B natural mask 255.255.0.0

- Class C natural mask 255.255.255.0

By separating the network and host portions of an IP address, masks facilitate the creation of subnets. Without the introduction of subnets, network numbers would be of very limited use. Each physical segment, such as an Ethernet, Token

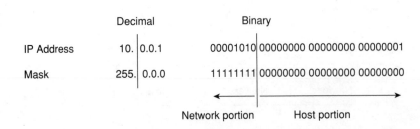

Network 10.0.0.0 with 16777216 hosts

Figure 3–5
Illustration of an unsubnetted class A address space.

Ring, or FDDI segment, is normally associated with one or more network numbers. If this is the case, then a class A network of the form 10.0.0.0 would accommodate one physical segment with about 16 million hosts on it, as indicated in figure 3–5.

With the use of masks, networks can be divided into subnetworks by extending the network portion of the address into the host portion. The subnetting technique increases the number of subnetworks and reduces the number of hosts.

In figure 3–6, a mask of 255.255.0.0 is applied to network 10.0.0.0. This will divide the IP address 10.0.0.1 into a network portion of 10, a subnet portion of 0, and a host portion of 0.1. The 255.255.0.0 mask has borrowed a portion of the host space and has applied it to the network space. As a result, the network space of the class 10 has increased from a single network 10.0.0.0 to 256 subnetworks ranging from 10.0.0.0 to 10.255.0.0. This would decrease the number of hosts per each subnet from 16777216 to 65536 (ignoring boundaries).

Variable Length Subnet Mask

The term *Variable Length Subnet Mask* (VLSM) refers to the fact that one network can be configured with different masks. The idea behind Variable Length Subnet Masks [3] is to offer more flexibility in dividing a network into multiple

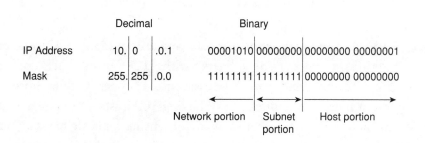

Figure 3–6
Basic subnetting.

subnets while still maintaining an adequate number of hosts in each subnet. Without VLSM, one subnet mask only can be applied to a network. This would restrict the number of hosts given the number of subnets required. If you pick the mask such that you have enough subnets, you might not be able to allocate enough hosts in each subnet. The same is true for the hosts; a mask that allows enough hosts might not provide enough subnet space.

Suppose, for example, that you were assigned a class C network 192.214.11.0 and you need to divide that network into three subnets, with 100 hosts in one subnet and 50 hosts for each of the remaining subnets. Ignoring the two end limits 0 and 255, you theoretically have available to you 256 addresses 192.214.11.0 to 192.214.11.255. The desired subdivision cannot be done without VLSM, as you shall see.

There are a handful of subnet masks of the form 255.255.255.X that can be used to divide the class C network 192.214.11.0 into more subnets. Remember that a mask should have a contiguous number of ones starting from the left, and the rest of the bits should be zeros. The following masks could be used to segment the theoretical 256 addresses available to you into more subnets.

- 252 (1111 1100)—64 subnets with 4 hosts each.

- 248 (1111 1000)—32 subnets with 8 hosts each.

- 240 (1111 0000)—16 subnets with 16 hosts each.

- 224 (1110 0000)—8 subnets with 32 hosts each.

- 192 (1100 0000)—4 subnets with 64 hosts each.

- 128 (1000 0000)—2 subnets with 128 hosts each.

Without VLSM, you have the choice of using mask 255.255.255.128 and dividing the addresses into two subnets with 128 hosts each or using 255.255.255.192 and dividing the addresses into 4 subnets with 64 hosts each. This would not meet the requirement of having 100 hosts on one segment and 50 hosts on each of the two other segments. By using multiple masks, you can use mask 128 to divide the addresses into two subnets with 128 hosts each and then use mask 192 to further subnet the second chunk of addresses into two subnets with 64 hosts each. Figure 3–7 and figure 3–8 illustrate how to divide the address space accordingly.

Not all routing protocols can handle VLSM. RIP Version 1[2] and IGRP[3] do not carry network masks in routing updates and hence have trouble dealing with variably subnetted networks. Today, even with the deployment of routing protocols such as OSPF[4], EIGRP[5], ISIS[6], and RIP Version 2 that can handle variable length masks, administrators still have difficulties adapting to this technique. Most early networks built on RIP version 1 and IGRP do not have their IP addresses assigned in a manner that would enable them to be grouped in blocks. Rather, their IP addresses are all over the place, and administrators would have to renumber their hosts to make them conform with the new addressing scheme. Such renumbering is so difficult that most administrators consider it out of the

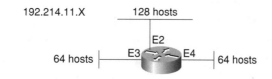

Figure 3–7
Example of a class C network divided into three subnets.

VLSM

128 addresses (E2)	
(mask 255.255.255.128)	
64 addresses (E3)	64 addresses (E4)
(mask 255.255.255.192)	(mask 255.255.255.192)

Figure 3–8
Use of VLSM to split network space into subnets of unequal size.

[2] Routing Information Protocol
[3] Interior Gateway Routing Protocol—Cisco proprietary
[4] Open Shortest Path First
[5] Enhanced Internet Gateway Protocol—Cisco proprietary
[6] Intermediate System-to-Intermediate System

question. So, the older protocols must co-exist with newer methods that do handle VLSM. This co-existence is a challenge, and administrators have resorted to much maneuvering and static routing to accommodate it.

IP ADDRESS SPACE DEPLETION

The growing demand for IP addresses has put a strain on the classfull model, especially class B address space, which was getting depleted at a fast pace. Most companies requesting IP addresses have estimated that a class B would meet their requirement because it is a fair balance between the number of networks and the number of hosts. A class A was overkill with more than 16 million hosts, and a class C had too few hosts per network. By 1991, it was becoming obvious that the class B consumption was not slowing down and actions needed to be taken to prevent its depletion. Some of these measures consisted of creative assignment of IP addresses and promoting the use of private IP addresses for organizations that do not have global connectivity needs. Other measures resulted in the initiation of working groups and directorates such as the Routing and Addressing (ROAD) working group and the IP next generation (IPng) directorate. In 1992, the ROAD working group proposed the use of Classless Interdomain Routing (CIDR) as a measure to move away from classfull IP addressing. At the same time, the IPng directorate was working on developing a new and improved IP addressing scheme, IP version 6 (IPv6), that would eventually solve the problems that IPv4 is encountering.

The measures to handle the IP depletion can be grouped in the following categories:

- Creative IP address space allocation

- Classless Interdomain Routing (CIDR) [4]

- Private addressing and Network Address Translation (NAT) [6,7]

- IP version 6 (IPv6) [8]

Along with depletion concerns, growing IP address demand generated a need to convert the IP addressing allocation process from a central registry. Originally, the Internet Assigned Numbers Authority (IANA) and the Internet Registry (IR) had total control for address assignment. IP addresses were assigned to organizations sequentially without any consideration of geographical factors and to how or where an organization would plug in into the Internet. This method had the effect of punching holes in the IP address space; that is, segregating individual or small numbers of IP addresses and eliminating large, contiguous ranges of numbers.

A different approach needed to be taken whereby a large, contiguous range of addresses is given to different administrations (such as service providers), and those providers in turn allocate addresses from their own space. In general, this funnel-down method of address allocation predicts a more controlled and hierarchical method of IP address distribution.

IP Address Allocation

Class A network numbers are limited resources, and the allocation from this space is restricted. Although the upper range of class A 64 to 127 will be distributed, there is still no definite plan on how this is going to be done.

Class B addresses are also restricted. They will be allocated only if the need for such addresses is fully justified. Due to the scarcity of class B network numbers and the under utilization of the address space by most organizations, the recommendation is to use multiple class Cs instead.

The class C network number space is now being divided and allocated in a way that is compatible with address aggregation techniques. *Address aggregation* is the practice of summarizing a contiguous block of addresses in a single notation, or advertisement. (Aggregation is also relevant to the CIDR model, to be discussed in the next section.)

Class C addresses are being distributed to ISPs with the requirement that the original allocation for the provider should last at least two years. In turn, each provider will allocate a block of addresses from its own range to each of its customers. Customers will not be granted more addresses from their ISPs until 80 percent of the original address space granted to the customer has been used. The allocation of class C addresses is illustated in table 3–1.

If a subscriber has a requirement for more than 4,096 IP addresses, a class B network number might be allocated.

Organizations are encouraged to use Variable Length Subnet Mask (VLSM) as much as possible to use the address space more efficiently.

As far as the geographic allocation of blocks of C addresses, there are four major areas: Europe, North America, the Pacific Rim, and South and Central America. The allocation is summarized in table 3–2. The multiregional area represents network numbers that have been assigned prior to the implementation of this plan. Ranges designated as "Others" are for geographical areas other than the areas named specifically.

Classless Interdomain Routing (CIDR)

In recent years, the IP routing tables held in the Internet routers have grown in a way that caused routers to start being saturated as far as processing power and memory allocation. Statistics and growth rate projections suggest that routing tables have doubled in size every 10 months between 1988 and 1991. Figure 3–9 illustrates this growth. Without any plan of action, the routing table would have grown to about 80,000 routes in 1995. Actual data in 1996, however, showed

	Organization Requirement	Address Assignment
Table 3–1 *Class C address assignment summary.*	Fewer than 256 addresses	1 class C network
	Fewer than 512 but more than 256	2 contiguous class C networks
	Fewer than 1,024 but more than 512	4 contiguous class C networks
	Fewer than 2,048 but more than 1,024	8 contiguous class C networks
	Fewer than 4,096 but more than 2,048	16 contiguous class C networks
	Fewer than 8,192 but more than 4,096	32 contiguous class C networks
	Fewer than 16,384 but more than 8,192	64 contiguous class C networks

Area of Allocation	Address Spaces
Multiregional	192.0.0.0 to 193.255.255.255
Europe	194.0.0.0 to 195.255.255.255
Others	196.0.0.0 to 197.255.255.255
North America	198.0.0.0 to 199.255.255.255
Central/South America	200.0.0.0 to 201.255.255.255
Pacific Rim	202.0.0.0 to 203.255.255.255
Others	204.0.0.0 to 205.255.255.255
Others	206.0.0.0 to 207.255.255.255

Table 3–2
Address space allocation among major geographic areas.

that the routing table size is around 42,000 routes. This reduction in growth is attributed to the IP address allocation scheme discussed in the previous section and to the adoption of CIDR.

CIDR is a move away from the traditional IP classes A/B/C. In CIDR, an IP network is represented by a prefix, which is an IP address and some indication of

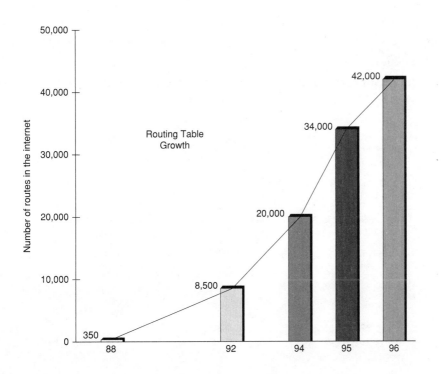

Figure 3–9
Routing table growth chart.

the leftmost contiguous significant bits within this address. For example, 198.32.0.0, which used to be an illegal class C network, is now a valid prefix with a notation 198.32.0.0/16. The /16 is an indication that you are using 16 bits of mask counting from the far left. This is similar to 198.32.0.0 255.255.0.0.

A network is called a *supernet* when the prefix boundary contains fewer bits than the network's natural mask. A class C network 198.32.1.0, for example, has a natural mask of 255.255.255.0. The representation 198.32.0.0 255.255.0.0 also represented as 198.32.0.0/16 has a shorter mask than the natural mask (16 < 24); hence, it is a supernet.

These address schemes are illustrated in figure 3–10.

This notation enables you to lump all the more specific routes of 198.32.0.0 (such as 198.32.1.0 and 198.32.2.0, and so on) into one advertisement called an *aggregate*.

It is easy to be confused by all this new terminology, especially because the terms *aggregate*, *CIDR block*, and *supernet* are often used interchangeably in casual discussion. Generally, the terms all indicate that a list of contiguous IP networks has been summarized into one announcement. More precisely, CIDR

Figure 3–10
CIDR-based addressing illustration.

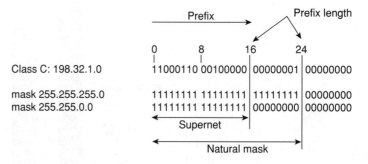

is the <prefix,length> notation; supernets have a prefix length shorter than the natural mask; and aggregates indicate any summary route.

All the networks that are a subset of an aggregate or a CIDR block are called "more specific" because they give more information about the location of a network. More specific prefixes have a longer prefix length than the aggregate:

- 198.213.0.0/16—aggregate of length 16

- 198.213.1.0/20—more specific prefix of length 20

Routing domains that are CIDR-capable are called *classless*, in contrast to the traditional classfull routing domains. CIDR has depicted a new, more hierarchical Internet architecture, where each domain takes its IP addresses from a higher hierarchical level. This gives tremendous savings in route propagation especially when summarization is done close to the so-called *leaf networks*. Leaf networks are endpoints on the global network; they do not, in turn, provide Internet connection to other networks. An ISP that supports numerous leaf networks subdivides its subnets into many smaller blocks of addresses to serve those customers. Aggregation permits the ISP to advertise the addresses in a single notation rather than many, thus resulting in more efficient routing strategies and propagation.

The efficiency of aggregation is illustrated in figure 3–11. In this example, ISP3 has been given the block 198.0.0.0 through 198.255.255.0. ISP3 has given two blocks of its addresses to ISP1 and ISP2. ISP1 has the range 198.32.0.0 through 198.32.255.0, and ISP2 has the range 198.33.0.0 through 198.33.255.0. In the same manner, ISP1 and ISP2 have allocated their own customers a block of addresses from their own ranges. The left side instance of figure 3–11 shows what happens if you do not use CIDR: ISP1 and ISP2 would have to advertise all the subnets coming from their customers, and ISP3 would have passed all these advertisements to the outside world. This would result in a major increment in the global IP routing tables.

The right side instance of figure 3–11 shows the same scenario when CIDR is applied. ISP1 and ISP2 are performing aggregation on their customer subnets,

ISP1 is advertising the aggregate 198.32.0.0/16, and ISP2 is advertising the aggregate 198.33.0.0/16. In the same manner, ISP3 is performing aggregating on its customer subnets, ISP1 and ISP2, and is sending only one aggregate 198.0.0.0/8. This results in tremendous savings in the global IP routing tables.

As you can see, aggregation results in more significant efficiency gains when done close to the leaf node because the majority of the subnets to be aggregated are deployed at the customer premises. Aggregation at higher levels, such as ISP3, results in less reduction because it is dealing with fewer networks to start with.

Aggregation works optimally if every customer connects to his provider via one connection only (a scenario called *single-homing*), and also if the customer has taken its IP addresses from its provider's prefixes. Unfortunately, this is not

Figure 3–11

Comparison of classful addressing and CIDR-based addressing.

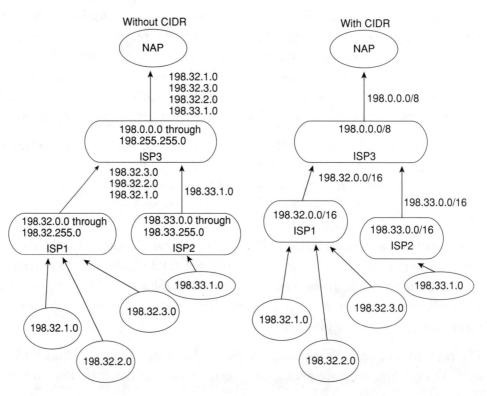

always the case in the real world. Situations arise, for example, where customers already have IP addresses that do not belong to their provider's range. As another example, some customers (who could be providers themselves) have found the need to connect to multiple providers at the same time (a scenario known as *multihoming*). These situations result in further complications and less flexibility in aggregation.

These complications to aggregation are discussed in more detail. But first, it is important to understand a couple of routing rules, as described in the next two subsections.

The Longest Match Routing Rule

Routing to all destinations is always done on a *longest match* basis: a router that has to decide between two different length prefixes of the same network will always follow the longer mask. Suppose, for example, that a router has the following two entries in its routing table:

–198.32.1.0/24 via path 1

–198.32.0.0/16 via path 2

When trying to deliver traffic to host 198.32.1.1, the router tries to match the destination with the longest prefix and would deliver the traffic via path 1. This is illustrated in figure 3–12 where Domain C is receiving the two updates 198.32.1.0/24 and 198.32.0.0/16; traffic toward 198.32.1.1 is following path 1. In case path 1 goes down for some reason, traffic will take path 2. In cases where Domain C is receiving identical routing updates with masks of equal length coming from Domain A and Domain B, Domain C would pick one path or the other or both depending on the load balancing techniques offered by the specific routing implemetation defined for that domain.

The longest match rule implies that destinations connected to multiple domains must always be explicitly announced—that is, announced in their most specific, not aggregate, forms—by these domains. In figure 3–12, because Domain B does not explicitly advertise route 198.32.1.0/24, traffic from the customer to the host must always go via the longest prefix match, through Domain A. Such a routing configuration might put an unacceptable burden on Domain A.

Less Specific Routes of a Network's Own Aggregate

Avoiding loops in default routing by use of pit buckets.

A specific rule of routing states that, for the sake of preventing routing loops, a network must not follow a less specific route for a destination that matches one of its own aggregated routes. A *routing loop* occurs when traffic circles back and forth between domains, never reaching its final destination. Default routes 0.0.0.0/0.0.0.0 are a special case of this rule. A network should not follow the default to destinations that are part of one of its aggregated advertisements. This is why routing protocols that handle aggregation of routes should always keep a *Pit Bucket* (*Null0 route* in Cisco's terminology) to the aggregate route itself. Traffic sent to the pit bucket will be dropped, which would stop the loop situation.

Figure 3–13 illustrates ISP1 aggregating its domain into a single route 198.32.0.0/13. Assume that the link between ISP1 and its customer Samnet (where network 198.32.1.0/24 exists) broke. Suppose also that ISP1 has a default route 0.0.0.0/0.0.0.0 that points to ISP2 for addresses not known within ISP1. Traffic toward 198.32.1.1 will follow the aggregate route to ISP1, will not find the destination, and will follow the default route back to ISP2. The traffic will bounce back and forth between ISP2 and ISP1. To prevent such a loop, a null0

Figure 3–12
Following the longest match.

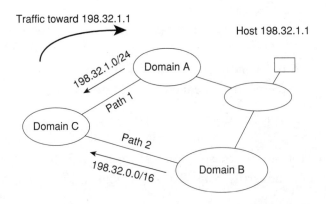

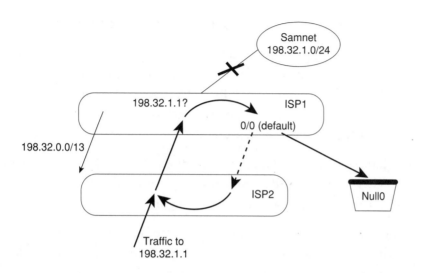

Figure 3–13
Following less specific routes of a network's own aggregate causes loops.

entry to the aggregate route, installed in ISP1's border router will drop all packets destined to an unreachable destination less specific than the aggregate route.

Aggregation, if not properly applied, could result in routing loops and black holes. A *black hole* occurs when traffic reaches and stops at a destination that is not its intended destination, but from which it cannot be forwarded. These and other routing challenges will become more apparent as you learn about multiple IP address allocation schemes and how they interact with aggregation.

Single-Homing Scenario: Addresses Taken from Outside the Provider's Address Space

In this scenario, the customer is connected to a single provider and has an IP address space totally different from the provider's. This could have happened because the customer changed providers and kept the addresses of the previous provider. Usually in this situation, customers are encouraged or forced to renumber. But if renumbering does not take place, the new provider cannot aggregate the customer addresses. Moreover, the old provider cannot aggregate as efficiently as it once did, because a hole has been punched in its address space. The overall effect of using addresses from outside the provider's address space is that more routes must be installed in the global routing tables.

Multihoming Scenario: Addresses Taken from One Provider

In this scenario, customers are connected to multiple providers. Customers are small enough that they need to take IP addresses from only one of their multiple providers. We will consider two ISPs, ISP1 and ISP2, and their customers: Jamesnet, Stubnet, and Lindanet. The IP address ranges for each domain, corresponding aggregate, and provider are listed in table 3–3.

Note that Jamesnet and Lindanet are multihomed to ISP1 and ISP2 with their address ranges taken from ISP1. Stubnet is single-homed to ISP1 with an address range taken from ISP1. This is illustrated in figure 3–14.

Advertising aggregates is a tricky business. Customers and ISPs have to be careful about the IP address ranges that the aggregate covers. No one is allowed to aggregate someone else's routes (proxy aggregation) unless the aggregating party is a superset of the other party or both parties are in total agreement. In the following, you will see how ISP2 can cause a routing black hole by aggregating the ranges coming from Jamesnet and Lindanet.

TROUBLESHOOTING

Black holes that result from inappropriate aggregation of others' routes.

If ISP2 were to send an aggregate that summarizes Jamesnet and Lindanet into one update (198.24.0.0/18), then a routing black hole will occur. Stubnet, for example, which is a customer of ISP1, has an IP address space that falls inside the aggregate 198.24.0.0/18. If ISP2 were to advertise that aggregate, then traffic to Stubnet will follow the longest match and end up in ISP2. This is why ISP2 will have to specifically list each of the IP address ranges that it has in common with ISP1 on top of its own address space 198.32.0.0/13.

	Domain	Address Range	Aggregate	Provider	Address Taken From
Table 3–3 *List of customers and corresponding providers.*	ISP1	198.24.0.0-198.31.0.0	198.24.0.0/13		
	Jamesnet	198.24.0.0-198.24.15.0	198.24.0.0/20	ISP1, ISP2	ISP1
	Stubnet	198.24.16.0-198.24.23.0	198.24.16.0/21	ISP1	ISP1
	Lindanet	198.24.56.0-198.24.63.0	198.24.56.0/21	ISP1, ISP2	ISP1
	ISP2	198.32.0.0-198.39.0.0	198.32.0.0/13		

Figure 3–15 shows the correctly advertised aggregates. ISP2 has to advertise the aggregates from Jamesnet and Lindanet explicitly. This way, traffic advertised to Stubnet would never go to ISP2.

Note in figure 3–15 that ISP1 is also advertising the explicit aggregates of Jamesnet and Lindanet. If ISP1 were to advertise the less-specific aggregate 198.24.0.0/13 only, all traffic toward Jamesnet and Lindanet would always follow the longest match via ISP2.

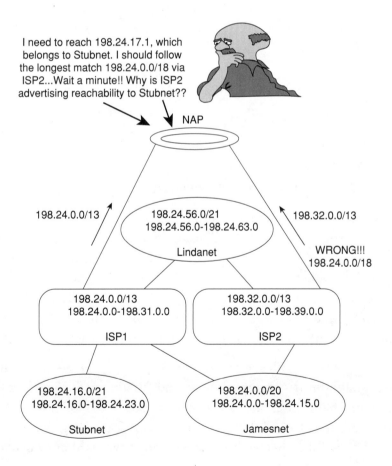

Figure 3–14
ISP2 advertising the wrong aggregate causes black holes.

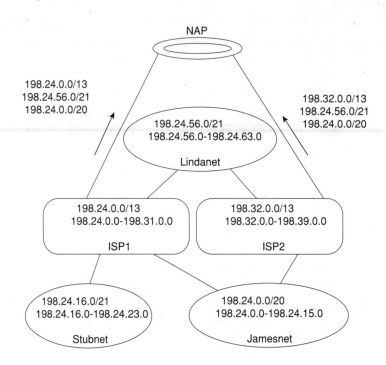

Figure 3–15
*Correctly
advertised
aggregates.*

Multihoming Scenario:
Addresses Taken from Different Providers

One possibility for large domains is to take addresses from different providers based on the geographic location. Consider figure 3–16. Largenet has taken its IP addresses from two different providers, ISP1 and ISP2. With this design, each provider will be able to aggregate its own address space without having to list specific ranges from the other provider. ISP1 would advertise the aggregate 198.24.0.0/13, and ISP2 would advertise the aggregate 1928.32.0.0/13. Both aggregates are supersets of an IP address block in Largenet.

The major drawback with the design illustrated in figure 3–16 is that backup routes to multihomed organizations are not maintained. ISP2 is advertising only its block of addresses and not the block taken from ISP1. In case ISP1 has problems and the 198.24.0.0/13 is lost, traffic to Largenet destined for 198.24.0.0/20 will be affected because it is not advertised anywhere else. The

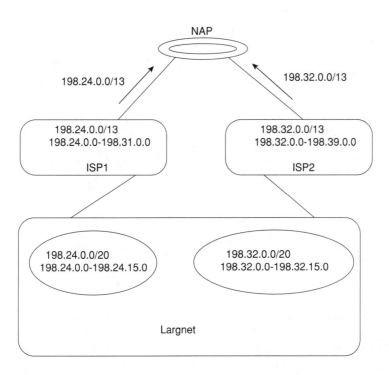

same reasoning applies for Largenet's addresses taken from ISP2. If the link to ISP2 fails, accessibility of the 198.32.0.0/20 range will be impaired. To remedy this situation, ISP1 has to advertise 198.32.0.0/20 and ISP2 has to advertise 198.24.0.0/20.

Multihoming Scenario:
Addresses Taken from None of the Providers

Figure 3–17 illustrates a situation in which addresses are taken from a range totally different from ISP1 or ISP2's address space. In this case, both ISP1 and ISP2 will advertise a specific aggregate (204.24.0.0/20) on top of their own ranges (198.24.0.0/13 and 198.32.0.0/13). The drawback of this method is that all routers in the Internet must have a specific route to the new range that is introduced. Too many of such instances would result in an increase in the overall routing tables.

Figure 3–17
*Addresses
obtained outside
ISP address space.*

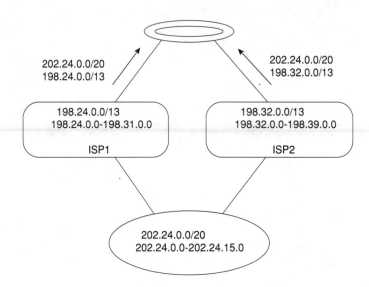

Aggregation Recommendations

In conclusion, a domain that has been allocated a range of addresses has the sole authority for aggregation of its address space. When a domain performs aggregation, it should aggregate as much as possible without causing ambiguity such as is possible in the case of multihomed networks.

Different situations require different designs. No one specific solution can handle all cases. It is recommended that single-homed customers obtain a single contiguous prefix from the direct provider. If they change providers, a plan should be put in place to transition the addressing to the new provider's address space. For multihomed customers, address assignments should be done in a way to maximize aggregation as much as possible. In the case where aggregation impacts redundancy, redundancy should prevail even if extra networks have to be listed.

The introduction of CIDR has helped damper the explosion of global routing tables tremendously over the last few years. The Border Gateway Protocol 4 (BGP4) is the routing protocol of choice on the Internet in part because it so efficiently handles route aggregation and propagation between different autonomous systems. As this book progresses, you will see more and more examples of the importance of CIDR in controlling traffic behavior and stability.

Private Addressing and Network Address Translation (NAT)

To find ways to slow down the pace at which the IP addresses were being allocated, it was important to identify different connectivity requirements and try to assign IP addresses accordingly.

Most organizations' connectivity needs fall in the following categories:

- Global connectivity

- Private connectivity (total or partial)

Global Connectivity

Global connectivity means that hosts inside an organization have access to both internal hosts and Internet hosts. In this case, hosts have to be configured with globally unique IP addresses that are recognized inside and outside the organization. Organizations requiring global connectivity must request IP addresses from their service providers.

Private Connectivity

Private connectivity means that hosts inside an organization have access to internal hosts only, not Internet hosts. Examples of hosts that require only private connectivity include bank ATM machines, cash registers in a retail company, or any host that does not really need to reach or be reached by hosts outside the company. Private hosts need to have IP addresses that are unique inside the organization, but do not have to be unique outside the organization. For this type of connectivity, the IANA has reserved the following three blocks of the IP address space for what is referred to as "private Internets:"

- 10.0.0.0 through 10.255.255.255 (a single class A network number)

- 172.16.0.0 through 172.31.255.255 (16 contiguous class B network numbers)

- 192.168.0.0 through 192.168.255.255 (256 contiguous class C network numbers)

An enterprise that picks its addresses from the preceding range does not need to get permission from the IANA or an Internet Registry. Hosts that get a private IP address can connect with any other host inside the organization, but cannot connect to hosts outside the organization without going through a proxy gateway. The reason is that IP packets leaving the company will have a source IP address that is ambiguous outside the company and cannot be replied to by outside hosts. Because multiple companies building private networks can use the same IP addresses, fewer unique global IP addresses need to be assigned.

Hosts having private addresses can co-exist with hosts having global addresses. Figure 3–18 illustrates such an environment. Companies might choose to have most of their hosts private and still keep particular segments with hosts having global addresses. The latter hosts can reach the Internet as usual. Companies that use private addresses and still have connectivity to the Internet have the responsibility of applying routing filters to prevent the private networks from being leaked to the Internet.

The drawback of this approach is that if an organization later on decides to open up its hosts to the Internet, the private IP addresses will have to be renumbered.With the introduction of new protocols such as the Dynamic Host Configuration Protocol (DHCP) [5], this task might become easy. DHCP provides a mechanism for transmitting configuration parameters (including IP addresses) to hosts using the TCP/IP protocol suite. Provided that the hosts are DHCP-compatible, hosts can get their new addresses dynamically from a central server.

Hosts that have private addresses can still reach the outside by going through a gateway or some kind of host that has a global address.

Figure 3–18
*General private
Connectivity
environment.*

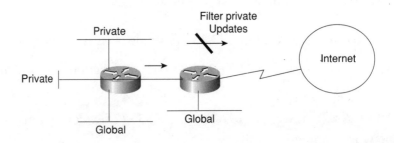

Host A in Figure 3–19 has a private IP address. If A wants to telnet to a destination outside the company, it can do so by first logging into host B and then telnetting from host B to the outside. Packets leaving the company now would have B's source IP address, which is global and can be replied to.

Network Address Translator

Companies migrating from a private address to a global address space can do so with the help of Network Address Translators (NAT). Cisco Systems offers this solution as part of its Cisco Internetwork Operating System (IOS)™ software running on its routers.

NAT technology enables private networks to connect to the Internet without resorting to renumbering IP addresses. A NAT router is placed at the border of a domain, and it translates the private addresses into global addresses before sending packets to the Internet.

As illustrated in figure 3–20, hosts A and B have private IP addresses 10.1.1.1 and 10.1.1.2. If A and B want to reach destinations outside the company, the NAT will convert the source IP addresses of the packets according to the predefined mapping in the NAT table. Packets from host A will reach the outside with a source IP address of 128.213.x.y, and packets from host B will reach the outside as coming from source IP address 128.213.z.w. Hosts in the global domains will not know the difference and will reply to hosts A and B as they would to any other host. On the way back, the destination address of the packets will be mapped back to the private IP address.

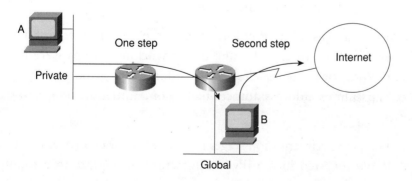

Figure 3–19
Privately addressed hosts accessing Internet resources.

Figure 3–20
*Network Address
Translator example.*

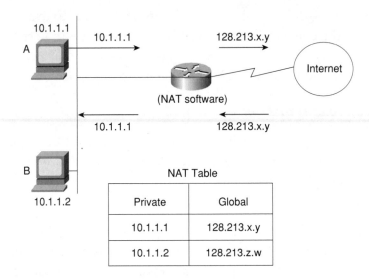

Discussions about NAT devices are beyond the scope of this book because they have to handle many "corner cases" and more involved situations. Such cases include enterprises that have used addresses that are not part of the IANA private addresses. In this case, addresses used could be already assigned by the IANA to some other company. Other situations involve enterprises that get assigned fewer global addresses than their number of hosts. In this case, the NAT has to dynamically map private IP addresses to a smaller pool of global addresses.

IP Version 6 (IPv6)

IP version 6 (IPv6), also known as IP next generation (IPng), is a move to improve the existing IPv4 implementation.

The IPng proposal was released in July 1992 at the Boston Internet Engineering Task Force (IETF) meeting, and a number of working groups were formed in response. IPv6 tackles issues such as the IP address depletion problem, quality of service capabilities, address autoconfiguration, authentication, and security capabilities.

IPv6 is still in its experimentation stage. It is not easy for companies and administrators deeply invested in the IPv4 architecture to migrate to a totally new architecture. As long as the IPv4 implementation keeps providing hooks and techniques (as cumbersome as they might be) to tackle all the major issues that IPv6 will solve, adopting IPv6 might not seem very compelling to many companies. How soon or how late people will migrate to IPv6 is yet to be seen.

As far as this book is concerned, we will only touch on part of the IPv6 addressing scheme and how it compares to what you already have seen in IPv4.

The IPv6 addresses are 128 bits long (compared to 32 bits in IPv4). This should provide ample address space to handle scalability issues in the Internet (128 bits of addressing will translate into 2^{128}—which is a lot of addresses).

The types of IPv6 addresses are indicated by the leftmost bits of the address in a variable length field called the *Format Prefix* (FP). This is illustrated in figure 3–21.

Table 3–4 outlines the initial allocation of these prefixes. IPv6 has defined multiple types of addresses; we are interested in the provider-based unicast addresses and the local use addresses for comparison with IPv4 techniques.

Provider-Based Unicast Addresses

Provider-based unicast addresses are similar to the IPv4 global addresses. The format of these addresses is illustrated in figure 3–22. Descriptions of the address fields are as follows:

- *Format Prefix*—First three bits are 010, indicating a provider-based unicast address.

- *REGISTRY ID*—Identifies the Internet address registry that assigns the PROVIDER ID.

- *PROVIDER ID*—Identifies the service provider responsible for this address.

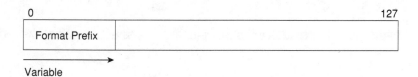

Figure 3–21
IPv6 prefix and address format.

Table 3–4	Description	Format Prefix
Allocation of IPv6 prefixes.	Reserved	0000 0000
	Unassigned	0000 0001
	Reserved for NSAP Allocation	0000 001
	Reserved for IPX Allocation	0000 010
	Unassigned	0000 011
	Unassigned	0000 1
	Unassigned	0001
	Unassigned	001
	Provider-Based Unicast Address	**010**
	Unassigned	011
	Reserved for Geographic Unicast Addresses	100
	Unassigned	101
	Unassigned	110
	Unassigned	1110
	Unassigned	1111 0
	Unassigned	1111 10
	Unassigned	1111 110
	Unassigned	1111 1110 0
	Link Local Use Addresses	**1111 1110 10**
	Site Local Use Addresses	**1111 1110 11**
	Multicast Addresses	1111 1111

- *SUBSCRIBER ID*—Identifies which subscriber is connected to the service provider.

- *SUBNET ID*—Identifies the physical link to which the address belongs.

- *INTERFACE ID*—Identifies a single interface among interfaces that belong to the SUBNET ID. For example, this could be the traditional 48-bit IEEE-802 Media Access Control (MAC) address.

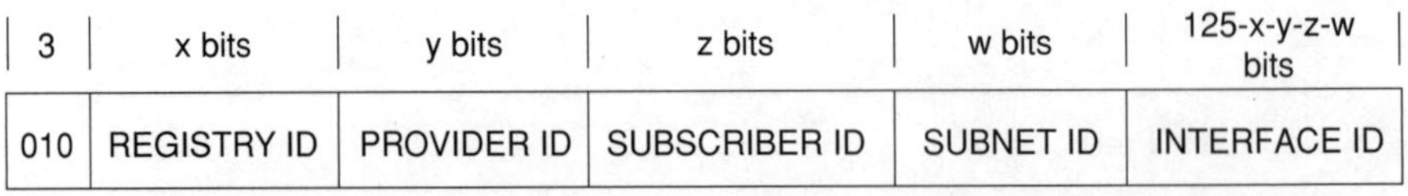

Figure 3–22
IPv6 address assignment hierarchy.

3	x bits	y bits	z bits	w bits	125-x-y-z-w bits
010	REGISTRY ID	PROVIDER ID	SUBSCRIBER ID	SUBNET ID	INTERFACE ID

The IPv6 global address incorporates the CIDR functions of the IPv4 scheme. Addresses are defined in such a way as to allow hierarchy, where each entity takes its portion of the address from an entity above it, as illustrated in figure 3–23.

Local-Use Addresses

Local-use addresses are similar to the IPv4 private addresses defined in RFC 1918. Local-use addresses are divided into two types: Link-Local Use (prefix 1111111010), which are private to a particular physical segment, and Site-Local Use (prefix 1111111011), which are private to a particular site. Figure 3–24 illustrates the format of these local use addresses.

The local-use addresses have local meaning. The link addresses have local meaning to a particular segment, and the site addresses have local meaning to a particular site.

Companies that are not connected to the Internet can easily assign their own addresses without a need for requesting prefixes from the global address space. If the company later decides to interconnect globally over the Internet, a REGISTRY ID, PROVIDER ID, and SUBSCRIBER ID will be assigned to be used with the already assigned local addresses. This is a major improvement over

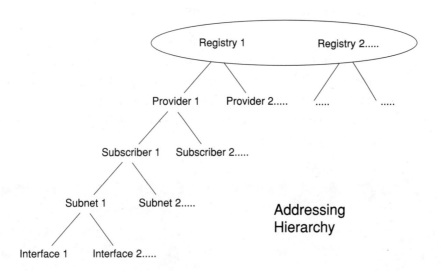

Figure 3–23
IPv6 address assignment hierarchy.

Figure 3–24
Local-use address
formats.

10 bits	x bits	118-x bits
1111111010	00000..	INTERFACE ID

Link Local-Use Addresses

10 bits	x bits	y bits	118-x-y bits
1111111011	00000..	SUBNET ID	INTERFACE ID

Site Local-Use Addresses

having to replace all private addresses with global addresses or using Network Address Translation tables to get things working in the IPv4 addressing scheme.

LOOKING AHEAD

IP addresses and addressing schemes are basic elements of interdomain routing. Addressing by itself defines where certain information can be found, but does not give any indication on how the information is to be accessed. A mechanism is needed to exhange information about destinations and to calculate the optimal way to reach a certain destination. This mechanism, of course, is routing.

This chapter concludes all the foundation material required before proceeding to study routing architecture itself. In the next chapter, the basics of interdomain routing are covered, building on concepts of addressing, global networks, and domains as discussed in this and previous chapters. Routing protocols in general, and BGP in particular, are discussed, with implementation details on BGP to follow in Chapter 5 and beyond.

FREQUENTLY ASKED QUESTIONS

Q— *How is VLSM different from the usual subnetting?*

A— It is not. VLSM is an extension of the basic subnetting where the same class A/B/C address is subnetted by using masks of different length.

Q— *Why do I need VLSM?*

A— VLSM provides a more efficient way of IP address assignment. It provides more flexibility in assigning adequate numbers of hosts and subnets given a limited number of IP addresses.

Q— *What is the difference between CIDR and supernetting ?*

A— Classless Interdomain Routing is the mechanism that allows to advertise both supernets and subnets outside of the normal bounds of a classfull network number. Supernetting is a representation that allows masks that are shorter than the natural masks, hence creating supernets.

Q— *Is the classfull model the cause of the growth in the global routing tables?*

A— No. The growth of the routing tables is due to the fact that more and more organizations are connecting to the Internet. The classfull model does not offer a solution to deal with such growth.

Q— *I have a network that uses older protocols such as RIP v.1 and IGRP. What issues should I consider in deciding whether to upgrade to newer protocols that support VLSM and CIDR?*

A— If you feel that implementing VLSM and CIDR can help you utilize your address space more efficiently and give you better route summarization capabilities, then you should upgrade. One issue could be whether your current hardware is capable of running newer protocols that might need extra processing or memory requirements. That of course depends on the protocol to which you are upgrading. Other issues have to deal with the co-existence of new and old protocols. Because network upgrades are usually done in stages, you will be faced with situations where both older and newer protocols are running concurrently. Because older protocols cannot deal with VLSM or CIDR, you should not be surprised that extensive use of static routing might be required to ensure connectivity in your domain during the transition period.

Q— *Can I aggregate any routes in my routing table?*

A— You can only aggregate routes that you administer. Aggregating routes that are not an extension of your domain could create black holes.

Q— *If I leave my provider, can I keep my IP addresses?*

A— For the purposes of better aggregation, today's routing practices recommend (sometimes require) that you return the old addresses and get addresses from your new provider. Ask your provider for its policies.

Q— *I have hosts that require Internet connectivity and others that do not. Can I use private addresses on some hosts and not others?*

A— Yes, you can use both private and global addresses in the same network. When advertising routes to your provider, you only advertise the legal networks.

Q— *I need to connect to the Internet, and not all my addresses are registered. I can't afford to renumber—what do I do?*

A— You could always use Network Address Translation (NAT) to map your illegal address to a legal pool of addresses you get from your provider.

REFERENCES

[1] RFC 791 Internet Protocol (IP)

[2] RFC 917 Internet Subnets

[3] RFC 1878 Variable Length Subnet Table for IPv4

[4] RFC 1519 Classless Interdomain Routing (CIDR)

[5] RFC 1541 Dynamic Host Configuration Protocol

[6] RFC 1918 Address Allocation for Private Internets

[7] RFC 1631 The IP Network Address Translator (NAT)

[8] RFC 1884 IP Version 6 Addressing Architecture

PART 2

Routing Protocol Basics

Although this book is primarily concerned with exterior gateway protocols—routing *between* different autonomous systems—it makes sense to look at internal gateway protocols as a first step because, conceptually and in practice, the two will affect each other's behavior. Thus, Chapter 4 begins with a consideration of protocols intended for routing *within* an autonomous system before moving into exterior gateway protocols. Chapter 4 concludes with an overview of the particular exterior gateway protocol, BGP, which we will focus on. Chapter 5 contains a more in-depth exploration of BGP's attribute manipulation and the use of route filtering in influencing the BGP decision process. Understanding the basics of BGP, as described in Part 2, is necessary before we can put the protocols's capabilities to use in practical routing design problems throughout the rest of the book.

THIS CHAPTER COVERS THE FOLLOWING KEY TOPICS:

- ## Overview of IGPs
  A brief consideration of interior gateway protocols as a point of contrast for this chapter's more in-depth consideration of exterior gateway protocols.

- ## Autonomous Systems
  An autonomous system is a set of routers sharing the same routing policies. Various configurations for autonomous systems are possible, depending on how many exit points to outside networks are desired and whether the system should permit through traffic.

- ## How BGP Works
  An overview of how the Border Gateway Protocol (version 4) operates, including its message header format, and how and what it negotiates with neighboring routers. The formats and purposes of BGP's four main message types—OPEN, NOTIFICATION, KEEPALIVE, and UPDATE—are covered.

CHAPTER 4

Interdomain Routing Basics

The Internet is a collection of autonomous systems that define the administrative authority and the routing policies of different organizations. Autonomous systems run Interior Gateway Protocols (IGPs), such as RIP, IGRP, EIGRP, OSPF, and ISIS, within their boundaries and interconnect via an Exterior Gateway Protocol (EGP) called the Border Gateway Protocol (BGP).

Routers are devices that direct traffic between hosts. Routers build routing tables that contain their collected information on all the best paths to all the destinations they know how to reach. They both announce and receive route information to and from other routers. This information goes into the routing tables.

OVERVIEW OF ROUTERS AND ROUTING

Routers develop a hop-by-hop mechanism by keeping track of "next hop" information that enables a data packet to find its destination through the network. A router that does not have a direct physical connection to the destination checks its routing table and forwards the packet to another next hop router

89

that is closer to that destination. The process repeats until the traffic finds its way through the network to its final destination.

EGPs, such as BGP, were introduced because IGPs do not scale in networks that go beyond the enterprise level. IGPs were never designed for the purpose of global internetworking because they do not have the necessary hooks to segregate enterprises into different administrations that are technically and politically independent from one another. This chapter touches upon basic IGP functionality and then explains the specifics of BGP.

Figure 4–1 describes three routers, RTA, RTB, and RTC, connecting three local area networks, 192.10.1.0, 192.10.5.0, and 192.10.6.0, via serial links. Each serial link is repesented by its own network number, which results in three additional networks, 192.10.2.0, 192.10.3.0, and 192.10.4.0. Each network has a metric associated with it indicating the level of overhead (cost) of transmitting traffic on that particular link. The link between RTA and RTB, for example, has a cost of 2,000, much higher than the cost of 60 of the link between RTA and RTC. In practice, the link between RTA and RTB is a 56 Kbps link with much bigger delays than the T1 link between RTA and RTC and the T1 link between RTC and RTB combined.

Routers RTA, RTB, and RTC would exchange network information via some interior gateway protocol and build their respective IP routing tables. Figure 4–1 shows examples of RTA's IP routing table for two different scenarios; the routers are exchanging routing information via RIP in one scenario and OSPF in another.

As an example of how traffic is passed between end stations, if host 192.10.1.2 is trying to reach host 192.10.6.2, it will first send the traffic to RTA. RTA will look in its IP routing table for any network that matches this destination and would find that network 192.10.6.0 is reachable via next hop 192.10.3.2 (RTC) out on Serial line 2 (S2). RTC would receive the traffic and would try to look for the destination in its IP routing table (not shown). RTC would discover that the host is directly connected to its Ethernet 0 interface (E0) and would send the traffic to 192.10.6.2.

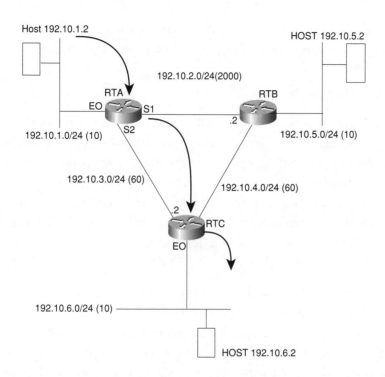

Figure 4–1
Basic routing behavior.

RTA IP Routing table (RIP)

Destination	Next Hop	Hop count
192.10.1.0	Connected (E0)	-
192.10.2.0	Connected (S1)	-
192.10.3.0	Connected (S2)	-
192.10.4.0	192.10.2.2 (S1)	1
	192.10.3.2 (S2)	1
192.10.5.0	192.10.2.2 (S1)	1
192.10.6.0	192.10.3.2 (S2)	1

RTA IP Routing table (OSPF)

Destination	Next Hop	Hop count
192.10.1.0	Connected (E0)	-
192.10.2.0	Connected (S1)	-
192.10.3.0	Connected (S2)	-
192.10.4.0	192.10.3.2 (S2)	120
192.10.5.0	192.10.3.2 (S2)	130
192.10.6.0	192.10.3.2 (S2)	70

In the preceding example, the routing is the same whether RTA is using the RIP or OSPF scenario. RIP and OSPF, however, fall into different categories of IGP protocols, namely distance vector protocols and link state protocols, respectively. For a different routing example in figure 4–1, the results might be different depending on whether you are looking at the RIP or OSPF scenario. It is useful at this point to consider characteristics of both IGP protocol categories, to see how protocols generally have evolved to meet increasingly sophisticated routing demands.

Distance Vector Protocols

Distance vector protocols such as RIP version 1 were mainly designed for small network topologies. The term *distance vector* derives from the fact that the protocol includes in its routing updates a vector of distances (hop counts). By using hop counts, distance vector protocols do not factor into the routing equation the overhead of sending information over a particular link. Low-speed links are treated equally or sometimes preferred over a high-speed link, depending on the calculated hop count in reaching a destination. This would lead to suboptimal and inefficient routing behaviors.

Consider, for example, the RTA routing tables shown in figure 4–1. In the RIP case, RTA has listed the direct link between RTA and RTB to reach network 192.10.5.0. RTA prefers this link because it requires just one hop via RTB versus two hops via RTC and then RTB. But the preferred route is inefficient because the total cost of the routing path via RTC and then RTB (60 + 60 = 120) is much less than the cost of crossing the RTA–RTB link (2,000).

Another issue with hop counts is the *count to infinity* restriction: distance vector protocols have a finite limit of hops (15) after which a route is considered unreachable. This would restrict the propagation of routing updates and would cause problems for large networks.

The reliance on hop counts is one deficiency of distance vector protocols; another deficiency is the way that the routing information gets exchanged. Distance vector algorithms work on the concept that routers exchange all the network numbers they can reach via periodic broadcasts of the entire routing table. In large networks, the routing table exchanged between routers becomes very large and very hard to maintain, leading to slower convergence.

Convergence refers to the point in time at which the entire network becomes updated to the fact that a particular route has appeared or disappeared. Distance vector protocols work on the basis of periodic updates and hold-down timers: If a route is not received in a certain amount of time, the route goes into a hold-down state and gets aged out of the routing table. The hold-down and aging process translates into minutes in convergence time before the whole network detects that a route has disappeared. The delay between a route's becoming unavailable and its aging out of the routing tables can result in routing loops and black holes.

Another major drawback of distance vector protocols is their classfull nature and their lack of support of Variable Length Subnet Masks or CIDR. Distance vector protocols do not exchange mask information in their routing updates. A router that receives a routing update on a certain interface will apply to this update its locally defined subnet mask. This would lead to confusion, in case the interface belongs to a network that is variably subnetted, and a misinterpretation of the received routing update.

Finally, distance vector networks are considered to be flat. They present a lack of hierarchy, which translates into a lack of aggregation. This flat nature has made distance vector protocols incapable of scaling to larger and more efficient enterprise networks.

RIP version 2 has added support for VLSM and CIDR, but it still carries most of the other deficiencies that its predecessor, RIP version 1, has.

Link State Protocols

Link state protocols, such as the Open Shortest Path First (OSPF) [1] and Intermediate System-to-Intermediate System (ISIS) [2], are more advanced routing protocols that have addressed the deficiencies of distance vector protocols. Link state protocols work on the basis that routers exchange information elements, called *link states*, which carry information about links and nodes. This means that routers running link state protocols do not exchange routing tables. Each router inside a domain will have enough bits and pieces of the big puzzle that it can run a shortest path algorithm and build its own routing table.

Following are some of the benefits that link state protocols provide over distance vector protocols:

- *No hop count*—No limits on the number of hops a route can take. Link state protocols work on the basis of metrics rather than hop counts.

  As an example of a link state protocol's reliance on metrics rather than hop count, turn again to the RTA routing tables shown in figure 4–1. In the OSPF case, RTA has picked the optimal path to reach RTB by factoring in the cost of the links. Its routing table lists the next hop of 192.10.3.2 (RTC) to reach 192.10.5.0 (RTB). This is in contrast to the RIP scenario, which resulted in a suboptimal path.

- *Bandwidth representation*—Link bandwidth and delays are factored in when calculating the shortest path to a certain destination. This leads to better load-balancing based on actual link cost rather than hop count.

- *Better convergence*—Link and node changes are flooded into the domain via link state updates. All routers in the domain will immediately update their routing tables.

- *Support for VLSM and CIDR*— Link state protocols exchange mask information as part of the information elements that are flooded in the domain. As a result, networks with variable length masks can be easily identified.

- *Better hierarchy*—Whereas distance vector networks are flat networks, link state protocols divide the domain into different levels and areas. This hierarchical approach provides better control over network instabilities and a better mechanism to summarize routing updates across areas, specifically, by lumping multiple contiguous routing updates into supersets of routing updates called *aggregates*.

Even though link state algorithms have provided better routing scalability, which enables them to be used in bigger and more complex topologies, they still should be restricted to interior routing. Link state protocols, by themselves, cannot provide a global connectivity solution required for Internet interdomain routing. In very large networks and in case of route fluctuation caused by link instabilities, link state retransmission and recomputation will become too large for any router to handle.

SEGREGATING THE WORLD INTO ADMINISTRATIONS

Exterior routing protocols were created to control the expansion of routing tables and to provide a more structured view of the Internet by segregating routing domains into separate administrations, called *autonomous systems* (AS) that each have their own independent routing policies.

During the early days of the Internet, an exterior gateway protocol called EGP[3] (not to be confused with Exterior Gateway Protocols in general) was used. The NSFNET used EGP to exchange reachability information between the backbone and the regional networks. Although the use of EGP was widely deployed, its topology restrictions and inefficiency in dealing with routing loops and setting routing policies created a need for a new and more robust protocol. Currently, BGP4 [4] is the de facto standard for Internet routing; it is an advanced exterior protocol that is providing the Internet with a controlled and loop-free topology.

Static Routing, Default Routing, and Dynamic Routing

Before introducing and looking at the basic ways in which autonomous systems can be connected to ISPs, we need to establish some basic terminology and concepts of routing. *Static routing* refers to routes to destinations being listed manually in the router. Network reachability in this case is not dependent on the existence and state of the network itself. Whether a destination is up or down, the static routes would remain in the routing table, and traffic would still be sent toward that destination. *Default routing* refers to a "last resort" outlet—traffic to destinations that are unknown to the router will be sent to that default outlet. Default routing is the easiest form of routing for a domain connected to a single exit point.

Dynamic routing refers to routes being learned via an internal or external routing protocol. Network reachability is dependent on the existence and state of the network. If a destination is down, the route would disappear from the routing table, and traffic would not be sent toward that destination.

These three routing approaches are possibilities for all the AS configurations considered in forthcoming sections, but usually there is an optimal approach. Thus, in illustrating different autonomous systems, this chapter considers whether static, dynamic, default, or some combination of these is optimal. This chapter also considers whether interior or exterior routing protocols are appropriate. A more detailed exploration of routing choices for different AS topologies, however, must wait until Chapter 5 "Tuning BGP Capabilities."

Always remember, static and default routing are not your enemy. The most stable (but not so flexible) configurations are the ones based on static routing. Many people feel that they are not technologically up-to-date just because they are not running dynamic routing. Trying to force dynamic routing on situations that do not really need it is just a waste of bandwidth, effort, and money.

Autonomous Systems

An *autonomous system* (AS) is a set of routers having a single routing policy, running under a single technical administration. The AS could be a collection of IGPs working together to provide interior routing. To the outside world, the whole AS is viewed as one single entity. Each AS has an identifying number, which is assigned to it by an Internet Registry or a provider. Routing information between ASs is exchanged via an exterior gateway protocol such as BGP4, as illustrated in figure 4–2.

What we have gained by segregating the world into administrations is the capability to have one large network—in the sense that the Internet could have been one huge OSPF or ISIS network—divided into smaller and more manageable networks. These smaller networks, called ASs, can now have their own set of rules and policies that will uniquely distinguish them from other ASs. Each AS can now run its own set of IGPs, independent of IGPs in other ASs.

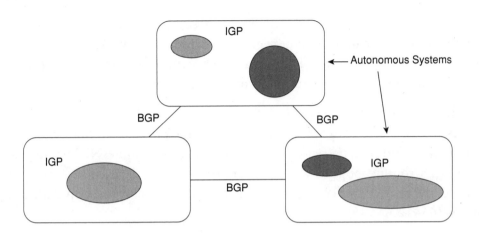

Figure 4–2
*General illustration
of AS relationships.*

Stub ASs

An AS is considered to be *stub* when it reaches networks outside its domain via a single exit point. These ASs are also called single-homed with respect to another provider. Figure 4–3 illustrates a single-homed or stub AS.

A single-homed AS does not really have to learn Internet routes from its provider. Because there is a single way out, all traffic can default to the provider. On the other hand, there are different methods for the provider to advertise the customer's routes. One possibility is for the provider to list the customer's subnets as static entries in its router. The provider would then advertise these static entries toward the Internet. This method would scale very well if the customer's routes can be represented by a small set of aggregate routes. When the customer has too many discontiguous subnets, listing all these subnets via static routes becomes inefficient.

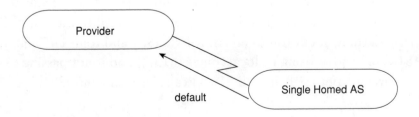

Figure 4–3
*Single-homed stub
AS.*

Alternatively, IGPs can be used for the purpose of advertising the customer's networks. An IGP can be used between the customer and provider for the customer to advertise its routes. This has all the benefits of dynamic routing where network information and changes are dynamically sent to the provider.

The third method by which the ISP can learn and advertise the customer's routes is to use BGP between the customer and the provider. In the stub AS situation, it is hard to get a registered AS number from the InterNIC because the customer's routing policies are an extension of the policies of the provider. Instead, the provider will give the customer an AS number from the private pool of ASs (65412-65535).

Quite a few combinations of protocols can be used between the ISP and the customer. Figure 4–4 illustrates some of the possible configurations, taking just stub ASs as an example. (The meaning of EBGP and IBGP will be discussed in the upcoming sections.) Providers might extend customer routers to their POPs or providers might extend their routers to the customer's network. Note that not every situation requires that a customer run BGP with its provider, as mentioned earlier.

Multihomed Nontransit AS

An AS is *multihomed* if it has more than one exit point to the outside world. An AS can be multihomed to a single provider or multiple providers. A *nontransit* AS does not allow transit traffic to go through it. *Transit traffic* is any traffic that has a source and destination outside the AS. Figure 4–5 illustrates an AS (AS1) that is nontransit and multihomed to two providers, ISP1 and ISP2.

A nontransit AS would only advertise its own routes and would not advertise routes that it learned from other ASs. This ensures that traffic for any destination that does not belong to the AS would not be directed to the AS. In figure 4–5, AS1 is learning about routes n3 and n4 via ISP1 and routes n5 and n6 via ISP2. AS1 is only advertising its local routes (n1,n2) and is not passing to ISP2 routes it learned from ISP1 or to IPS1 routes it learned from ISP2. This way,

AS1 will not open itself to outside traffic, such as ISP1 trying to reach n5 or n6 and ISP2 trying to reach n3 and n4 via AS1. Of course, ISP1 or ISP2 can force their traffic to be directed to AS1 via default or static routing. As a precaution against this, AS1 could filter any traffic coming toward it with a destination not belonging to AS1.

Multihomed nontransit ASs do not really need to run BGP4 with their providers, although it is recommended and most of the time required by the provider. As you will see later on in this book, running BGP4 with the providers has many advantages in controlling route propagation and filtering.

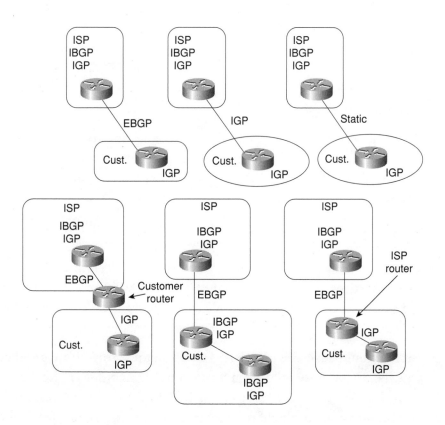

Figure 4–4
Example protocol implementation variations.

Figure 4–5
*Multihomed
nontransit AS
example.*

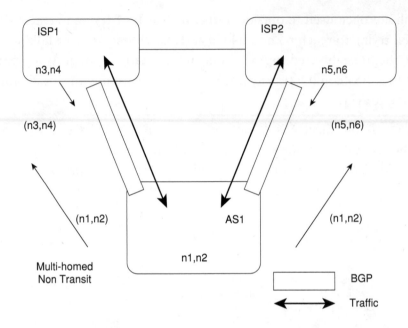

Multihomed Transit AS

A *multihomed transit AS* has more than one connection to the outside world and can still be used for transit traffic by other ASs (see figure 4–6). Transit traffic (relative to the multihomed AS) is any traffic with an origin and destination that does not belong to the AS.

Even though BGP4 is an exterior gateway protocol, it can still be used inside an AS as a pipe to exchange BGP updates. BGP connections inside an autonomous system are called Internal BGP (IBGP), whereas BGP connections between autonomous systems are called External BGP (EBGP). Routers that are running IBGP are called *transit routers* when they carry the transit traffic going through the AS. Routers that run EBGP with other ASs are usually called *border routers*.

A transit AS would advertise to one AS routes that it learned from another AS. This way, the transit AS would open itself to traffic that does not belong to it. Multihomed transit ASs are advised to use BGP4 for their connections to other ASs and also internally to shield their internal nontransit routers from Internet routes. Not all routers inside a domain need to run BGP; internal nontransit routers could run default routing to the BGP routers, which alleviates the number of routes the internal nontransit routers must carry.

Figure 4–6 illustrates a multihomed transit autonomous system, AS1, connected to two different providers, ISP1 and ISP2. AS1 is learning routes n3, n4, n5, and n6 from both ISP1 and ISP2 and in turn advertising all that it learned, including its local routes, to ISP1 and ISP2. In this case, ISP1 could use AS1 as a transit AS to reach networks n5 and n6, and ISP2 could use AS1 to reach networks n3 and n4.

BORDER GATEWAY PROTOCOL VERSION 4

BGP went through different phases and improvements from its earlier version, BGP1, in 1989 to today's version, BGP4, deployment of which started in 1993. BGP4 is the first version that handles aggregation (CIDR) and supernetting, as discussed earlier in this book.

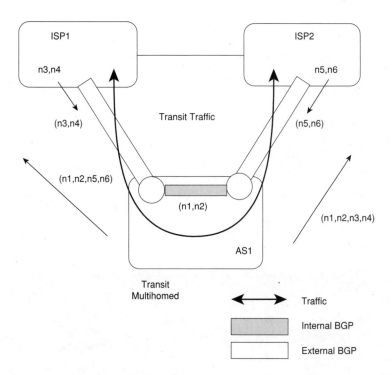

Figure 4–6
Multihomed transit AS using BGP internally and externally.

BGP imposes no restrictions on the underlying Internet topology. It assumes that routing within an autonomous system is done via an intra-autonomous system routing protocol. (For the purposes of this book, *intra* means routing within an entity, and *inter* means between entities.) BGP constructs a graph of autonomous systems based on the information exchanged between BGP neighbors. This directed graph environment is sometimes referred to as a *tree*. As far as BGP is concerned, the whole Internet is a graph of ASs, with each AS identified by an AS number. Connections between two ASs together form a path, and the collection of path information forms a route to reach a specific destination. BGP ensures that loop-free interdomain routing is maintained. Figure 4–7 illustrates this general path tree concept.

How BGP Works

BGP is a path vector protocol used to carry routing information between autonomous systems. The term *path vector* comes from the fact that BGP routing

Figure 4–7
Example AS_Path
tree.

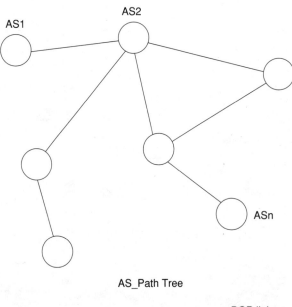

information carries a sequence of AS numbers, which indicates the path a route has traversed. BGP uses TCP as its transport protocol (port 179). This ensures that all the transport reliability such as retransmission is taken care of by TCP and does not need to be implemented in BGP itself.

Two BGP routers form a transport protocol connection between each other. These routers are called *neighbors* or *peers*. Figure 4–8 illustrates this relationship. Peer routers exchange multiple messages to open and confirm the connection parameters, such as the BGP version running between the two peers (for example, version 3 for BGP3 and version 4 for BGP4). In case of any disagreement between the peers, notification errors are sent, and the peer connection does not get established.

Initially, all candidate BGP routes are exchanged, as illustrated in figure 4–9. Incremental updates are sent as network information changes. The incremental update approach has shown an enormous improvement as far as CPU overhead and bandwidth allocation compared with complete periodic updates used by previous protocols, such as EGP.

Routes are advertised between a pair of BGP routers in UPDATE messages. The UPDATE message contains, among other things, a list of <length, prefix> tuples that indicate the list of destinations reachable via each system. The UPDATE message also contains the path attributes, which include such information as the degree of preference for a particular route.

In case of information changes, such as a route being unreachable or having a better path, BGP informs its neighbors by withdrawing the invalid routes and

N1
2.2.2.2
N2

N3
1.1.1.1
N4

Establish a neighboring
session with 1.1.1.1

Establish a neighboring
session with 2.2.2.2

Figure 4–8
*BGP routers
become neighbors.*

Figure 4–9
*Exchanging all
routing updates.*

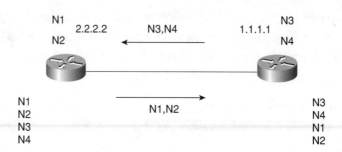

injecting new routing information. As illustrated in figure 4–10, withdrawn routes are part of the UPDATE message. These are the routes no longer available for use. Figure 4–11 illustrates a steady state situation: if no routing changes occur, the routers exchange only KEEPALIVE packets.

KEEPALIVE messages are sent periodically between BGP neighbors to ensure that the connection is kept alive. KEEPALIVE packets (19 bytes each) should not cause any strain on the router CPU or link bandwidth as they consume a minimal bandwidth (about 2.5 bits/sec for a periodic rate of 60 sec).

TROUBLESHOOTING

The meaning of
rapidly incre-
menting table
versions.

BGP keeps a table version number to keep track of the instance of the BGP routing table. If the table changes, BGP will increment the table version. A table version that is incrementing rapidly is usually an indication of instabilities in the network.

BGP Message Header Format

The BGP message header format is a 16-byte marker field, followed by a 2-byte length field and a 1-byte type field. Figure 4–12 illustrates the basic format of the BGP message header.

Figure 4–10
*N1 goes down;
partial update sent.*

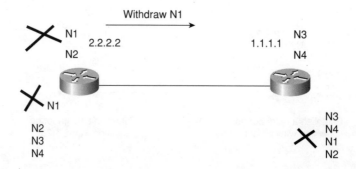

Figure 4–11
Steady state; N1 is still down.

There may or may not be a data portion following the header, depending on the message type. KEEPALIVE messages, for example, consist of the message header only, with no following data.

The marker field is used to either authenticate incoming BGP messages or to detect loss of synchronization between two BGP peers. The marker field can have two formats:

- If the type of the message is OPEN or if the OPEN message has no authentication information, the marker field must be all ones.

- Otherwise, the marker field will be computed based on part of the authentication mechanism used.

The length indicates the total BGP message length including the header. The smallest BGP message is no less than 19 bytes (16+2+1) and no greater than 4,096.

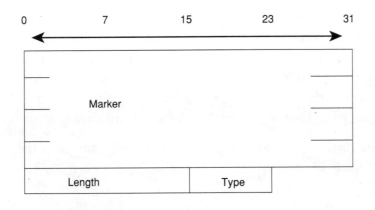

Figure 4–12
BGP message header format.

The type indicates the message type, from the following possibilities:

- OPEN

- UPDATE

- NOTIFICATION

- KEEPALIVE

The following sections examine the purpose and format of each of the four message types in more detail.

BGP Neighbor Negotiation

One of the basic steps of the BGP protocol is establishing neighbors between BGP peers. Without successful completion of this step, no exchange of updates will ever take effect. Neighbor negotiation is based on the successful completion of a TCP transport connection, the successful processing of the OPEN message, and periodic detection of the KEEPALIVE messages.

OPEN Message Format

Figure 4–13 illustrates the format of the OPEN message. The descriptions that follow summarize each of its fields:

- *Version*—A 1-byte unsigned integer that indicates the version of the BGP protocol, such as BGP3 or BGP4. During the neighbor negotiation, BGP peers agree on a BGP version number. BGP peers will try to negotiate the highest common version that they both support. Cisco Systems provides the option of predefining the version negotiated to cut down on the negotiation process. Setting the version statically is usually used when the versions of the BGP peers are already known.

- *My Autonomous System*—A 2-byte field that indicates the AS number of the BGP router.

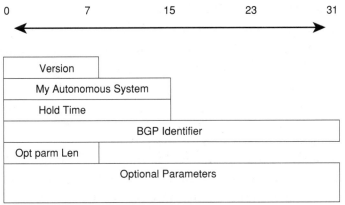

Figure 4–13
*OPEN message
format.*

- *Hold Time*—The maximum amount of time in seconds that may elapse between the receipt of successive KEEPALIVE or UPDATE messages. The hold timer is a counter that increments from zero to the hold time value. Receipt of a KEEPALIVE or UPDATE message causes the hold timer to reset to zero. If the hold time for a particular neighbor is exceeded, the neighbor would be considered dead. The hold time is a 2-byte unsigned integer.

  The BGP router negotiates with its neighbor to set the hold time at whichever value is lower—its own hold time or its neighbor's. The hold time could be 0, in which case the hold timer and the KEEPALIVE timers are never reset—that is, these timers never expire, and the connection is considered to be always up. If not set to zero, the minimum recommended hold time is three seconds.

- *BGP Identifier*—A 4-byte unsigned integer that indicates the sender's ID. In Cisco's implementation, this is usually the router ID (RID), which is calculated as the highest IP address on the router or the highest loopback address at BGP session startup. (*Loopback address* is Cisco's representation of the IP address of a virtual software interface that is considered to be up at all times, irrespective of the state of any physical interface.)

- *Optional Parameters*—This is a variable length field that indicates a list of optional parameters used in BGP neighbor session negotiation. This field is represented by the triplet <Parameter Type, Parameter Length, Parameter Value> with lengths of 1-byte, 1-byte, and variable length, respectively. An example of optional parameters is the authentication information parameter (type1), which is used to authenticate the session with a BGP peer.

- *Optional Parameter Length*—This is a 1-byte unsigned integer that indicates the total length in bytes of the Optional Parameters field. A length value of 0 indicates that no Optional Parameters are present.

Finite State Machine Perspective

BGP neighbor negotiation proceeds through different stages before the connection is fully established. Figure 4–14 illustrates a simplified finite state machine (FSM) that highlights the major events in the process with an indication of messages (OPEN, KEEPALIVE, NOTIFICATION) sent to the peer in the transition from one state to the other.

Figure 4–14
BGP neighbor negotiation finite state machine.

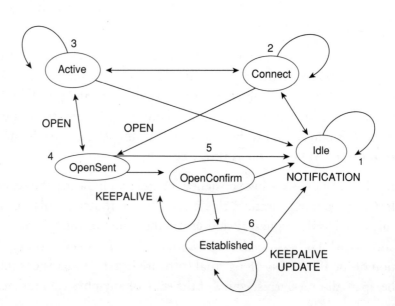

The following discussions summarize the key states in the FSM example illustrated in Figure 4–14:

1. *Idle*—This is the first stage of the connection. BGP is waiting for a Start event, which is normally initiated by an operator. A Start event is usually caused by an administrator establishing a BGP session through router configuration or resetting an already existing session. After the Start event, BGP initializes its resources, resets a connect retry timer, initiates a TCP transport connection, and starts listening for a connection that may be initiated by a remote peer. BGP then transitions to a Connect state. In case of errors, BGP falls back to the Idle state.

2. *Connect*—BGP is waiting for the transport protocol connection to be completed. If the TCP transport connection is successful, the state transitions to OpenSent (this is where the OPEN message is sent). If the transport connection is not successful, the state transitions to Active. If the connect retry timer expires, the state will remain in the connect stage, the timer will be reset, and a transport connection will be initiated. In case of any other event (initiated by system or operator), the state will go back to Idle.

3. *Active*—BGP is trying to acquire a peer by initiating a transport protocol connection. If it is successful, it will transition to OpenSent (an OPEN message is sent). If the connect retry timer expires, BGP will restart the connect timer and fall back to the connect state. Also, BGP is still listening for a connection that may be initiated from another peer. The state may go back to Idle in case of other events, such as a stop event initiated by the system or the operator.

   In general, a neighbor state that is flip-flopping between Connect and Active is an indication that something is wrong with the TCP transport connection not taking effect. It could be because of many TCP retransmissions or the inability of a neighbor to reach the IP address of its peer.

TROUBLESHOOTING

The meaning of flip-flopping between Connect and Active states.

4. *OpenSent*—BGP is waiting for an OPEN message from its peer. The OPEN message is checked for correctness. In case of errors, such as a bad version number or an unacceptable AS, the system sends an error NOTIFICATION message and goes back to Idle. If there are no errors, BGP starts sending KEEPALIVE messages and resets the KEEPALIVE timer. At this stage, the hold time is negotiated, and the smaller value is taken. In case the negotiated hold time is 0, the hold timer and the KEEPALIVE timer are not restarted.

At the OpenSent state, the BGP will recognize, by comparing its AS number to the AS number of its peer, whether the peer belongs to the same AS (Internal BGP) or to a different AS (External BGP).

When a TCP transport disconnect is detected, the state will fall back to Active. For any other errors, such as an expiration of the hold timer, the BGP will send a NOTIFICATION message with the corresponding error code and will fall back to the Idle state. Also, in response to a stop event initiated by system or operator, the state will fall back to Idle.

5. *OpenConfirm*—BGP waits for a KEEPALIVE or NOTIFICATION message. If a KEEPALIVE is received, the state will go to established, and the neighbor negotiation is complete. If the system receives an UP-DATE or KEEPALIVE message, it restarts the hold timer (assuming that the negotiated hold time is not 0). If a NOTIFICATION message is received, the state falls back to Idle. The system will send periodic KEEPALIVE messages at the rate set by the KEEPALIVE timer. In case of any transport disconnect notification or in response to any stop event (initiated by the system or the operator), the state will fall back to Idle. In response to any other event, the system will send a NOTIFI-CATION message with an FSM (Finite State Machine) error code and will go back to Idle.

6. *Established*—This is the final stage in the neighbor negotiation. At this stage, BGP starts exchanging UPDATE packets with its peers. Assuming that it is non-zero, the Hold timer is restarted at the receipt of an

UPDATE or KEEPALIVE message. If the system receives any NOTIFI-CATION message—that is, some error has occurred—the state will fall back to Idle.

The UPDATE messages are checked for errors, such as missing attributes, duplicate attributes, and so on. If errors are found, a NOTIFICATION is sent to the peer, and the state will fall back to Idle. In case the Hold timer expires, or a disconnect notification is received from the transport protocol, or a Stop event is received, or in response to any other event, the system will fall back to Idle.

NOTIFICATION Message

From the preceding examination of the finite state machine, it should be apparent that many opportunities exist among the various states, for errors to be detected. A NOTIFICATION message is always sent whenever an error is detected, after which the peer connection is closed. Network administrators will need to evaluate these NOTIFICATION messages to determine the specific nature of errors that emerge in the routing protocol. Figure 4–15 illustrates the general message format.

The NOTIFICATION message is composed of the Error code (1-byte), Error subcode (1-byte), and a Data field (variable).

The Error code indicates the type of the notification, the Error subcode provides more specific information about the nature of the error, and the Data field contains data relevant to the error such as a bad header, an illegal AS number, and so on. Table 4–1 lists possible errors and their subcodes.

TROUBLESHOOTING

Form and meaning of NOTIFICATION error messages.

0	7	15	23	31
Error	Error subcode	Data		

Figure 4–15
NOTIFICATION message format.

	Error Code	Error Subcode
Table 4–1 *Possible BGP error* *codes.*	1—Message Header Error	1—Connection Not Synchronized
		2—Bad Message Length
		3—Bad Message Type
	2—OPEN Message Error	1—Unsupported Version Number
		2—Bad Peer AS
		3—Bad BGP Identifier
		4—Unsupported Optional Parameter
		5—Authentication Failure
		6—Unacceptable Hold Time
	3—UPDATE Message Error	1—Malformed Attribute List
		2—Unrecognized Well-Known Attribute
		3—Missing Well-Known Attribute
		4—Attribute Flags Error
		5—Attribute Length Error
		6—Invalid Origin Attribute
		7—AS Routing Loop
		8—Invalid NEXT_HOP Attribute
		9—Optional Attribute Error
		10—Invalid Network Field
		11—Malformed AS_path
	4—Hold Timer Expired	NOT applicable
	5—Finite State Machine Error (for errors detected by the FSM)	NOT applicable
	6—Cease (for fatal errors besides the ones already listed)	NOT applicable

KEEPALIVE Message

KEEPALIVE messages are periodic messages exchanged between peers to determine whether peers are reachable. As discussed previously, the hold time is the maximum amount of time that may elapse between the receipt of successive KEEPALIVE or UPDATE messages. The KEEPALIVE messages are sent at a rate that ensures that the hold time will *not* expire (the session is considered alive). A recommended rate is one-third of the hold time interval. If the hold time interval is zero, periodic KEEPALIVE messages will not be sent. The KEEPALIVE message is a 19-byte BGP message header with no data following it.

UPDATE MESSAGE AND ROUTING INFORMATION

Central to the BGP protocol is the concept of routing updates. Routing updates contain all the necessary information that BGP uses to construct a loop-free picture of the Internet. The following are the basic blocks of an UPDATE message:

- Network Layer Reachability Information (NLRI)

- Path attributes

- Unreachable routes

Figure 4–16 illustrates these components in the context of an UPDATE message format.

The NLRI is an indication, in the form of an IP prefix route, of the networks being advertised. The path attribute list provides BGP with the capabilities of detecting routing loops and the flexibility to enforce local and global routing policies. An example of the BGP path attributes is the AS_path attribute, which is a sequence of AS numbers a route has traversed before reaching the BGP router.

AS3 in figure 4–17, for example, is receiving BGP updates from AS2 indicating that network 10.10.1.0/24 (NLRI) is reachable via two hops, first AS2 and then AS1. Based on this information, AS3 will be able to direct its traffic to 10.10.1.0/24.

The third part of the UPDATE message, is a list of routes that have become unreachable—or in BGP terminology, WITHDRAWN. With the example illustrated in figure 4–17, if 10.10.1.0/24 is no longer reachable or experiences a

Figure 4–16
BGP routing update.

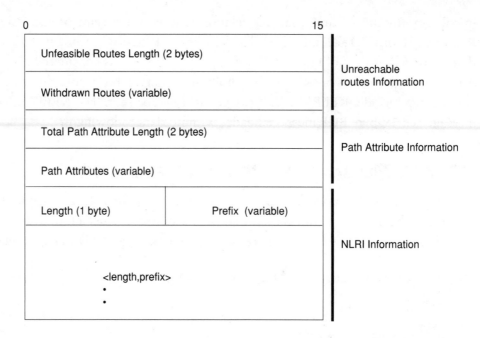

change in its attribute information, BGP can withdraw the route that it advertised by sending an UPDATE message that lists the new network information or the network being unreachable.

Network Layer Reachability Information

BGP4 provides a new set of mechanisms for supporting classless interdomain routing (CIDR). As discussed in Chapter 3, "Handling IP Address Depletion,"

Figure 4–17
BGP routing update example.

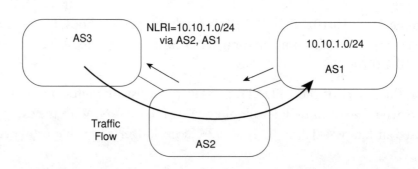

the concept of CIDR is a move from the traditional IP classes (A, B, C) toward a concept of IP prefixes. The IP prefix is an IP network address with an indication of the number of bits (left to right) that constitute the network number. The Network Layer Reachability Information (NLRI) is the mechanism by which BGP supports classless routing. The NLRI is the part of the BGP routing update that lists the set of destinations about which BGP is trying to inform its other BGP neighbors. The NLRI consists of multiple instances of the 2-tuples <length, prefix>, where length is the number of masking bits that a particular prefix has.

Figure 4–18 illustrates the NLRI <19, 198.24.160.0>. The prefix is 198.24.160.0, and the length is a 19-bit mask (counting from the far left of the prefix).

Withdrawn Routes

Withdrawn routes provide a list of routing updates that are not feasible, or that are no longer in service and need to be withdrawn (removed) from the BGP routing tables. The withdrawn routes have the same format as the NLRI: an IP address and the number of bits in the IP address counting from left, as illustrated in figure 4–19. Withdrawn routes are also represented by the tuple <length, prefix>. A tuple of the form <18,192.213.134.0> indicates a route to be withdrawn of the form 192.213.134.0 255.255.192.0 or 192.213.134.0/18 in the CIDR format.

The Unfeasible Routes Length is the length in bytes of the total withdrawn routes. An UPDATE message can list multiple routes to be withdrawn at the same time

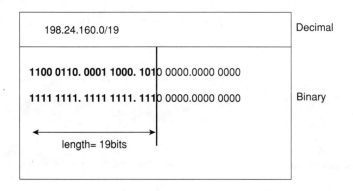

Figure 4–18
NLRI example.

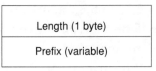

or no routes to be withdrawn. An Unfeasible Routes Length of 0 indicates that no routes are to be withdrawn. On the other hand, an UPDATE message can advertise at most one route, which can be described by multiple path attributes. An UPDATE message that has no NLRI or Path Attribute information is used to advertise only routes to be withdrawn from service.

Path Attributes

The BGP attributes are a set of parameters used to keep track of route-specific information such as path information, degree of preference of a route, next hop value of a route, and aggregation information. These parameters are used in the BGP filtering and route decision process. Every UPDATE message has a variable length sequence of path attributes. A path attribute is a triple of the form <attribute type, attribute length, attribute value> of variable length. The attribute type is a 2-byte field that consists of a 1-byte attribute flags and a 1-byte attribute type code. Figure 4–20 illustrates the general form of the path attribute type field.

Path attributes fall under four categories: well-known mandatory, well-known discretionary, optional transitive, and optional nontransitive. These four categories are described by the first two bits of the path attribute flags field.

The first bit of the flags field indicates whether the attribute is optional (1) or well-known (0). The second bit indicates whether the optional attribute is

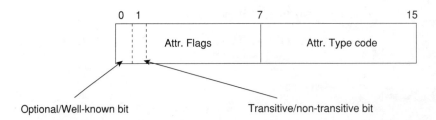

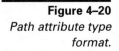

transitive (1) or nontransitive (0). Well-known attributes are always transitive (second bit is always 1). The third bit indicates whether the information in the optional transitive attribute is partial (1) or complete (0). The fourth bit defines whether the attribute length is 1-byte (0) or 2-bytes (1). The other four bits in the flags field are always set to 0.

The following descriptions elaborate on the significance of each attribute category:

- *Well-known mandatory*—An attribute that has to exist in the BGP UPDATE packet. It must be recognized by all BGP implementations. If a well-known attribute is missing, a notification error will be generated. This is to make sure that all BGP implementations agree on a standard set of attributes. An example of a well-known mandatory attribute is the AS_path attribute.

- *Well-known discretionary*—An attribute that is recognized by all BGP implementations, but may or may not be sent in the BGP UPDATE message. An example of a well-known discretionary attribute is the LOCAL_PREF.

In addition to the well-known attributes, a path can contain one or more optional attributes. Optional attributes are not required to be supported by all BGP implementations. Optional attributes can be transitive or nontransitive.

- *Optional transitive*—In case an optional attribute is not recognized by the BGP implementation, that implementation would look for a transitive flag to see whether it is set for that particular attribute. If the flag is set—that is, the attribute is transitive—the BGP implementation should accept the attribute and pass it along to other BGP speakers.

- *Optional nontransitive*—When an optional attribute is not recognized and the transitive flag is not set—the attribute is nontransitive—the attribute should be quietly ignored and not passed along to other BGP peers.

The Attribute Type code byte contains the attribute code. Currently, the following attributes are defined:

- 1—ORIGIN (Well-known mandatory, Type code 1)

- 2—AS_path (Well-known mandatory, Type code 2)

- 3—NEXT_HOP (Well-known mandatory, Type code 3)

- 4—MULTI_EXIT_DISC (Optional nontransitive, Type code 4)

- 5—LOCAL_PREF (Well-known discretionary, Type code 5)

- 6—ATOMIC_AGGREGATE (Well-known discretionary, Type code 6)

- 7—AGGREGATOR (Optional transitive, Type code 7)

- 8—COMMUNITY (Optional transitive, Type code 8, Cisco-defined)

- 9—ORIGINATOR_ID (Optional nontransitive, Type code 9, Cisco-defined)

- 10—Cluster List (Optional nontransitive, Type code 10, Cisco-defined)

- 11—Destination Preference (MCI-defined)

- 12—Advertiser (Baynet-defined)

- 13—rcid_path (Baynet-defined)

- 255—Reserved for development

Attributes type 1 to type 10 are discussed in detail in the next chapter. Attributes 11, 12, and 13 are not implemented by Cisco because they do not add additional functionality. These attributes are not covered.

LOOKING AHEAD

The Border Gateway Protocol has defined the basis of routing architectures in the Internet. The segregation of networks into autonomous systems has logically defined the administrative and political borders between organizations. Interior Gateway Protocols can now run independently of each other, but still interconnect via BGP to provide global routing.

BGP as a protocol presents some basic elements of routing that are flexible enough to allow total control from the administrator's perspective. The power of BGP lies in its attributes and its route filtering techniques. Attributes are simply parameters that can be modified to affect the BGP decision process. Route filtering can be done on a prefix level or a path level. A combination of filtering and attribute manipulation can acheive the optimal routing behavior. Because traffic follows a road map laid out by routing updates, modifying the routing behavior would eventually modify the traffic trajectories. The next chapter, "*Tuning BGP Capabilities*," gives you a hands-on approach to understanding the basics of setting routing policies with BGP.

FREQUENTLY ASKED QUESTIONS

Q— *What is the difference between a domain and an autonomous system?*

A— Both notations indicate a collection of routers. The domain notation is usually used to indicate a collection of routers running the same routing protocol, such as a RIP domain or an OSPF domain. The AS represents one or more domains under a single administration that have a unified routing policy with other ASs.

Q— *My company is connected to an ISP via RIP. Should I use BGP instead?*

A— If you are thinking of connecting to multiple providers in the near future, you should start discussing the option of using BGP with your provider. If your traffic needs do not require multiple provider connectivity, you should be okay with what you have.

Q— *I have a single IGP connection to a provider; I am thinking of connecting to the same provider in a different location. Can I connect via an IGP, or should I use BGP?*

A— This depends on the provider. Some providers will let you connect via IGP in multiple locations; others prefer that you use BGP. Practically speaking, when you use BGP, you will be in better control of your traffic, as you will see in the following chapters.

Q— *I thought that BGP is to be used between ASs; I am a bit confused about using BGP inside the AS.*

A— Think of BGP inside the AS (IBGP) as a tunnel through which routing information flows. If your AS is a transit AS, IBGP will shield all your internal nontransit routers from the potentially overwhelming number of external routing updates. On the other hand, even if you are not a transit AS, you will realize as this book progresses, that IBGP will give you better control in choosing exit and entrance points of your traffic.

Q— *You talk about BGP4, but is anybody still using BGP1, 2, or 3? What about EGP?*

A— BGP4 is the de facto interdomain routing protocol used on the Internet. EGP and BGP1, 2, and 3 are obsolete. BGP4's support of CIDR and better filtering and policy setting capabilities have prompted everybody to shift gears into using this new protocol.

Q— *Does BGP send periodic updates like RIP?*

A— No. BGP exchanges routing information once, when the BGP session is being established. After that, only network changes are exchanged between BGP peers.

Q— *Does the BGP session become "established" after all the routing updates have been exchanged between BGP neighbors?*

A— No. It is the other way around. No routing exchange can take effect until both BGP neighbors agree on all parameters and the session becomes established.

Q— *Is the Network Layer Reachability Information (NLRI) the actual BGP routing update?*

A— No. The NLRI is one of the elements that is carried in a BGP UPDATE message. Other elements are the attributes and the unreachable networks.

Q— *You talk about authentication as an example of the BGP optional parameters. How important is authentication?*

A— Authentication is a means to validate the BGP peer. This is to prevent hackers from assuming the identity of one of your peers and feeding you wrong routing information. With authentication, both peers will validate the connection via password mechanisms.

Q— *Where does BGP carry information about AS numbers?*

A— AS numbers are listed as part of the AS_path attribute carried in the UPDATE message.

REFERENCES

[1] RFC 1583 OSPF Version 2

[2] ISO 10589 Intermediate System-to-Intermediate System

[3] RFC 904 Exterior Gateway Protocol formal specification

[4] RFC 1771 A Border Gateway Protocol 4 (BGP-4)

THIS CHAPTER COVERS THE FOLLOWING KEY TOPICS:

- **Building Peer Sessions**

  A walk-through of the negotiation process between BGP and its neighbors.

- **Sources of Routing Updates**

  The source and method by which routes get injected into BGP has implications for the accuracy and stability of routing information.

- **Overlapping Protocols: Backdoors**

  When alternate routes into and out of a network are offered by overlapping protocols, a method of ranking them by preference is available.

- **The Routing Process Simplified**

  The decision model by which BGP receives, filters, selects for usage, and advertises routes, as a continuous process.

- **Controlling BGP Routes**

  At the core of BGP is a collection of attributes that administrators can apply to control routing according to their networks' needs.

- **Route Filtering and Attribute Manipulation**

  An example-oriented, step-by-step look at how BGP permits or denies routes, applies filters, and manipulates attributes to define the set of routing updates that enter and exit an AS.

- **BGP4 Aggregation**

  Several specific scenarios involving different aggregation choices and how BGP4 accommodates them.

CHAPTER 5

Tuning
BGP Capabilities

Up to this point, this book has been concerned primarily with general definitions of interior and exterior gateway protocols and an overview of their respective and interconnected tasks. The Border Gateway Protocol was also presented from the technical perspective of its functional elements. With this chapter, you will begin to consider more practical implementation details for BGP as part of the overall design problem in building reliable Internet connectivity. This chapter examines specific attributes of BGP and how they are applied individually and together to address this design problem. Although the terminology, attributes, and details of this chapter are specific to BGP, the general concepts and problems raised are pertinent to routing architecture design, regardless of what specific protocols are being utilized.

BUILDING PEER SESSIONS

The previous chapter began examining the process of BGP neighbor negotiation at a fairly technical level and with an emphasis on the formats of messages exchanged during negotiation. This chapter now expands the examination to consider additional subtleties of the negotiation process. In addition, distinctions between internal and external BGP, which have practical implications in building peer sessions, are introduced in this section.

Although BGP is meant to be used between autonomous systems to provide an interdomain loop-free topology, BGP can be used within an AS as a pipe between border routers running external BGP to other ASs. A neighbor connection, also called a *peer connection*, between two routers can be established within the same AS, in which case BGP is called *internal BGP* (IBGP). A peer connection can also be established between two routers in different ASs. BGP is then called *external BGP* (EBGP). Figure 5–1 contrasts these environments.

Upon neighbor session establishment and during the OPEN message exchange negotiation, peer routers compare AS numbers and determine whether they are peers in the same AS or in different ASs. The difference between EBGP and IBGP manifests itself in how each peer would process the routing updates coming from the other peer and in the way different BGP attributes are carried on external versus internal links.

Figure 5–1
Internal and external BGP implementations.

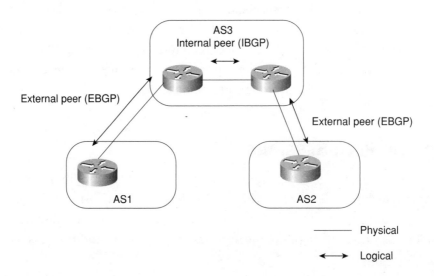

The neighbor negotiation process is mainly the same for internal and external neighbors as far as building the TCP connection at the transport level. It is essential to have IP connectivity between the two neighbors for the transport session to take place. IP connectivity has to be achieved via a protocol different from BGP; otherwise, the session will be in a *race condition*. An example of a race condition follows: neighbors can reach one another via some IGP, the BGP session gets established, and the BGP updates get exchanged. The IGP connection goes away for some reason, but still the BGP TCP session is up because neighbors can still reach each other via BGP. Eventually the session will go down because the BGP session cannot depend on BGP itself for neighbor reachability.

An Interior Gateway Protocol (IGP) or static route can be configured to achieve IP connectivity. In essence, a *ping* packet, containing a source IP address (the IP address of one BGP peer) and a destination IP address (the IP address of the second peer), must succeed for a transport session to initiate.

TROUBLESHOOTING

Verifying neighbor reachability for the TCP session to come up.

Physical Versus Logical Connections

External BGP neighbors have a restriction on being physically connected. BGP drops any updates from its external BGP peer if the peer is nonconnected. Some situations, however, arise where external neighbors cannot be on the same physical segment. Such neighbors are logically, but not physically connected. An example would be running BGP between external neighbors across non-BGP routers. In this situation, Cisco offers an extra knob to override this restriction. BGP would require some extra configuration to indicate that its external peer is not physically attached.

TROUBLESHOOTING

Nondirectly connected external neighbors need extra configuration.

In Cisco's implementation, nondirectly connected EBGP peers are referred to as *EBGP multihop*. In figure 5–2, RT2 is not able to run BGP, but RT1 and RT3 are. Thus, external neighbors RT1 and RT3 are logically connected and peer with one another via EBGP multihop.

On the other hand, neighbors within the same autonomous system (internal neighbors) have no restrictions whatsoever on whether the peer router is

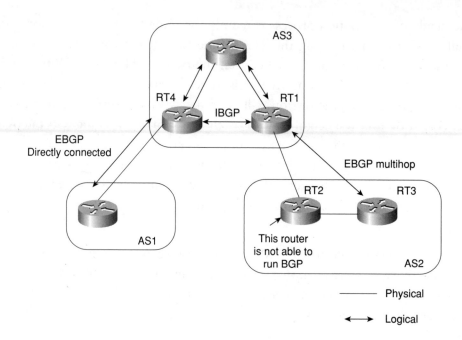

Figure 5–2
External BGP
multihop
environment.

physically connected. As long as there is IP connectivity between the two neighbors, BGP requires no extra configuration. In figure 5–2, RT1 and RT4 are logically but not physically connected. Because both are in the same AS, no additional configuration is needed for them to run IBGP.

Obtaining an IP Address

TROUBLESHOOTING

Session stability depends on stability of neighbor IP addresses.

The neighbor's IP address could be the address of any of the routers' interfaces, such as Ethernet, Token Ring, or Serial. Keep in mind that the stability of the neighbor connection will rely on the stability of the IP address you choose.

If the IP address belongs to an Ethernet card that has some hardware problems and is shutting down every few minutes, the neighbor connection and the stability of the routing updates will suffer. Cisco has introduced a *loopback interface*; this is actually a virtual interface that is supposed to be up at all times. Tying the neighbor connection to a loopback interface will make sure that the session is not dependent on any hardware interface that might be problematic.

Adding loopback interfaces is not necessary in every situation (it actually requires more configuration). If external BGP neighbors are directly connected and the IP addresses of the directly connected segment are used for the neighbor negotiation, a loopback address is of no added value. If the physical link between the two peers is problematic, then the session will break with or without loopback.

Ch. 10, pp. 300-305. Building Peering Sessions

Authenticating the BGP Session

As you have already seen in Chapter 4, "Interdomain Routing Basics," the BGP message header allows authentication. Authentication is a measure of precaution against hackers who might present themselves as one of your BGP peers and feed you wrong routing information. Authentication between two BGP peers gives the capability to validate the session between you and your neighbor by using a combination of passwords and keys upon which you both agree. A neighbor that tries to establish a session without the use of these specific passwords and keys will not be permitted. The authentication feature uses the Message-Digest Algorithm version 5 (MD5) [1]. The discussion of the authentication algorithm itself is beyond the scope of this book.

BGP Continuity Inside an AS

To avoid creating routing loops inside the AS, BGP does not advertise to internal BGP peers routes that are learned via other IBGP peers. Thus, it is important to maintain a full IBGP mesh within the AS—that is, every BGP router in the AS has to build a BGP session with all other BGP routers inside the AS. Figure 5–3 illustrates one of the common mistakes administrators make when setting BGP routing inside the AS.

TROUBLESHOOTING

Building full IBGP meshes to ensure connectivity.

In the situation illustrated in figure 5–3, an ISP has three POPs (Point Of Presence) in San Jose, San Francisco, and Los Angeles. Each POP has multiple non-BGP routers and a BGP border router running EBGP with other ASs. The administrator sets an IBGP connection between the San Jose border router and the San Francisco border router. He sets another IBGP connection between the

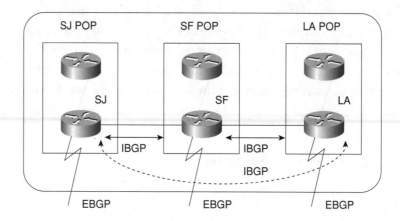

Figure 5–3
*Common BGP
continuity mistake.*

SF border router and the LA border router. In this configuration, EBGP routes learned via SJ will be given to SF, EBGP routes learned via SF are given to SJ and LA, and EBGP routes learned via LA are given to SF. Routing in this picture is not complete; EBGP routes learned via SJ will not be given to LA, and EBGP routes learned via LA will not be given to SJ. This is because the SF router will not pass on IBGP routes between SJ and LA. What is needed is an additional IBGP connection between SJ and LA (shown via the dotted line). You will see in Chapter 8, "Controlling Large-Scale Autonomous Systems," how this situation could be handled by using the concept of route reflectors, an option that scales much better in cases where the AS has a large number of IBGP peers.

Synchronization Within an AS

BGP must be synchronized with IGP in such a way that it waits until the IGP has propagated routing information across your autonomous system before advertising transit routes to other ASs. It is important that your AS be consistent about the routes it advertises. If, for example, your BGP were to advertise a route before all routers in your AS had learned about the route through the IGP, your AS could receive traffic that some routers cannot yet route.

Whenever a router receives an update about a destination from an IBGP peer, the router tries to verify internal reachability for that destination before advertising it to other EBGP peers. The router would do so by checking for the existence of this destination in the IGP. This would give an indication whether non-BGP routers can deliver traffic to that destination. Assuming that the IGP recognizes that destination, the router will announce it to other EBGP peers. Otherwise, the router will treat the route as not being synchronized with the IGP and would not advertise it.

Consider the situation illustrated in figure 5–4; ISP1 and ISP2 are using ISP3 as a transit AS. ISP3 has multiple routers in its AS and is running BGP only on the border routers. (Even though RTB and RTD are carrying transit traffic, ISP3 has not configured BGP on these routers.) ISP3 is running some Interior Gateway Protocol inside the AS for internal connectivity.

Assume that ISP1 is advertising route 192.213.1.0/24 to ISP3. Because RTA and RTC are running IBGP, RTA will propagate the route to RTC. Note that other routers besides RTA and RTC are not running BGP and have no knowledge so far of the existence of route 192.213.1.0/24.

TROUBLESHOOTING

Synchronizing BGP and IGP to advertise routes.

In the situation illustrated in figure 5–4, if RTC advertises the route to ISP2, traffic toward the destination 192.213.1.0/24 will start flowing toward RTC. RTC will do a recursive lookup in its IP routing table and will direct the traffic

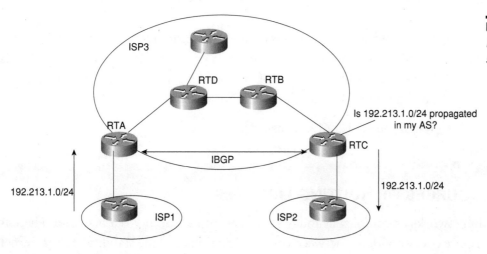

Figure 5–4
BGP route synchronization.

toward the next hop RTB. RTB, having no visibility to the BGP routes, will drop the traffic because it has no knowledge of the destination. This has happened because there is no synchronization between BGP and the IGP.

The BGP rule states that a BGP router should not advertise to external neighbors destinations learned from inside BGP neighbors unless those destinations are also known via IGP. If a router knows about these destinations via IGP, it assumes that the route has already been propagated inside the AS, and internal reachability is guaranteed.

The consequence of injecting BGP routes inside an AS is costly. Redistributing routes from BGP into the IGP will result in major overhead on the internal routers, which might not be equipped to handle that many routes. Besides, carrying all external routes inside an AS is not really necessary. Routing can easily be accomplished by having internal non-BGP routers default to one of the BGP routers. Of course, this will result in routing suboptimality (there is no guarantee for shortest path for each route), but this cost is minimal compared with maintaining thousands of routes inside the AS.

Cisco offers a software knob called "no synchronization" that enables BGP to override the synchronization requirement and enables it to advertise routes learned via IBGP irrespective of an existence of an IGP route. In practice, a couple of situations exist where synchronization can be safely turned off on border routers:

- When all transit routers inside the AS are running fully meshed IBGP. In this situation, internal reachability is guaranteed because a route that is learned via EBGP on any of the border routers will automatically be passed on via BGP to all other transit routers.

- When the AS is not a transit AS.

SOURCES OF ROUTING UPDATES

In networks as complex as today's Internet, route stability is a big issue. There is a close correspondence between route fluctuations and the stability of the Internet access links on one hand and how the routing information was injected into the Internet via BGP on the other hand. Information can be injected into BGP dynamically or statically. Dynamically injected routes come and go from the BGP routing table, depending on the status of the networks they identify. Statically injected routes are constantly maintained by the BGP routing tables, regardless of the status of the networks they identify. Thus, while a dynamic advertisement will cease if the network being advertised no longer exists, a static advertisement would not. Each method has its pros and cons, as you will see next.

Example: Ch. 10, pp. 315-324. Sources of Routing Updates

Injecting Information Dynamically into BGP

Dynamically injected information can be further divided into *purely dynamic*, where all the IGP routes are redistributed into BGP (**redistribute** command), and *semidynamic*, where only certain IGP routes are to be injected into BGP (**network** command). The distinction reflects both the level of user intervention and the level of control in defining the routes to be advertised.

Information is injected dynamically into BGP by enabling all the IGP routes to be redistributed into BGP. A variety of IGPs are used in autonomous systems these days, including Routing Information Protocol (RIP), Interior Gateway Routing Protocol (IGRP), Enhanced IGRP (EIGRP), Open Shortest Path First (OSPF), and Intermediate System-to-Intermediate System (ISIS) routing protocol. What dynamic redistribution offers is ease of configuration: all internal IGP routes will dynamically flow into BGP, regardless of what particular protocols are being used.

Example: Ch. 10, pp. 315-322. Injecting Information Dynamically into BGP

A semidynamic method of injecting information into BGP is to specify a subset of IGP networks to be advertised by individually listing them for injection into BGP by using the **network** command. This method is less than completely dynamic because a list of all the prefixes that need to be advertised must be maintained in the router—the router is not automatically injecting all IGP routes into BGP. If the list of prefixes is large, maintaining it would be impractical. Besides, router implementations might put an upper limit on the number of prefixes that can be listed. If the number of prefixes to be advertised is larger than that upper-bound limit, dynamically redistributing the IGP into BGP is a must.

TROUBLESHOOTING

Verification
requirement for
sending routing
updates with the
network com-
mand.

BGP assumes that networks defined with the **network** command are existing networks and will try to verify that by checking in the IP routing table. If BGP does not find an exact match for these networks, they will not be advertised. The verification step is smart because advertising a network not connected to or unknown by the router is misleading to other networks because the router cannot deliver traffic to this network anyway.

Injecting routes into BGP via the **network** command offers a more controlled way of route advertisement. Injecting IGPs into BGP via redistribution could result in the side effect of leaking unwanted or faulty information into BGP, as you will see next.

Injection of Unwanted or Faulty Information

Example: Ch. 10,
pp. 323-324.
Injecting Infor-
mation into BGP

Redistributing the whole IGP into BGP could result in some unwanted information being leaked into BGP. Such information could be private addresses, or illegal (not registered) addresses that are supposed to be used within the AS only. Other information could be routes with a prefix length that does not comply with the provider's aggregation policies; a host route with a prefix length of 32 is an example. This could be prevented by careful filtering.

Faulty information can also be injected into BGP due to the mutual exchange of routes between BGP and the IGP. In the same way that an IGP can be redistributed into BGP, BGP routes can be injected into an AS via redistribution into the IGP. When redistribution occurs in both directions, it is called *mutual redistribution*. In mutual redistribution, information that was injected from the outside into the AS could be sent back to the Internet as having originated from the AS. Figure 5–5 illustrates the danger of mutual redistribution between protocols.

In figure 5–5, AS100 is the source of NetA and is sending this information via BGP to AS200. The border router RTC injects that information into the IGP, and RTB learns about it. RTB is configured to redistribute the IGP information into BGP. NetA will end up being advertised via BGP back to the Internet as if it has originated from AS200. This is very misleading to ASs connected to the Internet because NetA now has two sources rather than one source (AS100).

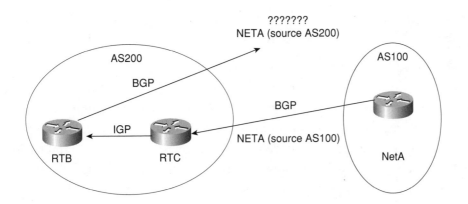

Figure 5–5
Mutual redistribution example.

Again, to remedy this situation, special filtering should be put on the border routers to specify what particular networks should be injected from the IGP into BGP. This would have stopped NetA from being redistributed back into BGP by RTB. For protocols that differentiate between internal and external routes such as OSPF, the administrator can configure the protocol to ensure that it will redistribute only internal routes into BGP. (In the Cisco implementation, external OSPF routes are automatically blocked from being redistributed into BGP; the administrator has the option of overriding this behavior.) For protocols that do not distinguish between internal and external routes such as RIP or IGRP, special route tagging should be performed to differentiate between external routes and internal routes.

Unstable Routes

Injecting the IGPs in BGP dynamically or semidynamically results in the dependency of the BGP routes on the IGP routes. Although you could argue that this is good because it reflects the actual status of networks, it can have drawbacks as well. Remember that with today's global network connectivity, route fluctuation within your AS will affect your provider if you are a customer or other providers if you are a provider. The IGP route you advertise will translate into a BGP route. If that route goes down, a WITHDRAWN message will be sent via BGP requesting peers to remove that route from their tables. A route constantly going up and down in your AS has the effect of being constantly sent and withdrawn by other ASs. The example of one fluctuating route is very simplistic; imagine having hundreds of these routes fluctuating in hundreds of ASs. Internet stability will be affected very negatively.

Strict measures are being put in place to try to mitigate the effect of route fluctuation on the Internet. As you will see in Chapter 9, "Designing Stable Internets," by a process called *route dampening*, fluctuating routes are penalized and stopped from being advertised depending on their degree of instability. Your routes might be "held hostage" for minutes and hours—until they stabilize—by an interconnected provider.

Controlling route instability is not an easy matter because it usually depends on factors that are beyond your control. Such factors could be instable access links or faulty hardware. One way to minimize route instability is aggregation. When the aggregate represents more than one route, the fluctuation of any single route does not cause fluctuation in the aggregate itself. Aggregation could be done on the customer boundary or the provider boundary, depending on the level of information exchanged between the customer and the provider. If done on the customer boundary, this would alleviate the provider from seeing the fluctuations of individual customer routes. If aggregation is done on the provider boundary, then the customer fluctuation would leak to the provider but will not be propagated to the Internet. BGP4 aggregation is discussed at the end of this chapter after you have acquired enough techniques in BGP tuning.

Another way of controlling route instability is to decouple route advertisement from the existence of the route itself. This is called *static injection of routes* into BGP, as described in the following section.

Injecting Information Statically into BGP

Example: Ch. 10, pp. 323-324. Injecting Information Statically into BGP

Today, injecting information statically into BGP has proven to be the most effective in ensuring route stability. Of course, this method also has drawbacks.

To statically inject information into BGP, IGP routes (or aggregates) that need to be advertised to other peers are manually defined as static routes. This ensures that these routes will never disappear from the IP routing table and hence will always be advertised. Because administrators are often uncomfortable advertising routes to networks that might be down or unreachable, the appropriateness of injecting information statically depends on the particular situation.

If, for example, the route is advertised to the Internet from a single point, then advertising a route that is actually down is not a big issue. Hosts trying to access that destination will fail irrespective of whether the route is advertised.

On the other hand, if a route is advertised to the Internet from multiple points, then advertising the route statically at all times might end up black-holing the traffic. If problems inside the AS prevent the border router from being able to reach the network it is advertising, traffic to that destination will be dropped even though it could have been reached from some other entry point.

The actual advertisement of the static route can be done with either of the methods described in the "Injecting Information Dynamically into BGP" section. Advertisement can be done by redistributing all the static routes via the **redistribute** command or a subset of the static routes via the **network** command. The latter method enables a more controlled route injection because redistribution might cause some unwanted static routes to be sent via BGP.

ORIGIN of Routes

BGP considers the networks advertised via the **network** command or via aggregation as being internal to the AS and will include the ORIGIN attribute in each route as being IGP (i). On the other hand, whenever a route is injected into BGP via redistribution (whether statically or dynamically), the ORIGIN of the route will be INCOMPLETE because the redistributed routes could have come from anywhere.

Figure 5–6 illustrates these issues. In Scenario 1, all networks have been listed under the BGP process via the **network** command. Note that BGP has considered 10.0.0.0 and 11.0.0.0 as having a known origin of IGP. Network 12.0.0.0

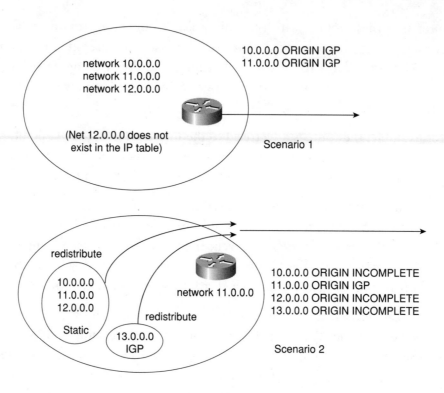

is the only network that is not known to the router (does not exist in the IP routing table). As you can see, 12.0.0.0 is not being advertised via BGP, even though it has been listed via the **network** command.

In Scenario 2, networks 10.0.0.0, 11.0.0.0, and 12.0.0.0 have been statically defined. Network 11.0.0.0 has also been defined via the **network** command. Finally, network 13.0.0.0 is learned dynamically by the router via IGP. All these networks have been injected into BGP via redistribution. As a result, networks 10.0.0.0, 12.0.0.0, and 13.0.0.0 have been advertised with an ORIGIN of INCOMPLETE because these networks have been injected into BGP via redistribution.

Although network 11.0.0.0 has been injected via redistribution, it is also defined natively to BGP via the **network** command, which is why it will be sent out with an ORIGIN of IGP. If it had not been defined natively, it would have been sent out with an ORIGIN of INCOMPLETE. Actually, network 11.0.0.0 did not need to be redistributed because defining it statically and listing it via the **network** command would suffice to inject it into BGP.

Although the ORIGIN is immaterial at this point, it is used later on to favor one route over the other by the BGP decision process.

An Example of Static Versus Dynamic Routing: Mobile Networks

It is common in the military for units to be mobile; this creates a problem for assigning IP addresses. Usually these mobile units would like to deploy their subnets and IP addresses wherever they go and operate as if they had never moved. If these networks are part of a global network and advertised via BGP, announcing them statically will not work easily. The static commands would have to be removed from the border router of one AS in one location and installed in the border router of another AS in the new location every time the unit moves.

To avoid such complications, injecting these networks dynamically into BGP becomes mandatory. One solution is to inject the IGP into BGP in all locations. This way, whenever the IP addresses are moved from one location to the other, the announcements will disappear from one location and reappear in the new one. In some cases, network administrators are not comfortable with this solution for reasons discussed earlier, such as mutual redistribution problems and the mandate for extensive filtering.

Another possibility is to define these networks in all the border routers of all the locations via the **network** command. Because BGP checks for the existence of these routes in the IP routing table before announcing them, BGP will only announce the routes in the location of the mobile unit. All other locations will automatically cease from announcing the routes because they are not part of the IGP of that particular AS.

Overlapping Protocols: Backdoors

Example: Ch. 10, pp. 324-326. Overlapping Protocols: (Backdoors)

With different IGPs and EGPs working together to achieve routing, networks can be learned via different protocols. Choosing one protocol over the other affects how the traffic flows. If, for example, traffic follows a RIP route, it might end up on one link; whereas if it follows an external BGP route, it might end up on another link. *Backdoor links* offer an alternate IGP path that can be used instead of the external BGP path. IGP routes reachable over the backdoor link are called *backdoor routes*. With the existence of such alternate routes, a mechanism that gives one protocol preference over other protocols is needed. Cisco Systems offers a preference parameter called the *distance* of a protocol. The lower a protocol's distance, the higher the preference for the protocol. Table 5–1 lists distances according to the Cisco implementation.

Table 5–1 indicates that a directly connected route is generally preferred over a static route, which in turn is preferred over an EBGP route, and so on. Note that EBGP routes with a distance of 20 are preferred over all the other IGP routes.

Table 5–1
Distance default values.

Protocol	Distance
Directly Connected	0
Static	1
EBGP	20
EIGRP (Internal)	90
IGRP	100
OSPF	110
ISIS	115
RIP	120
EGP	140
EIGRP (External)	170
IBGP	200
BGP Local	200
Unknown	255

Figure 5–7 illustrates the use of backdoor routes. In the figure, AS1 is receiving updates about NetA from two different sources. AS1 is receiving routes via EBGP on the link to AS3 and via the backdoor link running RIP between AS1 and AS2. According to the distance table, the router will give a distance of 20 to the EBGP route and a distance of 120 to the RIP route. In AS1, the EBGP route with the lower distance will be installed in the routing table. Hence, traffic toward NetA will follow the BGP route via AS3 and then AS2, rather than the direct RIP route via AS2.

Cisco provides a way to force IGP routes to take precedence over the EBGP routes. The concept is simple. EBGP routes can be tagged as backdoor routes. This would set the distance of these routes to be the same as the "BGP Local" route's distance (default is 200). According to table 5–1, this distance is higher than any IGP learned route, and the backdoor IGP route will be preferred.

THE ROUTING PROCESS SIMPLIFIED

Up until now, this chapter has examined discrete aspects of routing, specifically peer negotiation and static versus dynamic routing. Before diving into details of

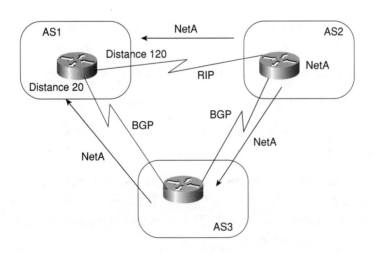

Figure 5–7
Backdoor routing conflicts.

routing configuration, it makes sense to pause here and briefly overview the BGP routing process in its entirety.

BGP is a fairly simple protocol, which is why it is so flexible. Routes are exchanged between BGP peers via UPDATE messages. BGP routers receive the UPDATE messages, run some policies or filters over the updates, and then pass on the routes to other BGP peers. Cisco's implementation of BGP keeps track of all BGP updates in a BGP routing table separate from the IP routing table. In case multiple routes to the same destination exist, BGP does not flood its peers with all those routes; rather, it picks the best route and sends it. In addition to passing along routes from peers, a BGP router may originate routing updates to advertise networks that belong to its own autonomous system. Valid local routes originated in the system, and the best routes learned from BGP peers are then installed in the IP routing table. The IP routing table is used for the final routing decision.

To model the BGP process, imagine each BGP speaker having different pools of routes and different policy engines applied to the routes. The model would involve the following components:

- A pool of routes that the router receives from its peers
- An Input Policy Engine that can filter the routes or manipulate their attributes
- A decision process that decides which routes the router itself will use
- A pool of routes that the router itself uses
- An Output Policy Engine that can filter the routes or manipulate their attributes
- A pool of routes that the router advertises to other peers

Figure 5–8 illustrates this model. The subsequent discussion provides more details about each component.

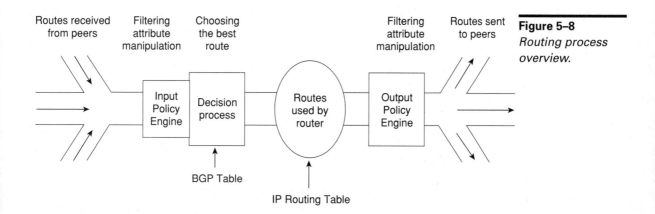

Figure 5–8
Routing process overview.

Routes Received from Peers

BGP receives routes from external or internal peers. Depending on what is configured in the Input Policy Engines, some or all of these routes will make it into the router's BGP table.

Input Policy Engine

This engine handles route filtering and attribute manipulation. Filtering is done based on different parameters such as IP prefixes, AS_path information, and attribute information. BGP also uses the Input Policy Engine to manipulate the path attributes to influence its own decision process and hence affect what routes it will actually use to reach a certain destination. If, for example, BGP chooses to filter a certain network number coming from a peer, it is an indication that BGP does not want to reach that network via that peer. Or, if BGP gives a certain route a better local preference (this attribute is discussed later on), it is an indication that BGP would like to prefer this route over other routes.

The Decision Process

BGP goes through a decision process to decide which routes it wants to use to reach a certain destination. The decision process is based on the routes that made it into the router after the Input Policy Engine was applied. The decision process is performed on the routes in the BGP routing table. The decision process looks at all the available routes for the same destination, compares the different attributes associated with each route, and chooses one best route. The decision process is discussed later in this chapter, after coverage of attributes.

Routes Used by the Router

The best routes, as identified by the decision process, are what the router itself uses and are candidates to be advertised to other peers and also to be placed in the IP routing table.

In addition to routes passed on from other peers, the router (if configured to do so) originates updates about the networks inside its autonomous system. This is how an AS injects its routes into the outside world.

Output Policy Engine

This is the same engine as the Input Policy Engine, applied on the output side. Routes used by the router (the best routes) in addition to routes that the router generates locally are given to this engine for processing. The engine might apply filters and might change some of the attributes (such as AS_path or metric) before sending the update.

The Output Policy Engine also differentiates between internal and external peers; for example, routes learned from internal peers cannot be passed on to internal peers.

Routes Advertised to Peers

This is the set of routes that made it through the Output Engine and are advertised to the BGP peers, internal or external.

Example Routing Environment

Figure 5–9 illustrates routing in an example environment. In the figure, AS5 is receiving routes from both AS1 and AS2 and is originating its own routes (172.16.10.0/24). To simplify, consider just the flow of updates in one direction, left to right. By applying the engine model to AS5, you will get the following.

Routes received from peers (these are the routes coming from AS1 and AS2):

- 192.213.1.0/24 via AS1.

- 0/0 (this is a default route) via AS1.

- 193.214.10.0/24 via AS2.

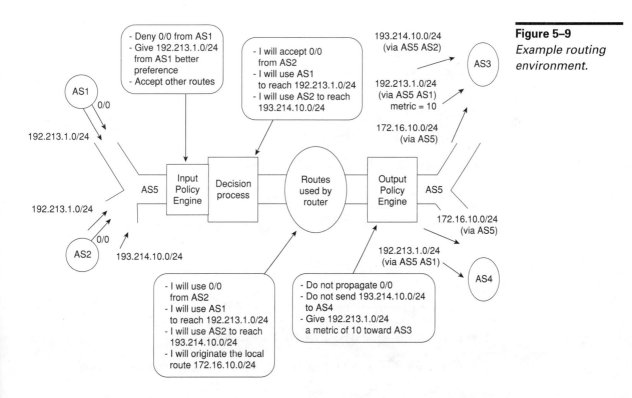

Figure 5–9
Example routing environment.

- 0/0 (this is a default route) via AS2.

- 192.213.1.0/24 via AS2.

Input Policy Engine:

- Do not accept default route 0/0 from AS1.

- Give route 192.213.1.0/24 coming from AS1 better preference than route 192.213.1.0/24 coming from AS2.

- Accept all other routes (this will accept 193.214.10.0/24).

The decision process:

- Because 192.213.1.0/24 has better preference via AS1, I will reach 192.213.1.0/24 via AS1.

- I will reach 193.214.10.0/24 via AS2.

- I will accept 0/0 via AS2.

Routes used by the router:

- I will use 0/0 as default from AS2.

- I can reach 192.213.1.0/24 via AS1.

- I can reach 193.214.10.0/24 via AS2.

- Network 172.16.10.0/24 is one of my local networks that I want to advertise.

Output Policy Engine:

- Do not propagate the default route 0/0.

- Do not advertise 193.214.10.0/24 to AS4.

- Give 192.213.1.0/24 a metric of 10 when sent to AS3.

Routes advertised to peers:

- Toward AS3:

    ○ 192.213.1.0/24 via (AS5 AS1) (this means, first AS5 then AS1) with a metric of 10.

    ○ 172.16.10.0/24 (via AS5).

    ○ 193.214.10.0/24 (via AS5 AS2).

- Toward AS4:

    ○ 192.213.1.0/24 (via AS5 AS1).

    ○ 172.16.10.0/24 (via AS5).

CONTROLLING BGP ROUTES

The preceding section discusssed the existence of policy engines that provide attribute manipulation and route filtering. This section discusses attribute manipulation and route filtering, the keys to controlling routing information, in detail. Each BGP attribute is examined to determine what it does and how to use it.

Traffic inside and outside an AS always flows according to the road map laid out by routes. Altering the routes translates to changes in traffic behavior. Among the questions that organizations and service providers ask about controlling routes are: How do I prevent my private networks from being advertised? How do I filter routing updates coming from a particular neighbor? How do I make sure that I use this link or this provider rather than another one? BGP provides the necessary hooks and attributes to address all these questions and more.

BGP Attributes

The BGP attributes are a set of parameters that describe the characteristics of a prefix (route). The BGP decision process uses these attributes to select its best routes. Remember that attributes are part of each BGP UPDATE packet. The

Example: Ch. 10, pp. 326-342. BGP Attributes

next few sections cover these attributes and how they can be manipulated to affect the routing behavior.

The NEXT_HOP Attribute

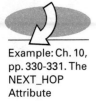

Example: Ch. 10, pp. 330-331. The NEXT_HOP Attribute

The NEXT_HOP attribute is a well-known mandatory attribute (type code 3). In IGP, the next hop to reach a route is the IP address of the connected interface of the router that has announced the route.

The next hop concept with BGP is slightly more elaborate and takes one of the following three forms:

1. For EBGP sessions: the next hop is the IP address of the neighbor that announced the route.

2. For IBGP sessions: for routes originated inside the AS, the next hop is the IP address of the neighbor that announced the route.

    For routes injected into the AS via EBGP, the next hop learned from EBGP is carried unaltered into IBGP. The next hop is the IP address of the EBGP neighbor from which the route was learned.

3. When the route is advertised on a multiaccess media (such as Ethernet, Frame Relay, and so on), the next hop is usually the IP address of the interface of the router, connected to that media, that originated the route.

Figure 5–10 illustrates the BGP NEXT_HOP attribute environment.

The SF router is running an EBGP session with the LA router and an IBGP session with the SJ router. The SF router is learning route 128.213.1.0/24 from the LA router. In turn, the SF router is injecting the local route 192.212.1.0/24 into BGP.

The SJ router learns route 192.212.1.0/24 via 2.2.2.2, the IP address of the IBGP peer announcing the route. Thus, 2.2.2.2 is the next hop, according to the definition, for SJ to reach 192.212.1.0/24. Similarly, the SF router sees 128.213.1.0/24 coming from the LA router via next hop 1.1.1.1. When it

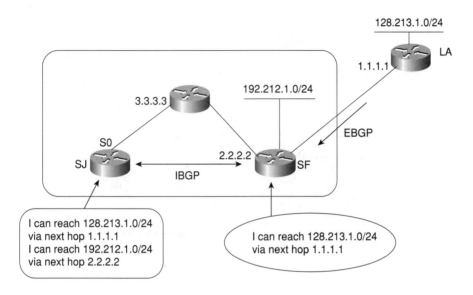

Figure 5–10
*BGP NEXT_ HOP
example.*

passes this route update to the SJ router via IBGP, SF includes the next hop information, unaltered. Thus, the SJ router would receive the BGP update about 128.213.1.0/24 with next hop 1.1.1.1. This is an example of the EBGP next hop being carried into IBGP.

As you can see from the preceding example, the next hop is not necessarily reachable via a direct connection. SJ's next hop for 128.213.1.0/24, for example, is 1.1.1.1, but reaching it requires a pathway through 3.3.3.3. Thus, the next hop behavior mandates a recursive IP lookup for a router to know where to send the packet. To reach the next hop 1.1.1.1, the SJ router will recursively look into its IGP routing table to see if and how 1.1.1.1 is reachable. This recursive search continues until the router associates destination 1.1.1.1 with an outgoing interface. The same recursive behavior is performed to reach next hop 2.2.2.2. If a hop is not reachable, BGP would consider the route as being inaccessible.

The following is a sample of how IP recursive lookup is used to direct the traffic toward the final destination. Table 5–2 and table 5–3 list the BGP and IP routing tables for the SJ router illustrated in figure 5–10.

Table 5–2	Destination	Next Hop
BGP table of SJ router.	192.212.1.0/24	2.2.2.2
	128.213.1.0/24	1.1.1.1

Table 5–3	Destination	Next Hop
IP routing table of SJ router.	192.212.1.0/24	2.2.2.2
	2.2.2.0/24	3.3.3.3
	3.3.3.0/24	Connected, Serial 0
	128.213.1.0/24	1.1.1.1
	1.1.1.0/24	3.3.3.3

Table 5–2 indicates that 128.213.1.0/24 is reachable via next hop 1.1.1.1. Looking into the IP routing table, network 1.1.1.0/24 is reachable via next hop 3.3.3.3. Another recursive lookup in the IP routing table indicates that network 3.3.3.0/24 is directly connected via Serial 0. This would indicate that traffic toward next hop 1.1.1.1 should go via Serial 0. The same reasoning applies to deliver traffic toward next hop 2.2.2.2.

TROUBLESHOOTING

Verifying next hop reachability.

Care must be taken to make sure that reachability of the next hop is advertised via some IGP or static routing. In case the BGP next hop cannot be reached, the BGP route would be considered inaccessible.

NEXT_HOP Behavior on Multiaccess Media

A media is considered multiaccess (MA) if routers connected to that media have the capability to exchange data in a many-to-many relationship. Routers on MA media share the same IP subnet and can physically access all other routers on the media in one hop (directly connected). Ethernet, FDDI, Token Ring, Frame Relay, and ATM are examples of multiaccess media.

IP has a rule on MA media that states that a router should always advertise the actual source of the route in case the source is on the same MA media as the router. In other words, if RTA (router A) is advertising a route learned from RTB, and RTA and RTB share a common MA media, when RTA advertises the route, it should indicate RTB as being the source of the route. If not, routers on the same media would have to make an unnecessary hop via RTA to get to a router that is sitting in the same segment.

In figure 5–11, RTA, RTB, and RTC share a common multiaccess media. RTA and RTC are running EBGP, while RTC and RTB are running OSPF. RTC has learned network 11.11.11.0/24 from RTB via OSPF and is advertising it to RTA via EBGP. Because RTA and RTB are running different protocols, you might think that RTA would consider RTC (10.10.10.2) as its next hop to reach 11.11.11.0/24, but this is incorrect. The correct behavior is for RTA to consider RTB (10.10.10.3) as the next hop because RTB shares the same media with RTC.

In situations where the media is broadcast, such as Ethernet and FDDI, physical connectivity is a given and the next hop behavior is no problem. On the contrary, in situations where the media is nonbroadcast, such as Frame Relay and ATM, special care should be taken as described in the following section.

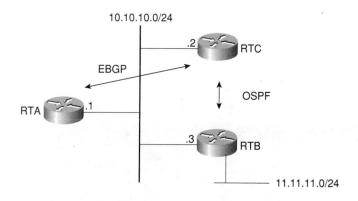

Figure 5–11
Example multiaccess media environment.

NEXT_HOP Behavior Over
Nonbroadcast Multiaccess Media (NBMA)

Media such as Frame Relay and ATM are nonbroadcast multiaccess. The many-to-many direct interaction between routers is not guaranteed unless virtual circuits are configured from each router to all other routers. This is called a *fully meshed* topology, and it is not always implemented for a number of reasons. In practice, Frame Relay or ATM virtual circuits are provided by the access carrier at a certain dollar amount per circuit, and additional circuits translate into extra money. In addition to this cost disincentive, most organizations use a *hub and spoke* approach, where multiple remote sites have virtual circuits built to one or more concentration routers at a central site (the hub site) where information resides. Figure 5–12 illustrates an example of next hop behavior in a nonbroadcast multiaccess environment.

The only difference between the environments illustrated in figure 5–12 and figure 5–11 is that the media in figure 5–12 is a Frame Relay cloud that is NBMA. RTC is the hub router; RTA and RTB are the spokes. Notice how the virtual circuits are laid out between RTC and RTA, and between RTC and RTB, but not between RTA and RTB. This is called a *partially meshed* topology.

RTA gets a BGP routing update about 11.11.11.0/24 from RTC and would try to use RTB (10.10.10.3) as the next hop (the same behavior as on MA media). Routing will fail because no virtual circuit exists between RTA and RTB.

Figure 5–12
Nonbroadcast multiaccess NEXT_HOP example.

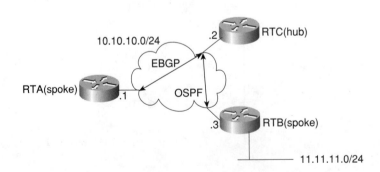

Cisco IOS software supports a special case parameter that remedies this situation. The next-hop-self parameter (when configured as part of the BGP neighbor connection) forces the router (in this case, RTC) to advertise 11.11.11.0/24 with itself as the next hop (10.10.10.2). RTA would then direct its traffic to RTC to reach destination 11.11.11.0/24.

Use of next-hop-self Versus Advertising DMZ

The demilitarized zone (DMZ) defines the shared network between ASs. The IP subnet used for the DMZ link might be part of any of the networked ASs or might not belong to any of them. As you have already seen, the next hop address learned from the EBGP peer is carried inside IBGP. It is important for the IGP to be able to reach the next hop. One way of doing so is for the DMZ subnet to be part of the IGP and have the subnet advertised in the AS. The other way is to override the next hop address by forcing the next hop to be the IP address of the border IBGP neighbor.

In figure 5–13, the SJ router is receiving updates about 128.213.1.0/24 with next hop 1.1.1.1 (part of the DMZ). For the SJ router to be able to reach this next hop, one option is for network 1.1.1.0/24 to be advertised inside the AS by the SF border router.

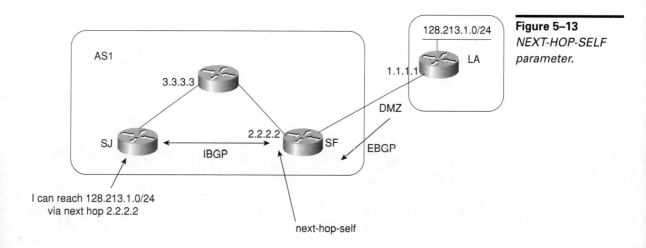

Figure 5–13
*NEXT-HOP-SELF
parameter.*

TROUBLESHOOTING

Use of
next-hop-self to
override carry-
ing the EBGP
next hop into
IBGP.

The other option is to have the SF router set the *next-hop-self* parameter as part of the IBGP neighbor connection to the SJ router. This will set the next hop address of all EBGP routes to 2.2.2.2, that is already part of the IGP. The SJ router can now reach the next hop with no problem.

Choosing one method over the other depends on whether you want to reach the DMZ. An example could be an operator trying to do a ping from inside the AS to a router interface that belongs to the DMZ. For the ping to succeed, the DMZ must be injected in the IGP. In other cases, the DMZ might be reachable via some suboptimal route external to the AS. Instead of reaching the DMZ from inside the AS, the router might attempt to use another EBGP link to reach the DMZ. In this case, using next-hop-self ensures that the next hop is reachable from within the AS. In all other cases, both methods are similar as far as the BGP routing functionality.

The AS_Path Attribute

Example: Ch. 10,
pp. 331-335. The
AS_Path
Attribute

An AS_path attribute is a well-known mandatory attribute (type code 2). It is a sequence of autonomous system numbers a route has traversed to reach a destination. The AS that originates the route adds its own AS number when sending the route to its external BGP peers. Thereafter, each AS that receives the route and passes it on to other BGP peers will prepend its own AS number to the list. *Prepending* is the act of adding the AS number to the beginning of the list. The final list represents all the AS numbers that a route has traversed with the AS number of the AS that originated the route all the way at the end of the list. This type of AS_path list is called an *AS_sequence*, because all the AS numbers are ordered sequentially.

BGP uses the AS_path attribute as part of the routing updates (UPDATE packet) to ensure a loop-free topology on the Internet. Each route that gets passed between BGP peers will carry a list of all AS numbers that the route has already been through. If the route is advertised to the AS that originated it, that AS will see itself as part of the AS_path attribute list and will not accept the route. BGP speakers prepend their AS numbers when advertising routing updates to other ASs (external peers). When the route is passed to a BGP speaker within the same AS, the AS_path information is left intact.

Figure 5–14 illustrates the AS_path attribute at each instance of the route 172.16.10.0/24, originating in AS1 and passed to AS2 then AS3 and AS4 and back to AS1. Note how each AS that passes the route to other external peers adds its own AS number to the beginning of the list. When the route gets back to AS1, the BGP border router will realize that this route has already been through its AS (AS number 1 appears in the list) and would not accept the route.

AS_path information is one of the attributes BGP looks at to determine the best route to take to get to a destination. In comparing two or more different routes, given that all other attributes are identical, a shorter path is always preferred. In case of a tie, other attributes are used to make the decision.

Using Private ASs

To conserve AS numbers, InterNIC generally does not assign a legal AS number to customers whose routing policies are an extension of the policies of their provider. Thus, in the situation where a customer is single-homed or multihomed

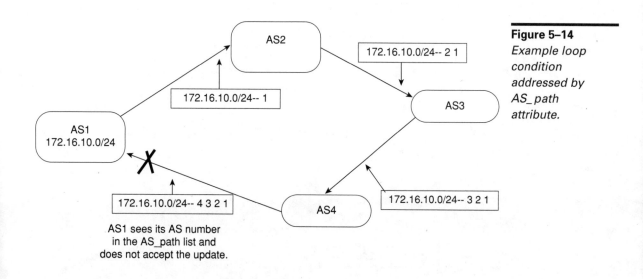

Figure 5–14
Example loop condition addressed by AS_path attribute.

Example: Ch. 10,
pp. 333-335.
Using Private
ASs

to the same provider, the provider generally requests that the customer use an AS number taken from the private pool of ASs (64512-65535). As such, all BGP updates the provider receives from its customer contain private AS numbers.

Private AS numbers cannot be leaked to the Internet because they are not unique. For this reason, Cisco has implemented a feature to strip private AS numbers out of the AS_path list before the routes get propagated to the Internet. This is illustrated in figure 5–15.

In figure 5–15, AS1 is providing Internet connectivity to its customer AS65001. Because the customer has only this provider and no plans for having an additional provider in the near future, the customer has been allocated a private AS number. If the customer later needs to connect to another provider, a legal AS number should be assigned.

Figure 5–15
*Stripping private
AS numbers.*

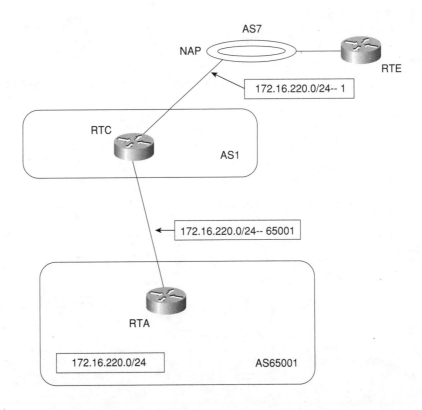

Prefixes originating from AS65001 have an AS_path of 65001. Note prefix 172.16.220.0/24 in figure 5–15 as it leaves AS65001. For AS1 to propagate the prefix to the Internet, it would have to strip the private AS number. When the prefix reaches the Internet, it would look like it has originated from the provider's AS. Note how prefix 172.16.220.0/24 has reached the NAP with AS_path 1.

NOTES

Chapter 1, "Evolution of the Internet," introduced the Network Access Points and their usage in interconnecting multiple providers. BGP connections to the NAP are usually done via a route server where multiple ASs peer via EBGP into a single system. The route server would have its own AS number. In figure 5–15, the NAP is represented by the route server RTE having AS number 7. Actually, the route server concept is not limited to the NAP; the NAP is a special case where the route server runs the RADB (Appendix A, "RIPE-181"). The route server concept would apply anytime multiple ASs rely on a single point for exchanging EBGP updates.

BGP will strip private ASs only when propagating updates to the external peers. This means that the AS stripping would be configured on RTC as part of its neighbor connection to RTE.

Private ASs should only be connected to a single provider. If the AS_path contains a mixture of private and legal AS numbers, BGP will view this as an illegal design and will not strip the private AS numbers from the list, and the update will be treated as usual. Only AS_path lists that contain private AS numbers in the range 64512 to 65535 are stripped.

AS_Path and Route Aggregation Issues

Route aggregation involves summarizing ranges of routes into one or more aggregates or CIDR blocks to minimize the number of routes in the global routing tables. A drawback of route aggregation is the loss of granularity that existed in the specific routes that form the aggregate. The AS_path information that exists in multiple routes, for example, will be lost when these routes get summarized into one single advertisement. This would lead to potential routing loops because a route that has passed through an AS might be accepted by the same AS as a new route.

BGP defines another type of AS_path list called an AS-SET where the ASs are listed in an unordered set. The set includes all the ASs a route has traversed. Aggregates carrying the AS-SET information would have a collective set of the attributes that form the individual routes they summarize.

In figure 5–16, AS1 is advertising 192.213.1.0/24, and AS2 is advertising 192.213.2.0/24. AS3 is aggregating both routes into 192.213.0.0/16. An AS that advertises an aggregate considers itself the originator of that route, irrespective of where that route came from. When AS3 advertises the aggregate 192.213.0.0/16, the AS_path information would be just 3. This would cause a loss of information because the originators of the route AS1 and AS2 are no longer listed in the AS_path. In a situation where the aggregate is somehow advertised back to AS1 and AS2 by some other AS, AS1 and AS2 would accept the route that would potentially lead to routing loops.

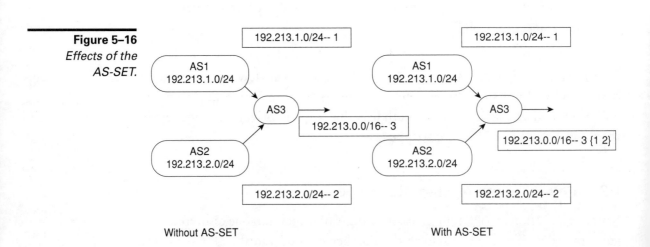

Figure 5–16
Effects of the
AS-SET.

With the notion of AS-SET, it is possible to have AS3 advertise the aggregate 192.213.0.0/16 while keeping information about the components of the aggregate. The set {1 2} indicates that the aggregate has come from both of these ASs in no particular order. The AS_path information of the aggregate with the AS-SET option would be 3 {1 2}.

AS_Path Manipulation

AS_path information is manipulated to affect interdomain routing behavior. Because BGP prefers a shorter path over a longer one, system operators are tempted to change the path information by including dummy AS path numbers that would increase the path length and influence the traffic trajectory one way or the other. Cisco's implementation enables a user to insert AS numbers at the beginning of an AS_path to make the path length longer. The following example shows how this feature can be used.

Example: Ch. 10, pp. 332-333. AS_Path Manipulation

In figure 5–17, AS50 is connected to two providers, AS200 and AS100. AS100 is directly connected to the NAP, whereas AS200 has to go through an extra hop via AS300 to reach the NAP. Figure 5–17 shows instances of prefix 192.213.1.0/24 as it traverses the ASs in its way to the NAP. When the 192.213.1.0/24 prefix reaches the NAP via AS300, it would have an AS_path of 300 200 50. If the same prefix reaches the NAP via AS100, it would have an AS_path of 100 50, which is shorter. ASs upstream from the NAP would prefer the shorter AS_path length and would direct their traffic toward AS100 at all times for destination 192.213.1.0/24.

AS50 is not too happy about this behavior because it prefers the traffic to come via its higher bandwidth T3 link to AS200. AS50 will manipulate the AS_path information by inserting dummy AS numbers when sending routing updates to AS100. One common practice is for AS50 to repeat its AS number as many times as necessary to tip the balance and make the path via AS200 become shorter.

In figure 5–18, AS50 will insert two AS numbers 50 50 at the beginning of the AS_path of prefix 192.213.1.0/24. When the prefix 192.213.1.0/24 reaches the NAP via AS100, it would have the AS_path 100 50 50 50, which is longer than

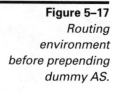
Figure 5–17
Routing environment before prepending dummy AS.

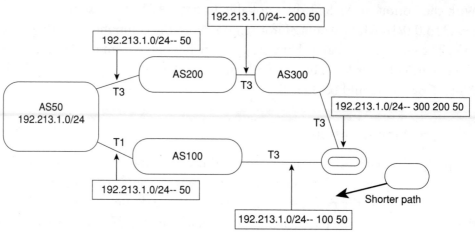

the AS_path 300 200 50 via AS300. ASs upstream of the NAP would prefer the shortest path and would direct the traffic toward AS300 for destination 192.213.1.0/24.

The bogus number should always be a duplicate of the AS announcing the route or the neighbor the route is learned from (in case an AS is increasing the path

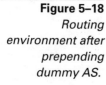
Figure 5–18
Routing environment after prepending dummy AS.

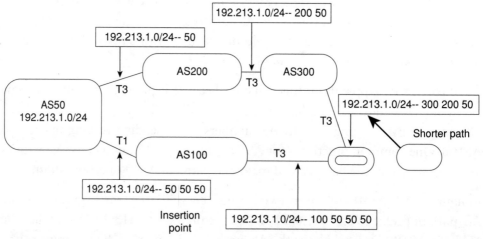

length for incoming updates). Adding any other number is misleading and could potentially lead to routing loops. Note the insertion point in figure 5–18.

The Local Preference Attribute

The local preference is a well-known discretionary attribute (type code 5). The local preference attribute is a degree of preference given to a route to compare it with other routes for the same destination. A higher local preference value is an indication that the route is more preferred. Local preference, as indicated by the name, is local to the autonomous system and gets exchanged between IBGP peers only and is not passed to EBGP peers.

Example: Ch. 10, pp. 335-337. The Local Preference Attribute

An AS connected via BGP to multiple other ASs will get routing updates about the same destinations from different ASs. Local preference is usually used to set the exit point of an AS to reach a certain destination. Because this attribute is communicated within all BGP routers inside the AS, all BGP routers will have a common view on how to exit the AS.

Consider the environment illustrated in figure 5–19. Suppose that company ANET has purchased Internet connections via two service providers XNET and YNET. ANET is connected to YNET via a primary T3 link and to XNET via a backup T1 link.

It is important for ANET to decide what path its outbound traffic is going to take. Of course ANET prefers to use the T3 link via YNET in normal operation because it is a high-speed link.

This is where local preference comes into play: the LA router will give the routes coming from YNET a local preference of 300. The SJ router will give the routes coming from XNET a lower value, say 200. Because both the LA and SJ routers are exchanging routing updates via IBGP, they both agree that the exit point of the AS is going to be via YNET because of the higher local preference. In figure 5–19, ANET learns route 128.213.0.0/16 via XNET and YNET. The SJ and LA routers will agree on using YNET as the exit point for destination 128.213.0.0/16 because of the higher local preference value of 300. The local preference manipulation discussed in this case affects the traffic going out of the AS and not traffic coming into the AS. Inbound traffic can still come via the T1 link.

Figure 5–19
*Local preference
attribute example.*

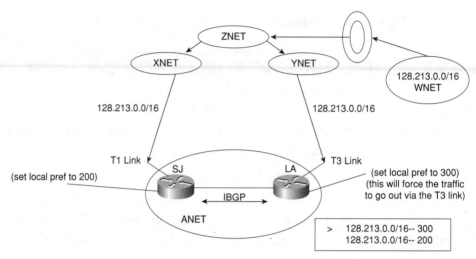

Cisco's proprietary weight parameter is similar to the local preference in that it gives higher preference to the route that has a higher weight. The difference is that the weight parameter is local to the router and does not get exchanged between routers. The weight parameter influences routes coming from different providers to the same router (one router with multiple connections to two or more providers). The weight parameter has a higher precedence than any other attribute; it is used as a main (proprietary) switch to determine route preference.

The MULTI_EXIT_DISC (MED) Attribute

Example: Ch. 10,
pp. 337-340. The
MULTI_EXIT_
DISC (MED)
Attribute

The MULTI_EXIT_DISC (MED) attribute is an optional nontransitive attribute (type code 4). It is a hint to external neighbors about the preferred path into an AS that has multiple entry points. The MED is also known as the external metric of a route. A lower MED value is preferred over a higher MED value.

Unlike local preference, the MED attribute is exchanged between ASs, but a MED attribute that comes into an AS does not leave the AS. When an update enters the AS with a certain MED value, that value is used for decision making within the AS. When BGP passes on the routing update to another AS, the MED is reset to zero (unless the outgoing MED is set to a specific value).

When the route is originated by the AS itself, the MED value follows the internal IGP metric of the route. This becomes useful when a customer has multiple connections to the same provider. The IGP metric reflects how close or how far a network is to a certain exit point. A network that is closer to exit point A than to exit point B will have a lower IGP metric in the border router connected to A. When the IGP metric translates to MED, traffic coming into the AS can enter from the link closer to the destination because a lower MED is preferred for the same destination. This can be used both by providers and customers to balance the traffic over multiple links between two ASs.

Unless otherwise specified, the router compares MED attributes for paths from external neighbors that are in the same AS. MEDs from different ASs are not comparable because the MED associated with a route usually gives some indication of the AS's internal topology. Comparing MEDs from different ASs would be like comparing apples and oranges. Still, for administrators who have a reason to do so, Cisco offers the **bgp always-compare-med** router command.

In the local preference example illustrated in figure 5–19, an AS was shown determining how to influence its own outbound decision. In the example illustrated in figure 5–20, the MED shows how an AS can influence the outbound decision of another AS. In figure 5–20, ANET and YNET try to influence XNET's outbound traffic by sending it different metric values.

XNET is receiving routing updates about 128.213.0.0/16 from three different sources; SJ (metric 120), LA (metric 200), and NY (metric 50). SF will compare the two metric values coming from ANET and will prefer the SJ router because it is advertising a lower metric (120). When the **bgp always-compare-med** router configuration command is used on the SF router, it will then compare metric 120 with metric 50 coming from NY and will prefer NY to reach 128.213.0.0/16. Note that SF could have influenced its decision by using local preference inside XNET to override the metrics coming from outside ASs. Nevertheless, MED is

Figure 5–20
Effects of the MED attribute.

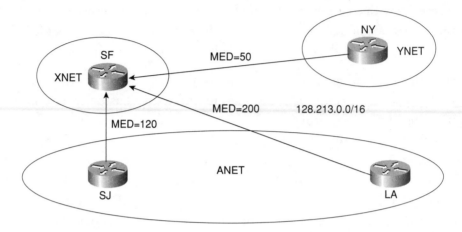

still useful in case XNET prefers to base its BGP decisions on outside factors to simplify router configuration on its end. Customers that connect to the same provider in multiple locations could exchange metrics with their providers to influence each other's outbound traffic, which leads to better load balancing.

The Community Attribute

Example: Ch. 10, pp. 340-342. The Community Attribute

In the context of BGP, a *community* is a group of destinations that share some common property. A community is not restricted to one network or one autonomous system; it has no physical boundaries. An example is a group of networks that belong to the educational or government communities. These networks can belong to any autonomous system. Communities are used to simplify routing policies by identifying routes based on a logical property rather than an IP prefix or an AS number. A BGP speaker can use this attribute in conjunction with other attributes to control which routes to accept, prefer, and pass on to other BGP neighbors.

The community attribute (type code 8) is an optional transitive attribute that is of variable length and consists of a set of 4-byte values. Communities in the range 0x00000000 through 0x0000FFFF and 0xFFFF0000 through 0xFFFFFFFF are reserved. These communities are well-known—that is, they have a global meaning. An example of well-known communities are:

- *NO_EXPORT (0xFFFFFF01)*: A route carrying this community value should not be advertised to peers outside a confederation (or the AS if it is the only AS in the confederation). Confederations are explained in Chapter 8.

- *NO_ADVERTISE (0xFFFFFF02)*: A route carrying this community value, when received, should not be advertised to any BGP peer.

Besides well-known community attributes, private community attributes can be defined for special uses. A common practice is to use the first two bytes of the community attribute for the AS number and the last two bytes to define a value in relation to that AS. A provider (AS256), for example, who wants to define a private community called "my-peer-routers" could use the community 256:1 represented in a decimal notation. The 256 indicates that this particular provider has defined the community, and the 1 has special meaning to the provider; in this case it is "my-peer-routers."

A route can have more than one community attribute. A BGP speaker that sees multiple community attributes in a route can act based on one, some, or all the attributes. A router has the option of adding or modifying community attributes before passing routes on to other peers.

Figure 5–21 shows a simple use of the community attribute. XNET is sending toward YNET routes X and Y with a NO_EXPORT community attribute, and route Z with no modification. The BGP router in YNET will propagate route Z only toward ZNET. Routes X and Y will not be propagated because of the NO_EXPORT community attribute.

The ATOMIC_AGGREGATE Attribute

Route aggregation causes a loss of information because the aggregate is coming from different sources that have different attributes. The ATOMIC_AGGREGATE

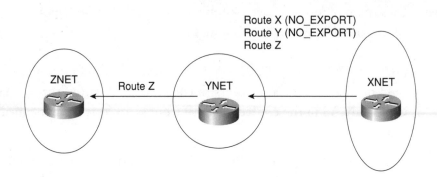

Figure 5–21
*Simple application
of community
attribute.*

attribute is a well-known discretionary attribute (type code 6) that gets set as an indication of information loss. Basically, if a system propagates an aggregate that causes loss of information, it is required to attach the ATOMIC_AGGREGATE attribute to the route.

Example: Ch. 10,
pp. 343-346.
Aggregate
Only, Suppress-
ing the More
Specific

The ATOMIC_AGGREGATE should not be set when the aggregate carries some extra information that gives an indication of where the aggregated information came. An example is an aggregate with the AS-SET parameter, as discussed earlier. An aggregate that carries the set of ASs that form the aggregate is not required to attach the ATOMIC_AGGREGATE attribute.

The AGGREGATOR Attribute

The AGGREGATOR attribute is an optional transitive attribute (type code 7). It specifies the autonomous system and the router that has generated an aggregate. A BGP speaker that performs route aggregation might add the AGGREGATOR attribute, which contains the speaker's AS number and IP address. In Cisco's implementation, the IP address is actually the Router ID (RID), which is the highest IP address on the router or the loopback address if it exists. The loopback interface is the virtual interface discussed earlier in this chapter. Figure 5–22 illustrates the AGGREGATOR attribute. AS300 is receiving routes 192.213.1.0/24 and 192.213.2.0/24 from AS100 and AS200, respectively. When RTA generates aggregate 192.213.0.0/16, it has the option of including

the AGGREGATOR attribute, which consists of the AS number 300 and the
RID 193.0.34.1 of the router (RTA) that originated the aggregate.

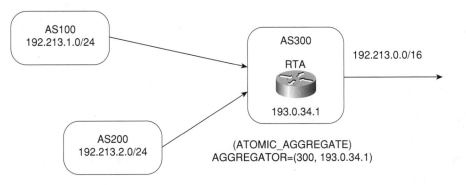

Figure 5–22
*AGGREGATOR
implementation
example.*

The ORIGIN Attribute

The ORIGIN attribute is a well-known mandatory attribute (type code 1). It
indicates the origin of the routing update (NLRI, which indicates prefix and
mask) with respect to the autonomous system that originated it. BGP considers
three types of origins:

- *IGP*—The Network Layer Reachability Information (NLRI) is internal
  to the originating AS.

- *EGP*—The Network Layer Reachability Information is learned via the
  Exterior Gateway Protocol (EGP).

- *INCOMPLETE*—The Network Layer Reachability Information is
  learned by some other means.

BGP considers the ORIGIN attribute in its decision-making process to establish
a preference ranking among multiple routes. Specifically, BGP prefers the path
with the lowest origin type, where IGP is lower than EGP, and EGP is lower
than INCOMPLETE. For more details on how the ORIGIN attribute is calculated, refer to the section, "ORIGIN of Routes," earlier in this chapter.

NOTES

The originator ID and cluster list attributes are discussed in Chapter 8.

BGP Decision Process Summary

BGP bases its decision process on the attribute values. When faced with multiple routes to the same destination, BGP chooses the best route for routing traffic toward the destination. The following process summarizes how BGP chooses the best route.

1. If the next hop is inaccessible, the route is ignored (this is why it is important to have an IGP route to the next hop).

2. Prefer the path with the largest weight (weight is a Cisco proprietary parameter).

3. If the weights are the same, prefer the route with the largest local preference.

4. If the routes have the same local preference prefer the route that was locally originated (originated by this router).

5. If the local preference is the same, prefer the route with the shortest AS_path.

6. If the AS_path length is the same, prefer the route with the lowest origin type (where IGP is lower than EGP, and EGP is lower than INCOMPLETE).

7. If the origin type is the same, prefer the route with the lowest MED.

8. If the routes have the same MED, prefer the route in the following manner: External (EBGP) is better than Confederation External which is better than Internal (IBGP). Confederations will be explained in Chapter 8.

9. If all the preceding scenarios are identical, prefer the route that can be reached via the closest IGP neighbor—that is, take the shortest internal path inside the AS to reach the destination (follow the shortest path to the BGP NEXT_HOP).

10. If the internal path is the same, the BGP router ID will be a tie breaker. Prefer the route coming from the BGP router with the lowest router ID. The router ID is usually the highest IP address on the router or the loopback (virtual) address. The router ID could be implementation specific.

ROUTE FILTERING AND ATTRIBUTE MANIPULATION

The concept of route filtering is straightforward. A BGP speaker can choose what routes to send and what routes to receive from any of its BGP peers. Route filtering is essential in defining routing policies. An autonomous system can identify the inbound traffic it is willing to accept from other neighbors by specifying the list of routes it advertises to its neighbors. Conversely, an AS can control what routes its outbound traffic uses by specifying the routes it accepts from its neighbors.

Example: Ch. 10, pp. 306-312. Route Filtering and Attribute Manipulation

Filtering is also used on the protocol level to limit routing updates flowing from one protocol to another. Recall that earlier this chapter discussed the possibility of injecting BGP routes in the IGP and IGP or static routes into BGP. Cisco's terminology for this process is *redistributing* between protocols. This chapter also discussed the dangers of mutual redistribution between protocols. Filtering is essential in specifying exactly what goes from BGP into the IGP and vice versa.

Routes permitted through a filter can have their attributes manipulated. Manipulating the attributes affects the BGP decision process of identifying best routes.

Inbound and Outbound Filtering

Both the *inbound* and *outbound* filtering concepts can be applied to the peer and to the protocol level; figure 5–23 illustrates this behavior.

At the peer level, inbound filtering indicates that the BGP speaker is filtering routing updates coming from other peers, whereas outbound filtering limits the routing updates advertised from the BGP speaker to other peers. Filtering behavior is the same whether the BGP peers are external (EBGP) or internal (IBGP).

Figure 5–23
Inbound outbound filtering example.

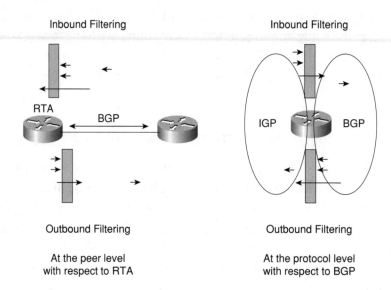

Inbound Filtering   Inbound Filtering

RTA   BGP

IGP   BGP

Outbound Filtering   Outbound Filtering

At the peer level   At the protocol level
with respect to RTA   with respect to BGP

At the protocol level, inbound filtering limits the routing updates being injected into a protocol. Outbound filtering limits the routing updates being injected from this protocol. With respect to BGP, for example, inbound filtering limits the updates being redistributed from other protocols such as IGP and static into BGP. Outbound filtering limits the updates being redistributed from BGP into IGP.

Route Filtering and Manipulation Process

Filtering and manipulating a route or a set of routes involves three actions:

1. Identifying Routes

2. Permitting or Denying the Routes

3. Manipulating Attributes

NOTES

Cisco uses the concept of *route maps* to achieve filtering and attribute manipulation. Route maps are discussed in Chapter 10, "Configuring Basic BGP Function and Attributes."

Identifying Routes

Identifying routes is the process of setting criteria to differentiate routes from each other. Such criteria could be based on the IP prefix of the route, the autonomous system from which a route was originated, a list of ASs a route has passed through, a specific attribute value inside the route, and so on. A list of criteria *instances* is contained in the filtering rules, and a route is compared to the first instance in the list. If the route does not match the first instance, it is checked against the next instance in the list. After a route matches an instance, it is considered identified and will not be compared to any further instances.

If the route proceeds to be compared against the entire list of instances and there is still no match, then the route is discarded.

Identifying routes based on the Network Layer Reachability Information (NLRI) or the AS_path list or both is the most common way of identifying routes. Each of these methods is discussed in more detail in the following sections, "Identifying Routes Based on the NLRI" and "Identifying Routes Based on the AS_Path."

Permitting or Denying the Routes

After the route has been identified, action can be taken upon it. The route is permitted or denied, depending on what filtering rules have been established for that juncture. The criteria for permitting or denying routes depends on the policies an AS is setting. If the route is permitted, then it is either accepted "as is," or submitted for modification of attributes, again, depending on what policies are to be set. If the route is denied, then that route is discarded.

Manipulating Attributes

If a route is permitted, its attributes can be changed to affect the decision process. In earlier sections, you saw how attributes such as local preference and MED can be added or made larger or smaller to prefer a route over another. As you will see later on, attribute manipulation is key to establishing route policies, load balancing, and route symmetry.

Figure 5–24 explains in detail how multiple instances can be applied on a set of routes to find a match. Note that each instance could have one or more criteria. A route could be checked based on its prefix and its AS_path information, for example.

Also note that after a route matches, it is not compared to any more instances. Hence, the order in which the instances are checked is important. An instance that permits all routes for example, if put at the beginning of the list, will override all the other instances.

Identifying Routes Based on the NLRI

Example: Ch. 10, pp. 308-310. Identifying and Filtering Routes Based on the NLRI

A BGP route could be identified by its Network Layer Reachability Information (NLRI), which is the prefix and the mask, as discussed in Chapter 4, "Interdomain Routing Basics." For filtering purposes, a prefix or a range of prefixes is defined. If the route falls within the range, it will be identified.

Figure 5–25 illustrates filtering criteria of 10.1.0.0 0.0.255.255, which represents a range of routes identified by a prefix 10.1.0.0 and an inverse mask 0.0.255.255. The 0s in the mask indicate a match, whereas the 1s indicate a do-not-care-bit. The 10.1.0.0 0.0.255.255 range will identify all routes of the form 10.1.X.X. Presented with the prefixes shown in figure 5–25, this filter will identify 10.1.1.0/24, 10.1.2.0/24, and 10.1.2.2/30, and will exclude 11.2.0.0/16 and 12.1.1.0/24.

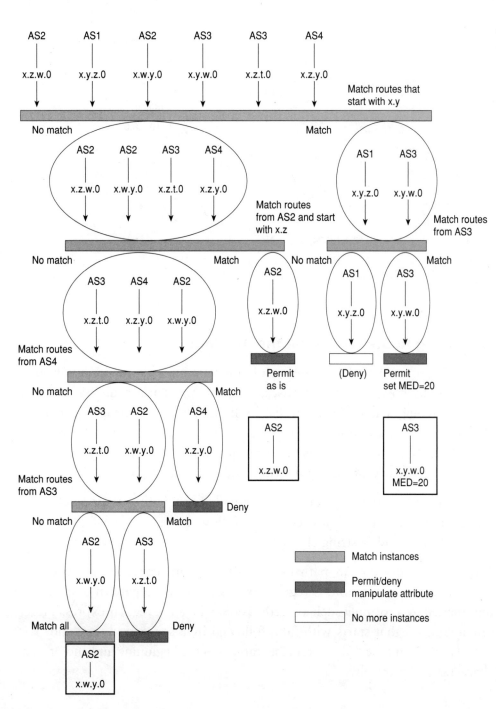

Figure 5–24
Summary example of route filtering and manipulation process.

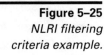

Figure 5–25
*NLRI filtering
criteria example.*

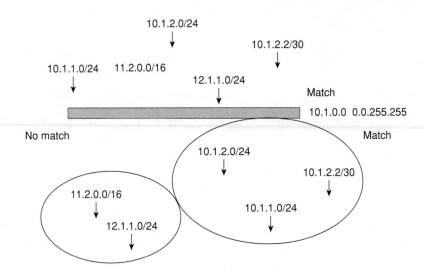

Identifying Routes Based on the AS_Path

Example: Ch. 10,
pp. 310-312.
Identifying and
Filtering Routes
Based on the
AS_Path

Identifying routes based on the AS_path information is a bit more involved. As you know by now, the AS_path list is a list of ASs that a route has traversed before reaching a BGP peer. The list itself is a character string that contains characters from the following set: 0,1,2,3,4,5,6,7,8,9, "space," left brace "{", right brace "}", left parenthesis "(", right parenthesis ")", the beginning of the input string, the end of the input string, and a comma ",".

The AS_path list 10 2, for example, is actually: a beginning of string character followed by character 1 followed by a 0 followed by a space followed by a 2 followed by an end of string character.

Trying to identify the AS_path list consists of comparing the list to what is called a *regular expression*. A regular expression is just a pattern of characters represented by a formula such as: ^200 100$, which is a regular expression representing a list that starts with 200, followed by a space, and then ends with 100. The "^" and the "$" are representations of the beginning and end of string characters, respectively.

A regular expression can be formed by using single-character patterns or multiple-character patterns.

Single-Character Patterns

A single-character pattern tries to match a single character. The single-character regular expression 3 tries to match the character 3 in an input string. You can specify a range of single characters to match against a string. Ranges are included within brackets ([]). The order in which the characters forming the range get listed is not important. The regular expression consisting of the range [efghEFGH], for example, is trying to match any of the above characters in an input string. Given the two input strings, "hello" and "there," the regular expression matches both of these lists because they both contain the character e.

Ranges can be listed by typing the end points of a range; for example, ranges [a–z] and [0–9] indicate any lowercase character between a and z and any numeric character between 0 and 9, respectively.

You can also reverse or negate the pattern matching by including a caret (^) at the beginning of the range. The range [^a-dA-D], for example, matches any character except a,b,c,d,A,B,C,D. Some characters have a special meaning, such as the dollar sign $ and the underscore _, as described in table 5–4.

Character	Symbol	Special Meaning
Period	.	Matches any single character, including white space.
Asterisk	*	Matches 0 or more sequences of the pattern.
Plus sign	+	Matches 1 or more sequences of the pattern.
Question mark	?	Matches 0 or 1 occurrences of the pattern.
Caret	^	Matches the beginning of the input string.
Dollar sign	$	Matches the end of the input string.
Underscore	_	Matches a comma (,), left brace ({), right brace (}), left parenthesis, right parenthesis, the beginning of the input string, the end of the input string, or a space.
Brackets	[range]	Designates a range of single-character patterns.
Hyphen	-	Separates the end points of a range.

Table 5–4
Regular expression special characters.

To list the special characters as part of an input list, they need to be preceded with a backslash (\). The range [abc\$], for example, will match an input string that contains the characters a,b,c, and $. Table 5–4 lists the special characters used in regular expressions.

Multiple-Character Patterns

Multiple-character regular expressions are just an ordered sequence of single-character patterns. The pattern is a combination of letters, numbers, any keyboard character, and special meaning characters. An example of a multiple-character regular expression follows: 100 1[0–9] . This regular expression matches any string that contains the exact sequence 100, followed by a space, followed by 1, followed by any number between 0 and 9. Any of the following input strings will match the regular expression: 123 **100 10** 11, or, **100 19**, or 19 **100 11** 200, and so on.

Building Complex Regular Expressions

The special characters in table 5–4 can be used to build complex but very practical regular expressions. The caret (^) and ($) dollar sign are used to match the regular expression pattern against the beginning and the end of the input string. Other characters such as the asterisk (*), the plus sign (+), and the question mark (?) enable you to repeat the patterns inside the regular expression.

The following example matches any number of occurrences of the letter "a," including none:

- a* is equivalent to any of the following: (nothing), a, aa, aaa, aaaa, and so on.

The following example requires that at least one letter "a" be present in the string to be matched:

- a+ is equivalent to a, aa, aaa, aaaa, and so on.

The following is an example of a list that may or may not contain the letter "a:"

- ba?b is equivalent to bb or bab.

To repeat instances of multiple-character patterns, the pattern is enclosed in parentheses; for example, the expression (ab)+ is equivalent to ab or abab.

The underscore character (_) matches the beginning of a string (^), the end of a string ($), parentheses (), space, braces, comma, or underscore. The dot character matches a single character, including a white space. Figure 5–26, table 5–5, and table 5–6 illustrate how characters can be strung together to create a useful regular expression.

Consider the network topology illustrated in figure 5–26. AS400, AS300, AS200, AS100, and AS50 are originating the routes NetA, NetB, NetC, NetD, and NetE, respectively. RTA in AS50 is receiving updates about all these networks from its neighbors AS100 and AS300. After running its BGP decision process, RTA has picked the best path to reach these networks according to table 5–5.

Table 5–6 reflects the regular expressions that would be used to create possible route filtering arrangements that RTA could apply when propagating routes to the NAP.

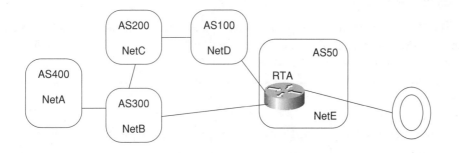

Figure 5–26
Network topology for complex regular expression example.

Network	AS_path
NetA	300 400
NetB	300
NetC	100 200
NetD	100
NetE	empty

Table 5–5
Best BGP route selection for RTA.

Routes to be Advertised from RTA to the NAP	Expression	Path Info	Outcome
Local routes only	^$	empty	NetE
All routes	.*	all paths	NetA, NetB, NetC, NetD, NetE
Routes that originated from directly connected customers	^300$ ^100$	300 100	NetB, NetD
Connected customer routes and their customers' routes	^300_ ^100_	300 400 300 100 200 100	NetA, NetB, NetC, NetD
Routes that originated in AS200	_200$	100 200	NetC
Routes that passed via AS100	_100_	100 200 100	NetC, NetD

NOTES

The ^$ expression indicates an empty path list, which is actually the local routes. The ^ and $ define the border of the string, and the underscore, such as in _200$, limits the AS number to being exactly 200 and not 1200 or 2200.

Filtering based on AS_path information is quite effective because it filters all the routing updates that belong to the AS_path at the same time. Without this type of filtering, thousands of routes would have to be listed individually.

Peer Groups

A BGP *peer group* is a group of BGP neighbors that share the same update policies. Instead of defining the same policies for each individual neighbor, you define a peer group name and assign policies to the peer group itself. An administrator, for example, setting policies toward its BGP peers will most probably set the same policies toward the majority of its peers, and therefore will define them as a peer group.

Not only do peer groups save the operator from repetitive configuration of each BGP peer, they save the BGP router itself from the effort of parsing the policies sequentially for each neighbor. With peer groups, the router formulates the UPDATE once, based on the policies of the peer group, and then floods the same UPDATE to all the neighbors that fall within the group.

In figure 5–27, RTA has three internal peers with which it has the same internal policies. RTA also has three external peers with which it has the same policies. RTA's configuration includes two sets of peer groups, one for inside the AS and one for outside the AS. Each peer group contains the set of policies that RTA has toward its peers. These policies could be a set of IP prefix filters or AS_path filters and possible attribute manipulation. After the peer groups have been defined, these policies are applied to the neighbors that make up the peer group.

Due to the route update optimization that peer groups offer, some restrictions need to be followed for peer groups to work correctly with external BGP peers. If the following guidelines are not followed, loss of routing information could occur.

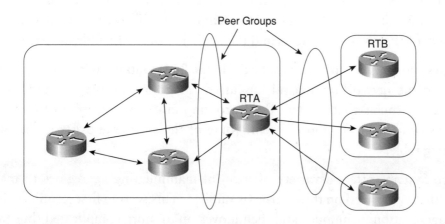

Figure 5–27
Peer group implementation.

When the peer group consists of external neighbors (EBGP), the following restrictions must apply:

- The hub router (such as RTA in figure 5–27) cannot be a transit router for the external ASs. In other words, updates from one EBGP neighbor in the peer group should not be passed to other EBGP neighbors in the same peer group.

- All the EBGP peer group members should belong to the same IP subnet.

Peer Group Exceptions

Example: Ch. 10, pp. 312-315. Peer Groups

Exceptions occur when some neighbors inside a peer group have slightly different policies from other neighbors. Additional policies can be added to the neighbor to complement the set of policies that fall within the peer group. Assume that RTA requires an additional set of filters to be set toward its peer RTB. RTA can apply the extra filters toward RTB while still keeping RTB within the external peer group.

BGP4 AGGREGATION

One of BGP4's main improvements over BGP3 and BGP2 is its capability to handle CIDR and supernetting. CIDR and supernetting were first discussed in Chapter 3, "Handling IP Address Depletion," with respect to controlling the growth of IP forwarding tables and the depletion of the IP address space.

Aggregation applies to routes that exist in the BGP routing table. This is in contrast to the **network** command, discussed earlier in this chapter, and which applies to routes that exist in the IP routing table. Aggregation can be performed if at least one more specific route of the aggregate exists in the BGP routing table.

Cisco Systems offers a variety of ways of manipulating aggregates to make sure that every need on the Internet is fulfilled. This section first examines simple aggregation techniques and then moves on to more complicated (but fun) scenarios.

Aggregate Only, Suppressing the More Specific

This scenario illustrates a case where an aggregate is advertised and all its specific routes are suppressed. This is usually done when the more specific routes do not offer any extra benefits, such as making better decisions in forwarding traffic. Figure 5–28 illustrates a situation in which all the routing updates are lumped into a single aggregate. Suppose that AS100 has the subnet ranges 172.16.0.0/24 to 172.16.15.0/24. This includes 172.16.0.X, 172.16.1.X, and so on. The list of specific attributes can be summarized into the range 172.16.0.0/20. The aggregate 172.16.0.0/20 is sent out, and all the more specific routes are suppressed.

Example: Ch. 10, pp. 343-346. Aggregate Only, Suppressing the More Specific

Aggregate Plus More Specific Routes

A number of situations exist in which an AS will send out an aggregate and its more specific routes. This usually occurs in situations where the customer is multihomed to a single provider. The provider would use the more specific routes to make better decisions when sending traffic toward the customer. At the same time, the provider can propagate the aggregate only toward the NAP to minimize the number of routes leaked to the Internet. This is illustrated in figure 5–29.

Example: Ch. 10, pp. 346-352. Aggregate Plus More Specific Route

AS100 is multihomed with provider AS200 via the San Francisco and New York links. AS100 can send AS200 either the aggregate 172.16.0.0/20 only, or

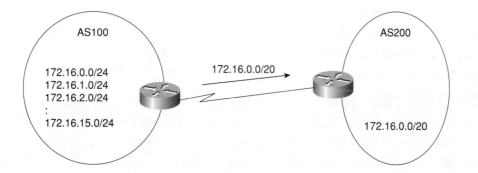

Figure 5–28
BGP4 aggregation example suppression specific routes.

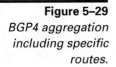

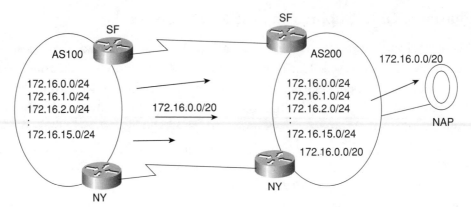

it can send the aggregate and all the more specific routes. If the aggregate only is sent over both the SF and NY links, then traffic from AS200 toward AS100 will always take one link or the other. This arrangement creates an unbalanced traffic load (balanced loading is discussed further in Chapter 6, "Redundancy, Symmetry, and Load Balancing"). To balance the load, AS100 sends the aggregate and all the more specific routes. Different metrics could be sent for different routes on each of the links. This way, based on the specific network number, AS200 can decide whether to use the SF or NY link when trying to reach AS100.

To avoid complicating routing tables beyond the provider level, more specific routes from customers are usually stopped at the provider level. AS200 would propagate only the aggregate 172.16.0.0/20 toward the NAP and suppress the more specific routes.

Usually providers like to minimize configuration and administration. In this situation, a dynamic approach can be used to stop all the more specific routes from being propagated to the NAP. This is done by having AS100 tag all the more specific updates with the community attribute **NO-EXPORT** while leaving the aggregate as is. This is illustrated in figure 5–30.

When AS200 gets the updates from AS100, it will recognize the community as a request not to forward the updates to its external peers. The aggregate will be propagated as usual to the NAP and other peers.

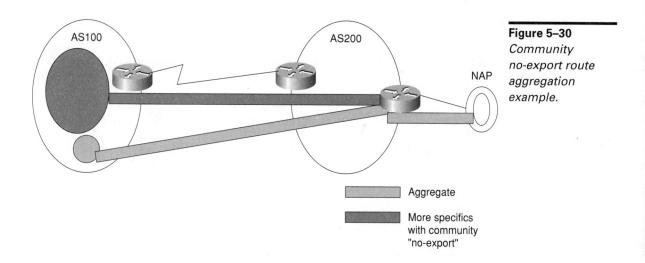

Figure 5–30
Community no-export route aggregation example.

Aggregate with a Subset of the More Specific Routes

In some situations, a subset of the more specific routes needs to be advertised in addition to the aggregate. Figure 5–31 illustrates a situation in which this might be useful.

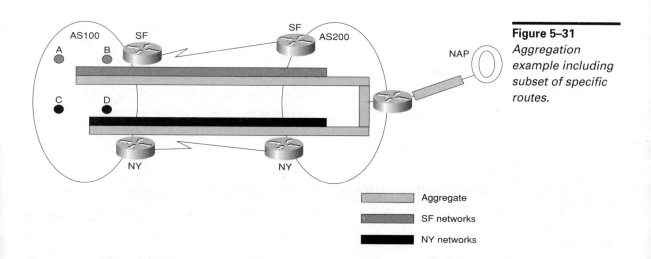

Figure 5–31
Aggregation example including subset of specific routes.

Example: Ch. 10,
pp. 352-356.
Aggregate with
a Subset of the
More Specific
Routes

In figure 5–31, AS100 is multihomed to AS200. AS100 would like the networks in the vicinity of SF to be accessed via the SF link and the networks in the vicinity of NY to be accessed via the NY link. This could be achieved in the following manner:

- On the SF link, advertise the aggregate and the SF networks only.

- On the NY link, advertise the aggregate and the NY networks only.

In this case, AS200 can only reach the SF networks via the SF link and the NY networks via the NY link. Networks in other locations could be sent on both links or either link. In case of a link failure, all networks can still be reached by following the aggregate route, which is advertised on both links. The no-export technique, discussed in the previous example, can be used to propagate only the aggregate to the NAP.

Loss of Information Inside Aggregates (AS-SET)

Example: Ch. 10,
pp. 356-359.
Loss of Informa-
tion Inside
Aggregates
(AS-SET)

Aggregation causes loss of information due to the fact that the attributes of individual routes that form the aggregate will be lost. As already discussed in this chapter, BGP defines an AS-SET, which is a mathematical set consisting of all elements contained in all paths that are being summarized. An example of such elements are the AS_path and community attributes.

Using AS-SET with the aggregate will cause additional route instabilities due to the fact that changes in the attributes of the individual routes being summarized will now translate into changes of the aggregate itself and will cause the aggregate to be constantly withdrawn and updated.

Changing the Attributes of the Aggregate

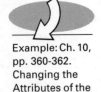

Example: Ch. 10,
pp. 360-362.
Changing the
Attributes of the
Aggregate

In some situations, it is required that the attributes of the aggregate be changed. One such situation is when the aggregate contains some unwanted attributes that it inherited from the routes it is summarizing (in case of

AS-SET). An example could be a "NO-EXPORT" community attribute that the aggregate got from one of the more specific routes and that causes the aggregate not to be exported to other ASs. Another situation that calls for changing the attributes of the aggregate is to reflect a level of preference for a certain aggregate. An example would be of customer's advertising an aggregate via multiple links to a certain provider. The customer might like to have the aggregate go out with different MEDs on different links to influence the entrance point into the AS. Cisco has developed techniques to enable the user to modify the attributes of an aggregate accordingly.

Forming the Aggregate Based on a Subset of More Specific Routes

You have seen that with AS-SET the aggregate will contain a set of all attributes (including AS numbers) that exist in the individual routes being summarized. If the aggregate is summarizing routes that come from different ASs, it becomes useful to specify which routes are being included in forming the aggregate. This would help in a hub and spoke situation where each of the leaf ASs contains a separate subset of the aggregate that is originated by the hub. When forming the aggregate, the hub AS would exclude the more specific routes that belong to the leaf AS that needs to receive the aggregate. The aggregate received by the leaf AS would not contain the AS number of the leaf AS, and hence it is not discarded. Figure 5–32 gives an example of where this could be used.

Example: Ch. 10, pp. 363-365. Forming the Aggregate Based on a Subset of More Specific Routes

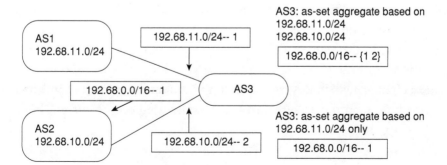

Figure 5–32
Forming aggregate based on a subset of more specifics.

AS3 is a hub AS receiving routes 192.68.11.0/24 and 192.68.10.0/24 from the leaf ASs AS1 and AS2. Prefix 192.68.11.0/24 has an AS_path of 1, and 192.68.10.0/24 has an AS_path of 2. When the AS-SET aggregate is being formed by AS3 based on all the more specific routes, the AS_path information would be {1 2}. The aggregate itself, if sent back to either AS1 or AS2, would be discarded for loop prevention. AS1 will see its AS number in the AS_path information and would drop the update; the same is true for AS2. If you are able to specify which more specific routes can form the aggregate, then you could, for example, specify that the aggregate is to be formed based on 192.68.11.0/24 only. This way, the AS_path information would be 1 and would not contain AS2. The aggregate can now be sent back to AS2 with no problem. AS2 can use this aggregate to forward traffic to all destinations in AS1.

LOOKING AHEAD

Having mastered the basics of routing protocols and examined the particular configuration tools of BGP, you are now in a position to begin applying these tools to specific internetworking topologies. In doing so, you will be juggling a number of overarching design goals—redundancy, symmetry, and load balancing—that are of varying importance depending on a particular network's needs and that sometimes conflict with one another. The meaning of these design goals is discussed in more detail in the next chapter. The attributes covered in this chapter are used in the following chapter to achieve the desired routing design goals.

Tuning BGP capabilities to satisfy a network's needs involves looking outside the AS as well as inside. That is, the policies set by the networks to which you are interconnected, although usually outside your direct control, have practical implications for how you configure BGP at your end. All this becomes clearer in the next chapter, which covers multiple redundancy, symmetry, and balancing scenarios by presenting architectures commonly used on the current Internet.

FREQUENTLY ASKED QUESTIONS

Q— *If my IBGP peers are not directly connected, do I have to use EBGP multihop?*

A— No. There is no restriction on IBGP peers to be connected. EBGP multihop is for EBGP only.

Q— *Should I inject my BGP routes into the IGP for synchronization to take effect?*

A— No. Injecting the BGP into your IGP is not recommended. You should turn the synchronization off. Make sure that this will not result in reachability problems inside your AS.

Q— *Does listing my IGP routes via the **network** command rather than redistributing the IGP into BGP give my BGP routes more stability?*

A— No. In both methods, the fluctuation of your IGP routes will translate in fluctuation in your BGP routes. The **network** command only gives you better control and less worry about what your IGP might carry into BGP if you use redistribution.

Q— *Do I have to list my connected interfaces by using the **network** command?*

A— If you want the directly connected subnets to be reachable via BGP, then you can advertise them; if not, you don't have to.

Q— *I have two border routers talking EBGP to my provider and IBGP internally. If I list my IGP routes via the **network** command on both routers, would that create a loop on the IBGP session?*

A— No, you will not create a loop. Actually, doing so gives you more redundancy. If one of your border routers fails, the other border router will still announce the same networks.

Q— *What happens if I use next-hop-self on my EBGP peers?*

A— Next-hop-self is used between IBGP peers. Using it between EBGP peers is a not an option because the next hop is always the IP address of the EBGP neighbor.

Q— *I need to receive only a few updates from my neighbor; can I filter on my side of the link?*

A— Yes, you can. Ask your neighbor to send you only the routes you need to minimize unnecessary link bandwidth usage and unnecessary route fluctuations. At the same time, use filtering on your end to protect yourself from potential accidents where your neighbor sends you more routes than you are expecting.

Q— *My provider needs me to send him different local preference on different links; is that possible?*

A— No. Local preference is defined inside the AS and is not carried on EBGP sessions.

Q— *I am receiving MED from my provider that is influencing my traffic in a way that conflicts with my IGP. What do I do?*

A— If receiving MEDs is causing you problems, call your provider and ask him to stop sending MEDs. Or, you can set MED to 0 on your end of the session.

Q— *I am connected to multiple providers. On some occasions, my AS gets hit with an enormous amount of traffic that does not belong to my AS. What could be wrong?*

A— You might be advertising routes that you receive from one provider to other providers. Other ASs might be using your AS as transit for their traffic. Make sure that you advertise only your routes to your providers.

Q— *I am multihomed to the same provider. Do I have to worry about advertising the routes I learn from one link back on the second link?*

A— BGP on your provider's end will detect that the routes it is receiving from you have passed through its AS already and will ignore them. Nevertheless, this is bad practice. You should not overload the links and routers with useless information; make sure that you send your own routes only.

Q— *I am a provider, and I have given one of my customers a private AS number. Now, the customer wants to have a different connection with another provider. What would happen if he keeps using a private AS number?*

A— This would be an illegal configuration. After you advertise this customer's network to the Internet, you are stripping the private AS number and announcing the routes as if they originated from your own AS. If the second provider does the same thing, then the customer's networks will have two origins—your AS and the AS of the other provider—and that is illegal.

Q— *I am connected to one provider in San Francisco, and I am advertising my routes via BGP. I am connecting to another provider in LA. Should I get a different AS number?*

A— If both the SF and LA networks fall under the same administration and have the same policies with other ASs, then they belong in the same AS. Remember that dividing networks via BGP is to define the boundaries of administration and policy. Geographical location is not the deciding factor.

REFERENCES

[1] RFC 1321 The MD5 Message-Digest Algorithm

[2] RFC 1997 BGP Communities Attribute

PART 3

Effective Internet Routing Designs

You are now in a position to begin applying the attributes and functionality of BGP to practical routing problems. Chapter 6 begins this process by introducing three fundamental design criteria—redundancy, symmetry, and load balancing—that network architects frequently must implement and balance in developing their routing policies. Chapter 7 considers how to integrate BGP with interior protocols, and Chapter 8 considers how to tap BGP's potential for managing large and growing networks. Chapter 9 takes up the problem of network stability, an increasingly challenging design goal in the wake of the ever-expanding Internet. BGP includes a number of built-in functions designed to help build stability. Part 3 takes an example-oriented approach, using specific topologies and scenarios to illustrate routing design concepts and applications.

THIS CHAPTER COVERS
THE FOLLOWING KEY TOPICS:

- **Redundancy**

  Building stability by providing alternate—default—routes in case of link failure is an important design goal of routing architecture.

- **Setting Default Routes**

  Configuring default routes is the fundamental method of building redundancy into network connections. When multiple default routes exist, methods of ranking them by preference are needed.

- **Symmetry**

  Configuring routes so that certain traffic enters and exits an AS at the same point is usually a design goal of routing architecture.

- **Specific Scenarios**

  Exploration is offered of several representative network designs with respect to developing redundancy, symmetry, and load balancing. Examples of attribute configuration to achieve these design goals for the different scenarios are offered.

CHAPTER 6

Redundancy, Symmetry, and Load Balancing

Redundancy, symmetry, and load balancing are crucial issues facing anyone implementing high-throughput connections to the Internet. ISPs and corporations connected to ISPs require adequate control over how traffic enters and exits their respective ASs.

Redundancy is achieved by providing multiple alternate paths for the traffic, usually by having multiple connections to one or more ASs. *Symmetry* means having traffic that leaves the AS from a certain exit point return through the same point. *Load balancing* is the capability to divide traffic optimally over multiple links. Putting these three requirements together, you can imagine how challenging it is to achieve an optimal routing solution.

No single switch exists that you can turn on that gives you all you need. On the Internet, multiple providers can control and manipulate traffic that transits any AS. Any provider along the way can direct the traffic. The art of balancing traffic depends on coordination between multiple entities.

The general design problem of how best to implement redundancy, symmetry, and load balancing is common to every network. The specific answer, however, depends on the needs and configuration of each particular network. This chapter considers the general design problem within the context of several specific network configurations. You might not see your exact network configuration in these examples, but the general issues and implementation methods they raise provide a model for your analysis and design of your own routing needs.

Before examining specific network scenarios, it is necessary to establish some basic concepts and definitions concerning redundancy.

REDUNDANCY

Although corporations and providers would prefer uninterrupted connectivity, connectivity problems occur for one reason or another from time to time. Connectivity is not the responsibility of one entity. A router's connection to the Internet involves the router, the CSU/DCU, cabling, physical access line, and numerous administrators—each with influence over different parts of the connection. At any time, the connectivity can be jeopardized by human error, software errors, physical errors, or adverse unforeseen conditions (such as bad weather or power outages).

For all these reasons, redundancy is generally desirable. But finding the correct balance between redundancy and symmetry is critical. Redundancy and symmetry can be conflicting design goals—the more redundancy a network has, the more unpredictable the traffic entrance and exit points would be. If a customer has multiple connections—one to a Point Of Presence (POP) in San Francisco and another to a POP in NY—traffic leaving San Francisco might come back from NY. Adding a third connection to a POP in Dallas makes connectivity even more reliable, but it also makes traffic symmetry more challenging. These are the trade-offs that network administrators must consider in implementing routing.

Geographical Restrictions Pressure

In addition to the reliability motivation, companies might feel geographical pressure to implement redundancy. Many contemporary companies are national, international, or multinational in nature. For them, the autonomous system is a logical entity that spans different physical locations. A corporation with an AS that spans several geographical points can take service from a single provider or from different providers in different regions. In figure 6–1, the San Francisco office of AS1 connects to the San Francisco POP of ISP1, and the NY office connects to the NY POP of ISP2. In this environment, traffic can take a shorter path to reach a destination by traveling via the geographically adjacent POP.

Because redundancy refers to the existence of alternate routes to and from a network, this translates into an additional number of routing information that needs to be kept in the routing tables. To avoid the extra routing overhead, *default routing* becomes an alternate practical tool. Default can provide us with backup routes in case primary connections fail. The next section attempts to define the different aspects of default routing and how it can be applied to achieve simple routing scenarios.

Setting Default Routes

Following defaults is a powerful technique in minimizing the amount of routes a router has to learn and providing networks with redundancy in the event of failures and connectivity interruptions. Cisco calls the default path the *gateway of last resort*. It is important to understand how default routing works, although it makes life easier when configured correctly; life is more difficult when routing is configured incorrectly.

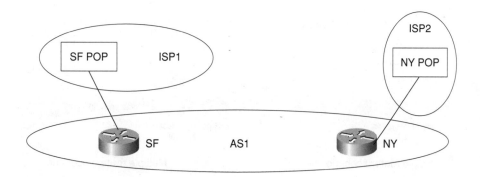

Figure 6–1
Geographically based multihoming situation.

By definition, a *default route* is a route in the IP forwarding table that is used if a routing entry for a destination does not exist. In other words, a default route is a last resort in case specific route information for a destination is unknown.

Dynamically Learned Defaults

Ch. 11, pp. 368-373. Dynamically Learned Defaults

The universally known default route is usually represented by the network mask combination 0.0.0.0/0.0.0.0 (also represented as 0/0). This route can be exchanged as a dynamic advertisement between routers. Any system advertising this route will be representing itself as a gateway of last resort for other systems. Figure 6–2 illustrates such an advertisement.

Dynamic defaults (0/0) can be learned via BGP or via IGP, depending on what protocol is running between two domains. For redundancy purposes and to accommodate potential failures, you should be receiving defaults from multiple sources. In the context of BGP, the local preference can be set for the default to give a degree of preference over which default is primary and which is backup. If one default goes away, the other will take its place.

In the left instance of figure 6–2, a single router is connecting AS1 to AS2 via two connections. If AS1 chooses to accept as few routes as possible from AS2, AS1 can accept only the 0/0 default route. In this example, AS1 is learning 0/0 from two links and giving preference by setting the local preference to 100 on

Figure 6–2
Dynamic default advertisement.

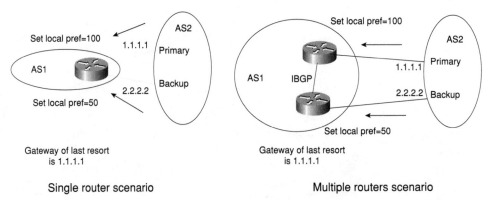

the primary link and 50 (or any number smaller than 100) on the backup link. This would set the gateway of last resort to 1.1.1.1.

In the multiple routers scenario (right instance of figure 6–2), the same behavior can be achieved with multiple routers as long as IBGP is running inside the AS. Local preference, which is exchanged between routers, will determine the primary and backup links.

Statically Set Defaults

It is also possible for an AS to statically set its own defaults by setting its own 0/0 route. Statically set defaults provide more control over routing behaviors because the operator has the option of defining his last resort rather than it being forced on him by some outside entity. Many operators choose to filter dynamically learned defaults to avoid situations where traffic ends up where it is not supposed to be.

Ch. 11, pp. 370-373. Statically Set Defaults

An operator can statically set the default route 0/0 to point to the following:

- The IP address of the next hop gateway

- A specific router interface

- A network number

Figure 6–3 illustrates the first two possibilities. On the left, a router is statically pointing its own 0/0 default toward the IP address 1.1.1.1. On the right, the same router is pointing its default toward an Ethernet interface. In the latter approach, further processing is needed to figure out to whom on the segment the traffic should be sent. Such processing usually involves sending Address Resolution Protocol (ARP) packets to identify the physical address of the next hop router.

A system can also set its default based on some network number it learns from another system. In figure 6–4, AS1 is dynamically learning route 192.213.0.0/16 from AS2. If AS1 points its default to 192.213.0.0/16, that network will

Figure 6–3
*Statically set
defaults.*

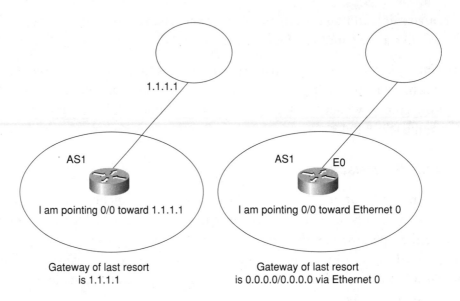

Gateway of last resort
is 1.1.1.1

Gateway of last resort
is 0.0.0.0/0.0.0.0 via Ethernet 0

automatically become the gateway of last resort. This approach uses recursive route lookup to find the IP address of the next hop gateway. In this example, the recursive lookup will determine that 192.213.0.0/16 was learned via the next hop 1.1.1.1, and traffic would be directed accordingly.

It is important for defaults to disappear dynamically if what they point to disappears. Cisco enables a statically defined default to follow the existence of the entity to which it is pointing. If the default, for example, is pointing to a network

Figure 6–4
*Pointing default
toward a network
number.*

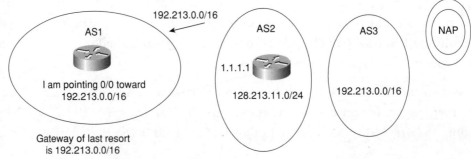

Gateway of last resort
is 192.213.0.0/16

number and that network is no longer reachable (does not show in the IP routing table), the default will also disappear from the IP routing table. This behavior is needed in situations where multiple defaults exist. One default can be used as primary and others as a backup in case the primary default is no longer valid.

Default networks should be selected as far upstream (closer to the Internet) as possible so that they are more representative of the whole link toward the NAP rather than a portion. This is important if the AS you are connected to has a single connection toward the NAP. In figure 6–4, AS1 can set the default toward its provider AS2 by pointing to prefix 128.213.11.0/24 or the supernet 192.213.0.0/16. Pointing the default to 128.213.11.0/24 makes it dependent on the stability of a portion of the link (AS1 to AS2) and not the whole link (AS1 to AS3) toward the NAP. If the link between AS2 and AS3 goes down, AS1 would be still sending traffic toward AS2 rather than directing it to some other default (assuming that AS1 has other providers). A better default choice would be the supernet, 192.213.0.0/16, because its existence is more representative of the whole link toward the NAP and is no longer dependent on any intervening links.

TROUBLESHOOTING

Setting and selecting reliable defaults.

Selected default networks should not be specific subnets. A subnet that is flip-flopping might cause your default to come and go constantly. It is much better to point the default to a major aggregate or supernet that reflects the stability of a whole provider rather than a particular link.

Multiple static defaults can be used at the same time. One way to set multiple static defaults is to point to multiple networks (use aggregates if possible for stability reasons) and establish a degree of preference by using the local preference attribute. This would apply to a single router connected to the provider via multiple connections, or multiple routers running IBGP inside the AS. Both scenarios are illustrated in figure 6–5. These are similar to the scenarios you saw in figure 6–2, the only difference being that the customer is setting its own default rather than relying on the provider to send the 0/0 default route. In this example, the customer will choose 128.213.0.0/16 with the local preference of 100 via the upper link. The lower link will be used as backup in case of failure in the primary link.

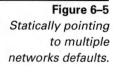

Figure 6–5
*Statically pointing
to multiple
networks defaults.*

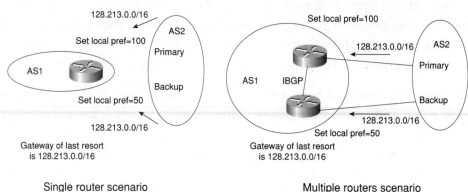

Single router scenario

Multiple routers scenario

Another way of setting defaults statically involves using the Cisco distance parameter (as described in Chapter 5, "Tuning BGP Capabilities," table 5–1) to establish a degree of preference. This would work only in the case of one router connected to multiple connections because the distance parameter is not exchanged between routers.

If two static default entries are defined with different distances, the default with the lowest distance wins. If the better default goes away, the second default becomes available. If both defaults have the same distance, then traffic will be balanced between the two defaults.

Figure 6–6 illustrates the use of the distance parameter in setting multiple defaults. AS1 is connected to AS2 via two links and is setting its own defaults

Figure 6–6
*Static defaults
pointing to multiple
connections.*

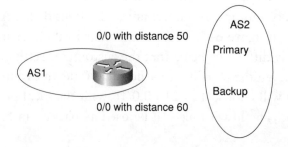

toward AS2. AS1 uses one link as primary by giving the static default a distance of 50, lower than the distance of 60 given to the backup link. In case of failure in the primary link, traffic will shift toward the backup.

SYMMETRY

Symmetry refers to the fact that traffic leaving the AS from an exit point comes back through the same point. This is easy to achieve if a single exit and entrance point exists. But, given the mandates of redundancy and the presence of multiple connections, traffic tends to be asymmetrical. When it is, customers and providers notice a lack of control over how traffic flows in and out of their ASs. Traffic leaving the AS from the East Coast might end up taking the "scenic route," coming back from the West Coast and traveling inside the AS multiple hops before returning to its origin.

Actually this is not as bad as it sounds, and in some situations asymmetrical traffic is acceptable depending on the overall physical topology as far as the speed of the links and the number of hops between locations. In general, customers and providers would like to see their traffic come back close to or at the same point it left the AS to minimize potential delays that could be incurred otherwise.

To accommodate symmetry, a primary link should be chosen, and a best effort should be made to enable the majority of traffic to flow on this link. Redundancy would be accommodated by enabling other links to be backup links that will be used if the primary link is problematic.

LOAD BALANCING

Load balancing deals with the capability to divide data traffic over multiple connections. A common misconception about balancing is that it means an equal distribution of the load. Perfectly equal distribution of traffic is elusive enough even in situations where traffic flows in a network that is under a single administration. Given the multiple players that traffic has to touch, equal distribution of the traffic is difficult to achieve in most scenarios. Load balancing tries to achieve a traffic distribution pattern that will best utilize the multiple links that are providing redundancy. To achieve this requires a good understanding of what traffic you are trying to balance, incoming or outgoing.

It is important not to think about traffic as a single entity. Traffic is two separate entities, inbound and outbound. With respect to an autonomous system, inbound traffic is received from other ASs, whereas outbound traffic is sent to other ASs.

Suppose that you are connected to two ISPs and traffic is overloading your link to ISP1. Your question should be: What traffic—inbound or outbound? Are you *receiving* all your traffic from ISP1, or are you *sending* all your traffic toward ISP1?

The patterns of inbound and outbound traffic go hand in hand with the way you advertise your routes and the way you learn routes from other ASs. Inbound traffic is affected by how the AS advertises its networks to the outside world, whereas outbound traffic is affected by the routing updates coming in from outside ASs. Make sure that you fully understand this behavior because it will be the basis of all future discussions. From now on, whenever we talk about taking steps to affect inbound traffic, we are really talking about applying attributes to outbound routing announcements because how our routes are learned by others affects how traffic is routed inbound. Similarly, whenever we talk about taking steps to affect outbound traffic, we are talking about applying attributes to inbound routing announcements, because how our network learns routes affects how outbound traffic is routed.

Figure 6–7 illustrates how inbound and outbound traffic behaves. As you can see, the path for outbound traffic to reach NetA depends on where NetA is learned from. Because NetA is received from both SF and NY, your outbound traffic toward NetA can go via SF or NY.

On the other hand, the path for inbound traffic to reach your local networks, NetB and NetC, depends on how you advertise these networks. If you advertise

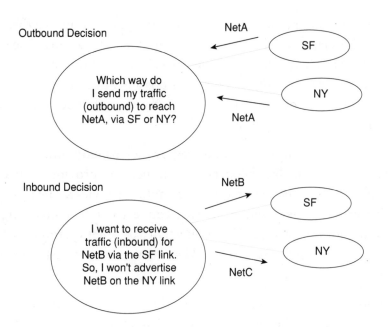

Figure 6–7
*Inbound and
outbound
decisions.*

NetC over the NY link only, then incoming traffic toward NetC will take the NY link. Similarly, if you advertise NetB over the SF link only, traffic toward NetB will take the SF link.

SPECIFIC SCENARIOS: DESIGNING REDUNDANCY, SYMMETRY, AND LOAD BALANCING

By now you recognize the general ways in which the design goals of redundancy, symmetry, and load balancing intersect with and potentially conflict with one another. How is it possible to balance traffic among multiple links and still achieve a single entrance and exit point as symmetry mandates? This becomes even harder when multiple links are spread out over multiple routers in the autonomous system. The routing attributes described in Chapter 5, "Tuning BGP Capabilities," are the tools for implementing the desired redundancy, symmetry, and load balancing. It is the responsibility of the operator to choose and configure the correct attributes and filtering to achieve the desired outcome.

This section presents specific scenarios and attempts to configure them in such a way as to optimize redundancy, symmetry, and load balancing. The scenarios are not representative of every possible network configuration, and the design solutions shown here are not the only ones possible. But the lessons they illustrate can be applied to other scenarios and will help you understand and implement better and more efficient designs.

The first scenario is a simple case followed by increasingly complex scenarios. Note that there is a fine line between a customer and provider in many cases because a provider can be the customer of another provider. The principal distinction is this: customers obtain Internet connectivity by connecting to providers, but do not themselves offer connectivity to other customers. Providers offer Internet connectivity services and can themselves be customers of other providers.

The scenarios to be considered in the following subsections are further divided depending on whether the customer is receiving minimal or no routes, partial routes, full routes, or some combination of these from the providers. In the case where the customer is accepting minimal or no routes (called default only), you can assume that the customer can still learn the 0/0 route or a couple of aggregate routes that enables him to statically set a default. *Partial routing* usually consists of the provider's local routes and the provider's other customers' routes. *Full routing* means all Internet routes in existence—about 42,000 routes in 1996. A combination of these scenarios can occur where a customer can receive a default route and partial routes from the same provider, or partial routes from one provider and full routes from another and so on.

Scenario 1: Single-Homing

Single-homed customers have sites that connect to the Internet via a single connection to a service provider. Figure 6–8 illustrates such a situation. These customers can usually be adequately served by pointing defaults toward the provider. The provider can also install static routing to reach the customer. This method is the least expensive and the most effective. The customer router does

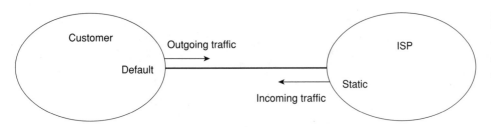

Figure 6–8
*Simple
single-homed site
situation.*

not need to learn any of the Internet routes. This substantially reduces memory usage and processing overhead. In this case, there is no issue of route symmetry because traffic has a single entrance and exit point.

Single-homed sites generally rely on a single connection to the Internet. Backup is not an issue. If the connection is lost, the customer can tolerate the outage until it is fixed. Obviously, such an arrangement would not satisfy mission-critical data communication requirements. A single-homed site with no backup access would not be appropriate for applications needing high levels of reliability.

Scenario 2: Multihoming to a Single Provider

A customer with multiple connections to the Internet via the same provider is considered to be multihomed to a single provider. For multihoming to a single provider, assume that BGP is used as a routing protocol. Although it is not necessary in all cases, it is recommended.

Default Only, One Primary, and One Backup Link

In this scenario, the customer configures default routing toward the provider and is not accepting partial or full routes. The customer can run default to both connections. In figure 6–9, the customer wants to use one link as the primary traffic conduit and the other as a backup in case the primary link goes down. (If there were more than two connections to the provider, the customer could set up multiple defaults with varying preference levels.)

Ch. 11, pp. 373-376. Default Only, One Primary, and One Backup Link

Figure 6–9
Basic mulithoming/single provider scenario.

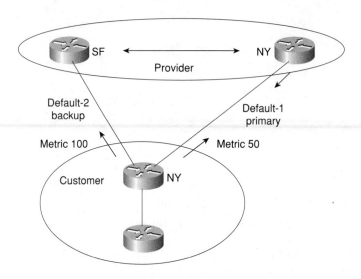

Customer's Outbound Traffic

In the scenario of figure 6–9, where a single router is used to connect to the provider in multiple locations, multiple static defaults with different distance values can be used, as already discussed in figure 6–6. The default with the lower distance will be the primary. The 0/0 default route or few aggregate routes can also be learned dynamically from the provider to enable the customer to set the default. Local preference can be used to prefer one default over the other.

Assume in figure 6–9 that the default to NY is more preferred than the default to SF. In normal operations, the customer will use the NY link as the primary link and the SF link as a backup.

For outbound traffic, load balancing is not an option because all traffic is sent over the primary line, and the secondary is kept as backup.

Absence of load balancing is offset by the fact that the customer's router requires less memory and processing power.

Customer's Inbound Traffic

The customer can advertise its networks to the provider via BGP. The provider will have two paths to reach the customer. Which path it chooses affects the customer's inbound traffic. Usually, the provider's default behavior (assuming that all attributes are the same) is for traffic to flow back to the customer's AS depending on which of the provider's exit points it is closest to. If traffic toward the customer is closer to the NY link, then it will enter the customer's AS via NY. If it is closer to SF, then it will enter via SF.

All the previous factors are outside the customer's control. Customers who want to override these influences and control incoming traffic via one path or the other can do so by advertising their routes with different metrics. The provider will direct its traffic toward the customer based on the metric value. In figure 6–9, the customer is advertising its routes with a metric of 50 toward NY and a metric of 100 toward SF. As such, traffic toward the customer will take the NY route.

Default, Primary, and Backup Plus Partial Routing

This is the same scenario as the default, primary, and backup case except that the customer can accept partial routing from the provider. Figure 6–10 illustrates this environment. This approach gives the customer better flexibility in choosing its exit point because more routing information is provided. As previously, both inbound and outbound traffic patterns are discussed.

Ch. 11, pp. 376-382. Default, Primary, and Backup Plus Partial Routing

Customer's Outbound Traffic

Consider a situation in which customer 1 is connected to the provider via two separate routers. The customer has the option of deciding which path to take for each of the partial routes it accepts from the provider. This is usually done by setting different local preference for different routes coming into the customer's AS. Local preference can be set on an AS_path or prefix basis or both. If set based on an AS_path, then the local preference will apply to all prefixes contained in a particular AS. In case routing decisions need to be made on a prefix basis, the local preference can be set based on each prefix. In figure 6–10, based on the physical location of certain ASs or prefixes, the customer can choose to forward traffic to customer 2 and customer 3 (C2 and C3) on the SF link and to C4 and C5 on the NY link. The customer can achieve this by doing the following:

- For routes being learned on the NY link, assign a local preference of 300 for the C4 and C5 routes. Give all other routes a preference of 250 (this would include C2 and C3).

- For routes being learned on the SF link, assign a local preference of 300 for the C2 and C3 routes. Give all other routes a preference of 200 (this would include C4 and C5).

Figure 6–10
Multihoming/single provider scenario with partial routing.

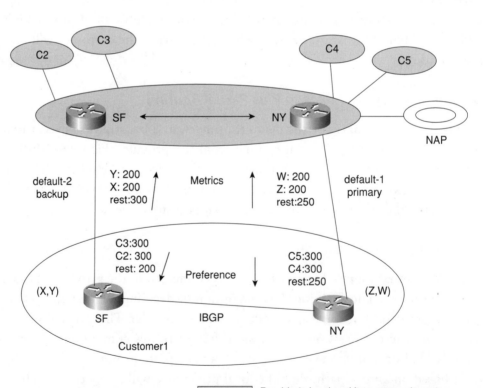

When presented with multiple routes for the same destination (via external and internal BGP), the customer will prefer the C4 and C5 routes via the NY link (300 > 200). In the same manner, the customer will prefer the C2 and C3 routes via the SF link (300 > 250). For customers other than C2, C3, C4, and C5, the NY link will be preferred (250 > 200).

For all other Internet routes not known to customer 1, default will be taken in the primary backup manner. The 0/0 default route could be dynamically learned from the provider from both ends, or could be statically configured to point to one of the provider's networks (as discussed in the "Setting Default Routes" section of this chapter). Local preference could be used to prefer one default over the other. Based on the way the local preference routes for the C2, C3, C4, and C5 customers were set, all other routes including the 0/0 will be preferred via the NY link (250 > 200).

A totally different approach that doesn't require as much configuration on the customer's side is for the provider to send its metrics toward the customer. This option was discussed in the MED section of Chapter 5. If metrics coming from the provider are representative of how close or how far networks are from the entrance points to the customer networks, then the customer will be able to load balance its outbound traffic accordingly. Traffic toward C4 and C5 will go out on the NY link, and traffic toward C2 and C3 will go out on the SF link. Other traffic will flow depending on what metrics are associated with the routes learned on each link. Although this method requires less configuration, it is also less deterministic on the customer's side because its traffic trajectory is totally dependent on the provider's setup. A combination of both approaches discussed might give the best behavior.

Customer's Inbound Traffic

The customer can influence inbound traffic by advertising different metrics on different links. Some providers encourage their customers to send their internal IGP metrics as BGP metrics (also discussed in Chapter 5). This way, the provider will deliver traffic to the customer via the link closer to the destination. In the example illustrated in figure 6–10, the customer has decided to manually set the metrics to force the following behavior:

- For routes being sent on the NY link, send the Z and W prefixes with a MED of 200. Give all other prefixes a metric of 250. (This includes X and Y.)

- For routes being sent on the SF link, send the X and Y prefixes with an MED of 200. Give all other prefixes a metric of 300. (This includes Z and W.)

When presented with multiple routes for the same destinations, the provider will access the Z and W prefixes over the NY link (200 < 300). In the same manner, the provider will access the X and Y prefixes over the SF link (200 < 250). For all prefixes other than X, Y, W, and Z, the provider will choose the NY link (250 < 300).

Default, Primary and Backup, Full and Partial Routing

For customers multihomed to a single provider, the customer can either get full routes on all its connections to the provider, or the customer can have a combination of full routes on one link and no routes (default) or partial routes on the other links. The same techniques discussed in the preceding sections would apply here: local preference is used to control the customer's outbound traffic, and the metric is used to control the inbound traffic. Also, if internal metrics are exchanged between customer and provider, a certain level of load balancing can be achieved.

NOTE

Careful! When dealing with outbound traffic, manipulating exit points for specific routes is dangerous. Routing loops can occur if outbound traffic following an IGP default toward the customer's BGP router gets directed toward another router following default to the BGP router. This situation might seem confusing now, but will become more clear in the next chapter.

Automatic Load Balancing

As is probably clear from the previous scenarios, load balancing is not a very intuitive task and requires extensive planning. To help, Cisco IOS software supports dynamic load balancing for identical destinations learned via EBGP by the same router and coming from the same autonomous system. This will reduce configuration efforts.

Ch. 11, pp. 382-385. Automatic Load Balancing

Figure 6–11 illustrates an example in which the same router (NY) is connected to its provider via two links and is getting identical routing on both links. A Cisco router will keep in its IP routing table up to six identical BGP routes to the same destination. When passing on the EBGP updates to the IBGP peers, however, the router will only pass on one best route. The next hop address of the route will automatically be changed to reflect the router's (NY) own IP address instead of having the EBGP next hop address carried into IBGP. Note that this is done automatically only in the case where load balancing is configured dynamically.

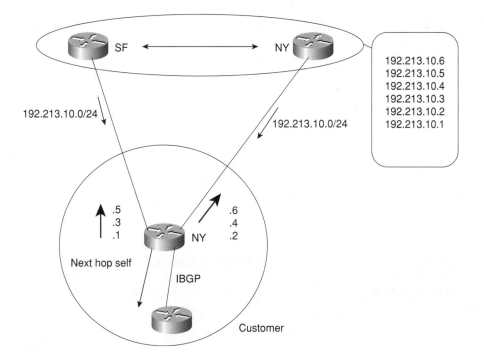

Figure 6–11
Router receiving identical routes from two sources.

By default, a Cisco router will load balance on a per destination (Host) basis. Balancing on a destination basis is done in round-robin fashion. One host will be locked to one path, the next host will be locked to the other path, and so on.

Figure 6–11 assumes that the customer is getting two identical routes to network 192.213.10.0/24. Without automatic load balancing, the BGP process prefers one path only. It is up to the administrator to try to affect the BGP decision by changing attributes to balance the traffic between paths.

With automatic balancing, BGP will keep two entries for the 192.213.10.0/24 prefix, one via the SF link and one via the NY link. Outbound traffic from the customer network will then be split over the two links on a round-robin basis, assuming that the customer needs to send traffic to the destinations 192.213.10.1 to 192.213.10.6. Destination 10.1 will be reached via the SF link, destination 10.2 will go over the NY link, destination 10.3 will go over the SF link, and so on.

NOTE

Load balancing in this manner works only when dealing with identical routing updates coming into the same router from the same provider. This method does not work to load balance in a multiprovider environment.

In the example illustrated in figure 6–11, automatic load balancing works well for outbound traffic. For inbound traffic, you must resort to manipulating metrics to influence the provider's decision.

Balancing Between Two Routers Sharing Multiple Paths

In some situations, two routers share multiple physical paths for backup or higher bandwidth services, as illustrated in figure 6–12.

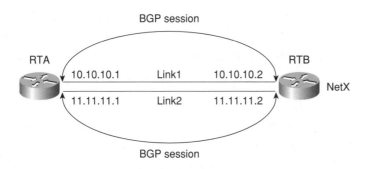

BGP session

RTA   10.10.10.1   Link1   10.10.10.2   RTB

NetX

11.11.11.1   Link2   11.11.11.2

BGP session

Figure 6–12
Load balancing between two routers sharing multiple paths.

To balance traffic in this environment, one option is to implement dynamic balancing. This is simply a special situation of the previous automatic load balancing case. Dynamic load balancing, however, will result in extra overhead for the routers. Each router would receive duplicate update messages from the other router. In the case of full routing, the result would be approximately 42,000 routes arriving on each link. Instead, it is possible (and preferable) to achieve load balancing for the situation illustrated in figure 6–12 by using a static approach.

Ch. 11, pp. 385-387. Balancing Between Two Routers Sharing Multiple Paths

In the normal behavior, BGP keeps the best next hop for each prefix it learns. As seen in table 6–1, RTA will receive two identical BGP routes for NetX. BGP will pick the best route and install it in its IP routing table. In this case, BGP has picked the route via next hop 10.10.10.2. Table 6–2 illustrates RTA's IP routing

Destination	Next Hop
NetX	10.10.10.2 (best)
NetX	11.11.11.2

Table 6–1
RTA's BGP table— NetX reachable via 10.10.10.2.

Destination	Next Hop
NetX	10.10.10.2
10.10.10.0/24	Link1

Table 6–2
RTA's IP routing table —NetX reachable via Link1.

table where the next hop 10.10.10.2 is reachable via link1. As a result of this configuration, traffic toward networks learned from RTB will be sent over link1. Hence, no load balancing is achieved.

BGP can be fooled by setting the next hop to a virtual interface rather than the physical link and by using the IP routing table to do the actual load balancing.In figure 6–13, RTB can be assigned a loopback interface (virtual interface), and RTA can use that address to set up the BGP neighbor connection. This way, the loopback interface itself and not the IP address of the physical link will be used as a next hop. Some dynamic IGP or static routing can be used to load balance between the links independent of BGP.

As seen in table 6–3, RTA will receive its BGP routes from its neighbor 12.12.12.12 and will be able to reach NetX via the next hop 12.12.12.12. Table 6–4 illustrates RTA's IP routing table. Next hop 12.12.12.12 can be reached via link1 and link2. Reachability of the 12.12.12.0/24 network can be achieved via IGP or by pointing multiple static routes toward link1 and link2. The router can

Figure 6–13
A single BGP session across multiple physical links.

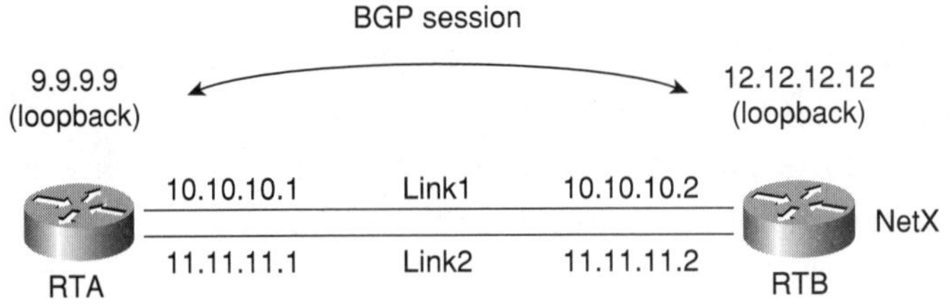

Table 6–3
RTA's BGP table— NetX reachable via 12.12.12.12.

Destination	Next Hop
NetX	12.12.12.12

Table 6–4
RTA's IP routing table —NetX reachable via Link1 or Link2.

Destination	Next Hop
NetX	12.12.12.12
12.12.12.0/24	Link1
12.12.12.0/24	Link2

now load balance the traffic. Due to the recursive route lookup in this scenario, load balancing is done per network rather than per destinations. Networks learned from RTB can now be reached round robin over multiple links.

Scenario 3: Multihoming to Different Providers

A customer connected to multiple providers is considered to be multihomed to different providers. Redundancy and geographical restrictions are strong motivations for multihoming. The outbound traffic behavior for each iteration of this scenario will be considered on a case-by-case basis. For all cases, the inbound traffic behavior is the same and is covered at the end of the section.

Default Only, Primary and Backup

In this case, the customer can follow defaults toward the provider. One link will be used as primary, and the second link as backup. Figure 6–14 illustrates a relevant situation.

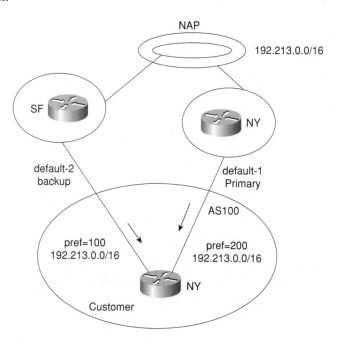

Figure 6–14
Multihoming to two providers.

A customer can set the default routes to the two providers statically or can dynamically learn 0/0 from both providers. The customer can prefer one default over another by using the "distance" or local preference. One good method of pointing defaults to both providers is to accept the same network from both providers. The customer will configure its 0/0 default based on that network and can manipulate local preference to choose one link over the other. In case one default goes away because of a link failure toward one provider, the other default will take its place. The customer can either negotiate with the providers to send him only the one network entry, or the customer can filter all updates on his end except for the one entry.

In figure 6–14, the customer is pointing the default toward the prefix 192.213.0.0/16 it is receiving from both providers and setting the local preference on the NY link to be higher (200). The NY link will be the primary link, and the SF link will be the backup.

Default, Primary, and Backup Plus Partial Routing

The addition of partial routing to the environment introduced in the previous discussion changes the traffic behavior. Figure 6–15 illustrates the new situation. The customer can accept partial routing from one or both providers and run default toward both providers with one default preferred over the other.

By accepting partial routing from the providers, a customer does not need to see all Internet routes and can still make a best route decision when routing toward its direct providers. (For some major providers, partial routes could represent a substantial number of routes.) In the case illustrated in figure 6–15, BGP will make the right choice, and the customer will choose the provider link closest to the destination network (shorter AS_path). For other Internet routes, the basic principal of primary and backup can be used. The customer can point to a specific network to be the default, accept that network from both providers, and use local preference to prefer one link over the other.

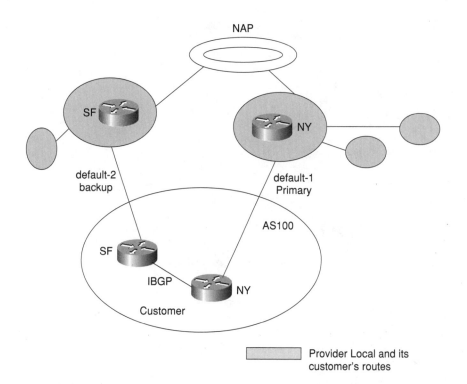

Figure 6–15
*Multimihoming to
two providers plus
partial routing.*

Provider Local and its
customer's routes

Default, Primary and Backup, Full and Partial Routing

In multihoming to different providers, accepting full routes from both or either providers is not really necessary unless the customer plans to be a provider itself and pass along full routes to its customers (act as a transit AS). Figure 6–16 illustrates a relevant environment.

Ch. 11, pp.
387-392. Multi-
homing to Dif-
ferent Providers

The customer can accept full routing from one or both providers depending on how much load balancing he wants to do. In the case of full routing from both (or multiple) providers, the customer can use local preference to decide which networks can be accessed via which provider. Decisions can be made based on AS or prefix information. In some cases, the customer might want to accept full routing from one provider and just do partial/default routing with the other provider. This way, the customer can get the best of both worlds without having to deal

Figure 6–16
*Multimihoming to
two providers with
full and partial
routing.*

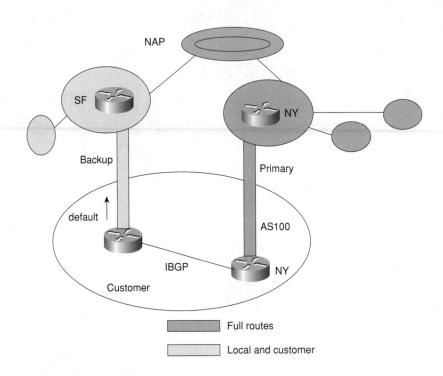

with managing full routes from different links. As you will see later, Internet instabilities caused by any provider could cause routers to become very CPU-intensive.

In figure 6–16, the customer is receiving full routes from the NY provider and partial routes from the SF provider. The customer is also pointing a default toward the SF provider. For the SF local and customer routes, the SF link will be used because of the shorter AS_path. For all other routes, the NY link will be used because the SF link is only providing partial routes. In case the SF link goes down, all networks can be reached via NY. In case the NY link goes down, the customer can still reach all Internet routes by following a default toward the SF link.

Customer Inbound Traffic (AS_Path Manipulation)

The inbound traffic is affected by how the customer advertises its networks to the providers. Note that with the multiprovider scenario, sending different metrics from the customer's end will not have any effect. This is because the

MED is always terminated at the provider's network and is not carried to the other provider.

To affect the providers' behavior dynamically, the customer can manipulate the AS_path attribute by inserting bogus entries in the AS_path to affect the AS_path length. The providers will receive the same prefix information with different path length and will pick the path with the shortest length. Note that in a multiprovider environment, it is not enough to influence the direct provider only because there is no guarantee that the direct provider will get the traffic itself. Path manipulation will have to influence providers all the way up to the NAP because this is where the balance (as far as path length) will be tipped one way or the other.

Figure 6–17 illustrates how bogus entries in the AS_path affect routing. The customer (AS100) has inserted a bogus entry (100) in its AS_path toward AS300. Providers at the NAP will get the same prefixes with different path length (300 100 100 versus 200 100) and will pick the shorter path via AS200. The bogus entry should be a repeat of the AS that originated the entry (in this case 100).

Scenario 4: Customers of the Same Provider with a Backup Link

In some cases, customers with common interests agree to provide each other with internal connectivity and backup connectivity to the Internet. The customers are connected to the same provider and at the same time have an alternate private link to each other. Two scenarios might typically arise:

- The private link can be used as a secondary (backup) link when an Internet link fails.

- The private link can be used as a primary link for internal traffic between the two companies *and* as a backup link in the event of an Internet link failure. If a backup strategy is to work, customers must advertise each other's networks to the provider. One customer must be able to act as a transit AS for the other customer when the other customer's Internet link fails.

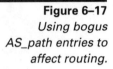

Figure 6–17
*Using bogus
AS_path entries to
affect routing.*

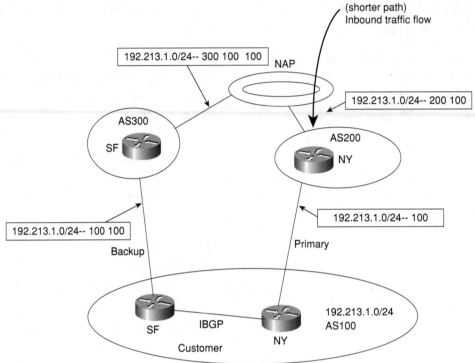

Private Link Used as a Pure Backup

Figure 6–18 illustrates the scenario where AS2 and AS3 are connected to the same provider—AS1. AS2 and AS3 have a private link that will be used only for backup. AS2 and AS3 will have the same policies.

For the backup environment illustrated in figure 6–18, AS2's outbound traffic considerations are of particular interest. Whether AS2 is getting full routing or a combination of default, full, and partial routing from the provider and AS3, AS2 will have to set its local preference for routes coming from AS1 to be higher (200) than the ones coming from AS3 (100). As a result, provider AS1 is always preferred, and the private link acts as a backup only. In case of partial routing being accepted by AS2, AS2 can set defaults to both the provider (AS1) and AS3. Setting a higher local preference ensures that all the traffic will be sent toward the provider. If AS2 is getting full routing from the provider and partial routing from AS3, AS2 can keep a default route to AS3 to be used if the provider link fails.

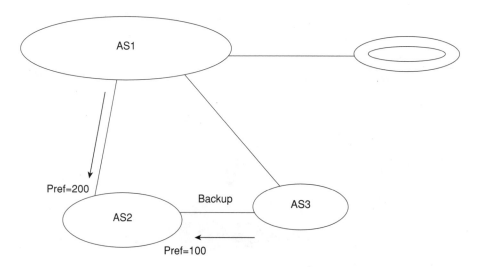

Figure 6–18
Private link used as backup.

Private Link Used as Primary Between AS2 and AS3

Figure 6–19 illustrates a case in which the link between AS2 and AS3 is used as a primary link for all traffic to AS3's local networks or to AS3's customers. For all other traffic, the link to the provider AS1 should be used. The two links (provider and private) should back up one another.

Ch. 11, pp. 392-394. Customers of the Same Provider with a Backup Link

Assume that the environment illustrated in figure 6–19 features default, full, and partial routing; the discussions that follow focus on outbound and inbound traffic implications from AS2's perspective. This scenario is usually handled by the default BGP behavior. Since the shortest path is always preferred AS2 and AS3 will always use the private link to reach each others networks. For the sake of experimenting with BGP policies we will attempt to address this scenario by manipulating the local preference attribute.

AS2's Outbound Traffic

Whether AS2 is accepting default, full, or partial routing from the provider and AS3, AS2 should set the local preference of all updates that do not contain AS3 to be higher than all other updates. In the case illustrated in figure 6–19, these routes are given a local preference of 300. Updates coming on the private link

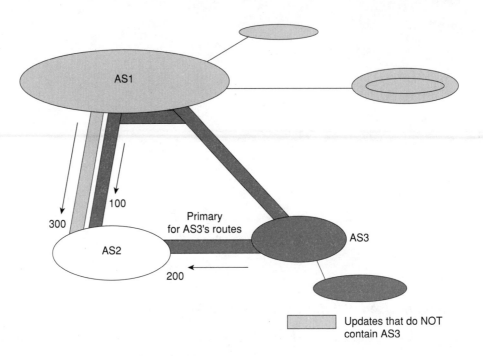

are given a local preference of 200. Updates that contain AS3 and that are passed on to AS2 via the provider are kept at a default local preference of 100 to make sure that the private link between AS2 and AS3 is taken (200 > 100).

For all other traffic, AS2 will accept defaults or set its own defaults to the provider and AS3, with the provider being preferred.

It is also possible for AS2 to accept local routing from AS3 and not to accept routing from the provider. AS2 then defaults to both, with the provider being preferred. This way, any traffic containing AS3 will take the private link; any other traffic will take the link to the provider (better default). In case of a failure of the provider's link, the default to the private link will kick in.

AS2's Inbound Traffic

All the cases discussed so far in scenario 4 have the same inbound traffic behavior. Because of the shorter path length, incoming traffic from the Internet will always take the provider to AS2 link. For all traffic originating from AS3 or its customers, the private link will be taken also because of the shorter path. This is the desired behavior.

Scenario 5: Customers of Different Providers with a Backup Link

It is not unusual for separate ASs to require Internet interconnection and to have different Internet service providers. Whenever multiple providers are involved and the customers of these providers agree to back up one another, support can get complicated. This section takes the previous discussions one step further and discusses how this backup connectivity is addressed from the provider's point of view.

Ch. 11, pp. 394-399. Customers of Different Providers with a Backup Link

In figure 6–20, AS1 is the customer of ISP1, and AS2 is the customer of ISP2. AS1 and AS2 have also entered a bilateral agreement under which the private link between the two ASs will be used as a backup in the event of a failure of either primary Internet link. Normally, an individual AS does not want to be used as transit for another AS. In the case illustrated in figure 6–20, AS1 wants ISP1 to set its routing configuration so that ISP1 reaches AS2 via ISP2. Similarly,

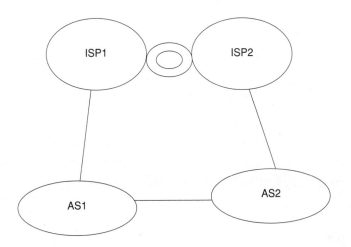

Figure 6–20
Customers of multiple providers with a backup link.

AS2 would prefer ISP2 to set its routing configuration so that ISP2 reaches AS1 via ISP1. In this scenario, for the backup link to work, AS1 advertises AS2's networks to ISP1, and AS2 advertises AS1's networks to ISP2.

The discussions about primary and backup are the same as with the scenario discussed in the preceding section, "Scenario 4: Customers of the Same Provider with a Backup Link." The private link can be a pure backup or can be used for interior traffic between customers.

The requirement to have the provider not use one customer to reach the other customer is more complicated. ISP1 will have to set the local preference for AS2 routes coming from ISP2 to be higher than the routes coming from AS1.This would cause ISP2 to be used under normal operational conditions. The same strategy might be deployed for ISP2.

Providers, however, would like to minimize configuration on their end as much as possible. In cases where a provider has multiple customers coming online every day, tracking the local preference for each can be cumbersome. Providers would also like to set their policies based on AS numbers rather than specific networks.

A couple of approaches can be used to implement the required policies. The first approach is the community approach, which requires coordination between providers and their customers. The second approach is the AS_path manipulation approach. AS_path manipulation is easier to implement, but might not be available in all vendor products.

Ch. 11, pp. 394-399. Customers of Different Providers with a Backup Link

The Community Approach

The use of the community attribute becomes very effective. Providers want to map certain community values to corresponding local preference values. Routing updates coming from customers having a specific community will automatically be given the corresponding local preference.

To keep this scenario manageable, only routing and policy setting from ISP1's point of view is addressed. An identical discussion would apply to ISP2. Traffic flow for the case illustrated in figure 6–21 can be divided into a minimum of three patterns.

NOTE

There can be more flow patterns, depending on how many connections a customer has to its provider, but the basic set of three illustrates required considerations.

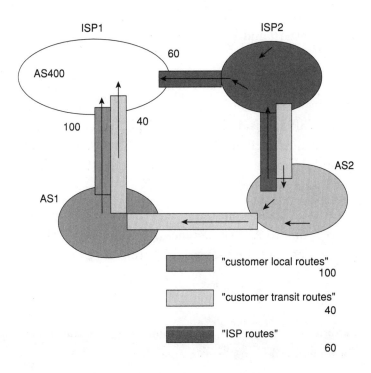

Figure 6–21
Community approach solution.

Flow patterns from ISP1's point of view can be summarized as follows:

- *Pattern 1*—Routes originated by the customer AS1, or *customer local routes*.

- *Pattern 2*—Routes transiting via AS1. These routes come from AS2 and consist of AS2's routes and all other routes that AS2 is receiving from ISP2. ISP1 uses this information to reach AS2 via AS1 as a backup in the event that AS2's link to ISP2 fails. This pattern is referred to as *customer transit routes*.

- *Pattern 3*—All other routes coming from ISP2, or *ISP routes*. These can include routes learned from AS2.

Having divided the routes into different categories, ISP1 will assign a community value to each pattern and will dynamically map it to the local preference, as listed in table 6–5.

ISP1 will inform all its customers and connected ISPs that its local preference values are dynamically set according to table 6–5. Customers can then dynamically influence the ISP's decision by sending the corresponding community values. In the example illustrated in figure 6–21, AS1 will send its local routes with no community and the transit routes with community 400:40. ISP2 will send its routes with community 400:60.

According to the preferences summarized in table 6–5, ISP1 prefers AS1's local routes via its direct link to AS1 (preference 100 is the highest). ISP1 prefers all other routes, including AS2 routes, via ISP2 (preference 60 is higher than 40.)

Table 6–5
Dynamic mapping of local preference.

Pattern	Community	Local Preference
Customer local routes	none	100
Customer transit routes	400:40	40
ISP routes	400:60	60

The AS_Path Approach

The AS_path manipulation approach is the same as was discussed for multi-homing to different providers, under "Customer Inbound Traffic (AS_Path Manipulation)." It is straightforward and has proven to be one of the the most efficient methods of influencing a provider's routing decisions. Figure 6–22 illustrates an environment in which AS_path manipulation is used to direct routing processes.

Ch. 11, pp. 398-399. The AS_Path Approach

For the case illustrated in figure 6–22, assume that all local preference attributes are kept at their default values to avoid overriding the AS_path attribute. With this assumption in mind, ISP1 will use the direct link to AS1 for AS1's local traffic and the direct link to ISP2 to reach ISP2's traffic. This is done based on the shorter AS_path.

For traffic going to AS2, ISP1 has an equal path via ISP2 and AS1. ISP1's AS_path to AS2 via AS1 is 1 2 and the AS_path via ISP2 is 500 2, which are of equivalent length.

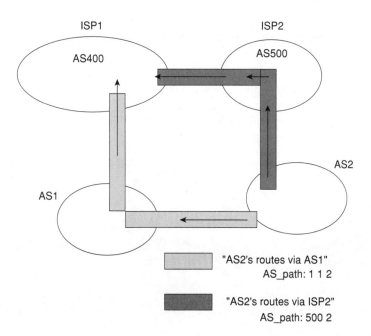

Figure 6–22
AS_path manipulation example.

To influence ISP1's decision, AS1 must increase the AS_path length when advertising AS2's routes to ISP1 by prepending an additional AS number to the AS_path list. Normally, AS1 will repeat its own AS number. ISP1's new AS_path to reach AS2 via AS1 will be 1 1 2, which is longer than ISP1's AS_path to reach AS2 via ISP2 500 2. As a result, ISP1 will use ISP2 to reach AS2.

LOOKING AHEAD

Mastering routing at the edges of your domain gives you full control over traffic in and out of your autonomous system. Still, another piece of the puzzle is how the traffic flows inside the AS before it gets out. Not all routers inside the AS run BGP. IGP-only routers usually do not carry a full list of Internet routes due to memory constraints. Running defaults inside the AS to reach external routes is one of the most common ways for internal routers to reach destinations outside the AS. With defaults comes the threat of routing loops if conflicting policies exist between your BGP and your IGP. The following chapter discusses these issues of how to make BGP policies flow hand-in-hand with IGP defaults. The chapter also discusses the use of policy routing in achieving total control over routing behaviors based on the sources of IP addresses rather than the traditional destination-based routing.

FREQUENTLY ASKED QUESTIONS

Q— *I statically defined a default toward my provider by pointing toward a network I am learning via BGP. What happens if that network goes up and down?*

A— Your default will appear and disappear. That is why you should not point your default to a specific subnet. Always point to an aggregate or supernet because they are less likely to flip-flop.

Q— *I have the option of getting the 0/0 default via BGP or defining a static default. What do you think is best?*

A— For the border router, both methods are the same as long as the aggregate you are pointing to is stable. On the other hand, after you receive the 0/0 via BGP, it will get flooded to all your IBGP peers and there is a chance that you will end up sending it out to your other EBGP peers. When you define the default statically, you will have better control.

Q— *I need to have a primary link where all my traffic flows and a backup link in case of failure. I also need to load balance my traffic. Is that possible?*

A— That is not possible. If you are using your primary link for all inbound and outbound traffic, this would dictate that no other traffic will flow on the other link. These are two contradicting requirements.

Q— *My AS is connected to two providers, one in SF and one in NY. I want the traffic from and toward my SJ site to go in and out on the SF link. All other traffic should flow over the NY link. What do I need to do to achieve this behavior?*

A— For your inbound traffic toward San Jose, you can use the AS_path manipulation technique to make your path longer for all SJ routes advertised on the NY link. The problem is with your outbound traffic. If you know exactly what networks the SJ users are trying to reach, you can give those destinations better local preference on the SF exit. If the SJ site needs to reach any destination, then setting a better local preference on the SF link will cause all your outbound traffic to leave via the SF link. That doesn't meet your requirement about the NY link carrying all other traffic.

Another way of dealing with this scenario is policy routing, where a router can track source addresses and direct traffic accordingly. This is described in Chapter 7, "Controlling Routing Inside the Autonomous System."

Q— *I am prepending AS numbers to my routes to tip the balance of my traffic. I am not seeing any effect. Why?*

A— Remember that your updates are exchanged by multiple providers. A provider along the way can use local preference to override your path length. Check with your provider.

Q— *Do I have to set BGP policies? Why can't I leave it to BGP to figure out the correct path?*

A— You do not have to set policies. Remember, though, that BGP is not taking into account the speed of your links and your user traffic requirements. If you are happy with your traffic pattern the way it is, then you do not need to change any attributes.

CHAPTER 7

Controlling Routing Inside the Autonomous System

The preceding chapter focused on the interaction between different ASs and how BGP attributes can be manipulated to address symmetry and load balancing. Our discussion concentrated on the behavior of the BGP border routers that connect the AS to other ASs.

ISPs usually have most of their routers running BGP, with some leaf nodes running IGP. On the other hand, most customers have few routers running BGP and the majority of their internal IGP routers running defaults toward the BGP routers. In these scenarios, it is important to have the BGP policies go hand-in-hand with routing inside the AS. Conflicting policies might result in routing loops if the AS's physical layout does not complement the logical layout. This chapter discusses the interaction of BGP routes with IGPs inside the AS and presents the options of controlling routes via policy routing.

INTERACTION OF NON-BGP ROUTERS WITH BGP ROUTERS

Non-BGP routers inside the AS can reach the outside world by using the following two methods:

- Injecting BGP into the IGP
- Following defaults inside the AS

233

Injecting BGP into the IGP

Injecting full BGP routes into an IGP is *not* recommended. Doing so will add excessive routing overhead to any IGP. Interior routing protocols were never meant to handle more than the networks inside your AS, plus some exterior routes from other IGPs.

This does not mean that BGP routes should never be injected into IGPs. Depending on the number of the BGP routes and how critical the need for them to be in the IGP, injecting partial BGP routes into IGP may well be appropriate.

Injecting partial BGP routes into the IGP from specific points of the AS can help direct the corresponding outbound traffic toward specific exit points. Outbound traffic toward other Internet routes will still have to follow defaults toward the BGP routers. Although injecting BGP routes into the IGP seems like the optimal routing solution, it has its drawbacks. If, for instance, the IGP is classfull (such as RIP v1 or IGRP), information about CIDR blocks will be lost. The other major problem is the potential instabilities in the injected BGP routes causing instabilities in the IGP. Some major network meltdowns have occured because the fluctuations of a large number of external routes have caused IGPs to fail.

Following Defaults Inside an AS

Ch. 11, pp. 399-418. Following Defaults Inside an AS

The more practical solution is to follow defaults inside your AS to the closest router that can get you outside the AS. A default route can be injected into the AS from each autonomous system border router. Each IGP router might receive the default route from one or multiple routers. The IGP router chooses the best path based on the internal cost or metric to reach the default. After the traffic reaches the BGP routers, the traffic will propagate according to how BGP has picked the best path.

Figure 7–1 illustrates non-BGP routers inside an AS following defaults to reach the closest BGP router. RTC and RTD are BGP border routers that are injecting the default 0/0 inside AS1. RTB is an internal BGP transit router running a full

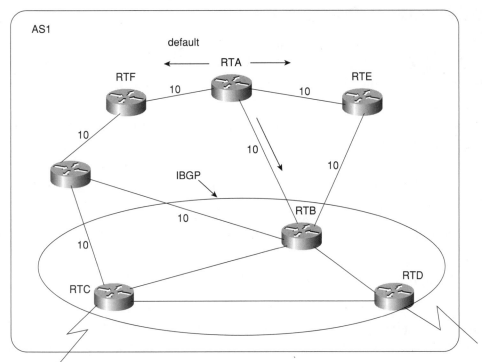

Figure 7–1
*Example of
following defaults.*

IBGP mesh with RTC and RTD. Internal non-BGP routers, such as RTA, will receive the default from different directions and choose the default with the smallest IGP metric. In figure 7–1, RTA is receiving the 0/0 from RTB with a metric of 10, from RTE with a metric of 20 (10 + 10), and from RTF with a metric of 30 (10 + 10 + 10). RTA will prefer the default via its link to RTB because it has the lowest internal metric (10). After the traffic arrives at RTB, it follows the BGP routing table to reach destinations external to the AS.

Running IBGP inside an AS is an important element in helping to control how traffic exits the AS and to carry transit traffic in case there is a need to do so. Also, most of the symmetry techniques discussed in the preceding chapter cannot be applied if multiple BGP routers are not running IBGP.

BGP POLICIES CONFLICTING WITH INTERNAL DEFAULTS

Ch. 11, pp.
402-418. BGP
Policies Conflict-
ing with Internal
Defaults

Depending on the physical topology of an AS and how policies are set, some odd situations might arise. Traffic following defaults inside the AS toward a border router might end up in a loop, if the border routers have some BGP policies that cause the traffic to be sent back inside the AS. This section discusses situations where loops might occur and experiments with possible solutions for the problem. Two cases will be considered:

- Defaults inside the AS in conjunction with a Primary/Backup BGP policy

- Defaults inside the AS in conjunction with other BGP policies

Defaults Inside the AS: Primary/Backup BGP Policy

Consider the routing scenario in figure 7–2; AS1 is connected to the Internet via two connections. RTC in SF is running EBGP with one provider, whereas RTD in NY is running EBGP with another provider. Inside the AS, RTC and RTD are running IBGP, but are not physically connected. Traffic between RTC and RTD has to go via routers RTA and RTB.

Assume that RTC and RTD are both receiving full routes from their respective providers. RTC and RTD are also injecting a 0/0 default route inside AS1. Assume also that AS1 wants to run the primary/backup technique to enable the NY T3 link to be the primary. AS1 would set the local preference higher for routes coming from NY, which makes that link primary. The SF link will be used as backup, and hence all outbound traffic that reaches RTC will be directed back toward RTD.

RTA and RTB are interior non-BGP routers and exchange routes via IGP with all other routers in the AS. RTA and RTB do not see any of the exterior routes and follow defaults toward RTC and RTD according to the lower IGP metric. Traffic for outside networks reaching RTA will end up following the default toward RTC, whereas traffic reaching RTB will end up following the default toward RTD.

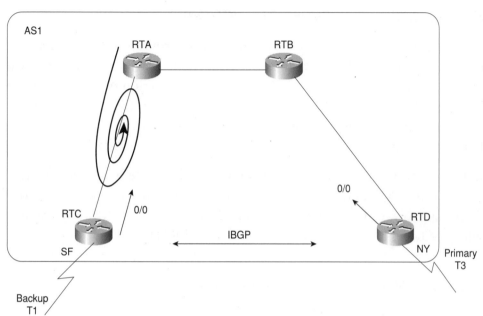

Figure 7–2
Following defaults: loop situation.

When RTC receives the traffic, it will divert it toward RTD because of the BGP policy that makes NY the primary link. Because RTC has no direct connection to RTD, it will send the traffic toward RTA. RTA will receive the traffic and send it back toward RTC, and a loop will occur.

Next, multiple scenarios are examined for avoiding the potential looping behavior when using defaults within the AS for primary/backup routing.

Scenario 1: Manipulating the IGP Metric

In this scenario, we want to try to avoid a loop condition by having all traffic for external destinations follow the default toward RTD. This could be done by having RTC inject the 0/0 default inside the IGP with a very high metric to make the 0/0 default for any internal router shorter via RTD. Traffic will never go to RTC unless the NY link goes down.

Scenario 2: IBGP Path Shorter Than IGP Path

The existence of a shorter path between the IBGP routers will make sure that traffic will not go back over the IGP-only routers to reach its destination. This is only required if BGP policies necessitate the redirection of traffic from one BGP router to the other. Such situations occur when an IBGP router does not have an external link to send the traffic, or if it does have an external link, that link is not used as the best path (RTC's situation in figure 7–2).

In the scenario of figure 7–2, a loop can be avoided if the border routers RTC and RTD that run IBGP also share a physical segment such as a serial link. Traffic coming toward RTC from RTA would be redirected over the physical link, which provides a shorter path between RTC and RTD.

Scenario 3: Running BGP on Transit Routers

Running BGP on all transit routers will make sure that once traffic reaches any of these routers, it can be directed outside the AS. In the example of figure 7–2, if RTA and RTB were to run an IBGP full mesh with RTC and RTD, all traffic that reaches RTA or RTB will find its way out. Note that even though AS1 might not be a transit AS, RTA and RTB are still used to carry traffic between border routers. Internal IGP-only routers will use the IBGP cloud to reach the outside word, as already illustrated in figure 7–1.

Scenario 4: Who Generates the Default, and How Does it Get Generated?

In this scenario, a loop can be avoided if the primary router generates the default into IGP while the secondary router does not. In this example, RTD would inject the 0/0 into the IGP, and RTC would not. All the traffic would follow the default toward RTD.

This solution works only in normal conditions and fails in backup situations. If the NY link fails, the IGP routers would lose the 0/0 default. Because RTC is not generating any default, traffic to outside the AS will fail.

The ideal situation is for RTC to inject a default into the IGP only if the NY link fails. If the NY link goes down, RTD should stop injecting a default into the IGP and RTC should start injecting the default into the IGP. For this mechanism to take place, the routers must engage in the following behaviors:

- A BGP router should stop injecting default into the IGP if the router's external link fails.

- A BGP router should inject default into the IGP only if the default it prefers points to the external link.

The first requirement can be easily achieved if the IGP allows redistribution of the external default 0/0 into the IGP. Whenever the external 0/0 ceases to exist, the IGP default disappears with it. The availability and behavior of redistribution depends on what IGP you are running and on the particular vendor implementation. The way Cisco implements redistribution could differ from other vendors.

The second requirement mandates that a router stop generating the default if the default it prefers comes from inside rather than outside the AS. When the secondary router prefers the default from inside the AS, it means that the primary link is still up. When the primary goes down, the secondary will prefer the default from outside the AS and will inject the default into IGP. This situation is easier to explain and understand by example. The next two examples study the difference between a RIP- and OSPF-generated default in a Cisco implementation.

RIP-Generated Default

In the example in figure 7–3, RTC and RTD can learn a 0/0 default or statically configure a 0/0 default toward their respective providers. In normal conditions, RTD will automatically (or via controlled redistribution) inject the 0/0 into RIP. RTC will detect the presence of a default coming from RTD and will stop generating a default. All traffic will be directed toward RTD.

In case of a failure in the NY link, RTD will stop generating the default into RIP. RTC will detect the loss of 0/0 via RIP and will inject its own default.

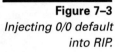

Figure 7–3
*Injecting 0/0 default
into RIP.*

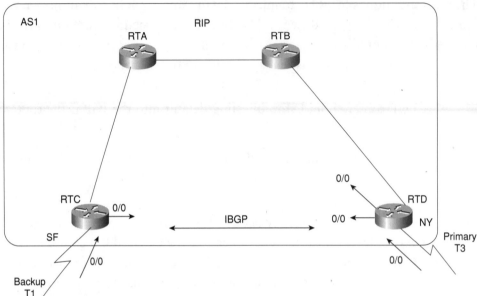

Note that RTC is receiving the 0/0 default via EBGP, RIP, and possibly IBGP if RTD is passing the 0/0 in the IBGP session. Because of the higher local preference via RTD, RTC would prefer the 0/0 via IBGP. Because the IBGP distance is 200, higher than the RIP distance of 120 (see table 5–1), the 0/0 default via RIP is preferred.

OSPF-Generated Default

OSPF behaves differently from RIP. The BGP 0/0 cannot be passed into OSPF via redistribution. OSPF has different hooks that enable the protocol to generate the 0/0 into the OSPF at any time, or even better, if the presence of a 0/0 is detected in the IP routing table. Now apply this behavior to the example in figure 7–4.

RTD and RTC will receive the 0/0 via EBGP or point a static default toward their respective providers. If RTD and RTC are configured such that the 0/0 is injected into OSPF as long as they themselves have a 0/0 in their IP routing table, the primary/backup model will fail. It fails because both RTD and RTC are receiving the 0/0 via IBGP. RTC will always inject the 0/0 into OSPF whether the NY link is up or down. Also, unlike the RIP scenario, RTC will ignore the OSPF default coming from RTD because RTC is also configured to generate a default.

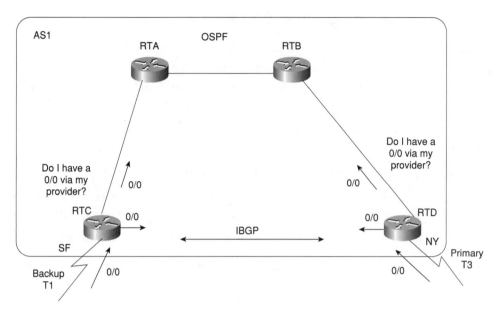

Figure 7–4

Injecting 0/0 default into OSPF.

To remedy this situation, further configuration is needed to instruct the routers RTC and RTD to generate the 0/0 into OSPF only if their own default points to their respective providers.

In essence, if RTD chooses, from all defaults, the default that points to its provider, RTD will inject the 0/0 into OSPF. In the same manner, if RTC prefers the default that points to its provider, RTC will inject the 0/0 into OSPF.

With this new model, this is what will happen: in normal operation, the NY link is up. RTD will prefer the external default over any other default. RTD will inject the 0/0 into OSPF. RTC will receive the 0/0 via EBGP, IBGP, and OSPF. RTC will ignore the OSPF default, as mentioned earlier. RTC would prefer the 0/0 coming from RTD via IBGP because of the higher local preference. Because the 0/0 is not learned via RTC's provider, RTC will not inject any default into OSPF.

If the NY link goes down, RTD will lose the 0/0 from its provider. RTD will still receive a 0/0 via IBGP and would not generate a 0/0 into OSPF because the 0/0 was not learned via RTD's provider. RTC will stop receiving the 0/0 via IBGP and will prefer the 0/0 via its provider. RTC will then start injecting the 0/0 into OSPF.

Ch. 11, pp. 405-418. Using OSPF as IGP

Defaults Inside the AS: Other BGP Policies

As you have already seen, loop situations can occur any time if the IGP defaults conflict with the BGP policies. In the primary/backup scenarios, you were able to control which border router should generate the default because you decided in advance which should be the primary router for all traffic external to the AS. In some situations, routing policies might be imposed on your AS by outside factors. In other cases, normal IBGP/EBGP routing will make the exit point from your ASs unspecified, which would conflict with your own defaults.

Consider figure 7–5. AS1 is connected to its provider AS2 in two locations, SF and NY. AS1 is injecting defaults from both its SF router RTC and its NY router RTD in such a way that internal locations will exit from the closest exit point.

Assume also that AS1 is very careful about injecting defaults. The SF router will never inject a default if the SF link is down, and the NY router will never inject a default if the NY link is down. All is well and working great until one day provider AS2 starts advertising metrics (MED) toward AS1.

Figure 7–5
*Policies inflicted
from outside
sources.*

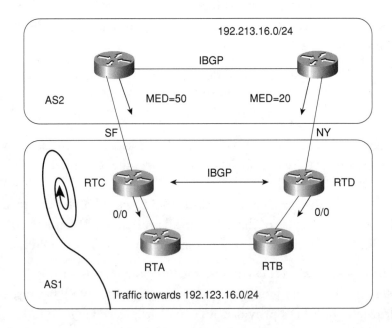

Assume in figure 7–5 that AS2 is sending its updates toward AS1 with the internal IGP metrics as MED. AS1 will receive the same networks on both the SF and NY links with different MED values. For each network, BGP will follow the path with the lowest metric. If, for example, RTC receives network 192.213.16.0/24 with MED 50 on the SF link and MED 20 on the NY link, RTC will prefer the NY link. This would mean that to reach 192.213.16.0/24, RTA might follow the interior default toward RTC and then be instructed to go toward RTD. Similarly, RTB might follow a default toward RTD and then be directed toward RTC. In both cases, a loop will occur.

As you can see, the exit point for all networks cannot be predetermined as in the primary/backup case. To deal with this situation, you have the following options:

- Ignore the MED and base the routing on a primary/backup scenario.

- Have a shorter path connection between RTC and RTD so that traffic redirected between exit points follows the shortest path between the IBGP routers.

- Run an IBGP mesh between, RTA, RTB, RTC, and RTD.

Other normal situations can also cause loops. You could end up in a looping situation whenever you have multiple links and you are running defaults inside the AS. If you are connected to two providers, you might prefer some destinations via one provider and others via the second provider. If your IGP is following defaults, you might end up at the wrong exit point with no way to go back.

As you can see by now, the solution to solve looping problems is to either have the BGP and your IGP be more deterministic about where to exit the AS or prevent traffic between IBGP routers from going back over IGP-only routers. The more you are aware of your traffic behavior, the better you can avoid loop situations.

POLICY ROUTING

Ch. 11, pp.
418-422. Policy
Routing

Policy routing is a means of controlling routes that relies on the source, or source and destination, of traffic rather than destination alone. Policy routing can be used to control traffic inside an AS as well as between ASs. Policy routing is a glorified form of static routing. It is used when you want to force a routing behavior different from what the dynamic routing protocols dictate.

Static routing enables you to direct traffic based on the traffic destination. Traffic toward destination 1 can go via point A whereas traffic toward destination 2 can go via point B.

Policy routing, on the other hand, enables you to direct traffic based on traffic source or a combination of source and destination. Traffic coming from network 1 can go via point A, or traffic coming from network 1 and going toward network 2 can go via point B.

Consider the example illustrated in figure 7–6. Assume that AS1 was assigned network numbers from two different providers. The 10.10.10.0/24 range was taken from AS3, and the 11.11.11.0/24 range was taken from AS4. AS1 wants to have any traffic originated from its 10.10.10.0/24 networks to be directed toward AS3 and traffic from its 11.11.11.0/24 networks to be directed to AS4, irrespective of the destination of the traffic. AS1 could use policy routing to

Figure 7–6
*Policy routing
scenario based on
source.*

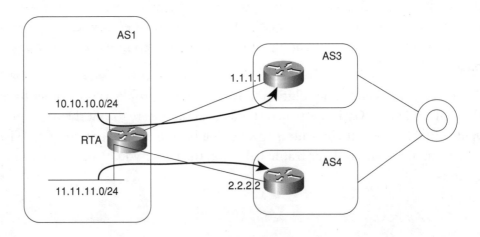

achieve this requirement by forcing all traffic with a source IP address belonging to 10.10.10.0/24 to have a next hop of 1.1.1.1, and traffic with source IP belonging to 11.11.11.0/24 to have a next hop of 2.2.2.2.

Policy routing can also be based on a source/destination combination. This is illustrated in figure 7–7. Assume that RTA wants to use the SF link for any traffic originating from network 10.10.10.0/24 and reaching network 12.12.12.0/24 in NY. Also, RTA wants to use the SJ link for any traffic originating from network 10.10.10.0/24 and reaching network 13.13.13.0/24 in NY. Policy routing can be used to set the next hop for the traffic combination (Source = 10.10.10.0/24, Destination = 12.12.12.0/24) to be 1.1.1.1. The traffic combination (Source = 10.10.10.0/24, Destination = 13.13.13.0/24) will be set with next hop 2.2.2.2.

Whenever static behavior is enforced, backup becomes an issue. It is important to make sure that if policy routed traffic cannot be delivered because the next hop is down, some other alternative is available. Cisco offers a creative way of doing policy routing by offering multiple next hops for policy routed traffic. If the first next hop is down or not available, the second next hop will be tried, and so on. If none of the statically defined next hops are available, the router can be configured to send the traffic according to the normal dynamic routing (that is, based on destination). This is illustrated in figure 7–8.

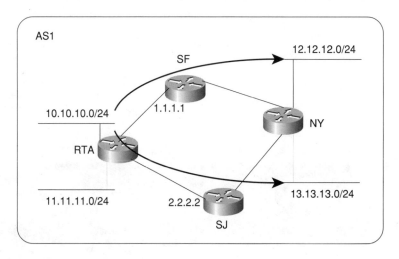

Figure 7–7
*Policy routing
scenario based on
source and
destination.*

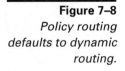

Figure 7–8
Policy routing defaults to dynamic routing.

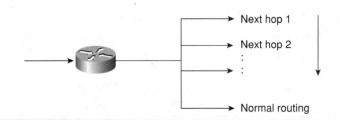

Other Applications of Policy Routing

One practical application of policy routing is its use with *firewalls*. Firewalls are devices that apply security requirements to traffic. Firewall implementations include packet filtering, authentication, and encryption. Depending on the network setup, administrators might want to direct some or all incoming (or outgoing) traffic toward a firewall device (see figure 7–9).

An applicable situation might involve traffic entering an organization through dialup services. Perhaps the organization requires that the dialup users from remote sites pass through a firewall before reaching the Internet. If the firewall is in the traffic trajectory, this is not a problem. Any inbound or outbound traffic will pass through the firewall on its way to a destination. In some cases, however, (such as that shown in figure 7–9), traffic bypasses the firewall in its normal path. Policy routing can be configured on a router bordering external networks, to force the incoming traffic to be directed to the firewall. After the firewall applies its policies or encryption, traffic will be sent to its destination.

Figure 7–9
Incoming or outgoing traffic can be routed to a firewall.

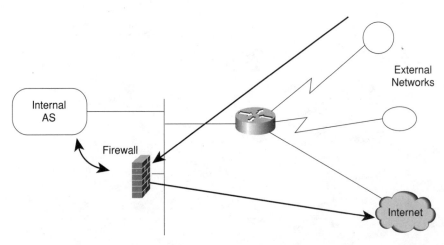

Policy routing does not change the traffic destination. It affects only the next hop to which traffic is directed prior to being sent along toward its destination.

Policy routing can also be used with dialup services for better traffic balancing, as illustrated in figure 7–10. Dialup users accessing a certain point of presence can be directed toward certain providers based on their source IP address. As illustrated in figure 7–10, dialup users in region 1 can be directed toward provider 1, whereas dialup users from region 2 can be directed toward provider 2.

Policy routing should not replace dynamic routing, but instead should complement it. Policy routing has its own set of drawbacks.

1. Extra configuration is needed to identify sources of traffic or a combination of source and destination. Care should be taken not to disrupt other traffic and to specify other alternatives for traffic in case of backup situations.

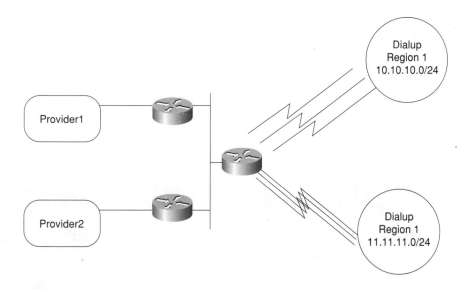

Figure 7–10
Balancing dialup traffic based on source.

2. Policy routing is CPU-intensive because it is based on the source IP addresses, unlike dynamic and static routing, which are based on the destination IP addresses. Sophisticated caching and switching techniques have been implemented all along based on the destination of the traffic. Most implementations have not yet optimized routing and caching techniques based on the source of the IP packet. As such, policy routing takes additional CPU cycles to detect source addresses. This behavior should change as implementations move toward better understanding of IP traffic flows that enable caches to keep track of source and destination information. This new caching methodology would alleviate routers from disruptive processing on matching sources of IP traffic and make policy routing much more effective and practical.

LOOKING AHEAD

Autonomous systems can grow in size beyond administrators' control. Service providers might find themselves with a large internal BGP mesh that is both cumbersome and inefficient to control. On the other hand, enterprise networks might grow in a manner that causes internal gateway protocols to struggle in keeping up with instabilities. Controlling large-scale autonomous systems lies in the art of dividing these large domains into smaller and more manageable entities. The following chapter offers concepts and techniques that can help providers and customers in applying architectural designs to achieve structured routing inside their domains.

FREQUENTLY ASKED QUESTIONS

Q— *I am not running IBGP between my border routers; do I have to worry about routing loops?*

A— As far as the interaction between IGP and BGP, loops cannot occur. If your internal routers are following a default toward the BGP border routers, after the traffic reaches the border router, it has only one way out via the EBGP session.

Q— *I have two BGP border routers running IBGP and connected via a serial link. I am using local preference to control my exit points. What happens if the serial line goes down?*

A— If you are setting BGP policies that cause traffic to be directed between BGP routers, this would be the same scenario as if you do not have a link between the border routers. While the serial line is down, your traffic might end up looping inside the AS.

Q— *If I use a serial link between my IBGP border routers to direct traffic from one router to the other, should that link be as fast as my links to my providers?*

A— The only traffic that line will carry is outbound traffic that is redirected between border routers and a portion of incoming traffic. Try to figure out what percentage of your total traffic that constitutes to estimate the appropriate link bandwidth.

Q— *I need to direct traffic toward destination X over my serial line and toward destination Y over my Ethernet line. Can I do that via policy routing?*

A— What you have just described can be done via static routing, which works based on the basis of destination. There is no need for policy routing, which works on the basis of source or source and destination combined.

Q— *Do I apply policy routing over my outbound or inbound router interface?*

A— Policy routing checks source addresses coming into an interface. Configure on the inbound interface.

THIS CHAPTER COVERS THE FOLLOWING KEY TOPICS:

- **Route Reflectors**

  A method of managing expanding mesh requirements in large ASs by using selected routers as focal points for internal BGP sessions

- **Confederations**

  A method of managing expanding mesh requirements in large ASs by creating sub-ASs

- **Controlling IGP Expansion**

  Methods of managing networks in which expansion is characterized by the use of multiple IGPs

- **Virtual Private Networks with Route Reflectors**

  A method of developing restricted network access, within an AS, using route reflectors

CHAPTER ■ 8

Controlling Large-Scale Autonomous Systems

Autonomous systems consisting of hundreds of routing nodes can pose a serious routing management problem for network administrators. Service providers and customers each have their own set of problems when dealing with large networks. On the service provider side, the majority of routers run BGP. The IBGP mesh will grow beyond the provider's control. On the customer side, however, the majority of routers run IGPs, which also may grow beyond the customer's control.

This chapter discusses methods and techniques that can be used to better control the deployment of BGP and IGPs inside large autonomous systems. There are no absolute rules that say a provider or customer should or should not use one of the methods discussed in this chapter, or which method to prefer. Keep in mind that any new technique brings with it its own complexities. Imposing complex techniques on situations that do not really need them could hurt more than help.

ROUTE REFLECTORS

In some ISP networks, the internal BGP mesh becomes quite large (more than 100 internal BGP sessions per router), which strongly suggests that some new peering mechanism be implemented. The *route reflector* [1] concept is based on the idea of specifying a *concentration* router to act as a focal point for internal BGP sessions. Multiple BGP routers can peer with a central point (the route reflector), and then multiple route reflectors peer together.

Ch. 11, pp. 422-426. Route Reflectors

Route reflectors are only recommended for ASs with a large internal BGP mesh, on the order of more than 100 sessions per router. The route reflector concept introduces processing overhead on the concentration router and, if configured incorrectly, can cause routing loops and routing instability. As a result, route reflectors are not recommended for every topology. If it can be tolerated, a full mesh is the better solution.

Internal Peers Without Route Reflectors

Without route reflectors, BGP speakers in an AS will have to be fully meshed. We have already discussed this behavior in this book; the following illustration is just a reminder. In figure 8–1, RTA, RTB, and RTC form an internal BGP full mesh. Each router acts as a BGP peer with the other two routers. RTA and RTB are physically connected, as are RTB and RTC. No physical connection exists between RTA and RTC.

Figure 8–1
Internal peers in mesh environment.

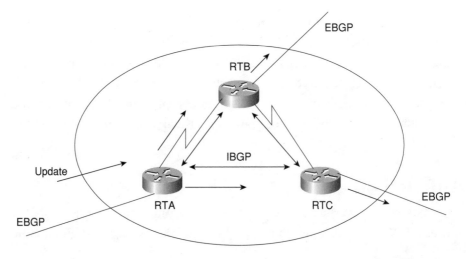

RTA gets an update from an external peer and will pass it on to its two internal peers, RTB and RTC. Note that even though there is no physical connectivity between RTA and RTC, RTA will manage to pass the update to RTC via the BGP peering session. RTB and RTC, in turn, will pass on the update to their external peers.

RTB will not pass on the update to RTC, because RTC is an internal peer and the update received by RTB also comes from an internal peer. Without the internal BGP session between RTA and RTC, RTC would never get the update; hence, the full mesh is necessary.

Internal Peers with Route Reflectors

The route reflector acts as a concentration point for other routers called *clients*. The clients peer with the route reflector and exchange routing information with it. In turn, the route reflector will pass on (reflect) the information between clients.

In figure 8–2, RTA gets an update from an external peer and passes it on to RTB. RTB is configured as a route reflector with two clients, RTA and RTC.

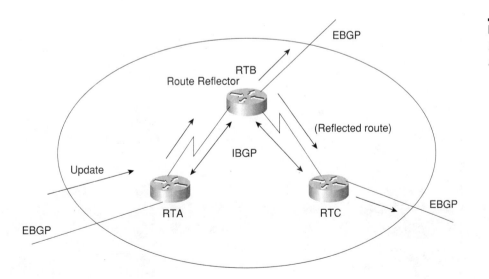

Figure 8–2
Internal peers using a route reflector.

RTB will reflect the update from client RTA to client RTC. In this configuration, a peering session between RTA and RTC is not really needed because the route reflector is propagating the BGP information to RTC.

In an AS where routers have to build BGP sessions with too many other routers, the route reflector concept becomes very helpful and very scalable.

Naming Conventions and Rules of Operation

The route reflector is a router that can perform the route reflection function. The IBGP peers of the route reflector fall under two categories, *clients* and *non-clients*. A route reflector and its clients form a *cluster*. All peers of the route reflector that are not part of the cluster are non-clients. Figure 8–3 illustrates these components.

Non-clients must be fully meshed with the route reflector and each other because they follow the basic rules of the IBGP mesh. Clients should not peer with internal speakers outside their associated cluster. As you can see, these conditions have been met for the clients and non-clients in figure 8–3.

The route reflector function is implemented only on the route reflector; all clients and non-clients are normal BGP peers that have no notion of the route

Figure 8–3
Route reflection process components.

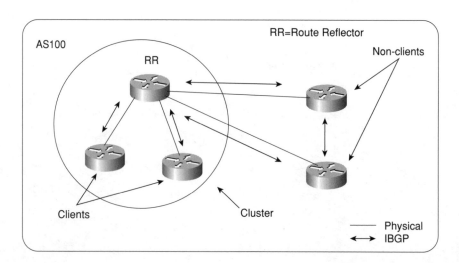

reflector. Clients are only considered as such because the route reflector lists them as clients.

Any route reflector that receives multiple routes for the same destination will pick the best path based on the usual BGP decision process.The best path would be propagated inside the AS based on the following rules of operation (propagation to EBGP runs as usual):

- If the route is received from a non-client peer, reflect to clients only.

- If the route is received from a client peer, reflect to all non-client peers and also to client peers, except the originator of the route.

- If the route is received from an EBGP peer, reflect to all client and non-client peers.

Redundancy Issues and Multiple Route Reflectors in an AS

With the lack of a full BGP mesh inside the AS, redundancy and reliability become issues. If a route reflector fails, clients will be isolated. Redundancy requires the existence of multiple route reflectors in an AS where clients can simultaneously peer with multiple routers. If one peer connection fails, the other will back it up.

The importance of complementing logical redundancy with physical redundancy cannot be overstated. It does not make sense to build route reflector redundancy if the physical redundancy itself does not exist.The logical redundancy arrangement on the left in figure 8–4 shows RTA as the client of both RR1 and RR2. RTA is peering with both route reflectors in an effort to create a redundant link. Unfortunately, if the connection to RR1 is broken, or if RR1 itself fails, RTA is isolated. The logical connectivity between RTA and RR2 is of no practical use and is simply more memory and processing overhead.

The physical redundancy configuration on the right in figure 8–4 illustrates how logical redundancy can be backed up with physical redundancy. In the event of a failure in the link to RR1, RTA can reach RR2.

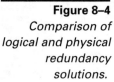

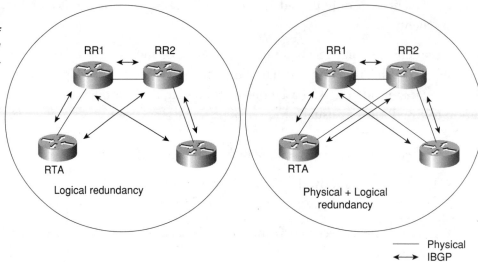

The Big Picture

National networks are usually laid out in concentration points per geographical regions. Providers have POPs (sometimes called *hubs*) in different regions in the U.S. with high-speed DS3 or OC3/OC12 links connecting different locations in a partially meshed topology. The route reflector concept can be used to logically interconnect the routers running BGP in a pattern that follows the physical connectivity. Figure 8–5 illustrates a complex arrangement featuring route reflectors (indicated as RR in this figure and those that follow).

Except for the fact that the route reflector needs to keep up with more BGP sessions than normal routers, any router could be configured as a route reflector. Your physical topology should be the main indicator of which is the best router to choose to be the route reflector.

In figure 8–5, AS100 is divided into three clusters: San Francisco, Dallas, and New York. The Dallas cluster has multiple RRs for redundancy. RTA and RTD physically connect San Francisco to New York. It makes sense to follow the

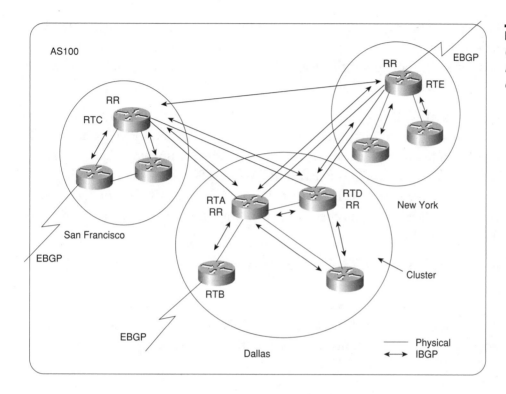

Figure 8–5
Complex multiple route reflector environment.

actual physical traffic flow in selecting RRs, so RTA and RTD are the obvious choices for RRs in the Dallas cluster.

In San Francisco, router RTC physically connects San Francisco to Dallas, so RTC would be the best candidate to become a RR. The same reasoning applies for the New York cluster: RTE physically connects New York to Dallas and is the best candidate for RR.

The Route Reflector Preserves IBGP Attributes

The route reflector concept does not change the IBGP behavior. The route reflector is not allowed to change the attributes of the reflected IBGP routes. The next hop attribute, for example, remains the same when exchanged between RRs. This is necessary for avoiding loops in the AS.

Figure 8–6 illustrates why the RR should not modify the attributes of the IBGP reflected routes. The next hop attribute is used as an example. Figure 8–6 focuses on the portion of the network from figure 8–5 where Dallas connects to San Francisco.

Assume that RTB is specified as the route reflector, rather than RTA, and that an IBGP session is configured between RTB (2.2.2.2) and RTC (1.1.1.1). This looks odd because physically RTA is passing the traffic, while logically RTB is reflecting the BGP updates between RTA and RTC. RTB will receive the prefix 192.213.11.0/24 from its IBGP neighbor RTC with a next hop of 1.1.1.1. RTB will reflect the route to its client RTA with the next hop 1.1.1.1 also. This is the desired behavior.

Alternatively, if RTB were to change the next hop to its IP address, 2.2.2.2, RTA would try to use RTB to reach destination 192.213.11.0/24. A loop would occur between RTA and RTB, with RTA sending the traffic to RTB, and RTB trying to use RTA to reach the final destination. This hypothetical situation exemplifies why the route reflector must not change IBGP behavior and attributes.

Figure 8–6
The route reflector preserves IBGP attributes.

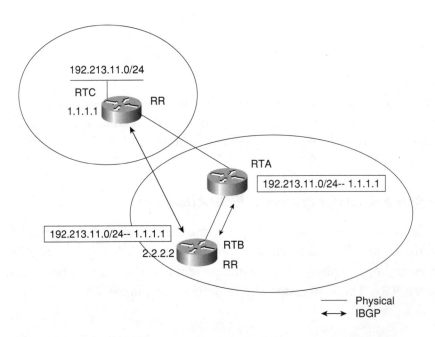

Avoiding Loops

When dealing with the possibility of routing updates making their way back into an AS, BGP relies on the information in the AS_path for loop detection. An update that tries to make its way back into the AS it was originated from will be dropped by the border router.

With the introduction of route reflectors, there is a potential for having routing loops within an AS. A routing update that leaves a cluster might find its way back inside the cluster. Loops inside the AS cannot be detected by the traditional AS_path approach because the routing updates have not left the AS yet. BGP offers two extra measures for loop avoidance inside an AS when route reflectors are configured.

Using an Originator ID

The *originator ID* is a 4-byte, optional, nontransitive BGP attribute (type code 9) that is created by the route reflector. This attribute carries the router ID of the originator of the route in the local AS. If, because of poor configuration, the update comes back to the originator, the originator ignores it.

⚠ TROUBLESHOOTING

Using originator IDs and cluster lists to avoid loops in ASs using route reflectors.

Using a Cluster List

The *cluster list* is an optional, nontransitive BGP attribute (type code 10). Each cluster is represented with a cluster ID.

A cluster list is a sequence of cluster IDs that an update has traversed. When a route reflector sends a route from its clients to nonclients outside the cluster, it appends the local cluster ID to the cluster list. If the route reflector receives an update whose cluster list contains the local cluster ID, the update is ignored. This is basically the same concept as the AS_path list applied between the clusters inside the AS.

Route Reflectors and Peer Groups

Recall from Chapter 5, "Tuning BGP Capabilities," that a peer group is a group of BGP neighbors that shares the same routing policies. Route reflectors can be used in conjunction with peer groups only when the clients of a route reflector are fully meshed. The reasoning is as follows: in a normal situation, a router A that learns a prefix from a router B will send a WITHDRAWN message back to that router to poison that route. In other words, router A is telling B that this prefix is not reachable via A. This is to prevent a situation where A claims that a prefix is reachable via B, and B claims it is reachable via A. In a peer group, the same UPDATE or WITHDRAWN message is sent to all members of the group. In a peer group/route reflector situation, a route reflector that has learned a prefix from one of the clients and is trying to poison that route will end up withdrawing that prefix from all the other clients. Because the clients are not talking to one another via BGP, that prefix will be lost. That is why an IBGP mesh between the clients is needed for the other clients to learn that prefix directly from the source. Even with this design, the network administrator is still avoiding a full IBGP mesh between all IBGP routers in the AS and concentrating the mesh between route reflectors and clients.

With the use of peer groups, the AS design would look like rings of fully meshed BGP speakers. Route reflectors are fully meshed among each other, and clients of each route reflector are also fully meshed. Figure 8–7 illustrates such an environment; each circled area represents a distinct peer group.

Figure 8–7
Route reflectors and peer groups.

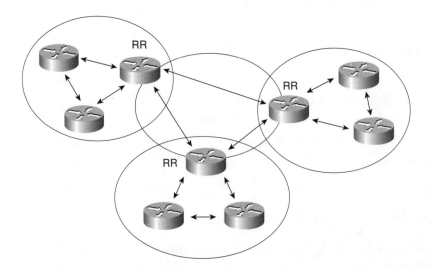

In conclusion, the route reflector concept is growing in popularity for large networks due to the fact that it is a simple approach that enables scalability without too much overhead. Migrating from a non-route reflector to a route reflector design is easy because only the route reflectors need to be modified to behave as route reflectors; all other routers would be running as usual. Routers that do not implement the route reflector behavior could be part of the AS without any loss of BGP routing information.

CONFEDERATIONS

Confederation [2] is another way to deal with the explosion of an IBGP mesh within an AS. As with route reflection, confederation is recommended only for cases in which the IBGP peering exceeds about 100 peering sessions per router.

Ch. 11, pp. 426-432. Confederations

Confederation is based on the concept that an AS can be broken into multiple sub-ASs. Inside each sub-AS, all the rules of IBGP apply. All BGP routers inside the sub-AS, for example, must be fully meshed. Because the sub-ASs each have a different AS number, external BGP must run between them. Even though EBGP is used between sub-ASs, routing inside the confederation behaves like IBGP routing in a single AS. In other words, the next hop, MED, and local preference information is preserved when crossing the sub-AS boundaries. To the outside world, a confederation looks like a single AS. Figure 8–8 illustrates an example of a confederation.

In figure 8–8, AS100 is split into two sub-ASs: AS65050 and AS65060. The AS as a whole is now one large confederation, identified by a single confederation number, 100. All the sub-ASs are shielded from the outside world and can be given any AS numbers. The numbers could be chosen from the private AS list in order not to use up any formal AS numbers.

IBGP full mesh is used within the sub-ASs, and EBGP is used between the sub-ASs, as well as between the confederation itself and outside ASs. Confederations can easily detect routing loops inside the AS because EBGP is run between sub-ASs. The AS_path list is used to detect routing updates that leave

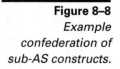

Figure 8–8
*Example
confederation of
sub-AS constructs.*

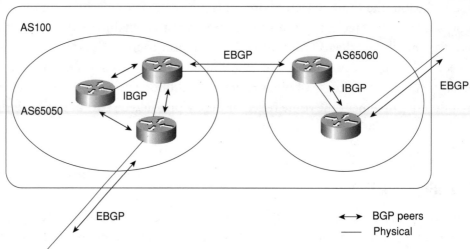

a sub-AS and try to reenter the same sub-AS. A routing update that tries to reenter a sub-AS it originated from will be detected because the sub-AS will see its own sub-AS number listed in the AS_path of the update.

The drawback with confederations is that migration from a nonconfederation to a confederation design requires major reconfiguration of the routers and a major change in the logical topology. In addition, routing through a confederation might not take an optimal path without manually setting BGP policies. Figure 8–9 illustrates this issue.

Confederation 100 is composed of three sub-ASs: 65010, 65020, and 65030. The AS_path within confederation 100 is represented by the sequence of ASs the route has traversed all considered to be the same length, which would introduce routing suboptimality inside the AS. From the point of view of sub-AS 65030, AS_path (65010) is the same length as AS_path (65020 65010); traffic inside the confederation may take either path. Additional policies would have to be set to affect routing behavior. Local preference, for example, can be configured to make AS_path (65010) preferred over (65020 65010).

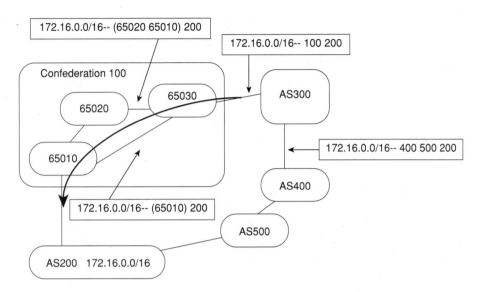

Figure 8–9
AS confederation internal and external routing.

For external ASs, the confederation is a single AS, and the route taken inside the confederation is not known. This is misleading for ASs that base their routing policies on the AS_path length. To reach AS200, AS300 will most likely prefer to go via confederation 100 because the path looks shorter than the path via AS400 and AS500. In actuality, of course, confederation 100 is not the shortest path because it includes a path via three ASs, whereas the alternative (AS400 AS500) only includes two. AS300 will never know of this pitfall unless the AS100 confederation design is disclosed.

Even though routes are exchanged between sub-ASs via EBGP, all the IBGP rules still apply to have the whole AS behave as a single entity. The EBGP next hop is still carried within the AS as well as the metric and local preference values.

As far as the BGP decision algorithm, the only changes are in the way BGP routes to outside the confederation compared to how BGP routes inside the confederation. Without confederations, EBGP routes are preferred over IBGP routes. With confederations, we have introduced new types of EBGP route between the sub-ASs, called a *confederation external route*. BGP prefers routes in the following manner: EBGP routes to outside the confederation > confederation exterior routes > IBGP routes. This means if BGP has a choice between two paths to the same destination, one outside the confederation and one inside, BGP will pick the exterior path. If BGP has a choice between two paths to the same destination—one inside the sub-AS and one outside the sub-AS—BGP will pick the one exterior to the sub-AS. This is, of course, assuming that all other attributes are the same.

Recommended Confederation Design

Choosing and connecting the sub-ASs randomly inside the confederation will lead to problems. Unnecessary processing will occur because each sub-AS will end up getting similar information from other sub-ASs. Besides, suboptimality will be introduced due to the fact that all paths inside the AS have exactly the same length, as already discussed.

Experience shows that a centralized confederation design leads to the best behavior. Centralized design means that all sub-ASs will exchange information with each other via a central sub-AS backbone.

With the example illustrated in figure 8–10, each sub-AS will have interaction with only one other sub-AS, and routing will be more uniform as far as path length and route exchange within the confederation.

Figure 8–10
Centralizing confederation.

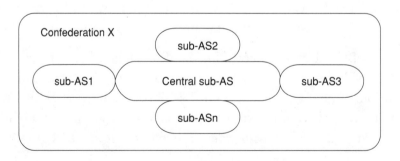

Confederations or Route Reflectors

Determining whether you should use route reflectors or confederations is not a simple decision. Different organizations have experienced different levels of stability with either approach. Cisco recommends the use of the route reflector technique to solve the IBGP mesh issues. Route reflectors have proven to be more flexible to deploy. On the other hand, confederations could be used to run an IGP in one sub-AS independently of IGPs in other sub-ASs, which would help in controlling the instabilities of large IGPs.

In some situations, both approaches, route reflectors and confederations, can be used in conjunction with each other. An AS can be divided into sub-ASs that are running route reflectors.

Whichever approach you use, you should always understand the restrictions and behavior of each method and design your network accordingly.

CONTROLLING IGP EXPANSION

One of the ways in which administrators push their networks to the limit is by letting them grow in size in such a way that the IGP will be hard to manage. Whether the IGP is as outdated as RIP version 1 or as advanced as OSPF and ISIS, the issue of scalability will arise. So far, this chapter has discussed route reflectors and confederations as ways of managing IBGP growth. A scalable way of managing IGP expansion is to segment the AS into multiple regions, each running a single, distinct IGP. The individual regions, in turn, must be connected via BGP. With this design, the stability of one region would not affect the stability of another.

What criteria should network designers and architects follow in deciding whether their networks need segmentation? One thing is for sure: the Internet is one huge network that cannot be handled by running an IGP, and that is why it is segmented by BGP.

So what constitutes a large or small network? Is it the number of routers or the number of routes, and if so, what number? You will hear different answers based on different administrators' experiences. The general answer to this question depends mainly on how robust the IGP, what tools it can offer to control the route explosion and instability, and whether BGP segmentation represents a more beneficial, less costly (in dollars and effort) method than relying on the IGP's tools.

Protocols such as OSPF and ISIS offer certain hierarchical methods that can control route instabilities and provide means for route summarization. But even with these methods, the IGP can grow beyond control. A working guideline for today's networks is that IP routing tables having 2,000 to 3,000 IGP interior routes may have reached a limit and need a closer look to make sure that they do not grow further. It is not the number of routes that cause problems, because BGP transit routers today are carrying more than 42,000 Internet routes with no problem. What causes problems is situations, such as hardware and access line instabilities, where these routes end up bouncing and trying to converge, causing what is known as a network "meltdown."

Does this mean that networks with 3,000 IGP routes need to be segmented via BGP? The answer is, not necessarily. In most cases, a redesign of the IGP itself with more emphasis on using the IGP segmentation and summarization techniques can bring down the number of routes to a manageable level.

To understand why the decision to control growth with BGP segmentation should be approached with caution, you need to understand what is compromised when ASs are segmented. The main strength of IGPs, especially IGPs based on Link State protocols, has always been convergence; that is, their capability to quickly adapt to network changes. Another strength is their capability to develop a level of redundancy and load balancing.

BGP, on the other hand, was created to implement policies across AS boundaries, with no major emphasis on convergence. When segmenting with BGP, convergence will be enhanced within the newly created smaller segments, but might diminish when crossing sub-AS boundaries because of the dependency of BGP on TCP sessions to carry routing updates.

Another drawback is the additional user intervention needed to control and manage the BGP policies that are automatically imposed on the routing behavior. As you have seen in this book, attribute manipulation is so far the only tool to manipulate routing behaviors. With the introduction of more ASs, what used to be simple IGP routing is no longer the case. Understanding all these issues will help designers develop a realistic approach to designing their networks.

This section discusses two methods of segmenting the AS:

- Multiple regions separated by IBGP
- Multiple regions separated by EBGP

Multiple Regions Separated by IBGP

The AS can be divided into multiple regions, each running different and independent IGPs. Regions will be logically interconnected via a full IBGP mesh. For better redundancy, regions could also be physically interconnected in a fully meshed topology. This is illustrated in figure 8–11.

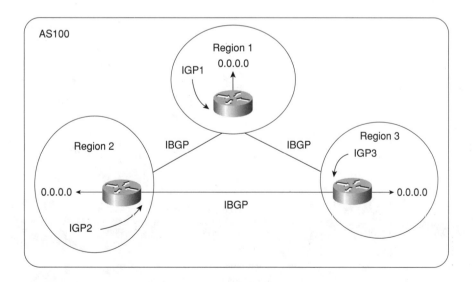

Figure 8–11
Multiple regions via IBGP.

Each region will inject its IGP routes into IBGP and would inject a default route inside the region. As a result, each region will default to the BGP border router for destinations that do not belong to the region. Border routers will carry all routes from all regions (exchanged via IBGP) and will be able to direct the traffic accordingly. Each region will be totally shielded from the instabilities of all the other regions because the internal non-BGP routers are only exposed to the routes in their respective region. In case there is need for a dynamic routing protocol to be run on top of the IBGP mesh for reachabilty between peers, a separate IGP can be used.

This design is still missing one important piece: Internet connectivity. Connecting to the Internet in this scenario needs further planning. As you can see in figure 8–11, each region is already following defaults to reach other regions. If the connection point to the Internet falls behind the BGP border router (inside the region), internal non-BGP routers will have to decide between the default to the Internet or the default to other regions. This is illustrated in figure 8–12.

To remedy this situation, all regions should always point to the BGP border router for default, whether reaching the Internet or other regions. This would

Figure 8–12
*Multiple conflicting
defaults.*

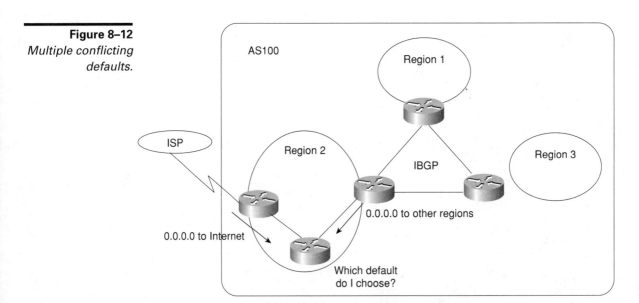

require the Internet connections to be part of the central IBGP mesh, as illustrated in figure 8–13.

Regions 1, 2, and 3 are interconnected via an IBGP mesh, which also provides Internet connectivity. Internal non-BGP routers in each region will default to the BGP border router, which contains all routes. If the destination belongs to any other region, the traffic will be directed to that region. Otherwise, the traffic will be sent to the Internet connections according to BGP policies.

This method does not have the flexibility for setting policies for each region. All regions run under the same autonomous system and cannot be easily differentiated from each other by BGP. More complex designs could utilize the "community" attribute to differentiate between regions. This could be used in conjuction with a route reflector hierarchy to create large, virtual, private networks, as you will see at the end of this chapter.

Multiple Regions Separated by EBGP

If multiple policies need to be set between regions, each region can be represented as a separate autonomous system. EBGP is run between ASs and IBGP is run within each AS. If there is a need for a dynamic routing protocol to be

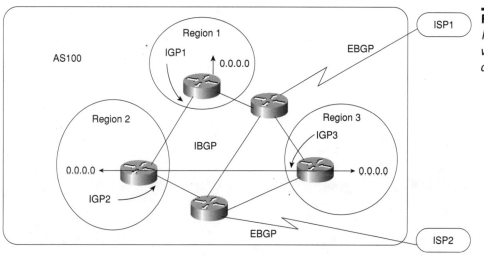

Figure 8–13
Multiple regions with Internet connectivity.

run for reachability between EBGP peers, a separate IGP can be used. This is illustrated in figure 8–14.

This seems to be the ideal solution for connectivity. Your AS is now divided into multiple ASs, with each region represented by a separate AS number and having a preferred connection to the Internet. Each AS will inject its IGP routes into BGP to be propagated to all other regions and the Internet. Internal non-BGP routers in each region will default to the BGP routers, which contain all routes. BGP policies using local preference can be set so that BGP routers prefer the interior company links for communications between regions instead of going via the Internet for interregional connectivity. Each region will prefer its own provider for Internet connectivity; if the link to the provider fails, other providers from other regions can be used.

This design looks good on paper until you try to implement it. You will realize that registering AS numbers from the InterNIC is very difficult. AS numbers are limited and could easily be depleted if misued. Good justification is needed before you receive multiple AS numbers. Getting multiple ASs for better IGP stability is usually not a good enough justification.

Figure 8–14
Multiple regions separated by EBGP.

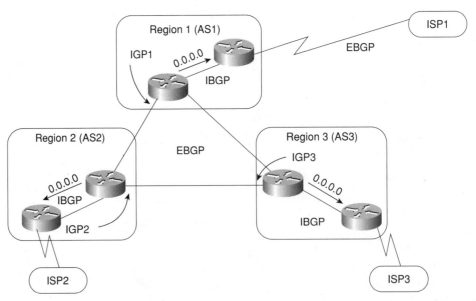

Using Private AS Numbers

Using private AS numbers is another way to divide a large AS into multiple regions connected by EBGP. Regions will be running IBGP internally and inter-connected via EBGP. Each IGP will be injected into BGP for interregional connectivity. Internal non-BGP routers in each region will default to the BGP routers, which contain all routes. In case a dynamic protocol is needed for the EBGP peering connectivity, a separate IGP can be run on top of EBGP.

This works well without Internet connectivity. To connect to the Internet, the private AS numbers should somehow be shielded from the outside world. This would require a more involved design. Figure 8–15 illustrates a method that can be used to remedy the situation of private ASs with Internet connectivity.

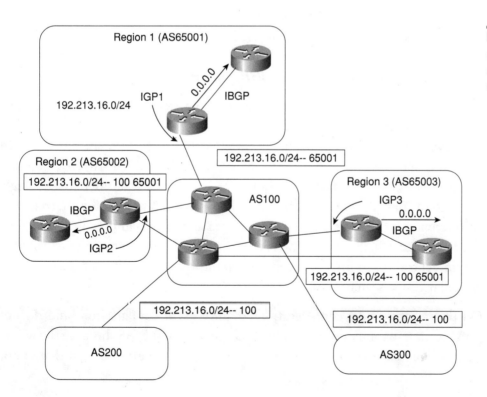

Figure 8–15
Private ASs in a multiprovider environment.

Figure 8–15 shows an AS that is broken into multiple private sub-ASs. Region 1 is now AS65001, region 2 is AS65002, and region 3 is AS65003. Different mutually exclusive IGPs are running in each private AS.

To provide multiple provider connectivity, AS100 is introduced as an interconnection point between all private ASs. Note that this central AS has a legal AS number. All private ASs would EBGP peer with the central AS100 for interregional and Internet connectivity.

To prevent private AS numbers from leaking to the providers, the AS_path stripping technique discussed in Chapter 5 can be used. AS100 will strip the private AS numbers before propagating the BGP updates to the Internet providers.

In figure 8–15, AS65001 is originating prefix 192.213.16.0/24. To all other private ASs, this prefix is seen with AS_path 100 65001. When the prefix gets propagated to AS200 and AS300, the private AS number will be stripped, and the remaining AS_path would be 100. To the Internet, all your networks will be advertised as if they originated from AS100.

Using Confederation to Control IGP Expansion

Confederations can also be used to control the expansion of IGPs. You have already seen how a confederation can divide the AS into multiple smaller sub-ASs. If each sub-AS is running a different IGP, then the centralized design described in figure 8–10 would be a viable approach. The IGPs are now running independently of one another, and the whole AS is still considered as a single entity to the outside world. Each IGP will be injected into BGP for interregional connectivity. Internal non-BGP routers in each region will default to the BGP border router, which contains all routes. Internet connectivity can be provided via the central AS to provide a central default for all the different regions. This is similar to the scenario in figure 8–15.

On the negative side, confederations require extra configuration and do not provide the capability of setting policies between the sub-ASs because the whole AS is still considered one entity. Besides, any confederation design that is not centralized could introduce further complications in route optimality inside the confederation.

VIRTUAL PRIVATE NETWORKS WITH ROUTE REFLECTORS

Virtual Private Networks (VPNs) are private networks in the sense that they require traffic exchange within their network boundaries and no access to or from other networks that are not part of the VPN. Providers and large enterprises are faced every day with the challenges of private data exchange. A large organization with different geographic locations, for example, serviced by a large provider, may want to restrict which regions can exchange traffic with each other. It is then the provider's duty to provide this level of privacy. Similarly, an enterprise that is a collection of smaller business units might want to implement data exchange restrictions between the units. So far, the only way to achieve this behavior is via packet filters and traffic pipes (tunnels), which protect information from being exchanged between private entities. This section attempts to find a solution to this problem using a route reflector hierarchical concept.

We will conceptualize a large AS, as shown in figure 8–16, as consisting of three hierarchical levels: customers (Level 3), distribution (Level 2), and core (Level 1). Customer, in this sense, means a unit or region that has the same data access and restriction criteria. Each distinct group of customers is served by a distinct Virtual Private Network. Figure 8–16 contains two such VPNs, VPN1 and VPN2.

Level 3 (L3), the customer level, is following a 0/0 default toward Level 2 (L2), the distribution level. At the customer level, the only routes exchanged are the ones generated locally. To reach other parts of the VPN, the customer will send its traffic toward the distribution level. The customer router is announcing its routes toward the distribution routers (L2) with a specific BGP community that is representative of its particular VPN. In figure 8–16, VPN1 is announcing its routes with a community C1, whereas VPN2 is announcing its routes with a community C2.

Figure 8–16
*Route reflector
hierarchy.*

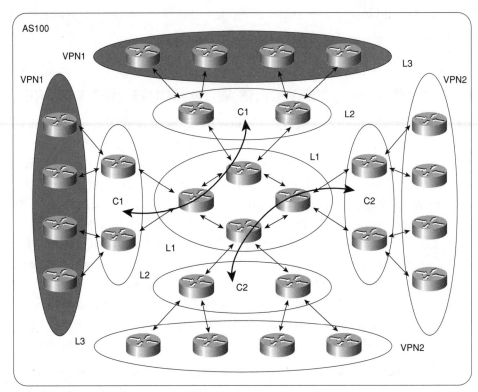

At Level 2, the distribution routers will receive the routing updates and will propagate (reflect) them to Level 1, the core routers. As such, the core routers will have all the VPN routes tagged with the VPN community. The core routers in turn will advertise these routes only to the distribution that can service a particular VPN. That means a distribution router that is servicing VPN1 will receive only routes that belong to VPN1. The distribution routers of VPN1 will not carry any routes of the other VPNs.

To understand the outcome of this design, consider two cases. In the first case, a customer in VPN1 is trying to access another customer in VPN1. In the second case, a customer in VPN1 is trying to access a customer not in VPN1.

In the first case, if the destination is within Level 3, the customer router would have the specific route in its routing table. If the destination is not in Level 3, the customer has no choice but to follow a 0/0 default toward Level 2. At Level 2, because the distribution router has knowledge of all VPN1 routes via the core, the distribution router will forward the traffic toward the core router. At the core, all destinations are known, and the traffic will be delivered to its destination in VPN1.

In the second case, the customer of VPN1 is trying to access a destination not inside VPN1. The traffic will follow the 0/0 default toward Level 2. At the distribution level, the routers have no knowledge of any destinations other than VPN1, and the traffic will be dropped. This will preserve the private aspects of the VPNs.

It is important to note, in this scenario, that the service provider is not providing global connectivity (Internet connectivity), but rather connectivity just among the different components of the organization (intranet connectivity). In fact, in this route reflector approach to servicing VPNs, Internet connectivity for the VPNs cannot be achieved. This is because Level 3 has to follow defaults toward the distribution and cannot follow a default toward the Internet. In addition, if Internet connectivity were provided on the distribution level, then customer traffic toward a different VPN could be rerouted to that VPN via the Internet, which defeats the purpose of VPNs. Finally, if Internet connectivity were provided via the core, then customer traffic would not be able to reach the Internet because the traffic will be dropped at the distribution router, which would not have the route in its routing table.

Given that private networks are supposed to be private, Internet connectivity might not be a requirement. For an organization that wants both VPNs and Internet connectivity, a method other than this specific hierarchical route reflector approach must be used.

LOOKING AHEAD

You have seen so far how BGP can be a powerful tool in giving routing a more structured look. You have learned how to manipulate traffic and how to segment the AS into more controlled elements. One more aspect that needs discussion is route instabilities on the Internet. Many factors induce route fluctuations and, in turn, traffic fluctuations. Some of these elements can be avoided and some are beyond your control. The Internet has become a necessity for everyday operations; it is in your best interest to respect and protect its integrity. The following chapter discusses the causes of route instability and some of the measures taken to stop or at least dampen its effect.

FREQUENTLY ASKED QUESTIONS

Q— *I have a SF hub and a SJ hub. Do you think it is better to separate them into different ASs and run BGP instead of running an IGP in between?*

A— This doesn't sound like a candidate for segmentation via BGP. Remember that even though segmentation gives better hierarchy and control, it introduces more routing policies dictated by the BGP behavior. In small networks such as yours, you could achieve the same stability by running an IGP.

Q— *I do not have enough BGP peers to justify using route reflectors. What happens if I use them anyway?*

A— You will achieve normal routing. You just need to understand that with this model, you rely on centralized routers for running BGP sessions. The RR has to do more processing, and it becomes a single point of failure. Hence, you have to do more provisioning for redundancy. You also will have to deal with other issues such as peer groups and attribute modification, as described in this chapter. If you think that the overhead is not an issue, configuring RRs is no problem.

Q— *With confederations, an EBGP external route is more preferred than a confederation external route. Does that mean that I can never use another sub-AS as an exit point?*

A— No. You could always use attributes such as local preference to prefer whichever exit point you want.

Q— *Because local preference is not passed between ASs, it won't be passed between sub-ASs inside a confederation, correct?*

A— That is not true. Using additional configuration, the sub-AS will know that it is talking to an external peer inside a confederation and will maintain all attributes that are normally maintained by IBGP.

Q— *I need to configure route reflectors, but the current software on my routers does not support it. Do I need to upgrade all my routers at the same time?*

A— No. You only need to upgrade the routers that will become RRs. Other routers will behave as any conventional IBGP speaker. This will help you migrate your network to the new design in a structured way.

REFERENCES

[1] RFC 1966 BGP Route Reflection an Alternative to Full Mesh IBGP

[2] RFC 1965 Autonomous System Confederations for BGP

CHAPTER 9

Designing Stable Internets

Establishing and maintaining route stability within and among networks is crucial to ensuring reliable Internet connectivity. A number of design flaws and problems can contribute to destabilizing connections to the Internet. This chapter explores some of the causes of route instability and techniques for reducing it.

ROUTE INSTABILITIES ON THE INTERNET

The central symptom of route instability is the disappearance of a route that previously existed in the routing table. This route might disappear and reappear intermittently, a condition sometimes referred to as *flapping*. What is happening at the routing protocol level is that BGP sends a routing update and then immediately withdraws it. A router that receives UPDATE or WITHDRAWN messages would have to propagate those messages to its peers. If this behavior continues to cascade, routing performance suffers.

Factors that affect route instabilities on the Internet include the following influences:

- Instabilities of IGPs
- Hardware Failures
- Software Problems
- Insufficient Horsepower
- Insufficient Memory
- Network Upgrades
- Human Error
- Backup Link Overloads

Instabilities of IGPs

Dynamically injecting IGPs into BGP can cause unnecessary route flapping. Problems that occur inside a domain can translate into problems outside the domain. As already discussed in Chapter 5, "Tuning BGP Capabilities," static injection of routing into BGP can solve this problem.

Route aggregation at the border routers can also reduce the potential unpleasant side effects associated with IGP injection into BGP. With aggregation, multiple route entries get injected into BGP as a summary aggregate. A route instability in any one element of the aggregate does not affect the stability of the aggregate itself.

Still, some network designers are forced to rely on dynamic routing for valid reasons:

- BGP implementations can only handle a fixed number of network entries to be advertised statically. The number of static routes permitted varies from vendor to vendor. Whatever that limit is, networks that want to go beyond this limit require that administrators inject the IGP into BGP.

- Some administrators are not too comfortable with the fact that the networks they are statically advertising might become unreachable by the router advertising them. This is understandable, especially in cases where routes are advertised from different points of the AS. Advertising a route that is not reachable can create black holes.

Hardware Failures

Faulty interfaces, faulty systems, or faulty lines can all affect route stability. An interface that is intermittently available might cause routing information to transition. Hardware failures are, to a certain degree, beyond the control of service users. System and link redundancy are important tools for reducing connectivity loss due to failures, but when a physical failure occurs, routing will be interrupted, and any interruption will initiate some kind of cascade effect down the routing path.

Software Problems

Software problems or "bugs" can cause system failures and network instabilities. Development teams try their best to catch these problems before the software is released to customers. Nevertheless, it is almost impossible to forsee every single situation that might occur in live networks. Administrators should experiment with new software or new features in test labs and low impact portions of their network in order to get some level of confidence before the software is fully deployed.

Insufficient Horsepower

The more routing updates and peering sessions the router handles, the more CPU power is required. Think of the router as your basic 4x4 truck, and think of the routing and traffic overhead as the load you carry. Would you be surprised if the truck has trouble moving with a 20-ton load? Picking the correct system with the correct CPU power is very important to satisfy your particular routing needs.

At the initial stages of building BGP tables after the BGP sessions are established, a system's processor can spend more than 90 percent of its time processing updates. When links become unstable and overloaded, the router might end up in a race condition: the CPU is too busy handling updates, which causes BGP sessions to drop, which in turn causes more instabilities.

Insufficient Memory

In addition to the memory needed by a router to run its own operating system, a router must store routing tables, cache tables, databases, and the other bits of software to permit operation. A router that reaches its memory limit might stop functioning, which causes all routes it knows of or advertises to be lost.

In BGP terms, a routing entry consists of the entry in the IP forwarding table and whatever corresponding information is available in the BGP routing table. Today, the Internet has reached more than 42,000 routes. Systems that are taking full routes from the Internet from a couple of providers are barely keeping up with 32 MB of memory. Most providers have upgraded their systems to 64 MB and even 128 MB.

Network Upgrades

Networks are dynamic. Performance improvement, site consolidation, and support expansion all require changes and adaptations. Changes might include upgrades to new versions of software or hardware, additions of more links, additions of more bandwidth, or reconfiguration of a network's layout.

For obvious reasons, administrators prefer to bring a system down for upgrading during some period when it usually experiences minimal usage. The downtime for some networks cannot exceed more than an hour, even at night, because of time zone differences. Despite these difficulties, the upgrade period itself is not usually the time when errors are most significant because administrators always keep a backup plan and can revert to the old setup if the new setup does not work. In case of configuration or software/hardware problems, network instabilities will take effect the next day when everybody is back online. At that point, reverting to the old setup is not likely to be a viable option. Unfortunately, to rectify the situation, administrators sometimes start adding or changing configuration on-the-fly, making the situation even worse.

To reduce the likelihood of causing disruptions, network changes should be simulated if possible in nonproduction environments. In addition, multiple major changes should not be deployed at the same time. It is, for example, unwise for a provider to perform major router software upgrades, switch hardware, and change cabling, all at the same time. Good planning and network simulation is the key to successful network upgrades.

Human Error

Most of the network instabilities caused by human error occur because an administrator circumvents an administration policy or makes a change without knowledge of possible effects. It *is easy* to make mistakes in complex network configurations. One wrong filter, and an entire AS can be isolated. Administrators should anticipate problems before they occur.

Here's an example of the kinds of errors that can happen: any router can send the default 0.0.0.0 via BGP to its neighbors. If you are not careful, traffic will take the wrong route. As much as it is somebody else's responsibility to send appropriate default routes, it is your responsibility to protect yourself by making sure that you filter any unwanted routes, default or otherwise, that come your way. The list of possible human errors is long: someone might advertise somebody else's networks; a provider might stop advertising your networks; somebody summarizes the *wrong* networks. The point is, don't expect everyone else to play by your rules. Other administrators can (usually inadvertently) deploy rules that directly conflict with your rules, which can lead to serious performance and connectivity degradation.

Backup Link Overloads

In some cases, a link failure will cause a backup link to be overloaded with traffic. This occurs because the backup link is handling all the additional traffic that is now being routed its way on top of its normal traffic. Even if the link can handle the load, a router might not be able to handle the additional load—depending on its horsepower. This can cause major performance degradation for the end-user.

In the process of trying to get a handle on network instabilities, BGP implementations have introduced several helpful features. Although these features do not provide a complete solution, they are significant preventative measures of route instability.

BGP STABILITY FEATURES

Of course, developing effective routing policies and configuring them correctly is at the core of building stability. BGP's attribute selections, as discussed throughout this book, are tools for building that core stability. In addition, BGP functions that can help provide a buffer against route instability effects include:

- Controlling Route and Cache Invalidation
- Route Dampening

Controlling Route and Cache Invalidation

Ch. 11, pp. 433-437. Controlling Route and Cache Invalidation

The basis of any BGP conversation is the TCP/IP session that takes place between two neighbors. The neighbor connection itself is based on the OPEN message, which contains parameters such as the BGP version number. In addition, exchanged routing updates carry different attributes such as the metric, communities, and AS_Path. Anytime an administrator changes attributes or policies, BGP implementations require that a BGP TCP session with its neighbor be reset (broken and restarted) for the modified routing behavior to take effect.

Unfortunately, every time the TCP session is reset, routing is interrupted. When a session is reset, the routing cache gets invalidated, routes disappear, and route instability cascades throughout the Internet. By the time the session is brought back up and routes/cache are re-established, real damage could result.

Cisco Systems introduced a mechanism called *soft reconfiguration* that enables administrators to reconfigure attributes on-the-fly without killing an already established TCP session. As a result, the routing cache is not cleared, and impact on the route is minimal.

Route Dampening

Another mechanism for controlling route instability is called *route dampening*. A route that appears and disappears intermittently causes BGP UPDATE and WITHDRAWN messages to be repeatedly propagated on the Internet. The tremendous amount of routing traffic generated can use up all the link's bandwidth and drive up CPU utilization of routers.

Dampening categorizes routes as either *well-behaved* or *ill-behaved*. A well-behaved route shows a high degree of stability during an extended period of time. On the other hand, an ill-behaved route experiences a high level of instability in a short period of time. Ill-behaved routes should be penalized in a way that is proportional to the expected future instability of the route. An unstable route should be suppressed (not advertised) until there is some degree of confidence that the route is stable.

Ch. 11, pp. 437-442. Route Dampening

The recent history of a route is used as a basis for estimating future stability. To track a route history, it is essential to track the number of times the route has flapped over a period of time. Under route dampening, each time a route flaps, it is given a penalty. Whenever the penalty reaches a predefined threshold, the route is suppressed. The route can continue to accrue penalties even after it is suppressed. The more frequently a route oscillates in a short amount of time, the faster the route will be suppressed.

Similar criteria are put in place to unsuppress a route and start readvertising it. An algorithm is implemented to decay (reduce) the penalty exponentially. The algorithm bases its configuration on a user-defined set of parameters. The following set of terms and parameters applies to the Cisco implementation:

- *Penalty*—An incremented numeric value that is assigned to a route each time it flaps.

- *Half-life-time*—A configurable numeric value that describes the amount of time that must elapse to reduce the penalty by one half.

- *Suppress limit*—A numeric value that is compared with the penalty. If the penalty is greater than the suppress limit, the route is suppressed.

- *Reuse limit*—A configurable numeric value that is compared with the penalty. If the penalty is less than the reuse limit, a suppressed route that is up will no longer be suppressed.

- *Suppressed route*—A route that is not advertised, even if it is up. A route is suppressed if the penalty is more than the suppressed limit.

- *History entry*—An entry used to store flap information. For the purposes of monitoring and calculating the level of oscillation of a route, it is important to store this information in the router when the route oscillates. When the route stabilizes, the history entry will become useless and will have to be flushed from the router.

Figure 9–1 illustrates the process of assessing a penalty to a route every time it flaps. The penalty is exponentially decayed according to parameters such as the half-life-time. The half-life-time parameter can be changed by the administrator to reflect the oscillation history of a route: a longer half-life might be desirable for a route that has a habit of oscillating frequently. A larger half-life-time value would cause the penalty to decay more slowly, which translates into a route being suppressed longer.

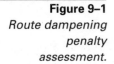

Figure 9–1
Route dampening penalty assessment.

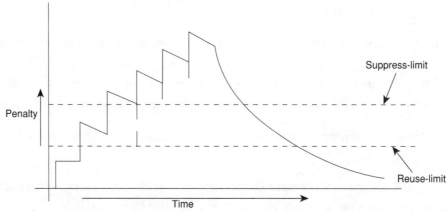

Stability Inside the AS

The benefits of route dampening are noticed inside as well as outside an autonomous system. When BGP is redistributed (injected) into an IGP, it is important that BGP instability does not affect internal routing in such a way as to cause a meltdown inside the AS. This is where route dampening can be useful. Routes that are flapping will be dampened and prevented from being injected into the AS until they show some degree of stability. Figure 9–2 compares the effects of EBGP flapping on an IGP with and without route dampening.

In figure 9–2, routes R1, R2, and R3 are injected from BGP into the AS. The up and down arrows next to R2 indicate that it is flapping. The routes will be carried via IBGP and/or IGP depending on how the administrator is injecting the routes into the AS. In either case, the oscillations of R2 create major overhead for the border router and also on the interior routers. IGPs will be flooding and removing the route as long as the route is instable. With route dampening, the ill-behaved route will be suppressed (after reaching the suppress limit) and will be prevented from entering the AS.

Instabilities Outside the AS

Route dampening can prevent unstable EBGP routes from being propagated to other peers. This can save on link bandwidth usage and processing overhead within border routers. If you are a provider with multiple customers using your services, it is important not to burden your own network (and the outside world) with instabilities that go on inside a customer's network. In the case where a provider advertises a customer's network as part of an aggregate, this

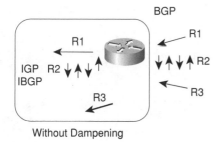

Without Dampening

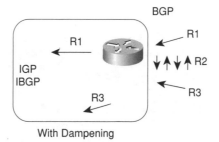

With Dampening

Figure 9–2
Effects of EBGP flapping on an IGP.

is not an issue. The aggregate will be stable (always advertised) even if most of its elements are not. Nonetheless, within the provider's AS, a customer's instabilities are a concern. When a customer's network cannot be aggregated (due to multihoming or addresses not being part of the provider's address space), then instabilities will be carried to the outside world.

With dampening, the provider's border router will suppress customer routes that are flapping. Suppression will take effect according to dampening rules and dampening parameters discussed earlier in this section.

One possible side effect of this is that the customer will experience some short outages even if his routes become stable. In figure 9–3, route R2 in the customer network is flapping. When the customer's ISP is running route dampening, R2 will be penalized and suppressed according to its level of oscillation. R2 could be dampened for minutes. Even if R2 stops oscillating, the penalty it had accumulated still might be far above the reuse limit, and it has to be decayed before the route can be used. In the meantime, some poor soul on the customer's network is pulling out his or her hair trying to figure out why some subnets are not reachable from the outside world. If administrators are unaware that their routes are being dampened, they might try to remedy the situation by some other means, which makes their routes flap even more and become more penalized. The better approach is to check with the provider on whether he is receiving the routes, and if he is, why they are not being advertised. Providers have strict policies and might not change the dampening behavior per the customer's request.

Figure 9–3
*Route dampening
ISP environment.*

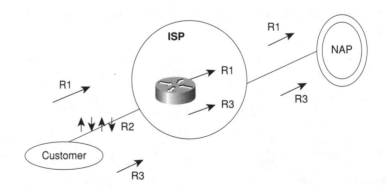

What the provider can do is "flush" the history information of the routes being dampened to advertise the route. This is, of course, under the condition that the customer will investigate the routing problems causing the routes to fluctuate.

On the other hand, instabilities can be caused by the providers themselves, and the effect can be much larger. If a link carrying full routes between a provider and customer or a provider and another provider oscillates, the border routers will feel the impact.

Suppose that you are getting full Internet routes (about 42,000 routes in 1996) from multiple providers. Now imagine that five percent of theses routes (about 2,100 routes) are toggling every two minutes. Your border router will be unable to handle this load.

Without route dampening, it will be difficult to determine what is really happening. All you know is that the process utilization on your border router is increasing rapidly. With route dampening, all the unstable routes will generate a history entry that shows the level of stability of the routes. After the unstable routes are identified, it is easy to determine where they are coming from by looking at the next hop address. Although route dampening in this case did not help solve the problem, it helped identify who is *causing* the problem. After you identify the culprit, you can temporarily remove your BGP session with the ISP at fault. Pick up the phone, call the ISP, and start complaining.

In conclusion, route instabilities in the Internet will affect everybody one way or the other. It is everyone's responsibility to minimize route oscillation by being more aware of the things we do and why we do them. Providers are becoming more tough on culprits; there is even talk about charging an additional fee per route flap. This might sound like overkill, but it is getting harder and harder to get the Internet under control. Having a "routing patrol" issue tickets whenever someone breaks the rules may become necessary.

LOOKING AHEAD

We have talked enough about architectures and routing behaviors. For the reader who wants to put things into perspective by learning actual routing implementations, the best is yet to come. The following chapters touch upon key designs and architectures already discussed in the book by presenting actual configuration by using the Cisco IOS software language.

The configuration examples are accompanied by complete explanations on why a certain action is taken and what outcome results from it. Actual displays are taken from Cisco routers to point out multiple BGP attributes and how the configuration has affected the routing tables. By going through the examples in the next two chapters, we hope that you will achieve a high-level of expertise in integrating your networks in the global Internet.

FREQUENTLY ASKED QUESTIONS

Q— *My border router is having problems because the link to my provider is oscillating, causing routes to flip-flop. Will configuring route dampening stabilize my router?*

A— To a certain extent. In this case, configuring route dampening might help stabilize your AS if you are injecting the BGP routes into your IGP. Your border router will still experience the instabilities caused by your provider. A better approach is to call your provider.

Q— *I am advertising my IGP routes into BGP. My IGP routes are very unstable, which causes the BGP routes I am advertising to fluctuate. Will route dampening solve the problem?*

A— No. Configuring route dampening on your border router will prevent your routes from being advertised. That will help others, but cause you outages. What you need to do is address the source of your IGP's instability.

Q— *Some of my internal routes are flip-flopping, which is causing my provider to dampen them. I cannot figure out the problem. What do I do in the meantime?*

A— You can always define these routes statically and inject them into BGP. This way they will always be advertised irrespective of their up or down state. Even better, if possible, you can define your routes as part of an aggregate route. The aggregate route will not disappear unless all the more-specific routes it represents disappear.

Q— *I am a provider. I do not want to penalize all prefixes in the same manner. Is there a way to assign different dampening parameters to different prefixes?*

A— Yes. Cisco offers you the flexibilty to selectively apply the dampening parameters depending on certain criteria such as IP prefixes or AS_path or community.

PART 4

Internet Routing
Device Configuration

In previous chapters, we developed concepts and approaches, but withheld the details of configuration code. In Chapters 10 and 11, you will find code examples for most of the concepts and functions described in Part 2 and Part 3. Chapter 10 focuses on configuration examples of basic BGP attributes, and Chapter 11 focuses on configuration examples for some of the more complex, realistic design problems faced by administrators developing routing policies. You cannot simply plug these code examples into your own network routing policies. Rather, they are models for the particular routing decisions you are likely to have to make as you develop, maintain, and extend routing policies to accommodate your evolving network and connectivity needs. You will need to extrapolate from and adjust the models to suit your particular situation.

Chapter 10—Configuring Basic BGP Functions and Attributes

Chapter 11—Configuring Effective Internet Routing Policies

THIS CHAPTER COVERS THE FOLLOWING KEY TOPICS:

- **Building Peering Sessions**

  Configuration examples for the first step in the routing task. This section overviews basic syntax used in configuration code.

- **Route Filtering and Attribute Manipulation**

  BGP route maps, filtering based on NLRI, and filtering based on AS_path.

- **Peer Groups**

  Configuration examples of defining and utilizing peer groups.

- **Sources of Routing Updates**

  Dynamic and static configuration for injecting information into BGP.

- **Overlapping Protocols (Backdoors)**

  Configuration examples for changing the distance parameter to favor certain routes over others.

- **BGP Attributes**

  Configuration examples for NEXT_HOP, AS_PATH, local preference, MED, and community attributes.

- **BGP4 Aggregation**

  Configuration examples for various aggregation scenarios.

CHAPTER 10

Configuring Basic BGP Functions and Attributes

This is the first of two chapters consisting primarily of configuration examples. Having covered all the important, prerequisite concepts, you can delve into these examples of how to write the code for basic BGP functions and attributes. This chapter focuses on those basics, and the next chapter considers some of the more complex design-oriented configuration problems.

Even if you have been using the references in previous chapters to flip ahead to these configuration examples, you are encouraged to reexamine them now, with the benefit of having read and assimilated all the concept-oriented chapters. In addition to the configuration code itself, be sure to look at the many routing tables that are included; they are intended to solidify your understanding of what results to expect.

Chapters 10 and 11 are not intended to replace Cisco manuals and do not cover every command and scenario. They present configurations for common situations that are encountered in connecting networks to the Internet. Your particular network might require a combination of scenarios—or a different approach—to achieve the most effective policies.

In the following discussions, an AS could play the role of a customer, provider, or both. Do not get confused by having AS numbers and AS roles being switched around, or by IP address numbering not being too realistic. These are just exercises that will help you understand BGP so that you can apply it accordingly in your own environment.

BUILDING PEERING SESSIONS

This example demonstrates the different types of BGP peering sessions you will encounter. Consider figure 10–1. An IBGP peering session is formed within AS3, between the loopback address of RTA and a physical address of RTF. An EBGP session is also formed between AS3 and AS1 by using the two directly connected IP addresses of RTA and RTC. Another EBGP session is formed between RTF in AS3 and RTD in AS2, using IP addresses that are not on the same segment (multihop).

It is important to remember that the BGP peers will never become established unless there is an IGP connectivity between the two peers or the two peers are on the same segment. We will use OSPF as an IGP to establish the required internal connectivity.

Figure 10–1
Building peering sessions.

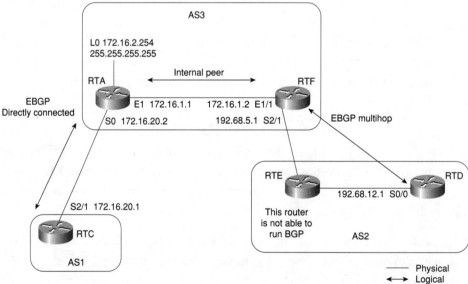

RTA's configuration is:

```
ip subnet-zero

interface Loopback0
 ip address 172.16.2.254 255.255.255.255

interface Ethernet1
 ip address 172.16.1.1 255.255.255.0

interface Serial0
 ip address 172.16.20.2 255.255.255.0

router ospf 10
 network 172.16.0.0 0.0.255.255 area 0

router bgp 3
 no synchronization
 neighbor 172.16.1.2 remote-as 3
 neighbor 172.16.1.2 update-source Loopback0
 neighbor 172.16.20.1 remote-as 1
 no auto-summary

ip classless
```

RTA's configuration shows some syntax that might be unfamiliar to you. All the syntax is explained here generically, as well as in relation to the particular routing scenario of figure 10–1. In subsequent examples throughout this chapter, however, the router's configuration will be reduced to necessary commands to configure BGP or IGP. Commands that assign IP addresses to interfaces will be omitted in many cases due to space limitations.

- **ip subnet-zero**: This global configuration command is necessary in case you are configuring interfaces that fall in subnet-zero subnets. With the introduction of classless routing, using subnet zero is very common.

- **interface** *type slot/port*: This command configures an interface type and number on the router. Any configuration that appears under the command will be specific to that particular interface. Note that RTA has three interface commands, one for each of its three connections. The *loopback* interface is a software-only interface that emulates an interface that is always up.

- **ip address** *ip-address mask* [**secondary**]: This is an interface command that configures an interface with an IP address/mask tuple. RTA's Ethernet IP address, for example, is configured by: **ip address** 172.16.1.1 255.255.255.0.

- **router** *process* [*process-id*]: This is a global command that defines a process such as OSPF, RIP, or BGP, and gives the process a process ID. Some processes such as RIP do not require a process ID.

  In RTA's configuration, "router ospf 10," for example, indicates an OSPF process with ID 10, whereas "router bgp 3" indicates a BGP process in autonomous system 3.

- **network**: This command indicates the networks or, in the case of OSPF, the interfaces that will run under a specific router process.

- **inverse mask**: In RTA's network command, you will notice a representation of the form 0.0.255.255 or basically a number of 0s followed with a number of 1s. This is an inverse mask with the 0s being an exact match, and the 1s being *do-not-care-bits*. For example: 172.16.0.0 0.0.255.255 indicates any IP address or network of the form 172.16.X.X. Inverse masks can be applied to access lists as well as the **network** command.

- **area** *area-number*: This is a representation of an OSPF area with a specified area number.

- **neighbor**: This command is used to define the BGP neighbor connection parameters and policies between this router and its peers. In RTA's configuration, "neighbor 172.16.1.2 remote-as 3," for example, is an indication that a BGP peer session is to be established between RTA and peer 172.16.1.2 in autonomous system 3.

- **no synchronization:** This command turns the synchronization off between BGP and IGP, as explained in Chapter 5, "Tuning BGP Capabilities."

- **no auto-summary:** This command will turn off the BGP automatic summarization at the major net boundary. Without this command, BGP will not send the subnets of a major net that are redistributed into BGP; that is, updates about 172.16.1.0/24, 172.16.2.0/24, and so on will be sent as a single major class B 172.16.0.0/16. Summarization at the major net boundary should be done only if the AS is the owner of the whole major net.

- **ip classless:** This command enables the router to forward packets that are destined for unrecognized subnets of directly connected networks. By default, when a router receives packets for a subnet that falls numerically within its subnetwork addressing scheme, if there is no such subnet number in the routing table and there is no network default route, the router discards the packets. When the **ip classless** command is enabled, however, the router forwards those packets to the best supernet route.

- **update-source** *interface*: This command, when associated with the BGP neighbor statement, specifies the interface to be used as a source IP address of the BGP session with the neighbor. In RTA's configuration, for example, the second neighbor statement indicates that Loopback 0 is to be used as a source IP address.

- **remote-as:** This command, when associated with the BGP neighbor statement, specifies the AS number of the remote BGP peer. In RTA's configuration, the first neighbor statement indicates that the internal BGP neighbor 172.16.1.2 belongs to the local AS3. The third neighbor statement indicates that the external BGP peer 172.16.20.1 belongs to AS1.

We turn now to RTF's configuration.

```
ip subnet-zero

interface Ethernet1/1
 ip address 172.16.1.2 255.255.255.0

interface Serial2/1
 ip address 192.68.5.1 255.255.255.0
```

```
router ospf 10
 network 172.16.0.0 0.0.255.255 area 0
 network 192.68.0.0 0.0.255.255 area 0

router bgp 3
 no synchronization
 neighbor 172.16.2.254 remote-as 3
 neighbor 192.68.12.1 remote-as 2
 neighbor 192.68.12.1 ebgp-multihop 2
 no auto-summary

ip classless
```

In RTF's configuration, you can see the **ebgp-multihop 2** command being used as part of the neighbor configuration. This is an indication that the exterior BGP peer is not directly connected and can be reached at maximum two hops away. Remember that **ebgp-multihop** is only applicable with EBGP and not IBGP.

RTC configuration:

```
ip subnet-zero

interface Serial2/1
 ip address 172.16.20.1 255.255.255.0

router bgp 1
 neighbor 172.16.20.2 remote-as 3
 no auto-summary

ip classless
```

RTD configuration:

```
ip subnet-zero

interface Serial0/0
 ip address 192.68.12.1 255.255.255.0

router ospf 10
   network 192.68.0.0 0.0.255.255 area 0

router bgp 2
 neighbor 192.68.5.1 remote-as 3
```

```
        neighbor 192.68.5.1 ebgp-multihop 2
        no auto-summary

        ip classless
```

The following is an example of how the peer connection will look after the neighbors are in an established state. From RTF's point of view, neighbor 172.16.2.254 is an internal neighbor that belongs to AS3. The neighbor connection is running BGP version 4 with a table version of 2. The table version changes every time the BGP table gets updated. A table version that increments rapidly is an indication of an unstable BGP neighbor session.

RTF's other neighbor 192.68.12.1 is also in an established state. This is an external neighbor that belongs to AS2. Note that the display indicates that this neighbor is two hops away (as configured in the ebgp-multihop).

```
        RTF#show ip bgp neighbor
        BGP neighbor is 172.16.2.254,  remote AS 3, internal link
          BGP version 4, remote router ID 172.16.2.254
          BGP state = Established, table version = 2, up for 22:36:09
          Last read 00:00:10, hold time is 180, keepalive interval is 60 seconds
          Minimum time between advertisement runs is 5 seconds
          Received 1362 messages, 0 notifications, 0 in queue
          Sent 1362 messages, 0 notifications, 0 in queue
          Connections established 2; dropped 1
        Connection state is ESTAB, I/O status: 1, unread input bytes: 0
        Local host: 172.16.1.2, Local port: 11008
        Foreign host: 172.16.2.254, Foreign port: 179

        BGP neighbor is 192.68.12.1,  remote AS 2, external link
          BGP version 4, remote router ID 192.68.5.2
          BGP state = Established, table version = 2, up for 22:13:01
          Last read 00:00:00, hold time is 180, keepalive interval is 60 seconds
          Minimum time between advertisement runs is 30 seconds
          Received 1336 messages, 0 notifications, 0 in queue
          Sent 1336 messages, 0 notifications, 0 in queue
          Connections established 1; dropped 0
          External BGP neighbor may be up to 2 hops away.
        Connection state is ESTAB, I/O status: 1, unread input bytes: 0
        Local host: 192.68.5.1, Local port: 11016
        Foreign host: 192.68.12.1, Foreign port: 179
```

ROUTE FILTERING AND ATTRIBUTE MANIPULATION

Route filtering and attribute manipulation are the basis of setting BGP policies. This section will describe the following:

- BGP route maps

- Identifying and filtering routes based on the NLRI

- Identifying and filtering routes based on the AS_path

For new BGP configuration, such as attribute manipulation or filtering, to take place, you should reset the BGP session by using the following command:

clear ip bgp [* | *address* | *peer-group*][**soft** [**in**|**out**]]

Refer to Chapter 11, "Configuring Effective Internet Routing Policies," for more details.

BGP Route Maps

Route maps are used with BGP to control and modify routing information and to define the conditions by which routes are redistributed between routing domains.

The format of a route map is as follows:

route-map *map-tag* [**permit** | **deny**] [*sequence-number*]

The *map tag* is a name that identifies the route map, and the *sequence number* indicates the position that an instance of the route map is to have in relation to other instances of the same route map. (Instances are ordered sequentially.)

You might, for example, use the following commands to define a route map named MYMAP:

```
route-map MYMAP permit 10
! First set of conditions goes here.
route-map MYMAP permit 20
! Second set of conditions goes here.
```

When BGP applies MYMAP to routing updates, it applies the lowest instance first (in this case, instance 10). If the first set of conditions is not met, the second instance is applied, and so on, until either a set of conditions has been met, or there are no more sets of conditions to apply.

The condition portion of a route map is set by using the **match** and **set** commands. The **match** command specifies criteria that must be matched, and the **set** command specifies an action that is to be taken if the routing update meets the conditions defined by the **match** command.

Following is an example of a simple route map:

```
route-map MYMAP permit 10
match ip address 1
set metric 5

access-list 1 permit 1.1.1.0 0.0.0.255
```

The access list is a way to identify routes. There are two types of access lists, standard and extended; the main difference is that a standard access list is applied to the source IP address, whereas an extended access list is applied to source and destination or source and network mask. The following global command defines a standard access list; the extended access list will be covered in this chapter at the point it is used in context.

access-list *access-list-number* {**deny** | **permit**} *source* [*source-wildcard*]

A standard access list is used to match on a particular source IP network or host, to permit or deny a specific routing update. The access list number falls between 1 and 99.

In this example, access-list 1 identifies all routes of the form 1.1.1.X (note the inverse mask notation 0.0.0.255). A routing update of the form 1.1.1.X will match the access list and will be propagated (because of the permit keyword) with a metric set to 5. The logic will then break out of the list of route map instances because a match has occurred.

When an update does not meet the criteria of a route map instance, BGP applies the next instance, and so on, until an action is taken, or there are no more route map instances to apply. If the update does not meet any criteria, the update is not redistributed or controlled.

The route map can be applied on the incoming (in) or the outgoing (out) BGP updates. The following is an example of the route map MYMAP applied on the outgoing updates toward BGP neighbor 172.16.20.2:

```
router bgp 1
neighbor 172.16.20.2 remote-as 3
neighbor 172.16.20.2 route-map MYMAP out
```

Identifying and Filtering Routes Based on the NLRI

To restrict the routing information that the router learns or advertises, you can filter based on routing updates to or from a particular neighbor. The filter consists of an access list that is applied to updates to or from a neighbor. In figure 10–2, RTD in AS2 is originating network 192.68.10.0/24 and sending it to RTF. RTF will pass the update to RTA via IBGP, which in turn will propagate

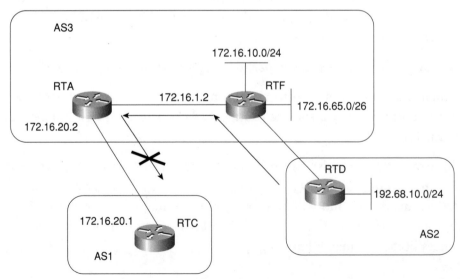

Figure 10–2
Identifying and filtering prefixes.

it to AS1. By doing so, AS3 could become a transit AS advertising reachability of network 192.68.10.0/24.

To prevent this situation from happening, RTA will configure a filter to prevent prefix 192.68.10.0/24 from propagating to AS1. This is demonstrated in the following configuration for RTA:

```
router bgp 3
 no synchronization
 neighbor 172.16.1.2 remote-as 3
 neighbor 172.16.20.1 remote-as 1
 neighbor 172.16.20.1 distribute-list 1 out
 no auto-summary

access-list 1 deny 192.68.10.0 0.0.0.255
access-list 1 permit 0.0.0.0 255.255.255.255
```

In the preceding configuration, the combination of the neighbor **distribute-list** router configuration command and access-list 1 prevents RTA from propagating prefix 192.68.10.0/24 to AS1. The access list portion of the configuration identifies the prefixes, whereas the distribute list portion applies the filtering on the outgoing updates (note the **out** keyword). Note that access-list 1 ended with a logic that permits all updates (permit 0.0.0.0 255.255.255.255). When using access lists for filtering, if no action is specified at the end of the access list statements, the logic of "deny everything else" applies. This means that anything that did not match any of the access list instances will be denied. This is why it is important to specify the default action; in this example, 192.68.10.0/24 will be denied, and everything else will be allowed.

NOTES

Route maps could have been used to filter updates in the previous example. The distribute list method was chosen to give you different options for doing filtering.

Using access lists to filter supernets or ranges of updates is a bit trickier. Assume, for example, that RTF in figure 10–2 has different subnets of 172.16.X.X, and you want to advertise an aggregate of the form 172.16.0.0/16 only. The following standard access list would not work because it permits more than is desired. The standard access list looks at the source IP address only and cannot check the length of the network mask. The following access list will permit 172.16.0.0/16, 172.16.0.0/17, 172.16.0.0/18, and so on:

```
access-list 1 permit 172.16.0.0 0.0.255.255
```

To restrict the update to 172.16.0.0/16 only, you have to use an extended access list of the form:

access-list *access-list-number* {**deny** | **permit**} *protocol source source-wildcard destination destination-wildcard | mask mask-wildcard*

This defines an extended access list that matches on a source destination or a source mask tuple, to permit or deny a specific routing update. The access list number falls between 100 and 199. In the case where the protocol is IP and we are checking on a source/mask tuple, this would translate into:

access-list *access-list-number* **permit** *ip network-number network-do-not-care-bits mask mask-do-not-care-bits*

For example:

```
access-list 101 permit ip 172.16.0.0 0.0.255.255 255.255.0.0 0.0.0.0
```

(where a "0" is an exact match bit, and a "1" is a do-not-care-bit).

The preceding extended access list indicates that aggregate 172.16.0.0/16 is to be sent only because we have indicated that the mask should match 255.255.0.0 exactly. An update of the form 172.16.0.0/17 will not be allowed.

Identifying and Filtering Routes Based on the AS_Path

Filtering routes based on AS_path information becomes handy when filtering is needed for all routes of the same or multiple ASs. It is an efficient alternative to listing hundreds of routes one-by-one as may be required to filter on a prefix basis. You can specify an access list on both incoming and outgoing updates based on the value of the AS_path attribute.

Referring still to figure 10–2, if AS3 wanted to prevent itself from becoming a transit AS for other ASs, AS3 can configure its border routers RTA and RTF to advertise only local networks. Local networks originated from the AS itself. This can be done with the following RTA configuration; RTF will be configured in the same manner.

RTA configuration:

```
router bgp 3
 no synchronization
 neighbor 172.16.1.2 remote-as 3
 neighbor 172.16.20.1 remote-as 1
 neighbor 172.16.20.1 filter-list 1 out
 no auto-summary

ip as-path access-list 1 permit ^$
```

In the preceding RTA configuration, the as-path access list 1 identifies only updates that originate from AS3. The filter list works in conjunction with the as-path access list to filter the updates. In this example, the filter list is applied on the outgoing updates (note the **out** keyword). The regular expression ^$ indicates an AS_path that is empty. The "^" symbol indicates the beginning of the AS_path, and the "$" symbol indicates the end of the AS_path. Because all networks originating from AS3 have an empty AS_path list, they will be advertised. All other prefixes will be denied.

If you want to verify that your regular expression works as intended, use the following EXEC command:

show ip bgp regexp *regular-expression*

The router displays all the paths that match the specified regular expression.

NOTES

Route maps could have been used to filter updates in the previous example. The filter list was chosen to give you a different option for filtering.

PEER GROUPS

A BGP *peer group* is a group of BGP neighbors that share the same update policies. Update policies are usually set by route maps, distribution lists, and filter lists. Instead of defining the same policies for each individual neighbor, you define a peer group name and assign policies to the peer group.

The use of BGP peer groups is demonstrated by the network shown in figure 10–3. RTC forms similar internal peering sessions with RTD, RTE, and RTH.

Figure 10–3
BGP peer groups.

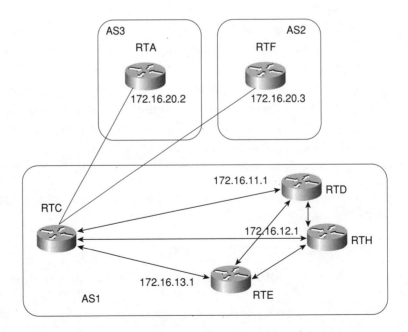

Instead of formulating and applying similar policies for each neighbor individually, RTC would define a peer group that contains the policies and would apply the peer group to its internal neighbors.

RTC configuration:

```
router bgp 1
 neighbor INTERNALMAP peer-group
 neighbor INTERNALMAP remote-as 1
 neighbor INTERNALMAP route-map INTERNAL out
 neighbor INTERNALMAP filter-list 1 out
 neighbor INTERNALMAP filter-list 2 in
 neighbor 172.16.11.1 peer-group INTERNALMAP
 neighbor 172.16.13.1 peer-group INTERNALMAP
 neighbor 172.16.12.1 peer-group INTERNALMAP
 neighbor 172.16.12.1 filter-list 3 in
```

The preceding configuration defines a peer group called INTERNALMAP that contains the following policies:

- A route map named INTERNAL

- A filter list for outgoing updates (filter list 1)

- A filter list for incoming updates (filter list 2)

The configuration applies the peer group to all internal neighbors—RTD, RTE, and RTH.

Members of a peer group inherit all the configuration options of the peer group. Peer group members can also be configured to override configuration options if the options do not affect outgoing updates. That is, peer group members can be configured to override options that affect incoming policies. The configuration of RTC, for example, also defines a filter-list 3 for incoming updates from the neighbor at IP address 172.16.12.1 (RTH). Filter-list 3 will override any incoming policies set by the peer group INTERNALMAP for neighbor RTH.

The following commands configure a BGP peer group named EXTERNAL-MAP on RTC and apply it to the exterior neighbors in AS3 and AS2:

RTC configuration:

```
router bgp 1
 neighbor EXTERNALMAP peer-group
 neighbor EXTERNALMAP route-map SETMED out
 neighbor EXTERNALMAP filter-list 1 out
 neighbor EXTERNALMAP filter-list 2 in
 neighbor 172.16.20.2 remote-as 3
 neighbor 172.16.20.2 peer-group EXTERNALMAP
 neighbor 172.16.20.3 remote-as 2
 neighbor 172.16.20.3 peer-group EXTERNALMAP
 neighbor 172.16.20.3 filter-list 3 in

ip as-path access-list 1 permit ^$
```

In the preceding configuration, the neighbor remote-as router configuration commands are placed outside the neighbor peer-group router configuration commands because different external ASs have to be defined. Also note that this configuration defines filter-list 3, which can be used to override configuration options for incoming updates from the neighbor at IP address 172.16.20.3 (RTF).

Note that the external BGP neighbors RTA and RTF that belong in the same peer group EXTERNALMAP were taken from the same subnet 172.16.20.0. This restriction is needed to prevent loss of information. Placing the external neighbors in different subnets could result in RTC sending updates to its neighbors (RTA and RTF) with a non-connected next hop IP address. These updates would be dropped due to the normal EBGP behavior of ignoring routes with non-connected next hop (remember that ebgp-multihop was implemented to override this behavior).

Another restriction that also applies is that peer groups should not be set on EBGP neighbors if the router is acting as a transit between these neighbors. If the router (RTC) is passing updates from one external neighbor to the other, placing external neighbors in peer groups might result in routes being mistakenly removed. Note that filter-list 1 has been defined to allow AS1's local routes only to be sent to neighbors RTA and RTF. This way RTC will not act as a transit router between RTA and RTF.

As you can see, using peer groups with external BGP peers is no longer intuitive because of limiting restrictions. Using peer groups with EBGP peers should be done with care in order not to cause loss of routes.

SOURCES OF ROUTING UPDATES

Routes can be injected dynamically or statically into BGP. The choice of method depends on the number and stability of routes.

Injecting Information Dynamically into BGP

The following example demonstrates how routing information can be injected dynamically into BGP. Consider figure 10–4. Assume that AS3 is getting Internet connectivity from AS1. AS3 is running OSPF as an IGP inside the AS and is running EBGP with AS1.

On the other hand, AS3 has also one customer, C1, with the following criteria:

- C1 is pointing a default toward AS3.

- C1 advertises all its routes to AS3 via RIP.

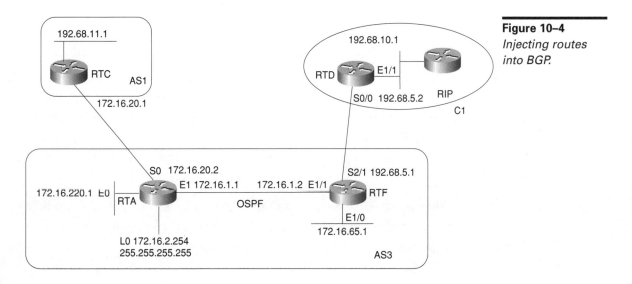

Figure 10–4
Injecting routes into BGP.

RTF is running two routing processes, the OSPF process and the RIP process. RTF will only listen to RIP on its connection to C1 and will redistribute the RIP updates it gets from C1 into OSPF. On the other hand, RTA will run two routing processes, the OSPF process and the BGP process. RTA will inject all its routes and customer routes dynamically into BGP.

RTF configuration:

```
interface Ethernet1/0
 ip address 172.16.65.1 255.255.255.192

interface Ethernet1/1
 ip address 172.16.1.2 255.255.255.0

interface Serial2/1
 ip address 192.68.5.1 255.255.255.0

router ospf 10
 redistribute rip subnets
 network 172.16.0.0 0.0.255.255 area 0

router rip
 passive-interface Serial2/1
 network 192.68.5.0
```

RTF's configuration has introduced two new commands, as described next:

- **passive-interface** *type number*: This router command disables sending routing updates on the specified interface. In our example, when used with RIP, this command prevents RIP updates from being sent on interface S2/1. This is in case RTF has multiple customers connected that do not need to see each other's networks.

  When used with OSPF, this command disables Hello packets from being sent on the specified interface, which eventually prevents Link State information from being exchanged on that interface.

- **redistribute** *protocol* [*process-id*]: The **redistribute** command injects routes from one routing domain into another routing domain. In this example, RTF is injecting the RIP routes into the OSPF domain (OSPF process 10). Numerous extensions (such as **subnets**) of the **redistribute** command exist; these extensions will be explained in context.

The **subnet** keyword is used to make sure that all subnetted information will be injected into the OSPF process. This is only needed in the case of redistributing routes into the OSPF protocol.

RTD configuration:

```
interface Ethernet1/1
  ip address 192.68.10.1 255.255.255.0

interface Serial0/0
  ip address 192.68.5.2 255.255.255.0

router rip
  redistribute static
  network 192.68.5.0
  network 192.68.10.0
  default-metric 1

ip route 0.0.0.0 0.0.0.0 192.68.5.1
```

Note that RTD has configured a static route pointing a 0/0 default toward RTF. For all destinations that are outside C1, RTD will direct the traffic to RTF. RTD will also redistribute the static default route into the internal RIP domain so that all other routers can follow a default toward AS3. The **default-metric** router command assigns a metric to the routes redistributed into a particular protocol. In this case, the default-metric assigns a hop count of 1 to the 0/0 route injected into RIP.

RTA configuration:

```
interface Ethernet0
  ip address 172.16.220.1 255.255.255.0
```

```
interface Ethernet1
 ip address 172.16.1.1 255.255.255.0

interface Serial0
 ip address 172.16.20.2 255.255.255.0

router ospf 10
 passive-interface Serial 0
 network 172.16.0.0 0.0.255.255 area 0

router bgp 3
 redistribute ospf 10 match  external 1 external 2
 neighbor 172.16.20.1 remote-as 1
 no auto-summary
```

RTA has a combination of OSPF routes that belong to AS3 and other external routes that came in from the RIP domain C1. Using the **redistribute** router command, RTA will dynamically inject all these routes into its BGP process. Note that RTA is using the keywords "match external 1 external 2" in conjunction with the **redistribute** router command. This is because OSPF does not inject external OSPF routes into BGP unless it is specifically instructed to do so. This measure was put in for loop avoidance in case the external OSPF information came from BGP.

The following is a snapshot of what the IP routing table of RTA looks like:

```
RTA#sh ip route
Codes: C - connected, S - static, I - IGRP, R - RIP, M - mobile, B - BGP
       D - EIGRP, EX - EIGRP external, O - OSPF, IA - OSPF inter area
       N1 - OSPF NSSA external type 1, N2 - OSPF NSSA external type 2
       E1 - OSPF external type 1, E2 - OSPF external type 2, E - EGP
       i - IS-IS, L1 - IS-IS level-1, L2 - IS-IS level-2,
       * - candidate default U - per-user static route, o - ODR
Gateway of last resort is not set
O E2 192.68.5.0/24 [110/20] via 172.16.1.2, 2d13h, Ethernet1
O E2 192.68.10.0/24 [110/20] via 172.16.1.2, 2d13h, Ethernet1
B    192.68.11.0/24 [20/0] via 172.16.20.1, 2d13h
```

```
        172.16.0.0/16 is variably subnetted, 5 subnets, 3 masks
C           172.16.2.254/32 is directly connected, Loopback0
C           172.16.220.0/24 is directly connected, Ethernet0
C           172.16.20.0/24 is directly connected, Serial0
C           172.16.1.0/24 is directly connected, Ethernet1
O           172.16.65.0/26 [110/20] via 172.16.1.2, 2d13h, Ethernet1
```

Note in RTA's IP table how networks 192.68.10.0/24 and 192.68.5.0/24 are listed as external OSPF routes (O E2). Dynamic redistribution will cause all these networks to be sent into BGP. The following is how the BGP table of RTC would look:

```
RTC#sh ip bgp
BGP table version is 20, local router ID is 192.68.11.1
Status codes: s suppressed, d damped, h history, * valid, > best,
i - internal Origin codes: i - IGP, e - EGP, ? - incomplete
    Network          Next Hop         Metric LocPrf Weight Path
*> 172.16.1.0/24    172.16.20.2           0              0 3 ?
*> 172.16.2.254/32  172.16.20.2           0              0 3 ?
*> 172.16.20.0/24   172.16.20.2           0              0 3 ?
*> 172.16.65.0/26   172.16.20.2          20              0 3 ?
*> 172.16.220.0/24  172.16.20.2           0              0 3 ?
*> 192.68.5.0       172.16.20.2          20              0 3 ?
*> 192.68.10.0      172.16.20.2          20              0 3 ?
*> 192.68.11.0      0.0.0.0               0          32768 i
```

Note how all networks running OSPF in AS3 have become BGP routes in AS1. Usually, not every network that belongs to your AS needs to be sent via BGP. You might be running private or illegal network numbers inside the AS that need not be advertised. Note how the loopback address 172.16.2.254/32 was also injected into BGP. No provider will enable you to advertise such prefixes and will instruct you to filter them, or the provider might filter them on its end. This restriction is put in place to make sure that customers are aggregating their routes as much as possible to prevent the explosion of the global IP routing tables. Also, the DMZ network 172.16.20.0/24 has been injected into BGP, which is not necessary. This is why redistribution should be accompanied by filtering to specify the exact routes that need to be advertised.

The following configuration of RTA gives an example of how filtering could be applied.

> **NOTES**
>
> From now on, due to space limitations, configuration examples will focus on commands that are directly relevant to the discussion at hand. Do not be alarmed if you notice commands that are missing, such as interface commands.

```
router ospf 10
 passive-interface Serial0
 network 172.16.0.0 0.0.255.255 area 0

router bgp 3
 redistribute ospf 10 match  external 1 external 2
 neighbor 172.16.20.1 remote-as 1
 neighbor 172.16.20.1 route-map BLOCKROUTES out
 no auto-summary

access-list 1 permit 172.16.2.254 0.0.0.0
access-list 1 permit 172.16.20.0 0.0.0.255

route-map BLOCKROUTES deny 10
 match ip address 1

route-map BLOCKROUTES permit 20
```

Filtering in the preceding example was performed with a route map, which is an indication of a set of actions to be taken in case certain criteria are found. Our criteria here are to find a match on the host route 172.16.2.254/32 and the network 172.16.20.0/24 and to prevent them from being sent via BGP. The access-list 1 will enable us to find a match on these routes, and the route map BLOCKROUTES specifies that they are to be denied. The second instance of the route map (20) permits all other routes to be injected into BGP. (Refer to the discussion of filtering in Chapter 5 for more details.)

This is how the BGP table of RTC would look after filtering has been applied. The host route 172.16.2.254/32 and the network 172.16.20.0/24 do not show anymore.

```
RTC#sh ip bgp
BGP table version is 34, local router ID is 192.68.11.1
Status codes: s suppressed, d damped, h history, * valid, > best,
i - internal Origin codes: i - IGP, e - EGP, ? - incomplete
   Network          Next Hop        Metric LocPrf Weight Path
*> 172.16.1.0/24    172.16.20.2          0           0 3 ?
*> 172.16.65.0/26   172.16.20.2         20           0 3 ?
*> 172.16.220.0/24  172.16.20.2          0           0 3 ?
*> 192.68.5.0       172.16.20.2         20           0 3 ?
*> 192.68.10.0      172.16.20.2         20           0 3 ?
*> 192.68.11.0      0.0.0.0              0       32768 i
```

To have better control over what is being redistributed from the IGP into BGP, the **network** command can be used. The **network** command is a way to individually listing the prefixes that need to be sent via BGP. The **network** command has a limit of 200. If more than 200 networks need to be listed, dynamic redistribution is a must. The **network** command specifies the prefix to be sent out (network and mask). The statement "network 172.16.1.0 mask 255.255.255.0," for example, is an indication for prefix 172.16.1.0/24 to be sent. Networks that fall on a major net boundary (255.0.0.0, 255.255.0.0, or 255.255.255.0) do not need to have the mask included; for example, the statement "network 172.16.0.0" is sufficient to send the prefix 172.16.0.0/16. Such networks are also listed in the BGP routing table without the /x notation. For example, the class C network 192.68.11.0 is equivalent to 192.68.11.0/24.

Considering figure 10–4, the following configuration of RTA will specify the networks that will be injected into BGP.

RTA configuration:

```
router ospf 10
 passive-interface Serial0
 network 172.16.0.0 0.0.255.255 area 0
```

```
router bgp 3
 network 172.16.1.0 mask 255.255.255.0
 network 172.16.65.0 mask 255.255.255.192
 network 172.16.220.0 mask 255.255.255.0
 network 192.68.5.0
 network 192.68.10.0
 neighbor 172.16.20.1 remote-as 1
 no auto-summary
```

The following is what the BGP table of RTC would look like. All routes have been injected into BGP except for 172.16.2.254/32 and 172.16.20.0/24. Note that the table looks similar to the one produced when redistributing the OSPF routes into BGP and applying filters. The only noticeable difference is with the origin code, which is indicated by the "i" at the end of the path information. The "i" origin code indicates that the source of these networks is internal (IGP) to the originating AS. If you look at the previous snapshot of RTC's BGP table, the origin code was "?", meaning incomplete, which is an indication that the origin of these networks is learned by some other means. Anytime routes are injected into BGP via redistribution, the origin code would be incomplete.

```
RTC#sh ip bgp
BGP table version is 34, local router ID is 192.68.11.1
Status codes: s suppressed, d damped, h history, * valid, > best,
i - internal Origin codes: i - IGP, e - EGP, i - incomplete
   Network          Next Hop          Metric LocPrf Weight Path
*> 172.16.1.0/24    172.16.20.2            0           0 3 i
*> 172.16.65.0/26   172.16.20.2           20           0 3 i
*> 172.16.220.0/24  172.16.20.2            0           0 3 i
*> 192.68.5.0       172.16.20.2           20           0 3 i
*> 192.68.10.0      172.16.20.2           20           0 3 i
*> 192.68.11.0      0.0.0.0                0       32768 i
```

The **network** command only takes effect if the prefixes listed are known to the router—that is, BGP will not go blindly advertising prefixes just because they were listed. The router will check for the availability of an exact match of the prefix in the IP routing table before the network is advertised. In the preceding example, if we list "network 172.16.192.0 mask 255.255.255.0," that network will not be originated because it is unknown by the router.

Injecting Information Statically into BGP

Listing prefixes with the **network** command has the same drawbacks as dynamic redistribution. If a route that is listed with the **network** command goes down, BGP will send an update; if the route comes back, BGP will send another update. If this behavior continues, the IGP instability will translate into BGP instabilities. The only way around this is to use a combination of statically defined prefixes in conjuction with the **network** command. This will make sure that the prefixes will always remain in the IP routing tables and will always be advertised.

In the previous example, if you wanted to make sure that the fluctuations of route 192.68.10.0/24 do not translate into fluctuations in the BGP, you would include in RTA a static route of the form:

```
ip route 192.68.10.0 255.255.255.0 Ethernet1
```

By using the static approach, the prefix entry will always be present in the IP routing table and will always be advertised. The drawback of this approach is that even when a route is down, it will still be advertised by BGP. Considering the gain in network stability compared to the damage an ill-behaved route or multiple ill-behaved routes can cause, administrators may find this approach very efficient.

RTA configuration:

```
router bgp 3
 network 172.16.1.0 mask 255.255.255.0
 network 172.16.65.0 mask 255.255.255.192
 network 172.16.220.0 mask 255.255.255.0
 network 192.68.5.0
 network 192.68.10.0
 neighbor 172.16.20.1 remote-as 1
 no auto-summary

ip route 192.68.10.0 mask 255.255.255.0 Ethernet1
```

The preceding configuration will make sure that 192.68.10.0/24 is always sent. Note that RTA itself is originating the 192.68.10.0/24 prefix and is not relying on the advertisement coming from RTF. In case an aggregate is advertised via a static route, it is better to point the static route to null 0 (pit bucket) for loop prevention.

OVERLAPPING PROTOCOLS: (BACKDOORS)

This example shows how the **backdoor** command can be used to change the EBGP **distance** to have IGP routes favored over EBGP routes for specific network numbers.

In figure 10–5, AS2 is running an IGP (OSPF) on the private link between it and AS1, and is running EBGP with AS3. RTC, in AS1, will receive advertisements about 192.68.10.0/24 from AS3 via EBGP with a distance of 20 and from AS2 via OSPF with a distance of 110. Because the lower distance is preferred, RTC will use the BGP link to AS3 to reach 192.68.10.0/24.

Looking at RTC's IP routing table, you see the following:

Figure 10–5
BGP backdoor routes.

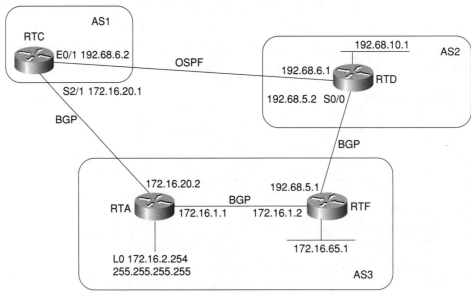

```
RTC#show ip route
Codes: C - connected, S - static, I - IGRP, R - RIP, M - mobile, B - BGP
       D - EIGRP, EX - EIGRP external, O - OSPF, IA - OSPF inter area
       E1 - OSPF external type 1, E2 - OSPF external type 2, E - EGP
       i - IS-IS, L1 - IS-IS level-1, L2 - IS-IS level-2,
       * - candidate default U - per-user static route
Gateway of last resort is not set
C    192.68.6.0/24 is directly connected, Ethernet0/1
B    192.68.10.0/24 [20/0] via 172.16.20.2, 00:21:36
     172.16.0.0/16 is variably subnetted, 3 subnets, 2 masks
C       172.16.20.0/24 is directly connected, Serial2/1
B       172.16.1.0/24 [20/0] via 172.16.20.2, 00:21:37
B       172.16.65.0/26 [20/20] via 172.16.20.2, 00:21:37
```

Prefix 192.68.10.0/24 is indeed learned via BGP. RTC will take the longer path via AS3 (next hop 172.16.0.2) to reach 192.68.10.0/24. Note the distance of [20] that the EBGP route has. If you wanted to have RTC prefer the OSPF entry, you would configure RTC in the following way:

RTC configuration:

```
router bgp 1
  neighbor 172.16.20.2 remote-as 3
  network 192.68.10.0 backdoor
  no auto-summary
```

The preceding configuration, "network 192.68.10.0 backdoor," changes the distance of the BGP route 192.68.10.0/24 from 20 to 200, which makes the OSPF route with a distance of 110 more preferred. Note that "network 192.68.10.0 backdoor" entry will not cause BGP to generate an advertisement for that network.

Following is the new routing table of RTC. Note that the 192.68.10.0/24 entry is now learned via OSPF with distance [110], and the private link between AS1 and AS2 will be used.

```
RTC#show ip route
Codes: C - connected, S - static, I - IGRP, R - RIP, M - mobile, B - BGP
       D - EIGRP, EX - EIGRP external, O - OSPF, IA - OSPF inter area
       E1 - OSPF external type 1, E2 - OSPF external type 2, E - EGP
       i - IS-IS, L1 - IS-IS level-1, L2 - IS-IS level-2,
       * - candidate default U - per-user static route
Gateway of last resort is not set
C    192.68.6.0/24 is directly connected, Ethernet0/1
O IA 192.68.10.0/24 [110/20] via 192.68.6.1, 00:00:21, Ethernet0/1
     172.16.0.0/16 is variably subnetted, 3 subnets, 2 masks
C       172.16.20.0/24 is directly connected, Serial2/1
B       172.16.1.0/24 [20/0] via 172.16.20.2, 00:29:07
B       172.16.65.0/26 [20/20] via 172.16.20.2, 00:29:07
```

BGP ATTRIBUTES

In this section, we will work with the network topology illustrated in figure 10–6 to demonstrate how the different BGP attributes are used.

Following is a first run of basic configuration for routers RTA, RTF, RTC, and RTD, illustrated in figure 10–6. Additional configuration will be added according to the topic under discussion.

Figure 10–6
Applying BGP attributes.

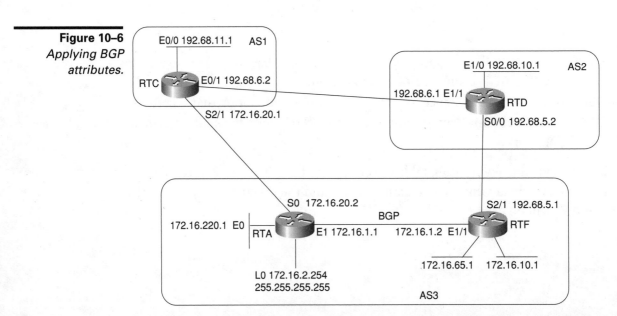

RTA configuration:

```
ip subnet-zero

interface Loopback0
 ip address 172.16.2.254 255.255.255.255

interface Ethernet0
 ip address 172.16.220.1 255.255.255.0

interface Ethernet1
 ip address 172.16.1.1 255.255.255.0

interface Serial0
 ip address 172.16.20.2 255.255.255.0

router ospf 10
 passive-interface Serial0
 network 172.16.0.0 0.0.255.255 area 0

router bgp 3
 no synchronization
 network 172.16.1.0 mask 255.255.255.0
 network 172.16.10.0 mask 255.255.255.0
 network 172.16.65.0 mask 255.255.255.192
 network 172.16.220.0 mask 255.255.255.0
 neighbor 172.16.1.2 remote-as 3
 neighbor 172.16.1.2 update-source Loopback0
 neighbor 172.16.20.1 remote-as 1
 neighbor 172.16.20.1 filter-list 10 out
 no auto-summary

ip classless
ip as-path access-list 10 permit ^$
```

RTF configuration:

```
ip subnet-zero

interface Ethernet0/0
 ip address 172.16.10.1 255.255.255.0

interface Ethernet 1/0
 ip address 172.16.65.1 255.255.255.192
```

```
        interface Ethernet1/1
         ip address 172.16.1.2 255.255.255.0

        interface Serial2/1
         ip address 192.68.5.1 255.255.255.0

        router ospf 10
         network 172.16.0.0 0.0.255.255 area 0

        router bgp 3
         no synchronization
         network 172.16.1.0 mask 255.255.255.0
         network 172.16.10.0 mask 255.255.255.0
         network 172.16.65.0 mask 255.255.255.192
         network 172.16.220.0 mask 255.255.255.0
         neighbor 172.16.2.254  remote-as 3
         neighbor 172.16.2.254 next-hop-self
         neighbor 192.68.5.2 remote-as 2
         neighbor 192.68.5.2 filter-list 10 out
         no auto-summary

        ip classless
        ip as-path access-list 10 permit ^$
```

RTC configuration:

```
        ip subnet-zero

        interface Ethernet0/0
         ip address 192.68.11.1 255.255.255.0

        interface Ethernet0/1
         ip address 192.68.6.2 255.255.255.0

        interface Serial2/1
         ip address 172.16.20.1 255.255.255.0

        router bgp 1
         network 192.68.11.0
         neighbor 172.16.20.2 remote-as 3
```

```
  neighbor 192.68.6.1 remote-as 2
  no auto-summary

ip classless
```

RTD configuration:

```
ip subnet-zero

interface Ethernet1/0
 ip address 192.68.10.1 255.255.255.0

interface Ethernet1/1
 ip address 192.68.6.1 255.255.255.0

interface Serial0/0
 ip address 192.68.5.2 255.255.255.0

router bgp 2
 network 192.68.10.0
 neighbor 192.68.5.1 remote-as 3
 neighbor 192.68.6.2 remote-as 1
 no auto-summary

ip classless
```

NOTES

AS3 is assumed to be a nontransit AS. This is why filter-list 10 is applied to force AS3 to originate its local routes only. Routes learned from AS1 or AS2 will not be propagated outside the AS. Also note that some networks such as 172.16.10.0/24 are advertised via the **network** command on both RTA and RTF. This will ensure that a link failure between AS3 and either AS1 or AS2 will not prevent such networks from being advertised.

The Next_Hop Attribute

Consider the BGP table of RTF:

```
RTF#sh ip bgp
BGP table version is 8, local router ID is 192.68.5.1
Status codes: s suppressed, d damped, h history, * valid, > best,
i - internal Origin codes: i - IGP, e - EGP, ? - incomplete
   Network          Next Hop         Metric LocPrf Weight Path
* i172.16.1.0/24    172.16.2.254          0    100      0 i
*>                  0.0.0.0               0         32768 i
* i172.16.10.0/24   172.16.2.254         20    100      0 i
*>                  0.0.0.0               0         32768 i
* i172.16.65.0/26   172.16.2.254         20    100      0 i
*>                  0.0.0.0               0         32768 i
* i172.16.220.0/24  172.16.2.254          0    100      0 i
*>                  172.16.1.1           20         32768 i
*> 192.68.10.0      192.68.5.2            0             0 2 i
*  192.68.11.0      192.68.5.2                          0 2 1 i
*>i                 172.16.20.1           0    100      0 1 i
```

Network 192.68.11.0/24 is learned via IBGP (note the "i" at the far left) with next hop 172.16.20.1, which is the IP address of the external neighbor of RTA. The EBGP next hop IP address is always carried inside the IBGP, which is why it is very important to have an internal route to the next hop. Otherwise, the BGP route would be unreachable. There are a couple of ways to make sure that you do not have problems reaching the EBGP next hop. The first way is to include the network that the next hop belongs to in the IGP. This is illustrated on RTA by including interface serial 0 in the OSPF; this way, RTF would know about 172.16.20.1. Note that even though OSPF is running on RTA serial 0, it need not exchange any OSPF "Hello" packets on serial 0, hence the **passive-interface** router command.

The second method is to use the **next-hop-self** (see RTF) neighbor command to force the router to advertise itself, rather than the external peer, as the next hop. On RTF, note how the next-hop-self is added at the end of the neighbor statement toward RTA. This way, when RTF advertises external networks such as

192.68.10.0/24 toward RTA, it will use itself as the next hop. Looking at RTA's BGP table that follows, prefix 192.68.10.0/24 is learned via next hop 172.16.1.2, which is its internal peer with RTF. Because 172.16.1.2 is part of the OSPF already, we have no problem reaching it.

```
RTA#sh ip bgp
BGP table version is 20, local router ID is 172.16.2.254
Status codes: s suppressed, d damped, h history, * valid, > best,
i - internal Origin codes: i - IGP, e - EGP, ? - incomplete
   Network          Next Hop          Metric LocPrf Weight Path
 * i172.16.1.0/24   172.16.1.2             0    100      0 i
 *>                 0.0.0.0                0          32768 i
 * i172.16.10.0/24  172.16.1.2             0    100      0 i
 *>                 172.16.1.2            20          32768 i
 * i172.16.65.0/26  172.16.1.2             0    100      0 i
 *>                 172.16.1.2            20          32768 i
 * i172.16.220.0/24 172.16.1.2            20    100      0 i
 *>                 0.0.0.0                0          32768 i
 *>i192.68.10.0     172.16.1.2             0    100      0 2 i
 *                  172.16.20.1                         0 1 2 i
 *> 192.68.11.0     172.16.20.1            0            0 1 i
```

Note in the preceding table that 192.68.10.0/24 is actually learned via two different paths, whereas 192.68.11.0/24 is learned via a single path. This might seem misleading, but actually routing is doing the right thing. In this situation, RTF has decided that the best path to reach 192.68.11.0/24 is via RTA (check RTF's BGP table) ; this is why RTF will not advertise network 192.68.11.0/24 back to RTA, and RTA will have a single entry for 192.68.11.0/24.

The AS_Path Attribute

Looking at RTF's BGP table that follows, you can see the AS_path information at the end of each line. Network 192.68.11.0/24 is learned via IBGP with AS_path 1 and via EBGP with AS_path 2 1. This means that if RTF wanted to reach 192.68.11.0/24 via IBGP, it can go to AS1, and if RTF wanted to reach 192.68.11.0/24 via EBGP, it has to go via AS2 then AS1. BGP always prefers the shortest path, which is why the path via IBGP with AS_path 1 is preferred. The ">" sign at the left is an indication that out of the two available paths that BGP has for 192.68.11.0/24, BGP has preferred the second one as being the "best" path.

```
RTF#sh ip bgp
BGP table version is 8, local router ID is 192.68.5.1
Status codes: s suppressed, d damped, h history, * valid, > best,
i - internal Origin codes: i - IGP, e - EGP, ? - incomplete
   Network          Next Hop         Metric LocPrf Weight Path
* i172.16.1.0/24    172.16.2.254          0    100      0 i
*>                  0.0.0.0               0         32768 i
* i172.16.10.0/24   172.16.2.254         20    100      0 i
*>                  0.0.0.0               0         32768 i
* i172.16.65.0/26   172.16.2.254         20    100      0 i
*>                  0.0.0.0               0         32768 i
* i172.16.220.0/24  172.16.2.254          0    100      0 i
*>                  172.16.1.1           20         32768 i
*> 192.68.10.0      192.68.5.2            0             0 2 i
*  192.68.11.0      192.68.5.2                          0 2 1 i
*>i                 172.16.20.1           0    100      0 1 i
```

AS_Path Manipulation

Considering RTF's BGP table, RTF has picked the direct path via AS1 to reach 192.68.11.0/24 because it is shorter. The following configuration shows how the AS_path information can be manipulated to make the AS_path longer by prepending AS path numbers. Considering figure 10–6, we will prepend two extra AS path numbers to the AS_path information sent from RTC to RTA to change RTF's decision about reaching 192.68.11.0/24.

RTC configuration:

```
router bgp 1
 network 192.68.11.0
 neighbor 172.16.20.2 remote-as 3
 neighbor 172.16.20.2 route-map AddASnumbers out
```

```
    neighbor 192.68.6.1 remote-as 2
    no auto-summary

    route-map AddASnumbers permit 10
    set as-path prepend 1 1
```

The preceding configuration prepends two additional AS_path numbers 1 and 1 to the AS_path information sent from RTC to RTA. If you look at RTF's BGP table, you will see that RTF can now reach 192.68.11.0/24 via next hop 192.68.5.2—that is, via path 2 1. RTF will prefer this path because it is shorter than the direct path via AS1, which has a path information of 1 1 1.

```
RTF#sh ip bgp
BGP table version is 18, local router ID is 192.68.5.1
Status codes: s suppressed, d damped, h history, * valid, > best,
i - internal Origin codes: i - IGP, e - EGP, ? - incomplete
     Network          Next Hop         Metric LocPrf Weight Path
* i172.16.1.0/24      172.16.2.254          0    100      0 i
*>                    0.0.0.0               0         32768 i
* i172.16.10.0/24     172.16.2.254         20    100      0 i
*>                    0.0.0.0               0         32768 i
* i172.16.65.0/26     172.16.2.254         20    100      0 i
*>                    0.0.0.0               0         32768 i
* i172.16.220.0/24    172.16.2.254          0    100      0 i
*>                    172.16.1.1           20         32768 i
*> 192.68.10.0        192.68.5.2            0             0 2 i
*> 192.68.11.0        192.68.5.2                          0 2 1 i
* i                   172.16.20.1           0    100      0 1 1 1 i
```

Using Private ASs

This example demonstrates how BGP can be configured to prevent the leakage of private AS numbers into the Internet. Consider figure 10–7; AS1 will prevent private AS number 65001 from being leaked to the Internet when BGP routes are propagated.

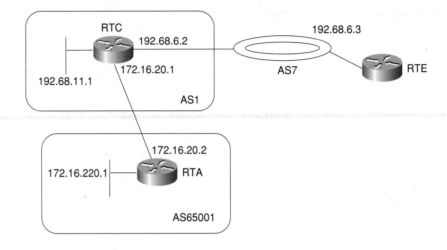

Figure 10–7
Stripping private AS numbers.

RTA configuration:

```
router bgp 65001
 network 172.16.220.0 mask 255.255.255.0
 neighbor 172.16.20.1 remote-as 1
 no auto-summary
```

RTC configuration:

```
router bgp 1
 network 192.68.11.0 mask 255.255.255.0
 neighbor 172.16.20.2 remote-as 65001
 neighbor 192.68.6.3 remote-as 7
 neighbor 192.68.6.3 remove-private-AS
 no auto-summary
```

Note how RTC is using the **remove-private-AS** keyword in its neighbor connection to AS7. The following output shows the BGP tables of RTC and RTE.

```
RTC#show ip bgp
BGP table version is 72, local router ID is 192.68.11.1
Status codes: s suppressed, d damped, h history, * valid, > best,
i - internal Origin codes: i - IGP, e - EGP, ? - incomplete
```

```
      Network          Next Hop         Metric LocPrf Weight Path
*> 172.16.220.0/24  172.16.20.2          0             0 65001 i
*> 192.68.11.0       0.0.0.0             0         32768 i

RTE#sh ip bgp
BGP table version is 245, local router ID is 192.68.30.1
Status codes: s suppressed, * valid, > best, i - internal
Origin codes: i - IGP, e - EGP, ? - incomplete

      Network          Next Hop         Metric LocPrf Weight Path
*> 172.16.220.0/24  192.68.6.2                         0 1 i
*> 192.68.11.0      192.68.6.2            0             0 1 i
```

Note that prefix 172.16.220.0/24 has an AS_path of 65001 in RTC's BGP table and an AS_path of 1 in RTE's BGP table. RTC has stripped the private AS path information when propagating the update to AS7.

The Local Preference Attribute

Setting the local preference also affects the BGP decision process. If multiple paths for the same prefix are available, the path with the larger local preference is preferred. Local preference is at the highest level of the BGP decision process (comes after the Cisco proprietary **weight** parameter); it is considered before the path length. A longer path with a higher local preference is preferred over a shorter path with a lower local preference. In the following example, still referring to figure 10–6, we will configure RTF to have a higher local preference for all BGP updates coming from RTD.

RTF configuration:

```
router bgp 3
 no synchronization
 network 172.16.1.0 mask 255.255.255.0
 network 172.16.10.0 mask 255.255.255.0
 network 172.16.65.0 mask 255.255.255.192
 network 172.16.220.0 mask 255.255.255.0
 neighbor 172.16.2.254  remote-as 3
 neighbor 172.16.2.254 next-hop-self
```

```
neighbor 192.68.5.2 remote-as 2
neighbor 192.68.5.2 filter-list 10 out
neighbor 192.68.5.2 route-map SETLOCAL in
no auto-summary

ip as-path access-list 10 permit ^$

route-map SETLOCAL permit 10
set local-preference 300
```

The route-map SETLOCAL will assign a local preference of 300 for all routes coming from RTD (note the keyword **in**). Note how BGP has decided that prefixes 192.68.10.0/24 and 192.68.11.0/24 are now reachable via next hop 192.68.5.2 having a local preference of 300.

```
RTF#sh ip bgp
BGP table version is 20, local router ID is 192.68.5.1
Status codes: s suppressed, d damped, h history, * valid, > best,
i - internal Origin codes: i - IGP, e - EGP, ? - incomplete
   Network          Next Hop          Metric LocPrf Weight Path
*> 172.16.1.0/24    0.0.0.0                0          32768 i
* i                 172.16.2.254           0    100       0 i
*> 172.16.10.0/24   0.0.0.0                0          32768 i
* i                 172.16.2.254          20    100       0 i
*> 172.16.65.0/26   0.0.0.0                0          32768 i
* i                 172.16.2.254          20    100       0 i
*> 172.16.220.0/24  172.16.1.1            20          32768 i
* i                 172.16.2.254           0    100       0 i
*> 192.68.10.0      192.68.5.2             0    300       0 2 i
*> 192.68.11.0      192.68.5.2                  300       0 2 1 i
```

Because the local preference attribute is carried inside the AS, RTF will pass the local preference value to RTA. This is illustrated in RTA's BGP table. Note how prefix 192.68.11.0/24 is preferred via IBGP with a local preference of 300, even though the AS_path via EBGP is shorter. Other prefixes learned via IBGP such as 172.16.10.0/24 have a default local preference of 100.

```
RTA#sh ip bgp
BGP table version is 43, local router ID is 172.16.2.254
Status codes: s suppressed, d damped, h history, * valid, > best,
i - internal Origin codes: i - IGP, e - EGP, ? - incomplete
   Network          Next Hop         Metric LocPrf Weight Path
* i172.16.1.0/24    172.16.1.2            0    100      0 i
*>                  0.0.0.0               0         32768 i
* i172.16.10.0/24   172.16.1.2            0    100      0 i
*>                  172.16.1.2           20         32768 i
* i172.16.65.0/26   172.16.1.2            0    100      0 i
*>                  172.16.1.2           20         32768 i
* i172.16.220.0/24  172.16.1.2           20    100      0 i
*>                  0.0.0.0               0         32768 i
*>i192.68.10.0      172.16.1.2            0    300      0 2 i
*                   172.16.20.1                      0 1 2 i
*>i192.68.11.0      172.16.1.2                 300    0 2 1 i
*                   172.16.20.1           0              0 1 i
```

The MULTI_EXIT_DISC (MED) Attribute

This example shows how metrics can be used by one AS to influence routing decisions of another AS. In figure 10–8, AS3 is the customer of provider AS1.

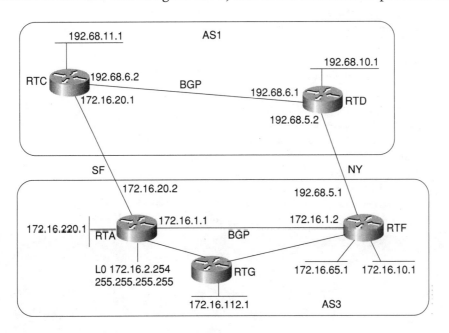

Figure 10–8
Setting the MED attribute.

AS3 wants to generate metrics toward AS1 to influence inbound traffic. In case all BGP attributes are the same, BGP will prefer routes with a lower metric over routes with a higher metric.

RTA and RTF are running IBGP internally and EBGP with the provider AS1. RTG is an internal non-BGP router, running OSPF only. Assume that RTA and RTF want to send MEDs toward AS1 to achieve the following:

1. Incoming traffic toward network 172.16.1.0/24 takes the SF link.
2. Incoming traffic toward all other networks should come in by using the border router that can reach these networks with a smaller internal metric. Incoming traffic toward network 172.16.112.0/24, for example, should come in on the SF link if RTA can reach this network with a smaller internal metric than RTF.

The following is the required configuration:

RTA configuration:

```
router ospf 10
 passive-interface Serial0
 network 172.16.0.0 0.0.255.255 area 0

router bgp 3
 no synchronization
 network 172.16.1.0 mask 255.255.255.0
 network 172.16.10.0 mask 255.255.255.0
 network 172.16.65.0 mask 255.255.255.192
 network 172.16.220.0 mask 255.255.255.0
 network 172.16.112.0 mask 255.255.255.0
 neighbor 172.16.1.2 remote-as 3
 neighbor 172.16.1.2 update-source Loopback0
 neighbor 172.16.20.1 remote-as 1
 neighbor 172.16.20.1 filter-list 10 out
 no auto-summary

ip as-path access-list 10 permit ^$
```

RTF configuration:

```
router ospf 10
 network 172.16.0.0 0.0.255.255 area 0

router bgp 3
 no synchronization
 network 172.16.1.0 mask 255.255.255.0
 network 172.16.10.0 mask 255.255.255.0
 network 172.16.65.0 mask 255.255.255.192
 network 172.16.220.0 mask 255.255.255.0
 network 172.16.112.0 mask 255.255.255.0
 neighbor 172.16.2.254  remote-as 3
 neighbor 172.16.2.254 next-hop-self
 neighbor 192.68.5.2 remote-as 1
 neighbor 192.68.5.2 route-map SETMETRIC out
 neighbor 192.68.5.2 filter-list 10 out
 no auto-summary

ip as-path access-list 10 permit ^$
access-list 1 permit 172.16.1.0 0.0.0.255

route-map SETMETRIC permit 10
 match ip address 1
 set metric 50

route-map SETMETRIC permit 20
```

The preceding configuration will make RTF generate prefix 172.16.1.0/24 with a MED of 50. When AS1 gets the prefix, AS1 will compare a metric of 50 coming from RTF versus a metric of 0 coming from RTA and will prefer the SF link. All other networks will be advertised with their internal metrics carried into BGP, and AS1 will choose the entrance with a smaller metric to the destination.

```
RTD#sh ip bgp
BGP table version is 17, local router ID is 192.68.10.1
```

```
Status codes: s suppressed, d damped, h history, * valid, > best,
i - internal Origin codes: i - IGP, e - EGP, ? - incomplete
   Network           Next Hop          Metric LocPrf Weight Path
*   172.16.1.0/24    192.68.5.1            50             0 3 i
*>i                  192.68.6.2             0    100      0 3 i
*> 172.16.10.0/24    192.68.5.1             0             0 3 i
*> 172.16.65.0/26    192.68.5.1             0             0 3 i
*   172.16.112.0/24  192.68.5.1            84             0 3 i
*>i                  192.68.6.2            74    100      0 3 i
*   172.16.220.0/24  192.68.5.1            20             0 3 i
*>i                  192.68.6.2             0    100      0 3 i
*> 192.68.10.0       0.0.0.0               0         32768 i
*>i192.68.11.0       192.68.6.2             0    100      0 i
```

Note how RTD has preferred network 172.16.1.0/24 via next hop 192.68.6.2, which is RTC (RTC is using **next-hop-self**). This is because of the lower metric (0 <50). For all other networks, RTD is preferring routes with the smaller metrics. Note that 172.16.112.0/24 is learned via metric 74 from RTA and metric 84 from RTF. RTD will prefer the SF link to reach 172.16.112.0/24.

For BGP learned routes, an AS can also advertise these routes to another AS with the internal IGP metric carried into BGP. This is achieved by using the following command as part of a route map towards a neighbor: **set metric-type internal**. This would cause BGP routes to carry the internal IGP metric as MED.

The Community Attribute

This example shows how the community attribute can be used to dynamically influence the routing decisions of another AS. With the network illustrated in figure 10–9, the following configuration example shows how AS3 can advertise route 172.16.65.0/26 to AS1 and dynamically instruct AS1 not to advertise this route externally. AS3 will assign route 172.16.65.0/26 the community attribute "no-export" when advertising it to AS1.

NOTES

The **send-community** option in the **neighbor** router subcommand is used to cause the assigned community to be sent out.

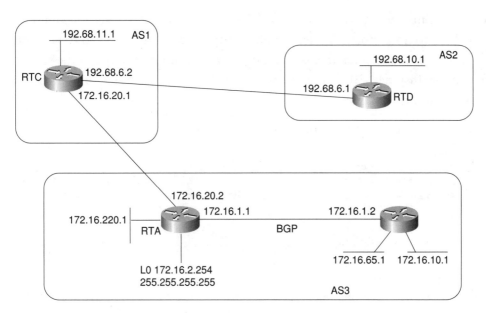

Figure 10–9
Setting the community attribute.

RTA configuration:

```
router bgp 3
 no synchronization
 network 172.16.1.0 mask 255.255.255.0
 network 172.16.10.0 mask 255.255.255.0
 network 172.16.65.0 mask 255.255.255.192
 network 172.16.220.0 mask 255.255.255.0
 neighbor 172.16.1.2 remote-as 3
 neighbor 172.16.1.2 update-source Loopback0
 neighbor 172.16.20.1 remote-as 1
 neighbor 172.16.20.1 send-community
 neighbor 172.16.20.1 route-map SETCOMMUNITY out
 no auto-summary

access-list 1 permit 172.16.65.0 0.0.0.63

route-map SETCOMMUNITY permit 10
match ip address 1
set community no-export

route-map SETCOMMUNITY permit 20
```

The preceding RTA configuration shows that RTA has defined a route map
SETCOMMUNITY toward neighbor 172.16.20.1 (RTC). Instance 10 of the

the route map will match on prefix 172.16.65.0/26 and will set its community attribute to **no-export**. The **send-community** keyword assigned to the neighbor session is required to enable the community attribute to be sent to the specified neighbor. Instance 20 of the route map will enable all other networks to be passed with no change.

RTC's BGP entry for 172.16.65.0/26 will show the following:

```
RTC#sh ip bgp 172.16.65.0 255.255.255.192
BGP routing table entry for 172.16.65.0/26, version 3
Paths: (1 available, best #1, not advertised to EBGP peer)
  3
    172.16.20.2 from 172.16.20.2 (172.16.2.254)
      Origin IGP, metric 20, valid, external, best
      Community: no-export
```

Note how the entry has been assigned the community no-export and instructions that it is not to be advertised to EBGP peers. RTC will not propagate this entry to its external peer RTD. Note that in the following RTD BGP table, RTD did not receive an update about 172.16.65.0/26.

```
RTD#sh ip bgp
BGP table version is 22, local router ID is 192.68.10.1
Status codes: s suppressed, d damped, h history, * valid, > best,
i - internal Origin codes: i - IGP, e - EGP, ? - incomplete
   Network          Next Hop          Metric LocPrf Weight Path
*> 172.16.1.0/24    192.68.6.2                        0 1 3 i
*> 172.16.10.0/24   192.68.6.2                        0 1 3 i
*> 172.16.220.0/24  192.68.6.2                        0 1 3 i
*> 192.68.10.0      0.0.0.0           0         32768 i
*> 192.68.11.0      192.68.6.2        0             0 1 i
```

BGP4 AGGREGATION

The following examples demonstrate different methods of aggregation that are seen on the Internet. The way aggregates are formed and advertised and whether they carry with them more specific routes will influence traffic patterns and sizes of BGP routing tables. Remember that aggregation applies to routes that exist in the BGP routing table. An aggregate can be sent if at least one more specific route of that aggregate exists in the BGP table.

Aggregate Only, Suppressing the More Specific

This example shows how an aggregate can be generated without propagating any of the more specific routes that fall under the aggregate. In the network illustrated in figure 10–10, RTA is sending prefixes 172.16.220.0/24, 172.16.1.0/24, 172.16.10.0/24, and 172.16.65.0/26 toward RTC. The following configuration shows how RTA can aggregate all these routes into a single prefix 172.16.0.0/16 and send it to RTC. This of course assumes that AS3 is the sole owner of the class B 172.16.0.0/16. RTF is also doing the same aggregation on its end with a configuration similar to RTA.

RTA configuration:

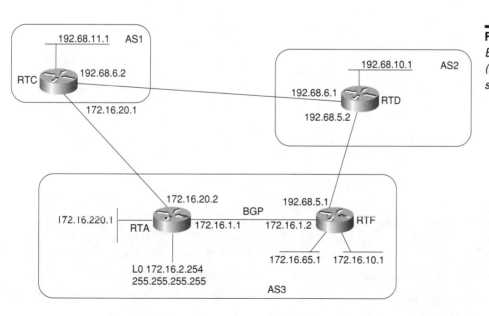

Figure 10–10
BGP aggregation (suppressing the specific routes).

```
router bgp 3
 no synchronization
 network 172.16.1.0 mask 255.255.255.0
 network 172.16.10.0 mask 255.255.255.0
 network 172.16.65.0 mask 255.255.255.192
 network 172.16.220.0 mask 255.255.255.0
 aggregate-address 172.16.0.0 255.255.0.0 summary-only
 neighbor 172.16.1.2 remote-as 3
 neighbor 172.16.1.2 update-source Loopback0
 neighbor 172.16.20.1 remote-as 1
 neighbor 172.16.20.1 filter-list 10 out
 no auto-summary

ip as-path access-list 10 permit ^$
```

RTA's configuration uses the aggregate-address command to aggregate all the more specific routes of 172.16.0.0/16 into a single address. RTA's BGP table (illustrated in the show command output that follows) indicates that a new aggregate 172.16.0.0/16 has been originated by this router (next hop is 0.0.0.0), whereas all the more specific prefixes have been suppressed (note the "s" at the far left). In this case, the same result could have been achieved by using auto-summary.

```
RTA#sh ip bgp
BGP table version is 14, local router ID is 172.16.2.254
Status codes: s suppressed, d damped, h history, * valid, > best,
i - internal Origin codes: i - IGP, e - EGP, ? - incomplete
    Network          Next Hop          Metric LocPrf Weight Path
*> 172.16.0.0        0.0.0.0                          32768 i
* i                  172.16.1.2                 100       0 i
s> 172.16.1.0/24     0.0.0.0                0         32768 i
s> 172.16.10.0/24    172.16.1.2            20         32768 i
s> 172.16.65.0/26    172.16.1.2            20         32768 i
s> 172.16.220.0/24   0.0.0.0                0         32768 i
*  192.68.10.0       172.16.20.1                          0 1 2 i
*>i                  172.16.1.2             0   100       0 2 i
*> 192.68.11.0       172.16.20.1           0              0 1 i
```

The output of RTC's BGP table shows that the only prefix that was learned from RTA is the aggregate 172.16.0.0/16. Because RTF is also performing the same aggregation, RTC will also learn an aggregate that is originated from RTF (next hop RTD via AS2).

```
RTC#sh ip bgp
BGP table version is 22, local router ID is 192.68.11.1
Status codes: s suppressed, d damped, h history, * valid, > best,
i - internal Origin codes: i - IGP, e - EGP, ? - incomplete
   Network          Next Hop         Metric LocPrf Weight Path
*> 172.16.0.0       172.16.20.2                        0 3 i
*                   192.68.6.1                         0 2 3 i
*> 192.68.10.0      192.68.6.1            0             0 2 i
*> 192.68.11.0      0.0.0.0              0         32768 i
```

Looking at the specific 172.16.0.0/16 aggregate entry, the following display provides more information about the aggregate itself. Note the presence of the "atomic-aggregate" attribute, which indicates that the prefix 172.16.0.0/16 is an aggregate. Also note the presence of the "aggregated by 3 192.68.5.1" and "aggregated by 3 172.16.2.254" statements, which represent the "aggregator" attribute. The "aggregator" attribute (Chapter 5) indicates the AS number and Router ID of the router who originated the aggregate; in this case, AS3 and the Router IDs of RTA and RTF.

```
RTC#sh ip bgp 172.16.0.0
BGP routing table entry for 172.16.0.0/16, version 22
Paths: (2 available, best #1, advertised over EBGP)
  3, (aggregated by 3 172.16.2.254)
    172.16.20.2 from 172.16.20.2 (172.16.2.254)
      Origin IGP, valid, external, atomic-aggregate, best
  2 3, (aggregated by 3 192.68.5.1)
    192.68.6.1 from 192.68.6.1 (192.68.10.1)
      Origin IGP, valid, external, atomic-aggregate
```

Aggregates can also be generated by using static routes. This is illustrated in the following RTA and RTF configuration.

RTA configuration:

```
router bgp 3
 no synchronization
 network 172.16.0.0
 neighbor 172.16.1.2 remote-as 3
 neighbor 172.16.1.2 update-source Loopback0
 neighbor 172.16.20.1 remote-as 1
```

```
    neighbor 172.16.20.1 filter-list 10 out
    no auto-summary

    ip route 172.16.0.0 255.255.0.0 null0
    ip as-path access-list 10 permit ^$
```

RTF configuration:

```
router bgp 3
 no synchronization
 network 172.16.0.0
 neighbor 172.16.2.254  remote-as 3
 neighbor 172.16.2.254 next-hop-self
 neighbor 192.68.5.2 remote-as 2
 neighbor 192.68.5.2 filter-list 10 out
 no auto-summary

    ip route 172.16.0.0 255.255.0.0 null0
    ip as-path access-list 10 permit ^$
```

The preceding configuration places a static instance of 172.16.0.0/16 in the routing table. Note that the static entry is pointing to null0 (pit bucket). If RTA or RTF have no knowledge of the more specific routes of 172.16.0.0, then traffic will be dropped. This is to prevent loops in case RTA or RTF are themselves following defaults to their providers (see "Aggregation and Loops," in Chapter 3, "Handling IP Address Depletion").

Aggregate Plus More Specific Routes

In some cases, more specific routes, in addition to the aggregate, need to be passed (leaked) to a neighboring AS. This is usually done in ASs multihomed to a single provider. An AS (the provider) that gets the more specific routes would be able to make a better decision about which way to take to reach the route. (You have already seen how an AS receiving different metrics can direct the traffic accordingly.)

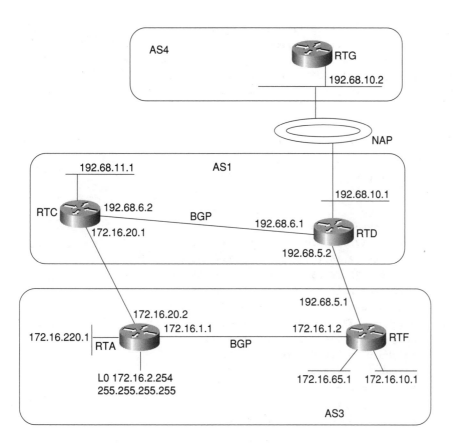

Figure 10–11
More BGP aggregation scenarios.

In figure 10–11, AS3 is multihomed to a single provider AS1. RTA and RTF in AS3 can send the aggregate 172.16.0.0/16 and the more specific routes toward AS1. The following configuration of RTA and RTF will do so:

RTA configuration:

```
router bgp 3
 no synchronization
 network 172.16.1.0 mask 255.255.255.0
 network 172.16.10.0 mask 255.255.255.0
 network 172.16.65.0 mask 255.255.255.192
 network 172.16.220.0 mask 255.255.255.0
```

```
        aggregate-address 172.16.0.0 255.255.0.0
        neighbor 172.16.1.2 remote-as 3
        neighbor 172.16.1.2 update-source Loopback0
        neighbor 172.16.20.1 remote-as 1
        neighbor 172.16.20.1 filter-list 10 out
        no auto-summary

        ip as-path access-list 10 permit ^$
```

RTF configuration:

```
        router bgp 3
         no synchronization
         network 172.16.1.0 mask 255.255.255.0
         network 172.16.10.0 mask 255.255.255.0
         network 172.16.65.0 mask 255.255.255.192
         network 172.16.220.0 mask 255.255.255.0
         aggregate-address 172.16.0.0 255.255.0.0
         neighbor 172.16.2.254  remote-as 3
         neighbor 172.16.2.254 next-hop-self
         neighbor 192.68.5.2 remote-as 1
         neighbor 192.68.5.2 filter-list 10 out
         no auto-summary

        ip as-path access-list 10 permit ^$
```

Note that the **aggregate-address** command in both the RTA and RTF configurations does *not* include the **summary-only** parameter, so both the aggregate
and specific routes will be advertised. The following output of RTC's BGP table
shows that RTC has learned the aggregate 172.16.0.0/16 in addition to the
more specific routes. RTD will also receive the same information.

```
        RTC#sh ip bgp
        BGP table version is 28, local router ID is 192.68.11.1
        Status codes: s suppressed, d damped, h history, * valid, > best,
        i - internal Origin codes: i - IGP, e - EGP, ? - incomplete
           Network          Next Hop          Metric LocPrf Weight Path
        * i172.16.0.0       192.68.6.1                 100      0 3 i
        *>                  172.16.20.2                          0 3 i
        * i172.16.1.0/24    192.68.6.1             0   100      0 3 i
        *>                  172.16.20.2            0            0 3 i
```

```
    * i172.16.10.0/24    192.68.6.1            0    100      0 3 i
    *>                   172.16.20.2          20             0 3 i
    * i172.16.65.0/26    192.68.6.1            0    100      0 3 i
    *>                   172.16.20.2          20             0 3 i
    * i172.16.220.0/24   192.68.6.1           20    100      0 3 i
    *>                   172.16.20.2           0             0 3 i
    *>i192.68.10.0       192.68.6.1            0    100        0 i
    *> 192.68.11.0       0.0.0.0               0         32768 i
```

Using the community "no-export" attribute, RTA and RTF can instruct RTC and RTD not to export the more specific routes and to only send the aggregate 172.16.0.0/16 toward AS4. This is very useful in controlling routing table expansion, assuming that AS4 can get by using the aggregate route only. The following is the needed configuration on RTF; RTA will have the same relative configuration.

RTF configuration:

```
router bgp 3
 no synchronization
 network 172.16.1.0 mask 255.255.255.0
 network 172.16.10.0 mask 255.255.255.0
 network 172.16.65.0 mask 255.255.255.192
 network 172.16.220.0 mask 255.255.255.0
 aggregate-address 172.16.0.0 255.255.0.0
 neighbor 172.16.2.254 remote-as 3
 neighbor 172.16.2.254 next-hop-self
 neighbor 192.68.5.2 remote-as 1
 neighbor 192.68.5.2 send-community
 neighbor 192.68.5.2 route-map SETCOMMUNITY out
 neighbor 192.68.5.2 filter-list 10 out
 no auto-summary

ip as-path access-list 10 permit ^$
access-list 101 permit ip 172.16.0.0 0.0.255.255 host 255.255.0.0

route-map SETCOMMUNITY permit 10
 match ip address 101

route-map SETCOMMUNITY permit 20
set community no-export
```

In the preceding configuration, RTF will use multiple instances of a route map SETCOMMUNITY to assign the more specific routes 172.16.1.0/24, 172.16.220.0/24, 172.16.10.0/24, and 172.16.65.0/26 with community "no-export," which instructs RTD not to send these routes to exterior ASs such as AS4. On the other hand, the aggregate itself, 172.16.0.0/16, is passed as is without any community and will be sent to AS4.

Instance 10 of the route map uses an extended access-list 101, which matches on the aggregate 172.16.0.0/16 only. Note how the host 255.255.0.0 part of the access list makes sure that no other entry that starts with 172.16 matches by specifiying the mask to be exactly 255.255.0.0 and nothing else. Instance 10 does not set any community values; hence, the aggregate will be passed as is.

Instance 20 will make sure that all the more specific routes will have a community "no-export."

The following are the required RTC and RTD configurations:

RTC configuration:

```
router bgp 1
 no synchronization
 network 192.68.11.0
 neighbor 172.16.20.2 remote-as 3
 neighbor 192.68.6.1 remote-as 1
 neighbor 192.68.6.1 next-hop-self
 neighbor 192.68.6.1 send-community
 no auto-summary
```

RTD configuration:

```
router bgp 1
 no synchronization
 network 192.68.10.0
 neighbor 192.68.5.1 remote-as 3
 neighbor 192.68.6.2 remote-as 1
 neighbor 192.68.6.2 next-hop-self
 neighbor 192.68.10.2 remote-as 4
 no auto-summary
```

Note the **send-community** neighbor parameter in RTC's configuration. Because RTA is also performing the same aggregation, RTD will receive the specific routes from its IBGP session with RTC. If RTC does not propagate the "no-export" community to RTD, RTD will advertise the specific routes to external peers.

The following are selected entries in RTD's BGP table. The first entry indicates that prefix 172.16.220.0/24 is not advertised to EBGP peer. This is because RTA and RTF have set this prefix (and all other specific routes) with community no-export. The second entry indicates that the aggregate itself has been originated by RTA and RTF as is. The aggregate will be passed on to AS4.

```
RTD#sh ip bgp 172.16.220.0
BGP routing table entry for 172.16.220.0/24, version 5
Paths: (2 available, best #2, not advertised to EBGP peer)
  3
    192.68.5.1 from 192.68.5.1
      Origin IGP, metric 20, valid, external
      Community: no-export
  3
    192.68.6.2 from 192.68.6.2 (192.68.11.1)
      Origin IGP, metric 0, localpref 100, valid, internal, best
      Community: no-export

RTD#sh ip bgp 172.16.0.0
BGP routing table entry for 172.16.0.0/16, version 8
Paths: (2 available, best #1, advertised over IBGP, EBGP)
  3, (aggregated by 3 192.68.5.1)
    192.68.5.1 from 192.68.5.1
      Origin IGP, valid, external, atomic-aggregate, best
  3, (aggregated by 3 172.16.2.254)
    192.68.6.2 from 192.68.6.2 (192.68.11.1)
      Origin IGP, localpref 100, valid, internal, atomic-aggregate
```

Looking at the BGP table of RTG, you will note that only the aggregate 172.16.0.0/16 has been propagated from AS3 to AS4. All the more specific routes do not show up.

```
RTG#sh ip bgp
BGP table version is 14, local router ID is 192.68.10.2
Status codes: s suppressed, d damped, h history, * valid, > best,
i - internal Origin codes: i - IGP, e - EGP, ? - incomplete
   Network          Next Hop          Metric LocPrf Weight Path
*> 172.16.0.0       192.68.10.1                          0 1 3 i
*> 192.68.10.0      192.68.10.1             0            0 1 i
*> 192.68.11.0      192.68.10.1                          0 1 i
```

Aggregate with a Subset of the More Specific Routes

In figure 10–12, we will show how AS3 can utilize a combination of aggregation
and more specific routes to influence what link AS1 uses to reach AS3's networks.
RTA will send over its direct link to AS1 the aggregate 172.16.0.0/16 plus the
more specific routes 172.16.1.0/24, 172.16.10.0/24, and 172.16.65.0/26. RTF
will send over its direct link to AS3, the aggregate 172.16.0.0/16, plus the more
specific route 172.16.220.0/24 only. As a result, AS1 is forced to reach
172.16.220.0/24 via RTF and all the other routes in AS3 via RTA.

Figure 10–12
*BGP aggregates
with subset of
specific routes.*

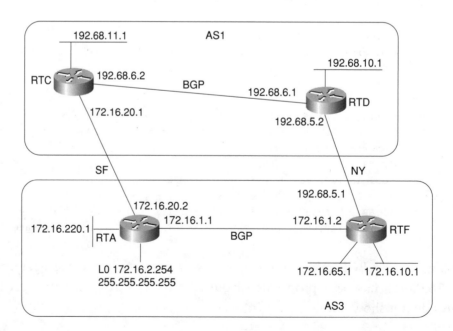

RTA configuration:

```
router bgp 3
 no synchronization
 network 172.16.1.0 mask 255.255.255.0
 network 172.16.10.0 mask 255.255.255.0
 network 172.16.65.0 mask 255.255.255.192
 network 172.16.220.0 mask 255.255.255.0
 aggregate-address 172.16.0.0 255.255.0.0 suppress-map SUPPRESS
 neighbor 172.16.1.2 remote-as 3
 neighbor 172.16.1.2 update-source Loopback0
 neighbor 172.16.20.1 remote-as 1
 neighbor 172.16.20.1 filter-list 10 out
 no auto-summary

ip as-path access-list 10 permit ^$
access-list 1 permit 172.16.220.0 0.0.0.255
access-list 1 deny any

route-map SUPPRESS permit 10
 match ip address 1
```

The **suppress-map** is another form of route-map that can be used to indicate the more specific routes to be suppressed or the more specific routes to be allowed. When a route is permitted through the suppress map, the route is suppressed. If the route is not permitted (denied), the route is not suppressed—that is, allowed. Note that the deny logic here does not prevent the route from being advertised; rather, it prevents it from being suppressed.

In RTA's configuration, we have used a suppress map called SUPPRESS that will prevent 172.16.220.0/24 from being advertised and enable all other routes. As a result, RTA will announce the aggregate 172.16.0.0/16, plus the more specific routes 172.16.1.0/24, 172.16.10.0/24, and 172.16.65.0/26. The following is RTA's BGP table; note how the suppressed entries have the "s" at the far left.

```
RTA#sh ip bgp
BGP table version is 17, local router ID is 172.16.2.254
Status codes: s suppressed, d damped, h history, * valid, > best,
i - internal Origin codes: i - IGP, e - EGP, ? - incomplete
```

```
       Network            Next Hop          Metric LocPrf Weight Path
  * i172.16.0.0          172.16.1.2                  100      0 i
  *>                     0.0.0.0                           32768 i
  *> 172.16.1.0/24       0.0.0.0                0          32768 i
  *> 172.16.10.0/24      172.16.1.2            20          32768 i
  *> 172.16.65.0/26      172.16.1.2            20          32768 i
  s> 172.16.220.0/24     0.0.0.0                0          32768 i
  * i192.68.10.0         172.16.1.2             0   100      0 1 i
  *>                     172.16.20.1                         0 1 i
  * i192.68.11.0         172.16.1.2             0   100      0 1 i
  *>                     172.16.20.1            0             0 1 i
```

On the other hand, RTF will use a similar logic to advertise the aggregate, plus the more specific route 172.16.220.0/24. RTF's configuration will include a suppress map called ALLOW that allows the prefix 172.16.220.0/24 and suppresses everything else. As a result, AS1 will be forced to use RTF to reach 172.16.220.0/24. The naming of the suppress maps SUPPRESS and ALLOW reflects the main function of the route map. In RTA's configuration, it made more sense to suppress a specific entry and allow the rest because the number of routes to be allowed is large. In RTF's configuration, it made sense to allow a specific entry and suppress the rest because the number of routes to be suppressed is large.

RTF configuration:

```
router bgp 3
 no synchronization
 network 172.16.1.0 mask 255.255.255.0
 network 172.16.10.0 mask 255.255.255.0
 network 172.16.65.0 mask 255.255.255.192
 network 172.16.220.0 mask 255.255.255.0
 aggregate-address 172.16.0.0 255.255.0.0 suppress-map ALLOW
 neighbor 172.16.2.254 remote-as 3
 neighbor 172.16.2.254 next-hop-self
 neighbor 192.68.5.2 remote-as 1
 neighbor 192.68.5.2 filter-list 10 out
 no auto-summary

ip as-path access-list 10 permit ^$
access-list 1 deny 172.16.220.0 0.0.0.255
access-list 1 permit any
```

```
route-map ALLOW permit 10
 match ip address 1
```

The preceding configuration of RTF will allow the aggregate 172.16.0.0/16 and the more specific route 172.16.220.0/24 to be advertised; all other more specific routes will be suppressed. The following is RTF's BGP table:

```
RTF#sh ip bgp
BGP table version is 17, local router ID is 192.68.5.1
Status codes: s suppressed, d damped, h history, * valid, > best,
i - internal Origin codes: i - IGP, e - EGP, ? - incomplete
    Network          Next Hop        Metric LocPrf Weight Path
*> 172.16.0.0        0.0.0.0                        32768 i
*  i                 172.16.2.254            100        0 i
s> 172.16.1.0/24     0.0.0.0              0         32768 i
s  i                 172.16.2.254         0  100        0 i
s> 172.16.10.0/24    0.0.0.0              0         32768 i
s  i                 172.16.2.254        20  100        0 i
s> 172.16.65.0/26    0.0.0.0              0         32768 i
s  i                 172.16.2.254        20  100        0 i
*> 172.16.220.0/24   172.16.1.1          20         32768 i
*> 192.68.10.0       192.68.5.2           0            0 1 i
*  i                 172.16.20.1             100      0 1 i
*> 192.68.11.0       192.68.5.2                        0 1 i
*  i                 172.16.20.1             100      0 1 i
```

Given the preceding configuration of RTA and RTF, AS1 will only be able to reach 172.16.220.0/24 via the RTD-RTF link and 172.16.1.0/24, 172.16.65.0/26, 172.16.10.0/24 via the RTC-RTA link. This is illustrated in the BGP table of RTD.

```
RTD#sh ip bgp
BGP table version is 19, local router ID is 192.68.10.1
Status codes: s suppressed, d damped, h history, * valid, > best,
i - internal Origin codes: i - IGP, e - EGP, ? - incomplete
    Network          Next Hop        Metric LocPrf Weight Path
*  i172.16.0.0       192.68.6.2              100      0 3 i
*>                   192.68.5.1                       0 3 i
*>i172.16.1.0/24     192.68.6.2           0  100      0 3 i
*>i172.16.10.0/24    192.68.6.2          20  100      0 3 i
*>i172.16.65.0/26    192.68.6.2          20  100      0 3 i
```

```
*> 172.16.220.0/24   192.68.5.1         20            0 3 i
*> 192.68.10.0       0.0.0.0             0        32768 i
*>i192.68.11.0       192.68.6.2          0   100      0 i
```

RTD has only one choice to reach 172.16.220.0/24, and that is via the RTD-RTF link. In case of link failure, the aggregate is still advertised via both links, and the route will follow the aggregate.

In some situations, administrators require that some neighbors receive some of the specific routes already suppressed. Suppression could have been done via the summary-only parameter or the **neighbor command**. In this case, Cisco provides a different form of route map called the unsuppress map that is applied on a per neighbor bases. The unsuppress map allows previously suppressed routes to be advertised. If for example, RTA wanted to prevent 172.16.220.0/24 from being suppressed toward 172.16.1.2 (RTF), the following RTA router configuration would be used:

```
neighbor 172.16.1.2 unsuppress-map AllowSpecifics

route-map AllowSpecifics permit 10
match ip address 1

access-list 1 permit 172.16.220.0 0.0.0.255
```

The preceding configuration will allow advertisement of prefix 172.16.220.0/24 toward RTF.

Loss of Information Inside Aggregates (AS-SET)

Aggregation causes loss of granularity. The detailed information that exists in the specific prefixes will be lost when summarized in the form of aggregates. The purpose of AS-SET is to try to save the attributes carried in the specific routes in a mathematical SET that gives a better idea of the elements of the aggregate.

In figure 10–13, RTA is aggregating prefixes 192.68.10.0/24 and 192.68.11.0/24 coming from AS2 and AS1, respectively. Without AS-SET, the aggregate 192.68.0.0/16 will be considered as having originated from AS3 and will lose all the specific attribute information that the individual prefixes 192.68.10.0/24 and 192.68.11.0/24 have. We will present two configuration possibilities for RTA—first without AS-SET and second with AS-SET. We will see how the aggregate 192.68.0.0/16 will look in both scenarios.

RTA configuration without AS-SET:

```
router bgp 3
 no synchronization
 network 172.16.1.0 mask 255.255.255.0
 network 172.16.10.0 mask 255.255.255.0
 network 172.16.65.0 mask 255.255.255.192
 network 172.16.220.0 mask 255.255.255.0
 aggregate-address 192.68.0.0 255.255.0.0
 neighbor 172.16.1.2 remote-as 3
 neighbor 172.16.1.2 update-source Loopback0
 neighbor 172.16.20.1 remote-as 1
 neighbor 172.16.20.1 filter-list 10 out
```

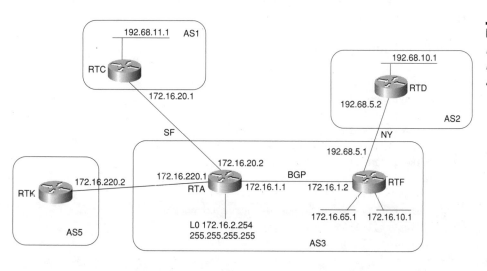

Figure 10–13
Dealing with loss of information with aggregates.

```
neighbor 172.16.220.2 remote-as 5
no auto-summary

ip as-path access-list 10 permit ^$
```

The following shows how the aggregate 192.68.0.0/16 will look when it is received by RTK. Note that the aggregate has lost the individual path information because the AS_path consists of AS number 3 only.

```
RTK#sh ip bgp
BGP table version is 8, local router ID is 172.16.220.2
Status codes: s suppressed, d damped, h history, * valid, > best,
i - internal Origin codes: i - IGP, e - EGP, ? - incomplete
   Network          Next Hop         Metric LocPrf Weight Path
*> 172.16.1.0/24    172.16.220.1          0            0 3 i
*> 172.16.10.0/24   172.16.220.1         20            0 3 i
*> 172.16.65.0/26   172.16.220.1         20            0 3 i
*> 172.16.220.0/24  172.16.220.1          0            0 3 i
*> 192.68.0.0/16    172.16.220.1                       0 3 i
*> 192.68.10.0      172.16.220.1                       0 3 2 i
*> 192.68.11.0      172.16.220.1                       0 3 1 i
```

Using the AS-SET concept, the aggregate will be sent out from RTA with a SET of the path information.

RTA configuration with AS-SET:

```
router bgp 3
 no synchronization
 network 172.16.1.0 mask 255.255.255.0
 network 172.16.10.0 mask 255.255.255.0
 network 172.16.65.0 mask 255.255.255.192
 network 172.16.220.0 mask 255.255.255.0
 aggregate-address 192.68.0.0 255.255.0.0 as-set
 neighbor 172.16.1.2 remote-as 3
 neighbor 172.16.1.2 update-source Loopback0
 neighbor 172.16.20.1 remote-as 1
 neighbor 172.16.20.1 filter-list 10 out
```

```
neighbor 172.16.220.2 remote-as 5
no auto-summary

ip as-path access-list 10 permit ^$
```

In the following BGP routing table for RTK, note how the aggregate 192.68.0.0/16 changed to include a SET {2,1} within its path information. This indicates that the aggregate actually summarizes routes that have passed via ASs 1 and 2. The AS-SET information becomes important in avoiding routing loops because it keeps an indication of where the route has been.

```
RTK#show ip bgp
BGP table version is 12, local router ID is 172.16.220.2
Status codes: s suppressed, d damped, h history, * valid, > best,
i - internal Origin codes: i - IGP, e - EGP, ? - incomplete

   Network          Next Hop         Metric LocPrf Weight Path
*> 172.16.1.0/24    172.16.220.1          0             0 3 i
*> 172.16.10.0/24   172.16.220.1         20             0 3 i
*> 172.16.65.0/26   172.16.220.1         20             0 3 i
*> 172.16.220.0/24  172.16.220.1          0             0 3 i
*> 192.68.0.0/16    172.16.220.1                        0 3 {2,1} i
*> 192.68.10.0      172.16.220.1                        0 3 2 i
*> 192.68.11.0      172.16.220.1                        0 3 1 i
```

In case the aggregate reaches AS1 or AS2, BGP's loop detection behavior will note the set information and drop the aggregate.

Given that the aggregate with the AS-SET contains information about each individual route that is summarized, changes in the individual route will cause the aggregate to be updated. In our example, if 192.68.11.0/24 goes down, the path information of the aggregate will change from 3 {2,1} to 3 2, and the aggregate will be updated. If the aggregate summarizes tens and hundreds of routes, the aggregate will be constantly flip-flopping if the routes forming the aggregate have problems.

Changing the Attributes of the Aggregate

In some situations, changing the attributes of the aggregate is required. This example shows one scenario where this could be useful.

As you have seen already, the aggregate can carry information about its individual elements if configured with the AS-SET option. If one or more of the routes forming the AS-SET aggregate are configured with "no-export" community attribute, then the aggregate itself will carry the same attribute. This will prevent the aggregate from being exported. To remedy this situation, the community attribute of the aggregate can be modified by using what Cisco calls an "attribute-map," which is another form of a route map that applies to aggregates only.

In figure 10–13, RTC has set the community of 192.68.11.0/24 to "no-export." If RTA is aggregating 192.68.11.0/24 into 192.68.0.0/16 using AS-SET, the aggregate itself will also contain the "no-export" community. The following are the configurations of RTC and RTA, which are needed to achieve this behavior:

RTC configuration:

```
router bgp 1
 network 192.68.11.0
 neighbor 172.16.20.2 remote-as 3
 neighbor 172.16.20.2 send-community
 neighbor 172.16.20.2 route-map SETCOMMUNITY out
 no auto-summary

access-list 1 permit 192.68.11.0 0.0.0.255

route-map SETCOMMUNITY permit 10
 match ip address 1
 set community no-export

route-map SETCOMMUNITY permit 20
```

RTA configuration:

```
router bgp 3
 no synchronization
 network 172.16.1.0 mask 255.255.255.0
 network 172.16.10.0 mask 255.255.255.0
 network 172.16.65.0 mask 255.255.255.192
 network 172.16.220.0 mask 255.255.255.0
 aggregate-address 192.68.0.0 255.255.0.0 as-set
 neighbor 172.16.1.2 remote-as 3
 neighbor 172.16.1.2 update-source Loopback0
 neighbor 172.16.20.1 remote-as 1
 neighbor 172.16.20.1 filter-list 10 out
 neighbor 172.16.220.2 remote-as 5
 no auto-summary


ip as-path access-list 10 permit ^$
```

Because RTA is doing the aggregation using the AS-SET, the aggregate itself will contain all the elements that the individual routes have; in particular, the community "no-export" coming from prefix 192.68.11.0/24 (originated by RTC). Note how the following display indicates that 192.68.0.0/16 is not to be advertised to EBGP peers.

```
RTA#show ip bgp 192.68.0.0
BGP routing table entry for 192.68.0.0 255.255.0.0, version 22
Paths: (2 available, best #2, not advertised to EBGP peer, advertised
over IBGP)
  Local (aggregated by 3 192.68.5.1)
    172.16.1.2 from 172.16.1.2 (192.68.5.1)
      Origin IGP, localpref 100, valid, internal, atomic-aggregate
  {2,1} (aggregated by 3 172.16.2.254)
    0.0.0.0
      Origin IGP, localpref 100, weight 32768, valid, aggregated, local,
best
        Community: no-export
```

By using the "attribute-map," we can manipulate the aggregate attributes. In this example, we can set the community to "none" and allow the aggregate to be advertised to EBGP peers.

RTA configuration:

```
router bgp 3
 no synchronization
 network 172.16.1.0 mask 255.255.255.0
 network 172.16.10.0 mask 255.255.255.0
 network 172.16.65.0 mask 255.255.255.192
 aggregate-address 192.68.0.0 255.255.0.0 as-set attribute-map
 SET_ATTRIBUTE
 neighbor 172.16.1.2 remote-as 3
 neighbor 172.16.1.2 update-source Loopback0
 neighbor 172.16.20.1 remote-as 1
neighbor 172.16.20.1 filter-list 10 out
 neighbor 172.16.220.2 remote-as 5
 no auto-summary

 ip as-path access-list 10 permit ^$

 route-map SET_ATTRIBUTE permit 10
  set community none
```

The preceding RTA configuration defines an "attribute-map" called SET_ATTRIBUTE that sets the community attribute of the aggregate to none. Note how the following display shows that the aggregate 192.68.0.0/16 is now being advertised to EBGP peers.

```
RTA#show ip bgp 192.68.0.0
BGP routing table entry for 192.68.0.0 255.255.0.0, version 10
Paths: (2 available, best #2, advertised over IBGP, EBGP)
  Local (aggregated by 3 192.68.5.1)
    172.16.1.2 from 172.16.1.2 (192.68.5.1)
      Origin IGP, localpref 100, valid, internal, atomic-aggregate
  {2,1} (aggregated by 3 172.16.2.254)
    0.0.0.0
      Origin IGP, localpref 100, weight 32768, valid, aggregated, local,
best
```

Forming the Aggregate Based on a Subset of Specific Routes

Having control over which individual prefixes form the aggregate is very useful in deciding which attributes the aggregate is going to carry. In the previous example, if we could exclude prefix 192.68.11.0/24 from being part of the prefixes that form the aggregate, the aggregate would not inherit the "no-export" community attribute.

The **advertise map** is yet another form of a route map that enables you to form the aggregated route based on a limited selection of the more specific routes.

In figure 10–14, RTA and RTF are getting routes 192.68.11.0/24 and 192.68.10.0/24 from ASs 1 and 2, respectively. If RTA and RTF are to aggregate these routes into 192.68.0.0/16 using the "as-set" option, the aggregate cannot be sent back to either AS1 or AS2 because it contains {1 2} in the AS_path information. This is due to the normal BGP behavior in detecting loops.

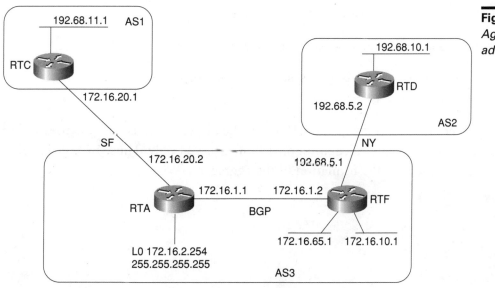

Figure 10–14
Aggregation with advertise-map.

Assume that the required behavior is to have the aggregate 192.68.0.0/16 be sent back to AS1 and not to AS2. The solution is to have AS1 not be part of the AS_path of the aggregate; then, AS1 will not drop the aggregate. This could be achieved by having RTA and RTF form the aggregate based on the 192.68.10.0/24 prefix only, using the advertise-map option.

RTA's configuration would be set as in the following example. RTF would have the same relative configuration.

RTA configuration:

```
router bgp 3
 no synchronization
 network 172.16.1.0 mask 255.255.255.0
 network 172.16.10.0 mask 255.255.255.0
 network 172.16.65.0 mask 255.255.255.192
 aggregate-address 192.68.0.0 255.255.0.0 as-set advertise-map
SELECT_MORE_SPECIF_ROUTES
 neighbor 172.16.1.2 remote-as 3
 neighbor 172.16.1.2 update-source Loopback0
 neighbor 172.16.20.1 remote-as 1
 neighbor 172.16.20.1 filter-list 10 out
 no auto-summary

ip as-path access-list 10 permit ^$

access-list 1 permit 192.68.10.0 0.0.0.255

route-map SELECT_MORE_SPECIF_ROUTES permit 10
 match ip address 1
```

By permitting prefix 192.68.10.0/24, the above advertise map causes RTA to base its aggregate calculation on 192.68.10.0/24 only. Thus, 192.68.11.0/24 is not included in the formation of the aggregate.

The following **show ip bgp** command output illustrates that the path information of the aggregate is now 2 and not {1 2}. This means that the aggregate can now be advertised to AS1 because the AS_path does not include AS1. AS2 will not be able to receive the aggregate.

```
RTA#show ip bgp 192.68.0.0
BGP routing table entry for 192.68.0.0 255.255.0.0, version 31
Paths: (2 available, best #2, advertised over IBGP)
  2 (aggregated by 3 192.68.5.1)
    172.16.1.2 from 172.16.1.2 (192.68.5.1)
      Origin IGP, localpref 100, valid, internal, atomic-aggregate
  2 (aggregated by 3 172.16.2.254)
    0.0.0.0
      Origin IGP, localpref 100, weight 32768, valid, aggregated, local,
atomic-aggregate, best
```

LOOKING AHEAD

The BGP attributes are the basic elements in interdomain network design. Combining and manipulating different attributes will result in a unique routing policy for your autonomous system. The next chapter takes what you have learned so far and goes further in showing implementations for major design problems facing every network. The chapter also shows examples of controlling Internet stabilty by using route dampening.

THIS CHAPTER COVERS THE FOLLOWING KEY TOPICS:

- **Symmetry, Redundancy, and Load Balancing**

  Configuration examples for dynamically and statically learned defaults, multihoming to single and multiple providers, load balancing, and customers sharing a backup link.

- **Following Defaults Inside an AS**

  Configuration examples for setting defaults in a variety of architectures. This section examines a particular routing problem assuming a variety of different IGPs.

- **Policy Routing**

  Configuration example for routing based on source rather than destination.

- **Route Reflectors**

  A practical example of using route reflectors in conjunction with peer groups.

- **Confederations**

  A practical example of how to configure confederations.

- **Controlling Route and Cache Invalidation**

  Syntax and practical example of BGP's soft reconfiguration feature.

- **Route Dampening**

  Syntax and practical example of BGP's route dampening feature.

11

Configuring Effective
Internet Routing Policies

The preceding chapter covered configuration examples for all the basic functions and attributes of BGP. In this chapter, we will consider examples that address the challenging, potentially conflicting design goals of routing architecture. We will also look at examples designed to help manage growing, complex ASs.

Perhaps the most challenging part of configuring your network's routing architecture is determining what your routing policies should be. This step, of course, must come before the actual configuration process, and there is no simple, lockstep method for determining your policies. A careful analysis of network needs, behavior, and potential growth will reveal a unique set of problems and optimal solutions for every network.

REDUNDANCY, SYMMETRY, AND LOAD BALANCING

The following examples will illustrate the implementation of different route redundancy, symmetry, and load balancing scenarios. Please remember that these scenarios are not cast in stone. Many variations of these techniques can be used to fit your situation. The examples presented here should guide you to a better understanding of how policies are set. We will first go over a brief implementation of default routes.

Dynamically Learned Defaults

It is important to control defaults in BGP because, if they are originated randomly, they could cause everybody serious problems. Problems occur when a BGP speaker that intends to originate a default to a specific peer ends up flooding the default over all its neighbors. Cisco provides a way to target the default toward a specific neighbor.

In figure 11–1, RTA is originating a default route 0.0.0.0 0.0.0.0 toward RTC only. IBGP neighbors, such as RTF, will not get the default. RTA's configuration follows.

RTA configuration:

```
router bgp 3
 no synchronization
 network 172.16.1.0 mask 255.255.255.0
 neighbor 172.16.20.1 remote-as 1
 neighbor 172.16.20.1 default-originate
 no auto-summary
```

Figure 11–1
Dynamically learned defaults.

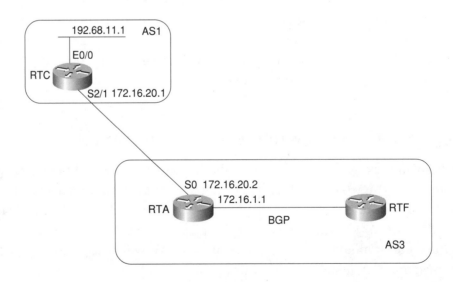

The **default-originate** option of the **neighbor** router subcommand will cause 0/0 to be sent toward RTC. This is shown in the BGP and IP routing tables of RTC:

```
RTC#show ip bgp
BGP table version is 14, local router ID is 192.68.11.1
Status codes: s suppressed, d damped, h history, * valid, > best,
i - internal Origin codes: i - IGP, e - EGP, ? - incomplete

   Network          Next Hop      Metric LocPrf Weight Path
*> 0.0.0.0          172.16.20.2                      0 3 i
*> 172.16.1.0/24    172.16.20.2        0             0 3 i
*> 192.68.11.0      0.0.0.0            0         32768 i

RTC#show ip route
Codes: C - connected, S - static, I - IGRP, R - RIP, M - mobile, B - BGP
       D - EIGRP, EX - EIGRP external, O - OSPF, IA - OSPF inter area
       E1 - OSPF external type 1, E2 - OSPF external type 2, E - EGP
       i - IS-IS, L1 - IS-IS level-1, L2 - IS-IS level-2,
       * - candidate default U - per-user static route

Gateway of last resort is 172.16.20.2 to network 0.0.0.0

C  192.68.11.0/24 is directly connected, Ethernet0/0
C    172.16.20.0/24 is directly connected, Serial2/1
B*  0.0.0.0/0 [20/0] via 172.16.20.2, 00:04:40
```

The routing table of RTC indicates that RTC has dynamically learned the 0/0 default from RTA and has set its gateway of last resort to 172.16.20.2, which is RTA.

Defaults can also be originated over all BGP peers by using the "network 0.0.0.0" router command, as long as the router advertising this default already has its own default. The following configuration can be used assuming that RTA has a default route itself (default could be created via a static route).

RTA configuration:

```
router bgp 3
 no synchronization
 network 0.0.0.0
```

```
network 172.16.1.0 mask 255.255.255.0
neighbor 172.16.20.1 remote-as 1
no auto-summary
```

Statically Set Defaults

Instead of dynamically learning the 0/0 default, a router can set its own default statically. This is illustrated in figure 11–2. RTC is using the following command:

ip route *network* [*mask*] {*address | interface*} [*distance*]

The 0/0 static route can point to a network number, a gateway address, or to a physical interface as being the default path. The distance is a means of giving preference to the static route in case multiple entries for the same network exist. Routes with a lower distance are preferred over routes with a higher distance.

The following configuration shows how RTC can set the default to point toward network 193.78.0.0/16.

RTC configuration:

```
router bgp 1
  network 192.68.11.0
  neighbor 172.16.20.2 remote-as 3
```

Figure 11–2
Dealing with 0/0 default.

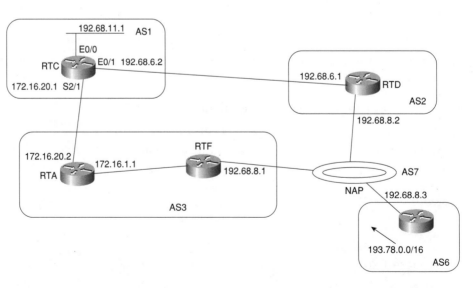

```
   neighbor 192.68.6.1 remote-as 2
   no auto-summary
 ip route 0.0.0.0 0.0.0.0 193.78.0.0
```

The following BGP table of RTC shows that 193.78.0.0/16 has been learned via two paths—the first via AS3 and the second via AS2. BGP has preferred the first path as being the best (BGP attributes can be used to influence which path BGP will use and hence influence the default path).

```
RTC#show ip bgp
BGP table version is 8, local router ID is 192.68.11.1
Status codes: s suppressed, d damped, h history, * valid, > best,
i - internal Origin codes: i - IGP, e - EGP, ? - incomplete

   Network          Next Hop        Metric LocPrf Weight Path
*> 192.68.11.0      0.0.0.0              0        32768 i
*> 193.78.0.0/16    172.16.20.2                      0 3 7 6 i
*                   192.68.6.1                       0 2 7 6 i
```

The following IP table of RTC shows how the gateway of last resort has been set to follow network 193.78.0.0/16. Recursive lookup in the IP routing table shows that 193.78.0.0/16 can be reached via 172.16.20.2, which is RTA.

```
RTC#show ip route
Codes: C - connected, S - static, I - IGRP, R - RIP, M - mobile, B - BGP
    D - EIGRP, EX - EIGRP external, O - OSPF, IA - OSPF inter area
    E1 - OSPF external type 1, E2 - OSPF external type 2, E - EGP
    i - IS-IS, L1 - IS-IS level-1, L2 - IS-IS level-2,
    * - candidate default U - per-user static route

Gateway of last resort is 193.78.0.0 to network 0.0.0.0

C  192.68.6.0/24 is directly connected, Ethernet0/1
C  192.68.11.0/24 is directly connected, Ethernet0/0
B  193.78.0.0/16 [20/0] via 172.16.20.2, 00:32:32
C   172.16.20.0/24 is directly connected, Serial2/1
S* 0.0.0.0/0 [1/0] via 193.78.0.0
```

In case you do not want to follow a single route, you can still use the **ip route 0.0.0.0 0.0.0.0** command to point to multiple networks or IP addresses. The "distance" keyword will give you the ability to prefer one default over the other. This is illustrated in the following:

RTC configuration:

```
router bgp 1
 network 192.68.11.0
 neighbor 172.16.20.2 remote-as 3
 neighbor 192.68.6.1 remote-as 2
 no auto-summary

ip route 0.0.0.0 0.0.0.0 172.16.20.2 40
ip route 0.0.0.0 0.0.0.0 192.68.6.1 50
```

Note how RTC is pointing to two different IP addresses. These could also have been two different network numbers that exist in the IP routing table. The "distance" 40 of the first static route will make sure that the route is preferred. In case the route to 172.16.20.2 goes away, the static entry will go with it, and the second entry will kick in. The following shows the output of RTC's routing table.

```
RTC#show ip route
Codes: C - connected, S - static, I - IGRP, R - RIP, M - mobile, B - BGP
    D - EIGRP, EX - EIGRP external, O - OSPF, IA - OSPF inter area
    E1 - OSPF external type 1, E2 - OSPF external type 2, E - EGP
    i - IS-IS, L1 - IS-IS level-1, L2 - IS-IS level-2,
    * - candidate default U - per-user static route

Gateway of last resort is 172.16.20.2 to network 0.0.0.0

C   192.68.6.0/24 is directly connected, Ethernet0/1
C   192.68.11.0/24 is directly connected, Ethernet0/0
B   193.78.0.0/16 [20/0] via 172.16.20.2, 00:45:08
C    172.16.20.0/24 is directly connected, Serial2/1
S*  0.0.0.0/0 [40/0] via 172.16.20.2
```

The following shows the same output in case the link between RTC and RTA goes down:

```
RTC#show ip route
Codes: C - connected, S - static, I - IGRP, R - RIP, M - mobile, B - BGP
```

```
      D - EIGRP, EX - EIGRP external, O - OSPF, IA - OSPF inter area
      E1 - OSPF external type 1, E2 - OSPF external type 2, E - EGP
      i - IS-IS, L1 - IS-IS level-1, L2 - IS-IS level-2,
      * - candidate default U - per-user static route

   Gateway of last resort is 192.68.6.1 to network 0.0.0.0

   C   192.68.6.0/24 is directly connected, Ethernet0/1
   C   192.68.11.0/24 is directly connected, Ethernet0/0
   B   193.78.0.0/16 [20/0] via 192.68.6.1, 00:01:14
   S*  0.0.0.0/0 [60/0] via 192.68.6.1
```

Note how the second static entry with distance 60 has now kicked in.

Multihoming to a Single Provider

For the case where one customer has multiple connections to the same provider, we will look at implementation examples that cover the following:

- Default only, one primary, and one backup link

- Default, primary, and backup plus partial routing

- Automatic load balancing

Default Only, One Primary, and One Backup Link

In figure 11–3, AS3 is multihomed to AS1. AS3 is not learning any BGP routes from AS1 and is sending its own routes via BGP. RTA will be running defaults toward AS1, with the NY link being the primary link and the SF link being the secondary link. The following policies should apply:

1. Outbound traffic from AS3 should always go on the NY link unless that link fails, in which case it should switch to the other link.

This can be achieved by configuring two static routes in RTA pointing the defaults toward the two links. The default via the NY link will be set with a lower distance to be more preferred.

2. Inbound traffic toward AS3 should always come on the NY link unless that link fails, in which case it should switch to the other link.

Figure 11–3
*Multihoming to a
single provider
(default only, one
primary, and one
backup link).*

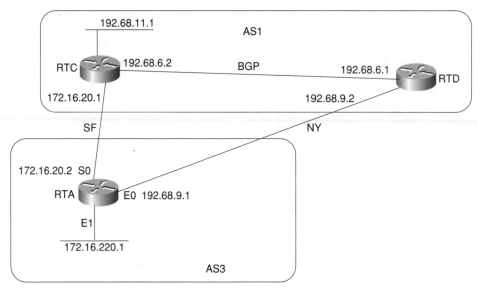

This can be achieved by having RTA send different metrics toward AS1 on both links, with a lower metric on the NY link. This way, inbound traffic coming from AS1 will always come via the NY link.

3. Prevent any BGP updates from coming into AS3.

This can be achieved by having AS3 configure a route map or distribute list that will block all incoming BGP routing updates. Usually, the provider (AS1, in this case) will not send you any updates per your request. Nevertheless, you should always protect the AS against the unknown. The provider could make a mistake and send you all his routes, and your AS would be vulnerable.

RTA configuration:

```
router bgp 3
 network 172.16.220.0 mask 255.255.255.0
 neighbor 172.16.20.1 remote-as 1
 neighbor 172.16.20.1 route-map BLOCK in
 neighbor 172.16.20.1 route-map SETMETRIC1 out
 neighbor 192.68.9.2 remote-as 1
 neighbor 192.68.9.2 route-map BLOCK in
```

```
    neighbor 192.68.9.2 route-map SETMETRIC2 out
    no auto-summary

  ip route 0.0.0.0 0.0.0.0 172.16.20.1 50
  ip route 0.0.0.0 0.0.0.0 192.68.9.2 40

  route-map SETMETRIC1 permit 10
   set metric 100

  route-map SETMETRIC2 permit 10
   set metric 50

  route-map BLOCK deny 10
```

In the preceding configuration, AS3 has used static routes to configure defaults toward AS1. The 0/0 toward RTD is given a distance of 40, lower than the distance of 50 toward RTC. The NY link will act as primary. Alternatively, AS3 could have accepted a single entry from AS1 and configured that entry as being the default.

Route maps SETMETRIC2 and SETMETRIC1 are used to set the outbound metric to 50 toward RTD and 100 toward RTC, respectively. Inbound traffic will prefer the NY link.

Route map BLOCK is used to block all incoming BGP updates from AS1.

The following RTA IP routing table shows how the default route is set. Note that distance 40 is being preferred over distance 50 for the 0/0 route, and the gateway of last resort is pointing to next hop 192.68.9.2.

```
    RTA#show ip route
    Codes: C - connected, S - static, I - IGRP, R - RIP, M - mobile, B - BGP
        D - EIGRP, EX - EIGRP external, O - OSPF, IA - OSPF inter area
        E1 - OSPF external type 1, E2 - OSPF external type 2, E - EGP
        i - IS-IS, L1 - IS-IS level-1, L2 - IS-IS level-2,
        * - candidate default

    Gateway of last resort is 192.68.9.2 to network 0.0.0.0

    C  192.68.9.0 is directly connected, Ethernet0
```

```
          172.16.0.0 255.255.255.0 is subnetted, 2 subnets
     C    172.16.220.0 is directly connected, Ethernet1
     C    172.16.20.0 is directly connected, Serial0
     S*  0.0.0.0 0.0.0.0 [40/0] via 192.68.9.2
```

The following is RTC's BGP table, and it shows that AS3 is always accessed via the RTD-RTA link because of the lower metric 50. Prefix 172.16.220.0/24 can be reached via IBGP and EBGP. The IBGP route has been chosen as the best route. Note in this table that RTC's next hop to reach prefix 172.16.220.0/24 is 192.68.6.1. This is because RTD has configured its neighbor connection with RTC using the **next-hop-self neighbor** command.

```
RTC#show ip bgp
BGP table version is 11, local router ID is 192.68.11.1
Status codes: s suppressed, d damped, h history, * valid, > best,
i - internal Origin codes: i - IGP, e - EGP, ? - incomplete

   Network          Next Hop      Metric LocPrf Weight Path
*>i172.16.220.0/24  192.68.6.1        50    100      0 3 i
*                   172.16.20.2      100             0 3 i
*> 192.68.11.0      0.0.0.0            0         32768 i
```

Default, Primary, and Backup Plus Partial Routing

This example shows how traffic can be manipulated in a situation where the AS is accepting partial routing from a single provider and running defaults toward the provider. Partial routes are usually the provider's local routes and its customers' routes. Figure 11–4 shows AS3 running IBGP internally and running EBGP at two different locations with its provider AS1. The following policies should apply:

1. AS3 will only accept AS1's local routes and its customers' routes such as AS6. AS3 will also accept one route from the Internet to set its default toward the provider AS1.
2. For all outbound traffic toward AS1 and AS6 (the partial routes), AS3 should use the SF link. In case of failure, the other link is used.
3. For all other outbound traffic toward the Internet, AS3 should use the NY link as the primary link by following a default route. In case of failure, the default via the other link should be used.

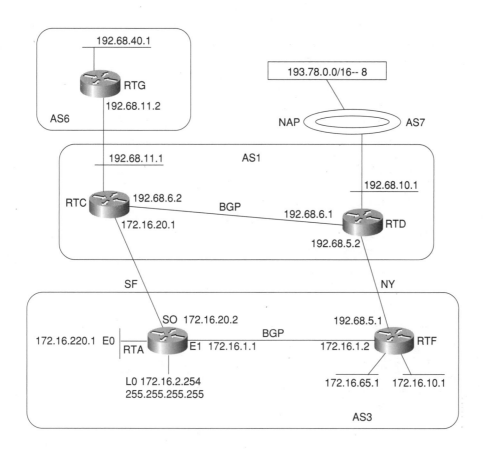

Figure 11–4
Default, primary, and backup plus partial routing.

4. For inbound traffic, AS3 will instruct AS1 to use the SF link for network 172.16.220.0/24.
5. For all other inbound traffic, the NY link is the primary.

The following partial configurations are needed for the BGP configuration in RTA and RTF:

RTA configuration:

```
router bgp 3
 no synchronization
 network 172.16.1.0 mask 255.255.255.0
 network 172.16.10.0 mask 255.255.255.0
```

```
        network 172.16.65.0 mask 255.255.255.192
        network 172.16.220.0 mask 255.255.255.0
        neighbor 172.16.1.2 remote-as 3
        neighbor 172.16.1.2 update-source Loopback0
        neighbor 172.16.1.2 next-hop-self
        neighbor 172.16.20.1 remote-as 1
        neighbor 172.16.20.1 route-map SET_OUTBOUND_TRAFFIC in
        neighbor 172.16.20.1 route-map SET_INBOUND_TRAFFIC out
        neighbor 172.16.20.1 filter-list 10 out
        no auto-summary

        ip route 0.0.0.0 0.0.0.0 193.78.0.0
        ip as-path access-list 10 permit ^$
        ip as-path access-list 4 permit ^1 6$
        ip as-path access-list 4 permit ^1$

        access-list 2 permit 172.16.220.0 0.0.0.255
        access-list 101 permit ip 193.78.0.0 0.0.255.255 255.255.0.0 0.0.0.0

        route-map SET_OUTBOUND_TRAFFIC permit 10
         match ip address 101
         set local-preference 200

        route-map SET_OUTBOUND_TRAFFIC permit 20
         match as-path 4
         set local-preference 300

        route-map SET_INBOUND_TRAFFIC permit 10
         match ip address 2
         set metric 200

        route-map SET_INBOUND_TRAFFIC permit 20
         set metric 300
```

RTF configuration:

```
        router bgp 3
         no synchronization
         network 172.16.1.0 mask 255.255.255.0
         network 172.16.10.0 mask 255.255.255.0
         network 172.16.65.0 mask 255.255.255.192
         network 172.16.220.0 mask 255.255.255.0
```

```
    neighbor 172.16.2.254 remote-as 3
    neighbor 172.16.2.254 next-hop-self
    neighbor 192.68.5.2 remote-as 1
    neighbor 192.68.5.2 route-map SET_OUTBOUND_TRAFFIC in
    neighbor 192.68.5.2 route-map SET_INBOUND_TRAFFIC out
    neighbor 192.68.5.2 filter-list 10 out
    no auto-summary

 ip route 0.0.0.0 0.0.0.0 193.78.0.0
 ip as-path access-list 10 permit ^$
 ip as-path access-list 4 permit ^1 6$
 ip as-path access-list 4 permit ^1$

 access-list 101 permit ip 193.78.0.0 0.0.255.255 255.255.0.0 0.0.0.0

 route-map SET_OUTBOUND_TRAFFIC permit 10
  match ip address 101
  set local-preference 250

 route-map SET_OUTBOUND_TRAFFIC permit 20
  match as-path 4
  set local-preference 250

 route-map SET_INBOUND_TRAFFIC permit 10
  set metric 250
```

The preceding configuration of RTA shows the following:

1. Route map SET_OUTBOUND_TRAFFIC is applied on RTA's EBGP link to AS1. This route map will help specify which outbound traffic goes over which link. The first instance (10) will allow only one network, 193.78.0.0/16, to be accepted from the Internet. This network is used to set the default. This will be given a local preference of 200, which is lower than the local preference 250 coming from RTF. This will cause all traffic toward the Internet to follow the default via the NY link.

   The second instance (20) will set all prefixes coming from AS1 and AS6 with a local preference of 300, which is higher than local preference 250 coming from RTF. This will make the SF link the primary link to reach AS1 and its customer AS6. Note that this route map will allow only partial routes (AS1 and AS6) to be injected into AS3 by specifying the AS_path to be either AS1 (^1$) or AS6 (^1 6$).

NOTES

Instead of listing all the customers of AS1 one by one as we did in as-path access-list 4, a regular expression of the form ^1 ?[0-9]*$ could have been used to identify all the AS_paths that start with 1 and of length 2—that is, AS1 and its direct customers. The form of the access list would have been: ip as-path access-list 4 permit ^1 ?[0-9]*$ (to enter the "?" press CTRL-V first). Careful: In the case where AS1 is directly connected to another major provider with a direct link (rather than via a NAP), the preceding regular expression would also give you the local routes of that second provider.

---

2. Route map SET_INBOUND_TRAFFIC is also applied on RTA's EBGP link to AS1. The first instance (10) will cause prefix 172.16.220.0/24 to be sent with a metric of 200, which is lower than the metric 250 sent by RTF. This will make sure that traffic from AS1 toward this destination will take the SF link. All other updates will be sent with a metric of 300, which is higher than metric 250 sent by RTF. This will cause all other inbound traffic to take the NY link.

3. The filter-list 10 will prevent AS3 from becoming a transit AS.

4. The **ip route 0/0** statement sets the default to be 193.78.0.0/16.

RTA's BGP table would have the following entries:

```
RTA#sh ip bgp
BGP table version is 19, local router ID is 172.16.2.254
Status codes: s suppressed, d damped, h history, * valid, > best,
i - internal Origin codes: i - IGP, e - EGP, ? - incomplete
  Network          Next Hop     Metric LocPrf Weight Path
* i172.16.1.0/24   172.16.1.2        0    100      0 i
*>                 0.0.0.0           0           32768 i
```

```
* i172.16.10.0/24   172.16.1.2        0    100      0 i
*>                  172.16.1.2       20            32768 i
* i172.16.65.0/26   172.16.1.2        0    100      0 i
*>                  172.16.1.2       20            32768 i
* i172.16.220.0/24  172.16.1.2       20    100      0 i
*>                  0.0.0.0           0            32768 i
*> 192.68.10.0      172.16.20.1           300      0 1 i
*> 192.68.11.0      172.16.20.1       0   300      0 1 i
*> 192.68.40.0      172.16.20.1           300      0 1 6 i
*>i193.78.0.0/16    172.16.1.2            250      0 1 7 8 i
*                   172.16.20.1           200      0 1 7 8 i
```

Note how RTA only sees networks that belong to AS1 and its customer AS6 (except for the default route). For network 193.78.0.0/16, which is the default, RTA follows the NY link because of the local preference 250. For traffic toward AS1 and AS6, RTA follows the RTA-RTC link (local preference 300). The following IP routing table of RTA shows that RTA has set its default to 193.78.0.0/16, which is reachable via 172.16.1.2.

```
RTA#sh ip route
Codes: C - connected, S - static, I - IGRP, R - RIP, M - mobile, B - BGP
       D - EIGRP, EX - EIGRP external, O - OSPF, IA - OSPF inter area
       N1 - OSPF NSSA external type 1, N2 - OSPF NSSA external type 2
       E1 - OSPF external type 1, E2 - OSPF external type 2, E - EGP
       i - IS-IS, L1 - IS-IS level-1, L2 - IS-IS level-2,
       * - candidate default U - per-user static route, o - ODR
Gateway of last resort is 193.78.0.0 to network 0.0.0.0
B    192.68.10.0/24 [20/0] via 172.16.20.1, 00:07:34
B    192.68.11.0/24 [20/0] via 172.16.20.1, 00:07:34
B    192.68.40.0/24 [20/0] via 172.16.20.1, 00:07:34
     172.16.0.0/16 is variably subnetted, 6 subnets, 3 masks
C       172.16.2.254/32 is directly connected, Loopback0
C       172.16.220.0/24 is directly connected, Ethernet0
C       172.16.20.0/24 is directly connected, Serial0
O       172.16.10.0/24 [110/20] via 172.16.1.2, 01:39:52, Ethernet1
C       172.16.1.0/24 is directly connected, Ethernet1
O       172.16.65.0/26 [110/20] via 172.16.1.2, 01:39:52, Ethernet1
S*   0.0.0.0/0 [1/0] via 193.78.0.0
B    193.78.0.0/16 [200/0] via 172.16.1.2, 00:03:07
```

The following is an output of RTD's BGP table:

```
RTD#sh ip bgp
BGP table version is 14, local router ID is 192.68.10.1
Status codes: s suppressed, d damped, h history, * valid, > best,
i - internal Origin codes: i - IGP, e - EGP, ? - incomplete
   Network          Next Hop       Metric LocPrf Weight Path
*> 172.16.1.0/24    192.68.5.1       250               0 3 i
*> 172.16.10.0/24   192.68.5.1       250               0 3 i
*> 172.16.65.0/26   192.68.5.1       250               0 3 i
*>i172.16.220.0/24 192.68.6.2       200   100         0 3 i
*                   192.68.5.1       250               0 3 i
*> 192.68.10.0      0.0.0.0            0           32768 i
*>i192.68.11.0      192.68.6.2         0   100         0 i
*>i192.68.40.0      192.68.6.2         0   100         0 6 i
*> 193.78.0.0/16    192.68.10.2                        0 7 8 i
```

RTD can reach all networks in AS3 via the RTD-RTF direct link except for prefix 172.16.220.0/24, which is reachable via the RTC-RTA link because of the better metric 200.

Automatic Load Balancing

Considering figure 11–5, we will show how the Cisco BGP implementation can do dynamic load balancing for identical updates received by the same router from the same autonomous system. RTA is EBGP peering with routers RTC and RTD in AS1. RTA is receiving identical updates about prefixes 192.68.11.0/24 and 192.68.40.0/24 from two links. We can configure RTA with the **maximum-paths** router subcommand to enable IP routing to load balance among up to six paths. In our example, the maximum-paths number is set to 2.

RTA configuration:

```
router bgp 3
 no synchronization
 neighbor 172.16.1.2 remote-as 3
 neighbor 172.16.1.2 update-source Loopback0
 neighbor 172.16.20.1 remote-as 1
```

```
neighbor 172.16.20.1 filter-list 10 out
neighbor 172.16.60.1 remote-as 1
neighbor 172.16.60.1 filter-list 10 out
maximum-paths 2
no auto-summary

ip as-path access-list 10 permit ^$
```

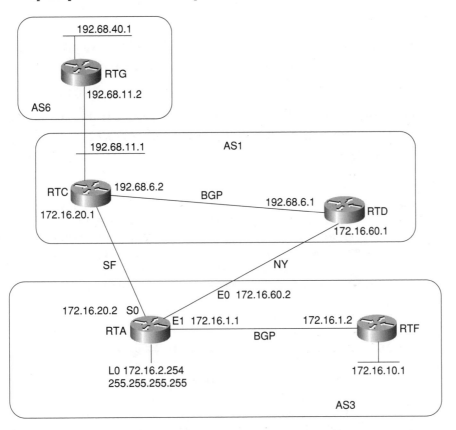

Figure 11–5
Automatic load balancing.

Looking at RTA's BGP table, we see that RTA has identical path information regarding 192.68.11.0/24 and 192.68.40.0/24. Normally, BGP will pick one of the entries as the "best" path and give it to the IP routing table.

```
RTA#show ip bgp
BGP table version is 8, local router ID is 172.16.2.254
Status codes: s suppressed, d damped, h history, * valid, > best,
```

```
  i - internal Origin codes: i - IGP, e - EGP, ? - incomplete

     Network          Next Hop      Metric LocPrf Weight Path
  *>i172.16.10.0/24   172.16.1.2          0    100      0 i
  *> 192.68.11.0      172.16.20.1         0             0 1 i
  *                   172.16.60.1                       0 1 i
  *> 192.68.40.0      172.16.20.1                       0 1 6 i
  *                   172.16.60.1                       0 1 6 i
```

Using the **maximum-paths** command will instruct BGP to give all the identical paths (up to six) to the IP routing table. Note that the requirement for these paths is that they come from the same AS.

The following shows how RTA will keep multiple entries from the same destination in its IP routing table. Note how prefixes 192.68.11.0/24 and 192.68.40.0/24 are learned from both links.

```
RTA#show ip route
Codes: C - connected, S - static, I - IGRP, R - RIP, M - mobile, B - BGP
       D - EIGRP, EX - EIGRP external, O - OSPF, IA - OSPF inter area
       N1 - OSPF NSSA external type 1, N2 - OSPF NSSA external type 2
       E1 - OSPF external type 1, E2 - OSPF external type 2, E - EGP
       i - IS-IS, L1 - IS-IS level-1, L2 - IS-IS level-2,
       * - candidate default U - per-user static route, o - ODR

Gateway of last resort is not set

B   192.68.11.0/24 [20/0] via 172.16.60.1, 00:03:20
                   [20/0] via 172.16.20.1, 00:03:18
B   192.68.40.0/24 [20/0] via 172.16.60.1, 00:03:20
                   [20/0] via 172.16.20.1, 00:03:18
    172.16.0.0/16 is variably subnetted, 5 subnets, 2 masks
C      172.16.2.254/32 is directly connected, Loopback0
C      172.16.60.0/24 is directly connected, Ethernet0
C      172.16.20.0/24 is directly connected, Serial0
O      172.16.10.0/24 [110/20] via 172.16.1.2, 00:20:23, Ethernet1
C      172.16.1.0/24 is directly connected, Ethernet1
```

When dealing with IBGP peers, RTA will only advertise a single BGP entry out of the multiple identical entries with a next-hop-self. Because RTA is IBGP

peered with RTF, RTA will advertise only one BGP update about
192.68.11.0/24 and 192.68.40.0/24 with a next-hop 172.16.2.254 rather than
the external next hop; this is illustrated in the following BGP table. For external
peers, BGP will still pass on the best path as usual.

```
RTF#show ip bgp
BGP table version is 56, local router ID is 172.16.10.1
Status codes: s suppressed, d damped, h history, * valid, > best,
i - internal Origin codes: i - IGP, e - EGP, ? - incomplete

    Network          Next Hop      Metric LocPrf Weight Path
*> 172.16.10.0/24   0.0.0.0          0            32768 i
*>i192.68.11.0      172.16.2.254     0      100      0 1 i
*>i192.68.40.0      172.16.2.254            100      0 1 6 i
```

Balancing Between Two Routers Sharing Multiple Paths

This example shows how load balancing can be achieved between two routers
sharing multiple paths without having routing updates being duplicated over
the two paths.

For the scenario in figure 11–6, we will configure loopback interfaces on RTA
and RTC and run a single peering session between the two routers. Using static
routes, we can point to the loopback interfaces via both of the physical interfaces. This way, the IP routing table will have two paths to reach the next hop
and will load balance.

RTA configuration:

```
interface Loopback0
  ip address 172.16.2.254 255.255.255.255

router bgp 3
  no synchronization
  neighbor 172.16.1.2 remote-as 3
  neighbor 172.16.1.2 update-source Loopback0
  neighbor 172.16.90.1 ebgp-multihop 2
  neighbor 172.16.90.1 update-source Loopback0
  no auto-summary
```

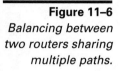

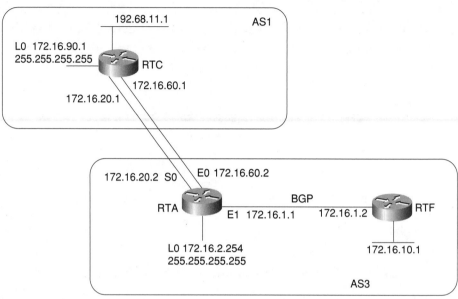

```
ip route 172.16.90.1 255.255.255.255 172.16.20.1
ip route 172.16.90.1 255.255.255.255 172.16.60.1
```

RTC configuration:

```
interface Loopback0
 ip address 172.16.90.1 255.255.255.255

router bgp 1
 network 192.68.11.0
 neighbor 172.16.2.254 remote-as 3
 neighbor 172.16.2.254 ebgp-multihop 2
 neighbor 172.16.2.254 update-source Loopback0
 no auto-summary

ip route 172.16.2.254 255.255.255.255 172.16.20.2
ip route 172.16.2.254 255.255.255.255 172.16.60.2
```

The following output shows how RTA is now learning BGP updates from RTC
via next hop 172.16.90.1, the loopback address.

```
RTA#show ip bgp
BGP table version is 4, local router ID is 172.16.2.254
```

```
Status codes: s suppressed, d damped, h history, * valid, > best,
i - internal Origin codes: i - IGP, e - EGP, ? - incomplete

  Network            Next Hop      Metric LocPrf Weight Path
*>i172.16.10.0/24  172.16.1.2         0     100     0 i
*> 192.68.11.0      172.16.90.1       0             0 1 i
```

The two static routes in RTA's routing table will provide multiple paths to reach the next hop 172.16.90.1, and hence the router will load balance between the two paths.

```
RTA#show ip route
Codes: C - connected, S - static, I - IGRP, R - RIP, M - mobile, B - BGP
       D - EIGRP, EX - EIGRP external, O - OSPF, IA - OSPF inter area
       N1 - OSPF NSSA external type 1, N2 - OSPF NSSA external type 2
       E1 - OSPF external type 1, E2 - OSPF external type 2, E - EGP
       i - IS-IS, L1 - IS-IS level-1, L2 - IS-IS level-2,
       * - candidate default U - per-user static route, o - ODR

Gateway of last resort is not set

B   192.68.11.0/24 [20/0] via 172.16.90.1, 00:00:41
     172.16.0.0/16 is variably subnetted, 6 subnets, 2 masks
C       172.16.2.254/32 is directly connected, Loopback0
C       172.16.60.0/24 is directly connected, Ethernet0
C       172.16.20.0/24 is directly connected, Serial0
O       172.16.10.0/24 [110/20] via 172.16.1.2, 02:17:34, Ethernet1
C       172.16.1.0/24 is directly connected, Ethernet1
S       172.16.90.1/32 [1/0] via 172.16.20.1
                       [1/0] via 172.16.60.1
```

Multihoming to Different Providers

For the case of one customer multihomed to multiple providers, we will discuss a scenario where updates are following a combination of defaults, partial, and full routing.

In figure 11–7, AS3 is multihomed to two different ASs, AS1 and AS2, which in turn exchange routing information and traffic with AS6 and each other via a network access point. AS6, AS2, and AS1 all peer with RTE, which is acting as a route server that has the function of only passing routing updates between all three ASs.

Figure 11–7
*Multiple providers
(default, primary
and backup,
full/partial).*

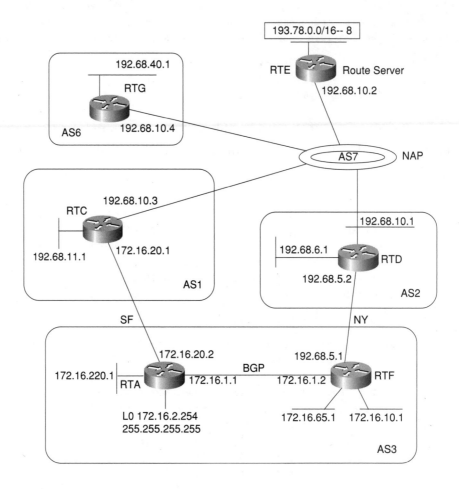

1. AS3 will be accepting AS1's local and customer routes only via the SF link. All other Internet routes will be accepted via the NY link (primary).
2. AS3 will accept a default route from AS1 just in case there is a failure in the NY link.
3. AS3 prefers that the SF network 172.16.220.0/24 be reachable by the outside world via the SF link, and the NY networks 172.16.10.0/24 and 172.16.65.0/26 be reachable via the NY link.
4. AS3 cannot be a transit network for AS1 and AS2, which means that under no circumstances will AS1 use AS3 to reach AS2.

The following configurations illustrate how to implement this routing arrangement.

RTA configuration:

```
router bgp 3
 no synchronization
 network 172.16.1.0 mask 255.255.255.0
 network 172.16.10.0 mask 255.255.255.0
 network 172.16.65.0 mask 255.255.255.192
 network 172.16.220.0 mask 255.255.255.0
 neighbor 172.16.1.2 remote-as 3
 neighbor 172.16.1.2 update-source Loopback0
 neighbor 172.16.1.2 next-hop-self
 neighbor 172.16.20.1 remote-as 1
 neighbor 172.16.20.1 route-map ACCEPT_LOCAL in
 neighbor 172.16.20.1 route-map PREPEND_PATH out
 no auto-summary

ip as-path access-list 1 permit ^1 ?[0-9]*$
ip as-path access-list 2 permit ^$

access-list 1 permit 172.16.65.0 0.0.0.63
access-list 1 permit 172.16.10.0 0.0.0.255

route-map PREPEND_PATH permit 10
 match ip address 1
 set as-path prepend 3

route-map PREPEND_PATH permit 20
 match as-path 2

route-map ACCEPT_LOCAL permit 10
 match as-path 1
```

RTA uses a route map called ACCEPT_LOCAL that accepts partial routes from AS1. The route map will try to match on any path of the form ^1 ?[0-9]*$, which, as already explained, enables AS1's local and customer routes.

RTA uses toward RTC a route map called PREPEND_PATH that will prepend an additional AS number to all NY prefixes such as 172.16.10.0/24 and 172.16.65.0/26. This will make the AS_path length of these prefixes shorter via the NY link. Doing the AS_path prepend should always be coordinated with the provider. Your provider might have policies that conflict with your path information. AS1, for example, might have a policy that advertises AS3 to the NAP, for example, using the form ^3$, which means an AS_path that starts with 3 and ends with 3. If AS3 starts sending AS_path information of the form 3 3 3 3, the provider will drop the routes because the AS_path will not match its policy.

Note that instance 20 of the route-map PREPEND_PATH enables AS3's local routes to be advertised only. This is done by matching on the local prefixes with empty AS_path information represented by the ^$ regular expression.

In the same manner, RTF will be configured to announce the SF prefixes on the NY link with an extra path length. This would make inbound traffic toward these networks preferred via the SF link.

RTF configuration:

```
router bgp 3
 no synchronization
 network 172.16.1.0 mask 255.255.255.0
 network 172.16.10.0 mask 255.255.255.0
 network 172.16.65.0 mask 255.255.255.192
 network 172.16.220.0 mask 255.255.255.0
 neighbor 172.16.2.254 remote-as 3
 neighbor 172.16.2.254 next-hop-self
 neighbor 192.68.5.2 remote-as 2
 neighbor 192.68.5.2 route-map PREPEND_PATH out
 no auto-summary

ip as-path access-list 2 permit ^$
access-list 1 permit 172.16.220.0 0.0.0.255

route-map PREPEND_PATH permit 10
 match ip address 1
 set as-path prepend 3

route-map PREPEND_PATH permit 20
 match as-path 2
```

Note that RTF is accepting all routes from AS2 and is advertising only the local routes ^$ with an extra path length added for the SF route 172.16.220.0/24.

The following is a snapshot of some of the BGP routing tables.

```
RTA#sh ip bgp
BGP table version is 13, local router ID is 172.16.2.254
Status codes: s suppressed, d damped, h history, * valid, > best,
i - internal Origin codes: i - IGP, e - EGP, ? - incomplete
   Network           Next Hop       Metric LocPrf Weight Path
*> 0.0.0.0           172.16.20.1                       0 1 i
*> 172.16.1.0/24     0.0.0.0             0         32768 i
*  i                 172.16.1.2          0    100      0 i
*> 172.16.10.0/24    172.16.1.2         20         32768 i
*  i                 172.16.1.2          0    100      0 i
*> 172.16.65.0/26    172.16.1.2         20         32768 i
*  i                 172.16.1.2          0    100      0 i
*> 172.16.220.0/24 0.0.0.0              0         32768 i
*  i                 172.16.1.2         20    100      0 i
*>i192.68.6.0        172.16.1.2          0    100      0 2 i
*> 192.68.11.0       172.16.20.1         0             0 1 i
*>i193.78.0.0/16     172.16.1.2               100      0 2 7 8 i
```

Note how RTA is learning a default 0/0 from RTC. RTA is also learning AS1's local routes (such as 192.68.11.0/24) and can reach those directly via the SF link. For all other routes, RTA will go via the NY link.

On the other hand, inbound traffic will follow the shortest path. The following table shows how an outside AS that falls behind the NAP, such as AS6, can reach AS3's networks.

```
RTG#sh ip bgp
BGP table version is 9, local router ID is 192.68.40.1
Status codes: s suppressed, d damped, h history, * valid, > best,
i - internal Origin codes: i - IGP, e - EGP, ? - incomplete
   Network           Next Hop       Metric LocPrf Weight Path
*> 172.16.1.0/24     192.68.10.1                       0 7 2 3 i
*> 172.16.10.0/24    192.68.10.1                       0 7 2 3 i
*> 172.16.65.0/26    192.68.10.1                       0 7 2 3 i
*> 172.16.220.0/24 192.68.10.3                         0 7 1 3 i
*> 192.68.6.0        192.68.10.1                       0 7 2 i
*> 192.68.11.0       192.68.10.3                       0 7 1 i
*> 192.68.40.0       0.0.0.0             0         32768 i
*> 193.78.0.0/16     192.68.10.2                       0 7 8 i
```

Note that the NY prefixes 172.16.10.0/24 and 172.16.65.0/26 are reachable via the NY link (path 7 2 3). The SF prefix 172.16.220.0/24 is reachable via the SF link (path 7 1 3).

Customers of the Same Provider with a Backup Link

Customers of the same provider can, by mutual agreement, interconnect via a private link. The private link will serve as a backup in case the Internet connectivity of any of the customers is broken. The following scenario discusses a case where the private link is used as the primary link between the two ASs and as a backup in case of Internet connectivity failures.

In this example, we will switch roles a bit. In figure 11–8, AS3 is the provider offering services to two of its customers, AS1 and AS2. AS1 and AS2 agree to

Figure 11–8
Backup—private link used as primary.

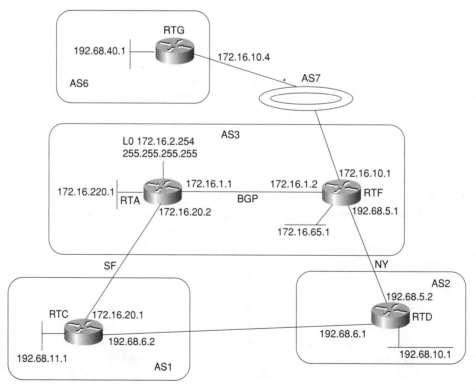

use each other as backup in case their links to AS3 fail. In normal conditions, AS1 and AS2 will use the private link only for traffic between AS1 and AS2; for all other Internet traffic, the direct link to the provider AS3 is used.

We will assume that AS1 and AS2 are getting full Internet routes. AS1 and AS2 should advertise each other's routes to AS3 because, for the backup behavior to occur, AS3 should be able to reach AS1's routes via AS2 and AS2's routes via AS1. Normally, this scenario is handled automatically by the BGP default behavior. Due to the shortest path rule, AS1 and AS2 will always reach each other's networks over the private link. For the sake of experimenting with setting BGP policies we will attempt to solve this problem by manipulating the local preference attribute. We will concentrate on the router configuration of RTC; RTD's configuration should be similar.

RTC configuration:

```
router bgp 1
 network 192.68.11.0
 neighbor 172.16.20.2 remote-as 3
 neighbor 172.16.20.2 route-map PREF_FROM_AS3 in
 neighbor 192.68.6.1 remote-as 2
 neighbor 192.68.6.1 route-map PREF_FROM_AS2 in
 no auto-summary

ip as-path access-list 1 permit _2_

route-map PREF_FROM_AS3 permit 10
 match as-path 1
 set local-preference 100

route-map PREF_FROM_AS3 permit 20
 set local-preference 300

route-map PREF_FROM_AS2 permit 10
 set local-preference 200
```

The preceding configuration shows a route map PREF_FROM_AS2, which sets all updates coming from AS2 with a local preference of 200. The other route map PREF_FROM_AS3 sets all updates coming from AS3 that have AS2 in them with a local preference of 100; all other updates will have a local preference of 300. Note the regular expression _2_, which indicates routes that have passed via AS2. With this configuration, all networks that originated from AS2 or customers of AS2 will be reachable directly via the private link. All other routes will be reachable via the provider AS3. The following is RTC's BGP table:

```
RTC#show ip bgp
BGP table version is 11, local router ID is 192.68.11.1
Status codes: s suppressed, d damped, h history, * valid, > best,
i - internal Origin codes: i - IGP, e - EGP, ? - incomplete

   Network          Next Hop      Metric LocPrf Weight Path
*> 172.16.1.0/24    172.16.20.2        0    300      0 3 i
*                   192.68.6.1              200      0 2 3 i
*> 172.16.10.0/24   172.16.20.2       20    300      0 3 i
*                   192.68.6.1              200      0 2 3 i
*> 172.16.65.0/26   172.16.20.2       20    300      0 3 i
*                   192.68.6.1              200      0 2 3 i
*> 172.16.220.0/24  172.16.20.2        0    300      0 3 i
*                   192.68.6.1              200      0 2 3 i
*  192.68.10.0      172.16.20.2            100      0 3 2 i
*>                  192.68.6.1         0    200      0 2 i
*> 192.68.11.0      0.0.0.0            0           32768 i
*> 192.68.40.0      172.16.20.2            300      0 3 6 i
*                   192.68.6.1              200      0 2 3 6 i
```

Note that prefix 192.68.10.0/24 coming from AS3 has a local preference of 100 because its AS_path 3 2 contains 2. All other routes coming from AS3 have a local preference of 300.

Customers of Different Providers with a Backup Link

Providers prefer to use as little configuration as possible when dealing with adding and removing customers. Every time a customer is added or removed, the provider will have to add policies to accommodate the customer's requirement. In the following examples, we will show how an AS can use the community attribute or path manipulation techniques in such a way that a new customer can have the provider dynamically set the customer's policies.

The Community Approach

In figure 11–9, customer AS1 is getting its service from provider AS4. Customer AS2 is getting its service from provider AS3. AS1 and AS2 have a private link that will be used for internal use between the two ASs. For all other traffic, both customers would like to go out via their direct providers, AS1 via AS4 and AS2 via AS3. In case the private link goes down, the customers should be able to talk to one another via the providers. If a link to the provider fails, the other customer should be used to reach the Internet.

The following is the relevant configuration of RTA, RTF, and RTC. RTD should be a mirror image of RTC.

RTA configuration:

```
router bgp 4
 network 172.16.220.0 mask 255.255.255.0
 neighbor 172.16.1.2 remote-as 3
 neighbor 172.16.1.2 route-map CHECK_COMMUNITY in
 neighbor 172.16.20.1 remote-as 1
 neighbor 172.16.20.1 route-map CHECK_COMMUNITY in
 no auto-summary
```

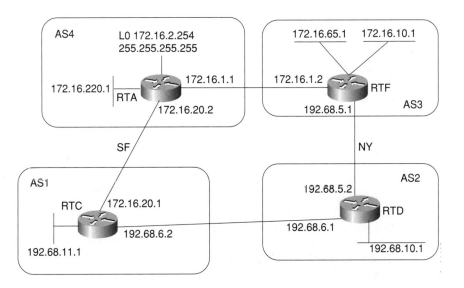

Figure 11–9
Multiple ASs with multiple providers.

```
ip community-list 2 permit 4:40
ip community-list 3 permit 4:60

route-map CHECK_COMMUNITY permit 10
 match community 2
 set local-preference 40

route-map CHECK_COMMUNITY permit 20
 match community 3
 set local-preference 60

route-map CHECK_COMMUNITY permit 30
 set local-preference 100
```

Note how RTA has configured the route map CHECK_COMMUNITY. The **match community** *value* statement under the route map corrolates with the **ip community-list** *value* list, which states the following:

- Instance 10: For routes with community 4:40, set the local preference to 40.

- Instance 20: For routes with community 4:60, set the local preference to 60.

- Instance 30: For all other routes, set the preference to 100.

RTC configuration:

```
router bgp 1
 network 192.68.11.0
 neighbor 172.16.20.2 remote-as 4
 neighbor 172.16.20.2 send-community
 neighbor 172.16.20.2 route-map setcommunity out
 neighbor 172.16.20.2 filter-list 10 out
 neighbor 192.68.6.1 remote-as 2
 no auto-summary

ip as-path access-list 2 permit _2_

ip as-path access-list 10 permit ^$
ip as-path access-list 10 permit ^2$
```

```
route-map setcommunity permit 10
 match as-path 2
 set community 4:40

route-map setcommunity permit 20
```

Note the route map "setcommunity," which is configured toward AS4. The route map states the following:

- Instance 10: For all routes that have passed via AS2 (_2_), set the community to 4:40.

- Instance 20: All other routes will go through and do not have any community set.

RTC also has a "filter-list 10 out," which prevents AS4 from learning about AS3 via AS1. The filter list only permits AS1 and AS2 routes. In case the link between AS4 and AS3 goes down, AS4 cannot use AS1 to reach AS3.

RTF configuration:

```
router bgp 3
 network 172.16.10.0 mask 255.255.255.0
 network 172.16.65.0 mask 255.255.255.192
 neighbor 172.16.1.1 remote-as 4
 neighbor 172.16.1.1 send-community
 neighbor 172.16.1.1 route-map setcommunity out
 neighbor 192.68.5.2 remote-as 2
 no auto-summary

route-map setcommunity permit 10
 set community 4:60
```

In RTF, the route map, **setcommunity neighbor** command sets all updates toward AS4 with a community of 4:60.

Consider RTA's BGP table to see what we have achieved.

```
RTA#show ip bgp
BGP table version is 7, local router ID is 172.16.2.254
```

```
Status codes: s suppressed, d damped, h history, * valid, > best,
i - internal Origin codes: i - IGP, e - EGP, ? - incomplete

     Network           Next Hop      Metric LocPrf Weight Path
*>  172.16.10.0/24    172.16.1.2        0      60      0 3 i
*>  172.16.65.0/26    172.16.1.2        0      60      0 3 i
*>  172.16.220.0/24   0.0.0.0           0          32768 i
*>  192.68.10.0       172.16.1.2               60      0 3 2 i
*                     172.16.20.1              40      0 1 2 i
*>  192.68.11.0       172.16.20.1       0     100      0 1 i
```

RTA has dynamically set the local preference for all routes from the provider AS3 to 60. All routes coming from AS2 via AS1 have a preference of 40, and routes local to AS1 have a preference of 100.

For all routes originated by AS1 (customer local routes) such as 192.68.11.0/24, AS4 will go directly to AS1. For routes belonging to AS2 (customer transit routes), such as 192.68.10.0/24, AS4 will use the other provider AS3. For other routes advertised by the provider (ISP routes), AS4 will go directly to AS3.

The AS_Path Approach

As an alternative to the community approach, AS_path can be be used to achieve the desired routing in figure 11–9. In our example, RTC will prepend an extra AS entry in its routing updates toward AS4 for all routes received from AS2. AS4 will see AS2's updates with a longer path via AS1 and will go via AS3.

RTC configuration:

```
router bgp 1
 network 192.68.11.0
 neighbor 172.16.20.2 remote-as 4
 neighbor 172.16.20.2 route-map setpath out
 neighbor 172.16.20.2 filter-list 10 out
 neighbor 192.68.6.1 remote-as 2
 no auto-summary

ip as-path access-list 2 permit _2_

ip as-path access-list 10 permit ^$
ip as-path access-list 10 permit ^2$
```

```
route-map setpath permit 10
 match as-path 2
 set as-path prepend 1

route-map setpath permit 20
```

RTC has prepended an additional AS number 1 to its updates toward RTA. This is how RTA's BGP table will look:

```
RTA#show ip bgp
BGP table version is 9, local router ID is 172.16.2.254
Status codes: s suppressed, d damped, h history, * valid, > best,
i - internal Origin codes: i - IGP, e - EGP, ? - incomplete

   Network          Next Hop       Metric LocPrf Weight Path
*> 172.16.10.0/24   172.16.1.2        0               0 3 i
*> 172.16.65.0/26   172.16.1.2        0               0 3 i
*> 172.16.220.0/24  0.0.0.0           0           32768 i
*> 192.68.10.0      172.16.1.2                        0 3 2 i
*                   172.16.20.1               100     0 1 1 2 i
*> 192.68.11.0      172.16.20.1       0       100     0 1 i
```

Note how RTA now prefers AS3 to reach prefix 192.68.10.0/24. Care must be taken to make sure that the provider AS1 is not using any access list to accept only routes of the form ^1$ or ^1 2$ from your AS. It is always good to coordinate with the provider regarding the changes you want to make.

FOLLOWING DEFAULTS INSIDE AN AS

The following examples show how border routers can inject defaults inside your AS for your IGP to follow. Figure 11–10 illustrates the following scenario: AS3 is multihomed to two providers, AS1 and AS2. RTA is running EBGP with RTC, and RTF is running EBGP with RTD. Inside AS3, RTA and RTF are running IBGP. We will experiment with two situations: first, RTA and RTF having a direct physical connection and second, RTA and RTF not having a direct physical connection. The latter scenario is used to demonstrate what could go wrong if your IGP traffic is following a default that conflicts with your BGP policies.

Figure 11–10
*Following defaults
inside the AS;
border routers
connected.*

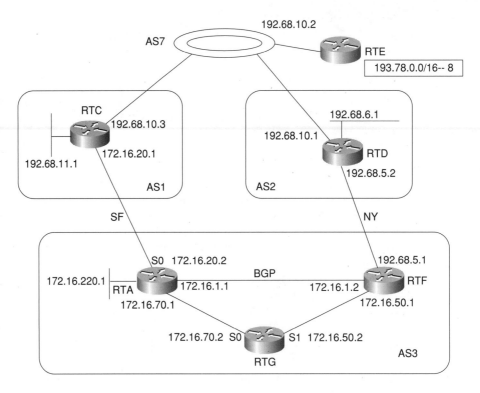

Finally, RTG is an interior router that is running an IGP; RTG is following the default route 0/0 to reach networks outside AS3.

The scenario where RTA and RTF are directly connected is easy; it is very hard for things to go wrong. As long as RTA and RTF are injecting defaults inside the IGP, traffic that reaches any of the BGP routers will find its way outside the AS. It is important that outbound traffic that reaches a BGP router does not go back to the non-BGP routers to avoid possible routing loops.

In case the border routers are not carrying full routes, they can accept a default to the providers to which they are connected. Both links can be used at the same time, or one link could be used as primary and the second as backup. Whichever policy you use, traffic will find its way out.

In the following configuration, RTA and RTF are accepting full routes from their respective providers. RTA and RTF are injecting defaults inside the AS (they are not getting any defaults themselves because they carry full routes). We will use OSPF as an IGP (other IGPs will be used in different scenarios later on).

RTA configuration:

```
router ospf 10
 passive-interface Serial0
 network 172.16.0.0 0.0.255.255 area 0
 default-information originate always

router bgp 3
 no synchronization
 network 172.16.1.0 mask 255.255.255.0
 network 172.16.70.0 mask 255.255.255.0
 network 172.16.220.0 mask 255.255.255.0
 neighbor 172.16.20.1 remote-as 1
 neighbor 172.16.20.1 filter-list 10 out
 neighbor 172.16.1.2 remote-as 3
 no auto-summary

ip as-path access-list 10 permit ^$
```

RTF configuration:

```
router ospf 10
 network 172.16.0.0 0.0.255.255 area 0
 default-information originate always

router bgp 3
 no synchronization
 network 172.16.1.0 mask 255.255.255.0
 network 172.16.50.0 mask 255.255.255.0
 neighbor 172.16.1.1 remote-as 3
 neighbor 172.16.1.1 next-hop-self
 neighbor 192.68.5.2 remote-as 2
 neighbor 192.68.5.2 filter-list 10 out
 no auto-summary

ip as-path access-list 10 permit ^$
```

RTG configuration:

```
router ospf 10
 network 172.16.0.0 0.0.255.255 area 0
```

Note that the RTA and RTF configurations use the router command **default-information originate** with the **always** keyword. This command forces OSPF to inject a 0/0 default route into the OSPF domain at all times. The internal router RTG, which is running OSPF only, will receive the default from multiple sources and will follow the shortest internal metric. Routers that are closer (metric-wise) to RTA will use RTA for default; routers closer to RTF will use RTF.

```
RTG#sh ip route
Codes: C - connected, S - static, I - IGRP, R - RIP, M - mobile, B - BGP
       D - EIGRP, EX - EIGRP external, O - OSPF, IA - OSPF inter area
       N1 - OSPF NSSA external type 1, N2 - OSPF NSSA external type 2
       E1 - OSPF external type 1, E2 - OSPF external type 2, E - EGP
       i - IS-IS, L1 - IS-IS level-1, L2 - IS-IS level-2,
       * - candidate default U - per-user static route, o - ODR
Gateway of last resort is 172.16.70.1 to network 0.0.0.0
    172.16.0.0/16 is subnetted, 5 subnets
O      172.16.220.0/24 [110/74] via 172.16.70.1, 00:03:27, Serial0
C      172.16.50.0/24 is directly connected, Serial1
O      172.16.20.0/24 [110/74] via 172.16.70.1, 00:03:27, Serial0
O      172.16.1.0/24 [110/74] via 172.16.70.1, 00:03:27, Serial0
C      172.16.70.0/24 is directly connected, Serial0
O*E2 0.0.0.0/0 [110/1] via 172.16.70.1, 00:03:27, Serial0
```

Note how RTG has set its gateway of last resort to RTA (172.16.70.1), which happens to be at a shorter internal metric than RTF.

BGP Policies Conflicting with the Internal Default

Anytime internal routers are following defaults to reach routes unknown to the AS, you should be careful not to create routing loops. A routing loop occurs when router X follows a default toward router Y, which in turn uses router X to reach the destination. The traffic will end up bouncing between routers X and Y.

The default route 0/0 is injected differently from BGP into the IGP, depending on what IGP you are using. Different scenarios will be considered, utilizing OSPF, RIP, EIGRP, and ISIS as the IGPs.

In the following scenarios, we will consider the case where routers RTA and RTF in figure 11–11 are not directly connected. As you will see, this will make configuration harder and more vulnerable to routing loops.

Consider figure 11–11. Assume that AS3 is setting its policies in a primary/backup environment where the NY link is primary, and the SF link is a backup. As such, RTA learns its IBGP routes with a higher local preference than

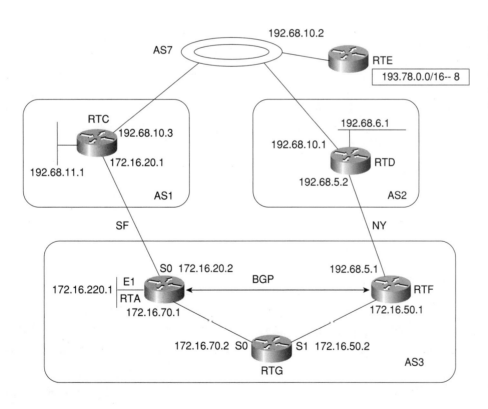

Figure 11–11
Following defaults inside the AS; border routers not connected.

its EBGP routes and will always direct its traffic toward its IBGP peer RTF. In case RTG is receiving the 0/0 from both RTA and RTF, RTG must pick the default via RTF (primary); otherwise, a routing loop will occur. The following sequence of events will explain why.

RTG tries to send traffic to a destination outside AS3. RTG will follow the default toward RTA. RTA has its BGP policies set to use RTF as the exit point. To reach RTF, RTA uses RTG as a first hop. RTG receives the traffic destined to the outside destination and sends it back to RTA, and the loop occurs.

To avoid the preceding situation, you can use any of the following methods:

1. Make sure that RTA does not inject a 0/0 in the IGP unless the primary link goes down. In normal conditions, all traffic will follow the default toward RTF and will be able to exit the AS. In case of a NY link failure, RTA should start sending defaults in the IGP.

NOTES

This method works most easily in a primary/backup environment. In cases were the exit point is not defined, it is hard to figure out which router should send the default. In such cases, any border router that receives the traffic should be able to send it on its direct external link.

2. Make sure that the border router (RTA) does not send the traffic back to the Internal router (RTG), which already used it (RTA) as default. This could be done by providing a shorter path (metric-wise) via the BGP routers; for example, by having a direct physical link between RTA and RTF. If RTG uses RTA as default, RTA will use its directly connected link to send the traffic back to RTF.
3. Run a full IBGP mesh between RTA, RTG, and RTF. RTG would learn all routes via BGP.
4. Manipulate the metrics in such a way that the internal router (RTG) always gets a lower metric via the primary.

We already used the second method in the previous example. The third method is straightforward and will not be covered. In each of the following scenarios, we will consider a different IGP and use either the first or fourth method to solve our problem. Even though we will use just one method in addressing each case, both methods 1 and 4 can be used with any of the IGPs.

To make our problem easier, we will assume that RTA and RTF are dynamically getting a 0/0 default from their providers (regardless of whether they need it). The following discussions experiment with how injecting defaults is treated in a Cisco environment.

Using OSPF as IGP

You can inject the 0/0 default into OSPF by using the following router command:

> **default-information originate** [**always**] [*metric value*] [*metric-type type*] [*route-map name*]

The **default-information originate** (without the **always** keyword) will inject a default 0/0 into OSPF only if the router itself has a default. The **always** keyword cannot be used here because, in case of a link failure, the border router would continue to inject a default in the IGP, even though it cannot deliver the traffic anymore (remember that there is no direct link between border routers).

If RTA and RTF are both configured with the router command **default-information originate,** this is what could happen: RTA receives a 0/0 via EBGP and IBGP. Because RTA is preferring everything via RTF (higher local preference), RTA will prefer the 0/0 via IBGP. Because RTA has a default (via BGP), it will start injecting the default into IGP. We are in a situation where both routers are generating defaults, and a loop may occur.

You might say, because the NY link is the primary, RTA should not send any defaults. This reasoning will fail because if the NY link goes down, RTF stops advertising a 0/0 into the IGP. RTA is not sending any defaults either, so traffic cannot exit the AS.

The solution to our problems is to have RTA and RTF inject a default only if they have a default themselves and only if the default they prefer comes from EBGP.

When RTA detects that it is preferring the 0/0 via EBGP rather than IBGP, it would get an indication that there is a problem with the NY link and would start sending the default. This could be achieved by using a route map in conjunction with the **default-information originate** router command.

RTA configuration:

```
router ospf 10
 passive-interface Serial0
 network 172.16.0.0 0.0.255.255 area 0
 default-information originate route-map SEND_DEFAULT_IF

router bgp 3
 no synchronization
 network 172.16.220.0 mask 255.255.255.0
 network 172.16.70.0 mask 255.255.255.0
 neighbor 172.16.20.1 remote-as 1
 neighbor 172.16.20.1 filter-list 10 out
 neighbor 172.16.50.1 remote-as 3
 neighbor 172.16.50.1 route-map setlocalpref in
 no auto-summary

ip as-path access-list 10 permit ^$

access-list 1 permit 0.0.0.0
access-list 2 permit 172.16.20.1

route-map setlocalpref permit 10
 set local-preference 300

route-map SEND_DEFAULT_IF permit 10
 match ip address 1
 match ip next-hop 2
```

Note the route map SEND_DEFAULT_IF associated with the **default-information originate** router command. This route map matches on the condition that the 0/0 default (access-list 1) has a next hop of 172.16.20.1 (access-list 2). This satisfies the condition that the 0/0 is learned via EBGP rather than IBGP. If this is the case, RTA will detect a link failure in NY and will start injecting its own 0/0 into OSPF.

The second route map "setlocalpref" assigns a value of 300 to all the RTA's IBGP routes. This makes all IBGP routes preferred over EBGP routes.

RTF is also originating a default into OSPF only on the condition that RTF is learning the default from its exterior link (next hop 192.68.5.2). In case of a NY link failure, RTF will stop advertising a 0/0, even though it might be getting a 0/0 from RTA via IBGP.

RTF configuration:

```
router ospf 10
 network 172.16.0.0 0.0.255.255 area 0
 default-information originate route-map SEND_DEFAULT_IF

router bgp 3
 no synchronization
 network 172.16.50.0 mask 255.255.255.0
 neighbor 172.16.70.1 remote-as 3
 neighbor 172.16.70.1 next-hop-self
 neighbor 192.68.5.2 remote-as 2
 neighbor 192.68.5.2 filter-list 10 out
 no auto-summary

ip as-path access-list 10 permit ^$

access-list 1 permit 0.0.0.0
access-list 2 permit 192.68.5.2

route-map SEND_DEFAULT_IF permit 10
 match ip address 1
 match ip next-hop 2
```

RTG is running OSPF only and following the 0/0 default for routes outside AS3.

RTG configuration:

```
router ospf 10
 network 172.16.0.0 0.0.255.255 area 0
```

The following is RTA's IP routing table. Note that RTA is preferring the 0/0 default via its IBGP peer RTF with next hop 172.16.50.1. Because the next hop is different from 172.16.20.1 (the external peer), RTA will not inject any default inside OSPF.

```
RTA#show ip route
Codes: C - connected, S - static, I - IGRP, R - RIP, M - mobile, B - BGP
       D - EIGRP, EX - EIGRP external, O - OSPF, IA - OSPF inter area
       N1 - OSPF NSSA external type 1, N2 - OSPF NSSA external type 2
       E1 - OSPF external type 1, E2 - OSPF external type 2, E - EGP
       i - IS-IS, L1 - IS-IS level-1, L2 - IS-IS level-2,
       * - candidate default U - per-user static route, o - ODR

Gateway of last resort is 172.16.50.1 to network 0.0.0.0

B   192.68.6.0/24 [200/0] via 172.16.50.1, 00:03:06
B   192.68.11.0/24 [200/0] via 172.16.50.1, 00:03:06
B   193.78.0.0/16 [200/0] via 172.16.50.1, 00:03:06
    172.16.0.0/16 subnetted, 4 subnets
C      172.16.20.0/24 is directly connected, Serial0
C      172.16.220.0/24 is directly connected, Ethernet1
O      172.16.50.0/24 [110/164] via 172.16.70.2, 02:17:37, Serial1
C      172.16.70.0/24 is directly connected, Serial1
B* 0.0.0.0/0 [200/0] via 172.16.50.1, 00:03:07
```

The following is RTG's IP routing table. Note how RTG is setting its default to RTF. Both the BGP policies and the IGP defaults are now in sync.

```
RTG#show ip route
Codes: C - connected, S - static, I - IGRP, R - RIP, M - mobile, B - BGP
       D - EIGRP, EX - EIGRP external, O - OSPF, IA - OSPF inter area
       N1 - OSPF NSSA external type 1, N2 - OSPF NSSA external type 2
       E1 - OSPF external type 1, E2 - OSPF external type 2, E - EGP
       i - IS-IS, L1 - IS-IS level-1, L2 - IS-IS level-2,
       * - candidate default U - per-user static route, o - ODR

Gateway of last resort is 172.16.50.1 to network 0.0.0.0
```

```
   172.16.0.0/16 is subnetted, 4 subnets
O    172.16.20.0/24 [110/128] via 172.16.70.1, 02:21:04, Serial0
O    172.16.220.0/24 [110/74] via 172.16.70.1, 02:21:04, Serial0
C    172.16.50.0/24 is directly connected, Serial1
C    172.16.70.0/24 is directly connected, Serial0
O*E2 0.0.0.0/0 [110/1] via 172.16.50.1, 00:41:26, Serial1
```

In case the NY link fails, RTA will learn the BGP 0/0 via its external link with next hop 172.16.20.1 and will inject a default into OSPF.

NOTES

Redistributing the 0/0 from BGP into OSPF via the **redistribute** router command is not allowed or implemented.

Using RIP as IGP

The Cisco RIP implementation behaves differently from OSPF when dealing with the 0/0 defaults. The BGP-learned 0/0 default is automatically injected into RIP. A **default-metric** router command is required under the RIP process to assign a metric (hop count) to the default. In our example (figure 11–11), assume that RTA, RTF, and RTG are running RIP. We will set the metric of the 0/0 injected into RIP by RTA in such a way that the internal router (RTG) always prefers RTF.

RTA will set the 0/0 default metric to 5. Note that no redistribution was necessary to inject the BGP default into RIP.

RTA configuration:

```
router rip
 passive-interface Serial0
 network 172.16.0.0
 default-metric 5
```

```
router bgp 3
 no synchronization
 network 172.16.220.0 mask 255.255.255.0
 network 172.16.70.0 mask 255.255.255.0
 neighbor 172.16.20.1 remote-as 1
 neighbor 172.16.20.1 filter-list 10 out
 neighbor 172.16.50.1 remote-as 3
 neighbor 172.16.50.1 route-map setlocalpref in
 no auto-summary

ip as-path access-list 10 permit ^$

route-map setlocalpref permit 10
 set local-preference 300
```

RTF will inject the 0/0 into RIP with a hop count of 1.

RTF configuration:

```
router rip
network 172.16.0.0
default-metric 1

router bgp 3
 no synchronization
 network 172.16.50.0 mask 255.255.255.0
 neighbor 172.16.70.1 remote-as 3
 neighbor 172.16.70.1 next-hop-self
 neighbor 192.68.5.2 remote-as 2
 neighbor 192.68.5.2 filter-list 10 out
 no auto-summary

ip as-path access-list 10 permit ^$
```

RTG is running RIP only and is following the 0/0 default for routes outside AS3.

RTG configuration:

```
router rip
network 172.16.0.0
```

The following is RTG's IP routing table. Note that RTG has set its default to RTF because of the lower metric of 1.

```
RTG#show
Codes: C - connected, S - static, I - IGRP, R - RIP, M - mobile, B - BGP
    D - EIGRP, EX - EIGRP external, O - OSPF, IA - OSPF inter area
    N1 - OSPF NSSA external type 1, N2 - OSPF NSSA external type 2
    E1 - OSPF external type 1, E2 - OSPF external type 2, E - EGP
    i - IS-IS, L1 - IS-IS level-1, L2 - IS-IS level-2,
    * - candidate default U - per-user static route, o - ODR

Gateway of last resort is 172.16.50.1 to network 0.0.0.0

    172.16.0.0/16 is subnetted, 4 subnets
R    172.16.220.0/24 [120/1] via 172.16.70.1, 00:00:03, Serial0
C    172.16.50.0/24 is directly connected, Serial1
R    172.16.20.0/24 [120/1] via 172.16.70.1, 00:00:03, Serial0
C    172.16.70.0/24 is directly connected, Serial0
R*  0.0.0.0/0 [120/1] via 172.16.50.1, 00:00:22, Serial1
```

NOTES

If more conditions are needed to inject the 0/0 into RIP, redistribution and route maps could be used to inject the default from BGP into RIP.

Using EIGRP as the IGP

BGP-learned defaults are injected into EIGRP via redistribution. The 0/0 metric needs to be converted into an EIGRP-compatible metric by using the **default-metric** router command. RTA will inject its default with a high metric in such a way that the internal router (RTG) always gets a lower metric via RTF.

RTA configuration:

```
router eigrp 1
  redistribute bgp 3 route-map DEFAULT_ONLY
  passive-interface Serial0
  network 172.16.0.0
  default-metric 5 100 250 100 1500
```

```
router bgp 3
 no synchronization
 network 172.16.70.0 mask 255.255.255.0
 network 172.16.220.0 mask 255.255.255.0
 neighbor 172.16.20.1 remote-as 1
 neighbor 172.16.20.1 filter-list 10 out
 neighbor 172.16.50.1 remote-as 3
 neighbor 172.16.50.1 route-map setlocalpref in
 no auto-summary

ip as-path access-list 10 permit ^$

access-list 5 permit 0.0.0.0

route-map setlocalpref permit 10
 set local-preference 300

route-map DEFAULT_ONLY permit 10
 match ip address 5
```

RTA uses a route map DEFAULT_ONLY to match on the default route 0/0. Any other updates will be prevented from being redistributed into EIGRP. RTA also sets the metric by using the **default-metric** router command.

In the same manner, RTF is redistributing only the 0/0 into EIGRP using the route map DEFAULT_ONLY. RTF uses the **default-metric 1000 100 250 100 1500** statement to set its default metric to an EIGRP-compatible metric. Note the bandwidth portion (1000) of the **default-metric** statement in RTF, which is much higher than the bandwidth (5) in RTA. This makes the metric from RTF much lower than the one from RTA.

RTF configuration:

```
router eigrp 1
 redistribute bgp 3 route-map DEFAULT_ONLY
 network 172.16.0.0
 default-metric 1000 100 250 100 1500

router bgp 3
 no synchronization
```

```
     network 172.16.50.0 mask 255.255.255.0
     neighbor 172.16.70.1 remote-as 3
     neighbor 172.16.70.1 next-hop-self
     neighbor 192.68.5.2 remote-as 2
     neighbor 192.68.5.2 filter-list 10 out
     no auto-summary

     ip as-path access-list 10 permit ^$

     access-list 5 permit 0.0.0.0

     route-map DEFAULT_ONLY permit 10
      match ip address 5
```

RTG is running EIGRP only and is following the default for all routes outside AS3.

RTG configuration:

```
     router eigrp 1
      network 172.16.0.0
```

The following is the IP routing table of RTG. Note that RTG follows the default toward RTF.

```
RTG#sh ip route
Codes: C - connected, S - static, I - IGRP, R - RIP, M - mobile, B - BGP
        D - EIGRP, EX - EIGRP external, O - OSPF, IA - OSPF inter area
        N1 - OSPF NSSA external type 1, N2 - OSPF NSSA external type 2
        E1 - OSPF external type 1, E2 - OSPF external type 2, E - EGP
     i - IS-IS, L1 - IS-IS level-1, L2 - IS-IS level-2,
     * - candidate default U - per-user static route, o - ODR

Gateway of last resort is 172.16.50.1 to network 0.0.0.0

   172.16.0.0/16 is subnetted, 4 subnets
D      172.16.220.0/24 [90/2195456] via 172.16.70.1, 00:12:17, Serial0
C      172.16.50.0/24 is directly connected, Serial1
D      172.16.20.0/24 [90/2681856] via 172.16.70.1, 00:12:17, Serial0
C      172.16.70.0/24 is directly connected, Serial0
D*EX 0.0.0.0/0 [170/3097600] via 172.16.50.1, 00:07:40, Serial1
```

Using IGRP as IGP

IGRP does not understand the 0.0.0.0 default. To set a default inside IGRP, the **ip default-network** global command needs to be set on RTA and RTF. The default network used needs to be redistributed into IGRP to set the default on the internal routers. A default-metric needs to be set for successful redistribution.

RTA is setting network 192.68.6.0/24 (or any other classfull network learned via BGP) to be the default network. RTA will redistribute that network only into IGRP.

RTA configuration:

```
router igrp 1
 passive-interface Serial0
 redistribute bgp 3 route-map DEFAULT_ONLY
 network 172.16.0.0
 default-metric 5 100 250 100 1500

router bgp 3
 no synchronization
 network 172.16.70.0 mask 255.255.255.0
 network 172.16.220.0 mask 255.255.255.0
 neighbor 172.16.20.1 remote-as 1
 neighbor 172.16.20.1 filter-list 10 out
 neighbor 172.16.50.1 remote-as 3
 neighbor 172.16.50.1 route-map setlocalpref in
 no auto-summary

ip default-network 192.68.6.0
ip as-path access-list 10 permit ^$

access-list 5 permit 192.68.6.0 0.0.0.255

route-map setlocalpref permit 10
 set local-preference 300

route-map DEFAULT_ONLY permit 10
 match ip address 5
```

RTF is also setting its default, to 192.68.6.0/24, and redistributing the default, with a better metric, into IGRP.

RTF configuration:

```
router igrp 1
 redistribute bgp 3 route-map DEFAULT_ONLY
 network 172.16.0.0
 default-metric 1000 100 250 100 1500

router bgp 3
 no synchronization
 network 172.16.50.0 mask 255.255.255.0
 neighbor 172.16.70.1 remote-as 3
 neighbor 172.16.70.1 next-hop-self
 neighbor 192.68.5.2 remote-as 2
 neighbor 192.68.5.2 filter-list 10 out
 no auto-summary

ip default-network 192.68.6.0
ip as-path access-list 10 permit ^$

access-list 5 permit 192.68.6.0 0.0.0.255

route-map DEFAULT_ONLY permit 10
 match ip address 5
```

RTG is running IGRP only and is following the default for all routes outside AS3.

RTG configuration:

```
router igrp 1
 network 172.16.0.0
```

The following is the IP routing table of RTG. Note that RTG follows the default toward RTF.

```
RTG#show ip route
Codes: C - connected, S - static, I - IGRP, R - RIP, M - mobile, B - BGP
```

```
         D - EIGRP, EX - EIGRP external, O - OSPF, IA - OSPF inter area
         N1 - OSPF NSSA external type 1, N2 - OSPF NSSA external type 2
         E1 - OSPF external type 1, E2 - OSPF external type 2, E - EGP
          i - IS-IS, L1 - IS-IS level-1, L2 - IS-IS level-2,
          * - candidate default U - per-user static route, o - ODR

Gateway of last resort is 172.16.50.1 to network 192.68.6.0

I*    192.68.6.0/24 [100/8576] via 172.16.50.1, 00:00:32, Serial1
      172.16.0.0/16 is subnetted, 4 subnets
I     172.16.220.0/24 [100/8576] via 172.16.70.1, 00:00:32, Serial0
C     172.16.50.0/24 is directly connected, Serial1
I     172.16.20.0/24 [100/10476] via 172.16.70.1, 00:00:32, Serial0
C     172.16.70.0/24 is directly connected, Serial0
```

Using ISIS as IGP

ISIS is similar to OSPF; it uses the **default-information originate** router command. RTA is originating a default into ISIS only on the condition that RTA is learning the default from its exterior link.

RTA configuration:

```
router isis 100
 redistribute connected
 default-information originate route-map SEND_DEFAULT_IF
 net 49.0001.0000.0c00.000a.00

router bgp 3
 no synchronization
 network 172.16.220.0 mask 255.255.255.0
 network 172.16.70.0 mask 255.255.255.0
 neighbor 172.16.20.1 remote-as 1
 neighbor 172.16.20.1 filter-list 10 out
 neighbor 172.16.50.1 remote-as 3
 neighbor 172.16.50.1 route-map setlocalpref in
 no auto-summary

ip as-path access-list 10 permit ^$

access-list 1 permit 0.0.0.0
access-list 2 permit 172.16.20.1
```

```
route-map SEND_DEFAULT_IF permit 10
 match ip address 1
 match ip next-hop 2
```

RTF is originating a default into ISIS on the condition that RTF is learning the default from its exterior link.

RTF configuration:

```
router isis 100
 default-information originate route-map SEND_DEFAULT_IF
 net 49.0001.0000.0c00.000c.00

router bgp 3
 no synchronization
 network 172.16.50.0 mask 255.255.255.0
 neighbor 172.16.70.1 remote-as 3
 neighbor 172.16.70.1 next-hop-self
 neighbor 192.68.5.2 remote-as 2
 neighbor 192.68.5.2 filter-list 10 out
 no auto-summary

ip as-path access-list 10 permit ^$

access-list 1 permit 0.0.0.0
access-list 2 permit 192.68.5.2

route-map SEND_DEFAULT_IF permit 10
 match ip address 1
 match ip next-hop 2
```

RTG is running ISIS and following the 0/0 default for routes outside AS3.

RTG configuration:

```
router isis 100
 net 49.0001.0000.0c00.000b.00
```

The following is RTG's IP routing table; note how RTG follows the default toward RTF.

```
RTG#show ip route
Codes: C - connected, S - static, I - IGRP, R - RIP, M - mobile, B - BGP
       D - EIGRP, EX - EIGRP external, O - OSPF, IA - OSPF inter area
       N1 - OSPF NSSA external type 1, N2 - OSPF NSSA external type 2
       E1 - OSPF external type 1, E2 - OSPF external type 2, E - EGP
        i - IS-IS, L1 - IS-IS level-1, L2 - IS-IS level-2,
        * - candidate default U - per-user static route, o - ODR

Gateway of last resort is 172.16.50.1 to network 0.0.0.0

    172.16.0.0/16 is subnetted, 4 subnets
i L1     172.16.220.0/24 [115/20] via 172.16.70.1, Serial0
i L1     172.16.20.0/24 [115/20] via 172.16.70.1, Serial0
C        172.16.50.0/24 is directly connected, Serial1
C        172.16.70.0/24 is directly connected, Serial0
i*L2 0.0.0.0/0 [115/10] via 172.16.50.1, Serial1
```

POLICY ROUTING

This example demonstrates how policy routing can be used to direct the traffic based on the source IP address rather than the destination IP address. Figure 11–12 shows a router RTA that is running BGP with two providers, AS1 and AS2. Internal routers such as RTG and RTF are running IGP only (OSPF) and are following a default route toward RTA.

RTA wants to set policy routing in such a way that traffic coming over the serial line S1 from RTG is directed toward AS2 if the source is network 172.16.10.0/24. Traffic coming from RTG with source 172.16.112.0/24 is to be directed toward AS1; in case of a link failure to AS1, the traffic will go to AS2. For all other source IP addresses, follow normal routing.

RTA will be configured in the following manner:

RTA configuration:

```
interface Ethernet0
  ip address 172.16.80.1 255.255.255.0
```

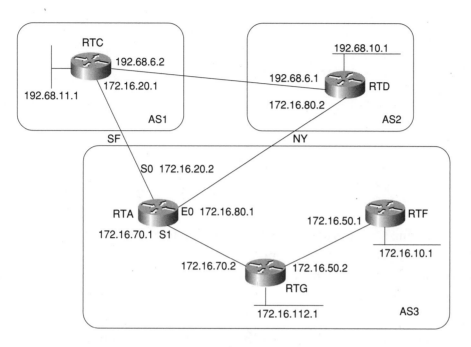

Figure 11–12
*Policy routing
scenario.*

```
interface Serial1
 ip address 172.16.70.1 255.255.255.0
 ip policy route-map CHECK_SOURCE

router ospf 10
 passive-interface Serial0
 passive-interface Ethernet0
 network 172.16.0.0 0.0.255.255 area 0
 default-information originate always

router bgp 3
 network 172.16.50.0 mask 255.255.255.0
 network 172.16.70.0 mask 255.255.255.0
 network 172.16.10.0 mask 255.255.255.0
 network 172.16.112.0 mask 255.255.255.0
 neighbor 172.16.20.1 remote-as 1
 neighbor 172.16.20.1 filter-list 10 out
 neighbor 172.16.80.2 remote-as 2
 neighbor 172.16.80.2 filter-list 10 out
 no auto-summary
```

```
ip as-path access-list 10 permit ^$

access-list 1 permit 172.16.10.0 0.0.0.255
access-list 2 permit 172.16.112.0 0.0.0.255

route-map CHECK_SOURCE permit 10
 match ip address 1
 set ip next-hop 172.16.80.2

route-map CHECK_SOURCE permit 20
 match ip address 2
 set ip next-hop 172.16.20.1 172.16.80.2
```

Policy routing is always applied to the incoming interface. Serial 1 is configured with the interface command **ip policy route-map** *map-name*. This will apply route map CHECK_SOURCE to all Serial 1 incoming traffic. The explanation of the route map follows:

- Instance 10: For all source IP addresses that come from 172.16.10.0/24, set the next hop to 172.16.80.2. If next hop 172.16.80.2 is unreachable, drop the packet.

- Instance 20: For all source IP addresses that come from 172.16.112.0/24, set the next hop to 172.16.20.1. If next hop 172.16.20.1 is unreachable, try sending the traffic to next hop 172.16.80.2.

For all other source IP addresses, follow normal routing.

The policy routing route maps give you the option to pick multiple next hops. This is necessary to always have a backup path. For all traffic that does not match the route maps, the router will follow normal routing. To illustrate, a trace route will be done from RTG to 192.68.10.1 from source IP address 172.16.112.1. The following is RTA's IP routing table:

```
RTA#show ip route
Codes: C - connected, S - static, I - IGRP, R - RIP, M - mobile, B - BGP
       D - EIGRP, EX - EIGRP external, O - OSPF, IA - OSPF inter area
```

```
            N1 - OSPF NSSA external type 1, N2 - OSPF NSSA external type 2
            E1 - OSPF external type 1, E2 - OSPF external type 2, E - EGP
             i - IS-IS, L1 - IS-IS level-1, L2 - IS-IS level-2,
             * - candidate default U - per-user static route, o - ODR

      Gateway of last resort is not set

      B   192.68.10.0/24 [20/0] via 172.16.80.2, 00:30:09
      B   192.68.11.0/24 [20/0] via 172.16.20.1, 00:30:14
          172.16.0.0/16 is subnetted, 5 subnets
      O       172.16.50.0/24 [110/69] via 172.16.70.2, 00:27:27, Serial1
      C       172.16.20.0/24 is directly connected, Serial0
      C       172.16.80.0/24 is directly connected, Ethernet0
      C       172.16.70.0/24 is directly connected, Serial1
```

Trace route from RTG with a source of 172.16.112.1 and a destination 192.68.10.1.

```
      RTG#traceroute
      Protocol [ip]:
      Target IP address: 192.68.10.1
      Source address: 172.16.112.1
      Numeric display [n]:
      Timeout in seconds [3]:
      Probe count [3]:
      Minimum Time to Live [1]:
      Maximum Time to Live [30]:
      Port Number [33434]:
      Loose, Strict, Record, Timestamp, Verbose[none]:
      Type escape sequence to abort.
      Tracing the route to gateway.aeg-aas.de (192.68.10.1)

       1 172.16.70.1 4 msec 4 msec 0 msec
       2 172.16.20.1 4 msec 4 msec 4 msec
       3 192.68.6.1 4 msec 4 msec 4 msec
```

Note how RTA has taken next hop 172.16.20.1 (second line in the trace route output) to reach 192.68.10.0/24, even though RTA's routing table indicates that 192.68.10.0/24 should be reached with next hop 172.16.80.2.

This second attempt shows what will happen if Serial 0 is down, and next hop 172.16.20.1 is unreachable. Trace route from RTG with a source of 172.16.112.1 and a destination 192.68.10.1 while Serial 0 is down.

```
RTG#traceroute
Protocol [ip]:
Target IP address: 192.68.10.1
Source address: 172.16.112.1
Numeric display [n]:
Timeout in seconds [3]:
Probe count [3]:
Minimum Time to Live [1]:
Maximum Time to Live [30]:
Port Number [33434]:
Loose, Strict, Record, Timestamp, Verbose[none]:
Type escape sequence to abort.
Tracing the route to gateway.aeg-aas.de (192.68.10.1)

 1 172.16.70.1 0 msec 4 msec 4 msec
 2 172.16.80.2 8 msec 4 msec 4 msec
```

RTA has taken the alternate next hop 172.16.80.2.

ROUTE REFLECTORS

This example will illustrate a practical use of route reflectors and peer groups. In figure 11–13, RTG and RTA form one cluster where RTG is the route reflector. RTF, RTE, and RTD form another cluster where RTF is the route reflector. RTG and RTF are part of a peer group called REFLECTORS; if there are other route reflectors, all can be IBGP peered in a full mesh. RTF puts all its clients in a peer group called CLIENTS, where common policies can be applied.

Clients are indicated by the route reflectors using the "route-reflector-client." Because clients are part of a peer group, client-to-client reflection needs to be turned off to avoid potential problems. Full IBGP mesh will be maintained inside the RTF-RTD-RTE cluster.

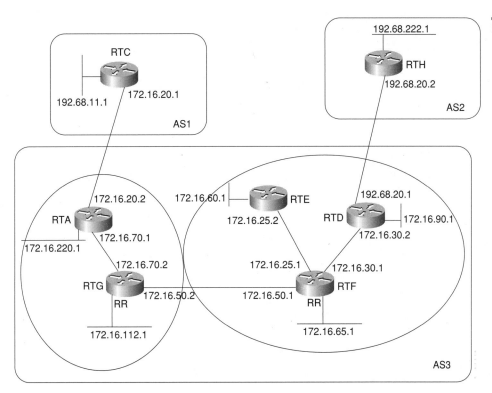

Figure 11–13
Route reflectors.

RTF configuration:

```
router bgp 3
 no synchronization
 no bgp client-to-client reflection
 network 172.16.65.0 mask 255.255.255.192
 network 172.16.50.0 mask 255.255.255.0
 network 172.16.25.0 mask 255.255.255.0
 network 172.16.30.0 mask 255.255.255.0
 neighbor REFLECTORS peer-group
 neighbor REFLECTORS remote-as 3
 neighbor CLIENTS peer-group
 neighbor CLIENTS remote-as 3
 neighbor CLIENTS route-reflector-client
 neighbor 172.16.25.2 peer-group CLIENTS
```

```
       neighbor 172.16.30.2 peer-group CLIENTS
       neighbor 172.16.50.2 peer-group REFLECTORS
       no auto-summary
```

RTD is a client of RTF. From RTD's perspective, the BGP peering session with RTF is a normal IBGP session. Note in the following configuration how RTD has a full IBGP mesh with RTF and RTE. The same goes for RTE.

RTD configuration:

```
       router bgp 3
        no synchronization
        network 172.16.90.0 mask 255.255.255.0
        network 172.16.30.0 mask 255.255.255.0
        neighbor 172.16.25.2 remote-as 3
        neighbor 172.16.25.2 next-hop-self
        neighbor 172.16.30.1 remote-as 3
        neighbor 172.16.30.1 next-hop-self
        neighbor 192.68.20.2 remote-as 2
        neighbor 192.68.20.2 filter-list 10 out
        no auto-summary

       ip as-path access-list 10 permit ^$
```

RTG configuration:

```
       router bgp 3
        no synchronization
        network 172.16.112.0 mask 255.255.255.0
        network 172.16.50.0 mask 255.255.255.0
        network 172.16.70.0 mask 255.255.255.0
        neighbor 172.16.50.1 remote-as 3
        neighbor 172.16.70.1 remote-as 3
        neighbor 172.16.70.1 route-reflector-client
        no auto-summary
```

RTA configuration:

```
       router bgp 3
        no synchronization
```

```
network 172.16.220.0 mask 255.255.255.0
network 172.16.70.0 mask 255.255.255.0
neighbor 172.16.20.1 remote-as 1
neighbor 172.16.20.1 filter-list 10 out
neighbor 172.16.70.2 remote-as 3
neighbor 172.16.70.2 next-hop-self
no auto-summary

ip as-path access-list 10 permit ^$
```

The following snapshot shows how RTD sees some of the routes that are being reflected into its own cluster. Note how RTD sees the originator of route 172.16.220.0/24 as 172.16.220.1, which is the router ID of RTA. The route also carries a cluster list that contains the router IDs of all the route reflectors that it passed through.

```
RTD#show ip bgp 172.16.220.0
BGP routing table entry for 172.16.220.0/24, version 52
Paths: (1 available, best #1)
 Local
   172.16.70.1 (metric 192) from 172.16.30.1 (172.16.220.1)
     Origin IGP, metric 0, localpref 100, valid, internal, best
     Originator : 172.16.220.1, Cluster list: 172.16.65.1, 172.16.112.1
```

In the case where multiple route reflectors are configured inside the cluster, all of them have to be configured with a common cluster-ID. This is needed to detect routing loops that might occur between clusters. If RTE, for example, were to be configured as a route reflector, then RTF's and RTE's configuration would need the additional router command **bgp cluster-id** *number*.

RTF configuration:

```
router bgp 3
 no synchronization
 no bgp client-to-client reflection
 network 172.16.65.0 mask 255.255.255.192
 network 172.16.50.0 mask 255.255.255.0
 network 172.16.25.0 mask 255.255.255.0
 network 172.16.30.0 mask 255.255.255.0
```

```
     neighbor REFLECTORS peer-group
     neighbor REFLECTORS remote-as 3
     neighbor CLIENTS peer-group
     neighbor CLIENTS remote-as 3
     neighbor CLIENTS route-reflector-client
     neighbor 172.16.25.2 peer-group CLIENTS
     neighbor 172.16.30.2 peer-group CLIENTS
     neighbor 172.16.50.2 peer-group REFLECTORS
     bgp cluster-id 1000
     no auto-summary
```

NOTES

The cluster-id 1000 is a number identifying the cluster. This is needed in case RTF and RTE are both configured as route reflectors in the same cluster.

CONFEDERATIONS

For the scenario in figure 11–14, we want to divide AS3 into two smaller sub-ASs, AS65050 and AS65060. The AS numbers of the sub-ASs are chosen from within the private AS pool range of 64512-65535. OSPF is used as the IGP in each sub-AS. The OSPF within AS65050 is running independently from the OSPF in AS65060, which means that the area numbers used in AS65050 can be reused in AS65060. This is taking advantage of one of the benefits of BGP, namely that IGPs in one AS run independently of IGPs in other ASs.

RTA's configuration shows that RTA has all its interfaces in OSPF area 5. RTA is running EBGP with RTC in AS1 and is running IBGP with RTG in AS65050. Note that RTA uses the **bgp confederation identifier 3** router command to present itself to RTC as being part of confederation 3.

RTA configuration:

```
     router ospf 10
      passive-interface Serial0
      network 172.16.0.0 0.0.255.255 area 5
```

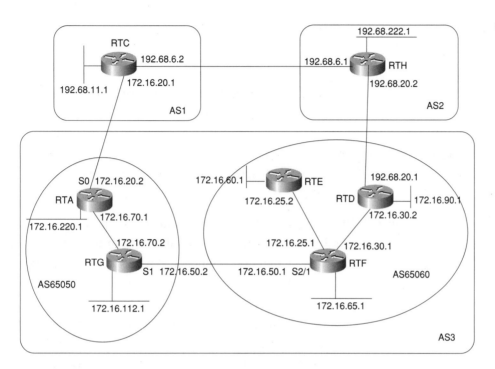

Figure 11–14
Confederation.

```
router bgp 65050
 no synchronization
 bgp confederation identifier 3
 network 172.16.220.0 mask 255.255.255.0
 network 172.16.70.0 mask 255.255.255.0
 neighbor 172.16.20.1 remote-as 1
 neighbor 172.16.20.1 filter-list 10 out
 neighbor 172.16.70.2 remote-as 65050
 no auto-summary

ip as-path access-list 10 permit ^$
```

RTC is running normal EBGP when talking to RTA. According to RTC, RTA belongs to AS3. RTC has no visibility to the sub-ASs inside confederation 3. RTC is also running EBGP with RTH in AS2.

RTC configuration:

```
router bgp 1
 network 192.68.11.0
```

```
neighbor 172.16.20.2 remote-as 3
neighbor 192.68.6.1 remote-as 2
no auto-summary
```

RTG is the sub-AS65050 border router that is running *confederation EBGP* with router RTF in sub-AS65060. RTG is also running IBGP with RTA. RTG is an OSPF area border router with a common area 5 with RTA and the rest of its interfaces in area 0. Note how RTG has disabled its OSPF processing on serial 1 (passive-interface Serial1), which is the common interface with RTF. Only EBGP is run on that link.

RTG also identifies itself as being part of confederation 3 (bgp confederation identifier 3). RTG uses the router command **bgp confederation peers 65060** to preserve all the attributes, such as local preference and next hop when traversing the EBGP session to AS65060. This will make the confederation EBGP session with sub-AS65060 look like an IBGP session. The **neighbor 172.16.50.1 next-hop-self** command will set the next hop address of routes going from RTG to RTF to RTG's IP address. Without this command, the next hop address of all EBGP routes from AS1 will be sent to RTF with the external next hop 172.16.20.1, which is acceptable only as long as routers in sub-AS65060 can reach it from within the confederation.

RTG configuration:

```
router ospf 10
 passive-interface Serial1
 network 172.16.70.2 0.0.0.0 area 5
 network 172.16.0.0 0.0.255.255 area 0

router bgp 65050
 no synchronization
 bgp confederation identifier 3
 bgp confederation peers 65060
 network 172.16.112.0 mask 255.255.255.0
 network 172.16.50.0 mask 255.255.255.0
 network 172.16.70.0 mask 255.255.255.0
 neighbor 172.16.50.1 remote-as 65060
```

```
  neighbor 172.16.50.1 next-hop-self
  neighbor 172.16.70.1 remote-as 65050
  no auto-summary
```

The same configuration that is in RTG applies to RTF, which is the border router of sub-AS65060. RTF is also an area border router in areas 0 and 5. Areas 0 and 5 in AS65060 are totally independent from areas 0 and 5 in AS65050. The two IGPs are shielded from each other by BGP. Full mesh IBGP sessions are configured between RTE, RTD, and RTF by using the peer group SUB_AS_65060.

RTF configuration:

```
  router ospf 10
   passive-interface Serial2/1
   network 172.16.25.1 0.0.0.0 area 5
   network 172.16.0.0 0.0.255.255 area 0

  router bgp 65060
   no synchronization
   bgp confederation identifier 3
   bgp confederation peers 65050
   network 172.16.65.0 mask 255.255.255.192
   network 172.16.50.0 mask 255.255.255.0
   network 172.16.25.0 mask 255.255.255.0
   network 172.16.30.0 mask 255.255.255.0
   neighbor SUB_AS_65060 peer-group
   neighbor SUB_AS_65060 remote-as 65060
   neighbor 172.16.25.2 peer-group SUB_AS_65060
   neighbor 172.16.30.2 peer-group SUB_AS_65060
   neighbor 172.16.50.2 remote-as 65050
   neighbor 172.16.50.2 next-hop-self
```

RTD is a border router for confederation 3. RTD is running EBGP with RTH in AS2 and a full IBGP mesh with routers RTE and RTF in sub-AS65060. RTD has all its interfaces in area 0. RTD is not running OSPF on the external link to AS2. This is why the next hop of external updates coming to RTD has to be set to self before the routes are propagated to RTF and RTE.

RTD configuration:

```
router ospf 10
 network 172.16.0.0 0.0.255.255 area 0.0.0.0

router bgp 65060
 no synchronization
 bgp confederation identifier 3
 network 172.16.90.0 mask 255.255.255.0
 network 172.16.30.0 mask 255.255.255.0
 neighbor 172.16.25.2 remote-as 65060
 neighbor 172.16.25.2 next-hop-self
 neighbor 172.16.30.1 remote-as 65060
 neighbor 172.16.30.1 next-hop-self
 neighbor 192.68.20.2 remote-as 2
 neighbor 172.16.20.2 filter-list 10 out
 no auto-summary

ip as-path access-list 10 permit ^$
```

RTE has all its interfaces in OSPF area 5 and is running a full IBGP mesh with RTF and RTD.

RTE configuration:

```
router ospf 10
 network 172.16.0.0 0.0.255.255 area 5

router bgp 65060
 no synchronization
 bgp confederation identifier 3
 network 172.16.60.0 mask 255.255.255.0
 network 172.16.25.0 mask 255.255.255.0
 neighbor 172.16.25.1 remote-as 65060
 neighbor 172.16.30.2 remote-as 65060
 no auto-summary
```

RTH is a BGP border router in AS2 that is running EBGP with AS1 and AS3. RTH has no visibility to the sub-AS in confederation 3.

RTH configuration:

```
router bgp 2
network 192.68.222.0
neighbor 192.68.6.2 remote-as 1
neighbor 192.68.20.1 remote-as 3
no auto-summary
```

Let us look at some excerpts from the BGP tables:

Note how RTH sees all routes via two paths—one via AS1 and one via AS3. As you can see, all the sub-ASs are hidden from RTH.

```
RTH#show ip bgp
BGP table version is 477, local router ID is 192.68.222.1
Status codes: s suppressed, * valid, > best, i - internal
Origin codes: i - IGP, e - EGP, ? - incomplete

     Network          Next Hop       Metric LocPrf Weight Path
*>  172.16.25.0/24    192.68.20.1                       0 3 i
*                     192.68.6.2                        0 1 3 i
*>  172.16.30.0/24    192.68.20.1         0             0 3 i
*                     192.68.6.2                        0 1 3 i
*>  172.16.50.0/24    192.68.20.1                       0 3 i
*                     192.68.6.2                        0 1 3 i
*>  172.16.60.0/24    192.68.20.1                       0 3 i
*                     192.68.6.2                        0 1 3 i
*>  172.16.70.0/24    192.68.20.1                       0 3 i
*                     192.68.6.2                        0 1 3 i
*>  172.16.90.0/24    192.68.20.1         0             0 3 i
*                     192.68.6.2                        0 1 3 i
*>  172.16.65.0/26    192.68.20.1                       0 3 i
*                     192.68.6.2                        0 1 3 i
*>  172.16.112.0/24   192.68.20.1                       0 3 i
*                     192.68.6.2                        0 1 3 i
*>  172.16.220.0/24   192.68.20.1                       0 3 i
*                     192.68.6.2                        0 1 3 i
*>  192.68.11.0       192.68.6.2          0             0 1 i
*                     192.68.20.1                       0 3 1 i
*>  192.68.222.0      0.0.0.0             0         32768 i
```

Looking at RTA's BGP table, all the sub-ASs are indicated between parentheses (). Any path taken between sub-ASs has a length of 0. Note how prefix 192.68.222.0/24 is learned via two paths, one internal via (65060) 2, and the other external via 1 2. The path length of the internal route via (65060) 2 is considered to be shorter because the sub-ASs are not counted in calculating the path length. This is why the internal path has been chosen over the external path.

```
RTA#show ip bgp
BGP table version is 13, local router ID is 172.16.220.1
Status codes: s suppressed, d damped, h history, * valid, > best,
i - internal Origin codes: i - IGP, e - EGP, ? - incomplete

   Network          Next Hop      Metric LocPrf Weight Path
*>i172.16.25.0/24   172.16.50.1        0    100      0 (65060) i
*>i172.16.30.0/24   172.16.50.1        0    100      0 (65060) i
*>i172.16.50.0/24   172.16.70.2        0    100      0 i
*>i172.16.60.0/24   172.16.50.1        0    100      0 (65060) i
*> 172.16.70.0/24   0.0.0.0            0         32768 i
*  i                172.16.70.2        0    100      0 i
*>i172.16.90.0/24   172.16.50.1        0    100      0 (65060) i
*>i172.16.65.0/26   172.16.50.1        0    100      0 (65060) i
*>i172.16.112.0/24  172.16.70.2        0    100      0 i
*> 172.16.220.0/24  0.0.0.0            0         32768 i
*> 192.68.11.0      172.16.20.1        0             0 1 i
*  192.68.222.0     172.16.20.1                     0 1 2 i
*>i                 172.16.50.1             100      0 (65060) 2 i
```

Note how the following excerpt shows how RTF considers all routes coming from sub-AS65050 as being confederation external routes (confed-external). BGP performs its decision process within a confederation in the following manner: EBGP is more preferred than confed-external, which is more preferred than internal.

```
RTF#show ip bgp 172.16.220.0
BGP routing table entry for 172.16.220.0/24, version 22
Paths: (1 available, best #1, advertised over IBGP)
  (65050)
    172.16.50.2 from 172.16.50.2 (172.16.112.1)
      Origin IGP, metric 0, localpref 100, valid, confed-external, best
```

CONTROLLING ROUTE AND CACHE INVALIDATION

A requirement of BGP is resetting the neighbors' TCP connection whenever a policy is changed for the new policy to take effect (**clear ip bgp** [* | *address* | *peer-group*]). Clearing the sessions in this manner will restart the neighbor negotiations from scratch, invalidate the cache, and cause a major impact on the operation of live networks.

Soft reconfiguration is a new approach that enables policies to be configured and activated without resetting the BGP TCP session. This enables new policies to take effect without significantly affecting the network. Soft configuration can be applied in two different ways, inbound and outbound. Use the following exec command:

> **clear ip bgp** [* | *address* | *peer-group*][**soft** [*in*|*out*]]

Outbound Soft Reconfiguration

Whenever outbound soft reconfiguration is applied, the new policies are automatically triggered, and appropriate updates are generated to enforce the new policy. Use the following exec command:

> **clear ip bgp** [* | *address* | *peer-group*] **soft out**

Inbound Soft Reconfiguration

Inbound soft reconfiguration is a bit more involved. All inbound updates (whether accepted or not accepted) need to be tracked by the router. Additional memory is required just to store this information.

An additional router subcommand is needed to configure inbound soft reconfiguration:

> **neighbor** {*address* | *peer-group*} **soft-reconfiguration inbound**

This command is required to start storing the received updates to do the soft reconfiguration. The exec command used to do the inbound reconfiguration is:

> **clear ip bgp** [* | *address* | *peer-group*] **soft in**

To avoid the memory overhead needed for the inbound soft reconfiguration, the same outcome could be achieved by doing an outbound soft reconfiguration at the other end of the connection.

If the "in/out" option is not specified (**clear ip bgp** [* | *address* | *peer-group*] **soft**), both inbound and outbound soft reconfiguration will be applied.

The following example demonstrates the difference between clearing a BGP session between two routers without and with the soft configuration BGP feature. While the session is cleared, an output log will be displayed to show the actual session being established and the route updates being exchanged.

Referring still to figure 11–14, RTA will be configured to send its updates to RTC with a metric of 5000. The following is RTA's configuration. Note the **neighbor 172.16.20.1 soft-reconfiguration inbound** command. This is needed only if clearing the session needs to take effect on the inbound; that is, in case we have no control over the neighbor router to clear the session on the outbound.

RTA configuration:

```
router bgp 65050
 no synchronization
 bgp confederation identifier 3
 network 172.16.220.0 mask 255.255.255.0
 network 172.16.70.0 mask 255.255.255.0
 neighbor 172.16.20.1 remote-as 1
 neighbor 172.16.20.1 soft-reconfiguration inbound
 neighbor 172.16.20.1 filter-list 10 out
 neighbor 172.16.20.1 route-map setmetric out
 neighbor 172.16.70.2 remote-as 65050
 no auto-summary

ip as-path access-list 10 permit ^$

route-map setmetric permit 10
 set metric 5000
```

For this information to take effect, the BGP session would have to be cleared between the two routers. Note how much overhead is caused by actually killing the TCP session between the two routers and starting over from scratch. The log will show that the BGP peer session is being first reset, then the neighbor election goes from Idle to Established, and then the actual routing updates will flow.

```
RTA#clear ip bgp 172.16.20.1

BGP: 172.16.20.1 reset requested
BGP: no valid path for 192.68.11.0/24
BGP: 172.16.20.1 reset by 0x27B740
BGP: 172.16.20.1 went from Established to Idle
BGP: nettable_walker 192.68.11.0/255.255.255.0 no best path selected
BGP: 172.16.20.1 went from Idle to Active
BGP: 172.16.70.2 computing updates, neighbor version 21, table version
23, starting at 0.0.0.0
BGP: 172.16.70.2 send UPDATE 192.68.11.0/24 -- unreachable
BGP: 172.16.70.2 1 updates enqueued (average=27, maximum=27)
BGP: 172.16.70.2 update run completed, ran for 0ms, neighbor version
21, start version 23, throttled to 23, check point net 0.0.0.0
BGP: scanning routing tables
BGP: 172.16.20.1 went from Active to OpenSent
BGP: 172.16.20.1 went from OpenSent to OpenConfirm
BGP: 172.16.20.1 went from OpenConfirm to Established
BGP: 172.16.20.1 computing updates, neighbor version 0, table version
23, starting at 0.0.0.0
BGP: 172.16.20.1 send UPDATE 172.16.25.0/24, next 172.16.20.2, metric
5000, path 3
BGP: 172.16.20.1 send UPDATE 172.16.30.0/24, next 172.16.20.2, path
(65060)
BGP: 172.16.20.1 send UPDATE 172.16.50.0/24, next 172.16.20.2, metric
5000, path 3
BGP: 172.16.20.1 send UPDATE 172.16.60.0/24, next 172.16.20.2, path
(65060)
BGP: 172.16.20.1 send UPDATE 172.16.70.0/24, next 172.16.20.2, metric
5000, path 3
BGP: 172.16.20.1 send UPDATE 172.16.90.0/24, next 172.16.20.2, path
(65060)
BGP: 172.16.20.1 send UPDATE 172.16.65.0/26, next 172.16.20.2, path
(65060)
BGP: 172.16.20.1 send UPDATE 172.16.112.0/24, next 172.16.20.2, path
BGP: 172.16.20.1 send UPDATE 172.16.220.0/24, next 172.16.20.2, path
BGP: 172.16.20.1 send UPDATE 192.68.222.0/24, next 172.16.20.2, metric
5000, path 3 2
BGP: 172.16.20.1 4 updates enqueued (average=58, maximum=68)
```

```
BGP: 172.16.20.1 update run completed, ran for 24ms, neighbor version
0, start version 23, throttled to 23, check point net 0.0.0.0
BGP: 172.16.20.1 rcv UPDATE about 192.68.11.0/24, next hop 172.16.20.1,
path 1 metric 2000
BGP: 172.16.20.1 rcv UPDATE about 192.68.222.0/24, next hop
172.16.20.1, path 1 2 metric 2000
BGP: 172.16.20.1 rcv UPDATE about 172.16.25.0/24 -- denied
BGP: 172.16.20.1 rcv UPDATE about 172.16.30.0/24 -- denied
BGP: 172.16.20.1 rcv UPDATE about 172.16.50.0/24 -- denied
BGP: 172.16.20.1 rcv UPDATE about 172.16.60.0/24 -- denied
BGP: 172.16.20.1 rcv UPDATE about 172.16.70.0/24 -- denied
BGP: 172.16.20.1 rcv UPDATE about 172.16.90.0/24 -- denied
BGP: 172.16.20.1 rcv UPDATE about 172.16.65.0/26 -- denied
BGP: 172.16.20.1 rcv UPDATE about 172.16.112.0/24 -- denied
BGP: 172.16.20.1 rcv UPDATE about 172.16.220.0/24 -- denied
BGP: nettable_walker 192.68.11.0/255.255.255.0 calling revise_route
BGP: revise route installing 192.68.11.0/255.255.255.0 -> 172.16.20.1
BGP: 172.16.70.2 computing updates, neighbor version 23, table version
24, starting at 0.0.0.0
BGP: NEXT_HOP part 1 net 192.68.11.0/24, neigh 172.16.70.2, next
172.16.20.1
BGP: 172.16.70.2 send UPDATE 192.68.11.0/24, next 172.16.20.1, metric
2000, path 1
BGP: 172.16.70.2 1 updates enqueued (average=59, maximum=59)
BGP: 172.16.70.2 update run completed, ran for 4ms, neighbor version
23, start version 24, throttled to 24, check point net 0.0.0.0
BGP: 172.16.20.1 rcv UPDATE about 172.16.25.0/24 -- withdrawn
BGP: 172.16.20.1 rcv UPDATE about 172.16.30.0/24 -- withdrawn
BGP: 172.16.20.1 rcv UPDATE about 172.16.50.0/24 -- withdrawn
BGP: 172.16.20.1 rcv UPDATE about 172.16.60.0/24 -- withdrawn
BGP: 172.16.20.1 rcv UPDATE about 172.16.70.0/24 -- withdrawn
BGP: 172.16.20.1 rcv UPDATE about 172.16.90.0/24 -- withdrawn
BGP: 172.16.20.1 rcv UPDATE about 172.16.65.0/26 -- withdrawn
BGP: 172.16.20.1 rcv UPDATE about 172.16.112.0/24 -- withdrawn
BGP: 172.16.20.1 rcv UPDATE about 172.16.220.0/24 -- withdrawn
BGP: 172.16.20.1 computing updates, neighbor version 23, table version
24, starting at 0.0.0.0
BGP: 172.16.20.1 update run completed, ran for 0ms, neighbor version
23, start version 24, throttled to 24, check point net 0.0.0.0
BGP: scanning routing tables
```

In the next display, the same session is being cleared by using the soft configuration feature. Note how the metric 5000 was sent without killing the BGP session, and the overhead is much smaller.

```
RTA#clear ip bgp 172.16.20.1 soft out
BGP: start outbound soft reconfiguration for 172.16.20.1
BGP: 172.16.20.1 computing updates, neighbor version 0, table version
24, starting at 0.0.0.0
BGP: 172.16.20.1 send UPDATE 172.16.25.0/24, next 172.16.20.2, metric
5000, path 3
BGP: 172.16.20.1 send UPDATE 172.16.30.0/24, next 172.16.20.2, metric
5000, path 3
BGP: 172.16.20.1 send UPDATE 172.16.50.0/24, next 172.16.20.2, metric
5000, path 3
BGP: 172.16.20.1 send UPDATE 172.16.60.0/24, next 172.16.20.2, metric
5000, path 3
BGP: 172.16.20.1 send UPDATE 172.16.70.0/24, next 172.16.20.2, metric
5000, path 3
BGP: 172.16.20.1 send UPDATE 172.16.90.0/24, next 172.16.20.2, metric
5000, path 3
BGP: 172.16.20.1 send UPDATE 172.16.65.0/26, next 172.16.20.2, metric
5000, path 3
BGP: 172.16.20.1 send UPDATE 172.16.112.0/24, next 172.16.20.2, metric
5000, path 3
BGP: 172.16.20.1 send UPDATE 172.16.220.0/24, next 172.16.20.2, metric
5000, path 3
BGP: 172.16.20.1 send UPDATE 192.68.11.0/24 -- unreachable
BGP: 172.16.20.1 send UPDATE 192.68.222.0/24, next 172.16.20.2, metric
5000, path 3 2
BGP: 172.16.20.1 5 updates enqueued (average=52, maximum=68)
BGP: 172.16.20.1 update run completed, ran for 24ms, neighbor version
0, start version 24, throttled to 24, check point net 0.0.0.0
BGP: scanning routing tables
```

ROUTE DAMPENING

Route dampening is a mechanism to minimize the instability caused by route flapping and oscillation over the network. The following are the commands used to control route dampening:

bgp dampening [[**route-map** *map-name*] [*half-life-time reuse-value suppress-value maximum-suppress-time*]]

- *half-life-time*—range is 1–45 minutes; current default is 15 minutes.
- *reuse-value*—range is 1–20000; default is 750.
- *suppress-value*— range is 1–20000; default is 2000.
- *max-suppress-time*—maximum duration a route can be suppressed. Range is 1–255; default is four times half-life-time.

A route map can be associated with bgp dampening to selectively apply the dampening parameters if certain criteria are found. Example criteria include matching on a specific IP route or AS_path or community.

Figure 11–15 shows two ASs, AS3 and AS1. RTA in AS3 is running IBGP with RTG in AS3 and EBGP with RTC in AS1. Information coming via EBGP from AS3 is injected into OSPF in AS1. RTC has noticed lots of fluctuations in network 172.16.220.0/24 coming from AS3, causing oscillation in its BGP and in turn in OSPF. The 172.16.220.0/24 keeps showing up and disappearing from RTH's routing table. To rectify the problem, RTC will apply dampening to the BGP by using a route map to selectively dampen route 172.16.220.0/24 only.

RTG configuration:

```
router bgp 3
 no synchronization
 network 172.16.112.0 mask 255.255.255.0
 neighbor 172.16.70.1 remote-as 3
 no auto-summary
```

RTA configuration:

```
router bgp 3
 no synchronization
 network 172.16.220.0 mask 255.255.255.0
 network 172.16.70.0 mask 255.255.255.0
```

```
neighbor 172.16.20.1 remote-as 1
neighbor 172.16.70.2 remote-as 3
neighbor 172.16.70.2 next-hop-self
no auto-summary
```

RTC is EBGP peered with RTA, and IBGP peered with RTH. RTC is injecting the BGP routes it receives into OSPF, which is running in AS1. RTC is applying BGP dampening with a route map SELECTIVE_DAMPENING, which applies the dampening parameters to network 172.16.220.0/24 only. All other routes such as 172.16.112.0/24 will not be dampened.

RTC has specified the dampening parameters in the following manner. The half-life-time is 20 minutes, the reuse limit for the penalty is 950, routes will be suppressed if the cumulative penalty exceeds 2500, and the maximum time a route could be suppressed is 80 minutes.

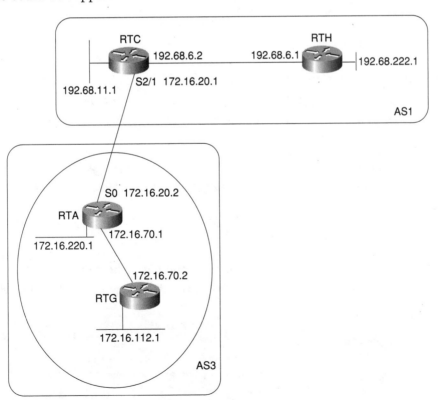

Figure 11–15
Route dampening.

RTC configuration:

```
router ospf 10
 redistribute bgp 1 subnets
 network 192.68.0.0 0.0.255.255 area 0

router bgp 1
 bgp dampening route-map SELECTIVE_DAMPENING
 network 192.68.11.0
 neighbor 172.16.20.2 remote-as 3
 neighbor 192.68.6.1 remote-as 1
 no auto-summary

access-list 1 permit 172.16.220.0 0.0.0.255

route-map SELECTIVE_DAMPENING permit 10
 match ip address 1
 set dampening 20 950 2500 80

route-map SELECTIVE_DAMPENING permit 20
```

The following output shows how RTC treats the flapping route
172.16.220.0/24. A flap is counted any time the path information changes for
a route. The first output shows the route before any flaps have occurred.

```
RTC#show ip bgp 172.16.220.0
BGP routing table entry for 172.16.220.0/24, version 326
Paths: (1 available, best #1, advertised over IBGP)
 3
   172.16.20.2 from 172.16.20.2 (172.16.220.1)
     Origin IGP, metric 0, valid, external, best
```

The following output shows the route after one flap. The route is down and is
put in "history" state. The route was given the default penalty of 1000, which
has already decayed to 997.

```
RTC#show ip bgp 172.16.220.0
BGP routing table entry for 172.16.220.0/24, version 327
Paths: (1 available, no best path, advertised over IBGP)
 3 (history entry)
```

```
    172.16.20.2 from 172.16.20.2 (172.16.220.1)
     Origin IGP, metric 0, external
     Dampinfo: penalty 997, flapped 1 times in 00:00:06
```

The following shows the route after a second flap (it has come back up again). Another penalty of 1000 has been added, and the cumulative penalty after decay has reached 1454.

```
RTC#show ip bgp 172.16.220.0
BGP routing table entry for 172.16.220.0/24, version 328
Paths: (1 available, best #1, advertised over IBGP)
  3
    172.16.20.2 from 172.16.20.2 (172.16.220.1)
     Origin IGP, metric 0, valid, external, best
     Dampinfo: penalty 1454, flapped 2 times in 00:01:20
```

The following shows the route after four flaps. The penalty is now 2851, which has exceeded the 2500 limit. The route is now suppressed (dampened) and will not be passed on to RTH. The route will be usable in 31 minutes and 40 seconds. At that time, the penalty would have decayed to the reuse limit of 950.

```
RTC#show ip bgp 172.16.220.0
BGP routing table entry for 172.16.220.0/24, version 329
Paths: (1 available, no best path, advertised over IBGP)
  3, (suppressed due to dampening)
    172.16.20.2 from 172.16.20.2 (172.16.220.1)
     Origin IGP, metric 0, valid, external
     Dampinfo: penalty 2851, flapped 4 times in 00:03:05, reuse in 00:31:40
```

The following output shows the same route after six flaps. The differences are that the half-life-time has been set to 5 minutes instead of 20 minutes, and the maximum suppress-time is 20 minutes instead of 80. With a shorter half-life-time, the penalty will be decayed much faster, and the route will be used a lot sooner. Note the reuse time of 8 minutes and 10 secs.

```
RTC#show ip bgp 172.16.220.0
BGP routing table entry for 172.16.220.0/24, version 336
```

```
Paths: (1 available, no best path, advertised over IBGP)
  3, (suppressed due to dampening)
    172.16.20.2 from 172.16.20.2 (172.16.220.1)
     Origin IGP, metric 0, valid, external
     Dampinfo: penalty 2939, flapped 6 times in 00:08:21, reuse in 00:08:10
```

Adjusting the dampening timers becomes essential when administators cannot afford to have a long outage for a specific route. BGP dampening with route maps is a powerful tool to selectively penalize ill-behaved routes in a user-configurable and controlled manner.

LOOKING AHEAD

The Internet has come a long way from the NSFNET backbone to the information highway of the 21st century—and there are no signs of its slowing down. And how could the Internet slow down when hundreds and thousands of users come online every day, attracted by the most advanced applications technology affords?

Routing protocols have struggled to keep up with the demand, from the early days of EGP to the latest in BGP. BGP started as a simple exterior routing protocol and has evolved into a de facto standard, gluing the Internet together. Indeed, every hook and tweak that BGP can offer has been used, and still it seems that more capabilities are requested every day. As a result, new protocols and new techniques will emerge. Whether they will make routing easier or more complicated, more robust or more shaky is yet to be seen. One thing is certain: common sense will never go away, and as long as it is the basis of all your designs, you will be the master of your domain.

RIPE-181

RIPE (Reséaux IP Européens) is a collaborative organization that consists of European Internet providers. RIPE and other contributors have developed a database language called RIPE-181 upon which all routing registries build their policies. The RIPE-181 language is now used to build the Routing Arbiter Database (RADB) that runs on the Route Servers (RS) of the Network Access Points (NAPs). The purpose of this Appendix is to make you familiar with some of the RIPE-181 objects and terminology.

RIPE OBJECTS

The RIPE-181 language defines a set of objects used to define routing and filtering policies between different autonomous systems. The main objects comprising the registry are defined as follows:

- maintainer: Indicating a registered maintainer of the autonomous system

- aut-num: Indicating a specific autonomous system

- route: Indicating a list of routes

Maintainer Object

The maintainer object specifies the registered party that is allowed to perform updates to the RADB. The first step in registering information in the database is to register one or more maintainer objects for the autonomous system. The format of the maintainer object looks like the following:

- mntner: MAINT-AS1239 (Describes the maintainer name.)

   ◦ descr: free text (A description of the Maintainer Object.)

   ◦ admin-c: Jane Doe (Name or uniquely assigned NIC-handle of an administrative contact person.)

   ◦ upd-to: bilx@ra.net (Update to any unauthorized update request of an object maintained by this maintainer will be forwarded to this address.)

   ◦ mnt-nfy: abc@Jean.net (Maintainer notification. A notification of changes, additions, and deletions will be e-mailed to this address.)

   ◦ auth: MAIL-FROM Joex@ddi.digital.n (Specifies a scheme to be used to identify and authenticate update requests from this maintainer. For example: MAIL-FROM specifies e-mail addresses of people allowed to modify the object.)

   ◦ changed: xx@sprint.net 950621 (Who changed this object last and when was this change made.)

   ◦ source: RADB (Defines the source of the information.)

AS Object

The AS object provides the contact information and the routing policies of an AS. The format of the AS object looks like the following:

- aut-num: AS1111

  - descr: MYNET backbone (Description of the autonomous system.)

  - as-in: AS123 AND NOT AS456 (Description of accepted routing information from AS peers; there can be multiple as-in and as-out lines, to describe all facets of the routing policy.)

  - as-in: AS789 AS888

  - as-out: AS1111 AS2222 (Description of generated routing information sent to other AS peers.)

  - admin-c: Jane Doe (Name or uniquely assigned NIC-handle of an administrative contact person.)

  - tech-c: Jean Doe (Name or uniquely assigned NIC-handle of a technical contact person.)

  - mnt-by: MAINT-AS1790 (Registered maintainer name.)

  - changed: xx@test.net 951126 (Who changed this object last and when was this change made.)

  - source: RADB (Defines the source of the information.)

This AS object indicates that autonomous system number AS1111 belongs to "MYNET backbone," its maintainer's object name is "MAINT-AS1790," the last changes for this object were done by xx@sprint.net on 11/26/95, and the source of the record is the Routing Arbiter Database.

Route Object

The route object indicates a route that is injected on the Internet. The route object keeps track of the autonomous system that originated the route and hence would provide contact information about the maintainer of the route.

The route object also references community objects (to be discussed in the next section) to group multiple routes under a single community name.

The following record indicates that the route aggregate 171.68.0.0/15 is part of Cisco Systems with origin AS200 and belongs to the COMM_NSFNET community.

- route: 171.68.0.0/15
  - descr: Cisco Systems, Inc.
  - descr: 1525 O'Brien Drive
  - descr: Menlo Park
  - descr: CA 94025, USA
  - origin: AS200 (The autonomous system announcing this route.)
  - comm-list: COMM_NSFNET (List of communities this route is part of.)
  - mnt-by: MAINT-AS200
  - changed: nsfnet-admin@merit.edu 950312
  - source: RADB

Community Objects

Community objects define a group of routes that have something in common but as yet cannot be represented by a single AS or a group of ASs. Communities are useful in setting special access and usage policies (but not routing policies) to a group of routes. An example of a community object is COMM_ESNET, which represents the Energy Science Community. Each community is represented in the database via a community tag (comm-list) and a community object. The community tag represents the routes belonging to a certain community. To illustrate, let us look at the following example:

- route: 13.13.0.0/16

  - descr: MYCOMPANY

  - origin: AS200

  - comm-list: COMM_ESNET COMM_US_FED

  - mnt-by: MAINT-AS200

  - changed: nsfnet-admin@merit.edu 950312

  - source: RADB

- community: COMM_ESNET

  - descr: The Energy Science Community

  - authority: Energy Sciences Network (ESnet)

  - guardian: routing@es.net (E-mail address of the guardian of the AS.)

  - tech-c: Joe Smith

  - admin-c: Jane Doe

  - mnt-by: MAINT-ESNET

  - changed: xx@yy.gov

  - source: RADB

The preceding example shows that route 13.13.0.0/16 belongs to COMM_ESNET and COMM_US_FED communities; the community object COMM_ESNET is a description of the maintainer of that community.

Communities are just a representation of access and usage policies of certain routes and by themselves cannot set routing policies. They can, however, be used in conjunction with an AS's routing policies to define a set of routes for which the AS sets policy. Communities can be used for statistical purposes. A list of ASs belonging to Energy Science Community, for example, could be easily found by querying the database and looking for the comm-list tags.

AS Macros

AS macros are a way of grouping multiple ASs under one name. This will save the AS guardian the trouble of updating the as-in and the as-out field in the aut-num object anytime a new AS is added. The guardian would simply add or remove an AS from the macro as-list and hence the new list would be automatically applied to the aut-num. Following is an example:

- aut-num: AS123

  ○ descr: SomeNet

  ○ as-in: from AS456 accept ANY

  ○ as-out: to AS456 announce AS-MYLIST

  ○ admin-c: Joe Smith

  ○ tech-c: Jane Doe

  ○ mnt-by: MAINT-AS123

  ○ changed: xx@xx.com

  ○ source: RADB

- as-macro: AS-MYLIST

  ○ descr: ASs that I would like to announce

  ○ as-list: AS1111 AS2222 AS3333

  ○ guardian: Joe@xx.net

  ○ admin-c: Joe Smith

  ○ tech-c: Jane Doe

- mnt-by: MAINT-AS123

- changed: xx@xx.com

- source: RADB

Based on the preceding descriptions, the as-list from the AS-MYLIST macro is applied where it is called by the AS object. Thus, the policy would be evaluated as follows:

- aut-num: AS123

  - descr: SomeNet

  - as-in: from AS456 accept ANY

  - as-out: to AS456 announce AS1111 AS2222 AS3333 (The macro AS-MYLIST was applied here.)

  - guardian: Joe@xx.net

  - admin-c: Joe Smith

  - tech-c: Jane Doe

  - mnt-by: MAINT-AS123

  - changed: xx@xx.com

  - source: RADB

SETTING POLICIES IN THE AS OBJECT

The AS object is used to identify the autonomous system and to set policies between it and other ASs. These policies are basically a list of ASs to be accepted or a list of ASs to be advertised. An example of the fields used to set the policies are "as-in," which indicates the ASs to be accepted, and "as-out," which indicates the ASs to be advertised. Given the previous AS object for MYNET, figure A–1 illustrates how the policies are set.

Given the connectivity illustrated in figure A–1, AS1111 chooses to accept any updates coming from AS123, AS789, and AS888 but no updates from AS456. AS1111 would like to advertise routes originating from AS1111 and its customer AS2222 to all other ASs, which leads to the following AS policy for AS1111:

- as-in: AS123 AND NOT AS456

- as-in: AS789 AS888

- as-out: AS1111 AS2222

The first statement indicates that AS1111 will accept routes from AS123 but not from AS456. The second statement indicates that AS1111 will also accept routes from AS789 and AS888. The third statement indicates that AS1111 will advertise to everybody its own AS1111 plus its customer AS2222.

Figure A–1
Setting policies in the AS object.

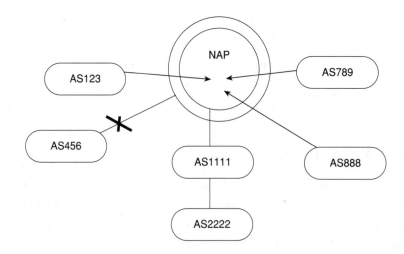

An AS that accepts routes from its neighbors and in turn advertises these routes to other neighbors is accepting to become a transit AS. ISPs are very careful about what routes they announce because no ISP wants to carry somebody else's traffic unless it is required to do so. In figure A–1, AS1111 is accepting routes from its neighbors and is only advertising its local and customer routes. This way, AS1111 will not receive any traffic destined to other than its own and customer networks.

The following are examples of policy setting using the AS object. In the first, AS123 accepts any routes coming from AS456 and only advertises its local routes (routes originated by AS123) to AS456.

- aut-num: AS123
  - descr: SomeNet
  - as-in: from AS456 100 accept ANY
  - as-out: to AS456 announce AS123
  - guardian: Sam@xx.com
  - admin-c: Joe Smith
  - tech-c: Joe Smith
  - remarks: SomeNet Services
  - mnt-by: MAINT-AS123
  - changed: Some@body.com
  - source: RADB

Note the 100 in the as-in statement. This number indicates a relative cost for the route. Later, if the AS learns this route from other sources, the numbers associated with the identical routes will help the AS determine which one to take; it prefers the route with the lower number (lower cost).

In this next example, AS123 accepts only routes originated from AS456, announces all its routes to AS456, and uses route 10.10.0.0/16 learned from AS789 as a default route:

- aut-num: AS123
    - descr: SomeNet
    - as-in: from AS456 100 accept AS456
    - as-out: to AS456 announce ANY
    - default: AS789 1 {10.10.0.0/16}
    - guardian: Sam@xx.com
    - admin-c: Joe Smith
    - tech-c: Joe Smith
    - remarks: SomeNet Services
    - mnt-by: MAINT-AS123
    - changed: Some@body.com
    - source: RADB

The 1 in the default statement is used in case multiple default statements are used in the same object; if one default goes away, the second will be used.

Setting Policies Based on Routes

In the same way that policies can be applied to the whole AS, they can be applied to specific routes. An autonomous system may choose to accept or deny a specific route out of all the routes that it announces or accepts from its neighbors. The routes are usually either a specific CIDR range or the default route 0.0.0.0/0.

In the following example, AS123 accepts only the route 10.10.0.0/16 from AS456 and advertises only the default route 0.0.0.0/0 to AS456.

- aut-num: AS123
  - descr: SomeNet
  - as-in: from AS456 100 accept {10.10.0.0/16}
  - as-out: to AS456 announce {0.0.0.0/0}
  - guardian: Sam@xx.com
  - admin-c: Joe Smith
  - tech-c: Joe Smith
  - remarks: SomeNet Services
  - mnt-by: MAINT-AS123
  - changed: Some@body.com
  - source: RADB

In the following example, AS123 will accept 10.10.0.0/16, 11.11.0.0/16, and 12.12.0.0/16 from AS456 and will announce all routes except 0/0 to AS456:

- aut-num: AS123
  - descr: SomeNet
  - as-in: from AS456 100 accept {10.10.0.0/16, 11.11.0.0/16, 12.12.0.0/16}
  - as-out: to AS456 announce ANY AND NOT {0.0.0.0/0}
  - guardian: Sam@xx.com

- admin-c: Joe Smith

- tech-c: Joe Smith

- remarks: SomeNet Services

- mnt-by: MAINT-AS123

- changed: Some@body.com

- source: RADB

A Practical Multi-AS Example of Routing Policies

Unless you are implementing and maintaining your AS routing policies at a NAP route server, you probably never will need to write RIPE language. However, understanding the logic behind policies is important; this logic can be applied to any situation where multiple ASs interconnect.

For a final example, we will consider policies not just with respect to a single AS, but in the more complex, more realistic situation of several interconnected networks. The AS object for each will reflect multiple in and out policies because of the multiple connections and the varying requirements of each network. We will begin with a textual description of the desired routing and then translate this into RIPE AS objects, one requirement at a time.

Figure A–2 illustrates an example in which AS4 is a major provider that is hooked up to the rest of the world via one of the NAPs. This environment has the following requirements:

1. AS1 is multihomed to AS2 and AS4. AS1 uses AS4 as a primary route for all its external destinations. In case of link failure with AS4, AS1 uses AS2 as an exit point. AS1 sets a default toward AS2 and AS4 based on the single route 10.10.0.0/16 that it accepts from both ASs. AS1 prefers the default toward AS4 in normal operation.

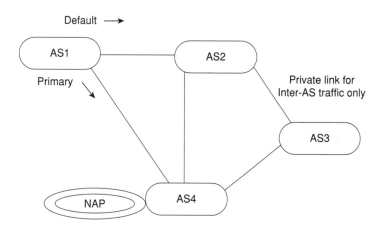

Figure A–2
Practical multi-AS example.

2. AS2 and AS3 are customers of AS4. AS2 and AS3 also have a private link to be used as the primary link for their inter-AS traffic. For all other Internet traffic, AS2 and AS3 will go via AS4.
3. In case of a link failure between AS2 and AS4 or AS3 and AS4, AS2 and AS3 would like to use each other as a transit network to reach the outside world.
4. In case of a direct link failure between AS2 and AS3, AS4 would be used to pass the traffic between the two ASs.
5. In normal situations, AS4 should always reach AS1, AS2, and AS3 via the direct link to each of those ASs.

The following discussions consider each of these requirements in turn:

Requirement 1

To fulfill the first requirement, AS1 will default to both AS2 and AS4 with a lower cost to AS4 (AS4 would be preferred). To set the default, AS1 will accept route 10.10.0.0/16 from both ASs. AS1 may choose to accept as many routes as it wants, but it does not need to. From the other end, AS2 and AS4 will send the single route 10.10.0.0/16 to AS1. The corresponding RIPE configuration would look like the following.

- aut-num: AS1
  - as-out: to AS2 announce AS1 (AS1 announces its routes only to AS2.)
  - as-out: to AS4 announce AS1 (AS1 announces its routes only to AS4.)
  - default: AS4 10 {10.10.0.0/16} (AS1 sets its default toward AS4 with a cost of 10.)
  - default: AS2 20 {10.10.0.0/16} (AS1 sets its default toward AS2 with a higher cost of 20.)

The 10 and 20 numbers above are relative costs with respect to AS2 and AS4. The peer with the lowest cost is used for default over ones with higher costs. The {10.10.0.0/16} is a route learned from both ASs and is used to indicate the default route. In normal cases, AS1 would prefer AS4. In case of a failure, the {10.10.0.0/16} route will not be learned from AS4, and the default will fall over to AS2. From AS2 and AS4 the configuration would be:

- aut-num: AS2
  - as-out: to AS1 announce {10.10.0.0/16} (Announce a single route to AS1.)
  - as-in: from AS1 1 accept AS1

- aut-num:AS4
  - as-out: to AS1 announce {10.10.0.0/16} (Announce a single route to AS1.)
  - as-in: from AS1 1 accept AS1

Requirement 2

To fulfill the second requirement, AS2 and AS3 would have to receive each other's routes from both the private link and AS4. To prefer the private link for inter-AS traffic, from AS2's perspective, the cost for the AS3 routes coming from AS3 should be lower than the cost of the AS3 routes coming from AS4. Similarly, from AS3's perspective, the cost of the AS2 routes coming from AS2 should be lower than the cost of the AS2 routes coming from AS4. The following RIPE configs should achieve this.

- aut-num: AS2
  - as-in: from AS3 5 accept AS3
  - as-in: from AS4 10 accept ANY
  - as-out: to AS3 announce ANY
  - as-out: to AS4 announce AS1 AS2

This also applies to AS3:

- aut-num: AS3
  - as-in: from AS2 5 accept AS2
  - as-in: from AS4 10 accept ANY
  - as-out: to AS2 announce ANY
  - as-out: to AS4 announce AS3

Requirement 3

With the preceding configuration, AS2 is accepting only AS3 routes from AS3 and AS3 is accepting only AS2 routes from AS2. In case of a link failure between AS2 and AS4, AS2 would not be able to reach the outside world because AS3 is not advertising these routes to it. In the same way, a link failure between AS3 and AS4 will prevent AS3 from reaching the outside world.

To take care of this situation AS2 and AS3 would have to announce all routes to each other and would have to accept all routes from each other. In normal situations (no link failures), AS2 would get all the outside routes from AS3 and from AS4; in the same way, AS3 would get the outside routes from AS2 and AS4. To prefer AS4, the cost of the routes from AS4 should be lower. The following will fulfill this requirement:

- aut-num: AS2 (This is AS2's final configuration.)

  - as-in: from AS1 1 accept AS1

  - as-in: from AS3 5 accept AS3 (From AS3, set AS3 originated routes with a cost of 5.)

  - as-in: from AS3 12 accept ANY (From AS3, set all other routes with a cost of 12.)

  - as-in: from AS4 10 accept ANY (From AS4, set all routes with a cost of 10.)

  - as-out: to AS1 announce {10.10.0.0/16} (Announce a single route to AS1.)

  - as-out: to AS3 announce ANY (Announce all routes to AS3.)

  - as-out: to AS4 announce AS1 AS2 AS3 (Announce AS1, AS2, AS3 routes to AS4.)

The preceding configuration will make AS2 prefer all AS3's local routes via the private link because of the better cost of 5. All other routes will be accessed via AS4 because of the better cost of 10. Also, because AS4 should be able to reach AS2 via AS3 in case of a direct link failure, AS2 should advertise AS3 routes to AS4.

The same reasoning is applied for AS3:

- aut-num: AS3 (This is AS3's final configuration.)
  - as-in: from AS2 5 accept AS2
  - as-in: from AS2 12 accept ANY
  - as-in: from AS4 10 accept ANY
  - as-out: to AS2 announce ANY
  - as-out: to AS4 announce AS3 AS2

Requirement 4

This requirement mandates that in case of a link failure between AS2 and AS3, the two ASs should be able to reach each other via AS4. This is achieved by allowing AS4 to announce all routes to AS2 and AS3.

- aut-num: AS4
  - as-out: to AS2 announce ANY
  - as-out: to AS3 announce ANY

Requirement 5

AS4 should always reach AS1, AS2, or AS3 via the direct link. This requirement is achieved by having AS4 always set a lower cost via the direct link.

- aut-num: AS4 (This is AS4's final configuration.)
  - as-in: from AS1 1 accept AS1
  - as-in: from AS2 5 accept AS1 AS2
  - as-in: from AS2 10 accept AS3

- as-in: from AS3 5 accept AS3

- as-in: from AS3 10 accept AS2

- as-out: to AS1 announce {10.10.0.0/16}

- as-out: to AS2 announce ANY

- as-out: to AS3 announce ANY

In the preceding configuration, AS4 is accepting AS2 routes from AS2 and AS3 with a lower cost from AS2. Also, AS4 is accepting AS3 routes from AS2 and AS3 with a lower cost from AS3. As such, AS4 will always use the direct link unless a failure occurs.

FINDING INFORMATION IN THE DATABASE

One way to search the database is to run WHOIS on a Unix machine connected to the Internet. The syntax is:

whois -h hostname -s <source-database> key

Where *<source-database>* is the database where the information is kept, such as RIPE or RADB. The key is a keyword such as an IP CIDR block from a route object, an autonomous system number, a maintainer, or a community-list, and so on. The following is the output of whois -h whois.ra.net -s radb 171.68.0.0, which shows Cisco Systems as the owner of that route.

- route: 171.68.0.0/15

  - descr: BN-CIDR-171.68

  - origin: AS109

  - mnt-by: MAINT-AS200

  - changed: vaf@valinor.barrnet.net 950517

  - source: RADB

- route: 171.68.0.0/15
  - descr: Cisco Systems, Inc.
  - descr: 1525 O'Brien Drive
  - descr: Menlo Park
  - descr: CA 94025, USA
  - origin: AS200
  - comm-list: COMM_NSFNET
  - mnt-by: MAINT-AS200
  - changed: nsfnet-admin@merit.edu 950312
  - source: RADB

Index